T5-BAE-941

Aboriginal Small Business and Entrepreneurship in Canada

edited by

Katherine Beaty Chiste

CAPTUS PRESS

Aboriginal Small Business and Entrepreneurship in Canada

Captus Press Inc.
Mail: York University Campus
            4700 Keele Street
            North York, ON
            Canada   M3J 1P3
Phone: (416) 736–5537
Fax: (416) 736–5793
Email: info@captus.com
Internet: http://www.captus.com

Canadian Cataloguing in Publication Data
Main entry under title:

Aboriginal small business and entrepreneurship in Canada

Includes bibliographical references.

ISBN 1–895712–67–X

1. Native peoples — Canada — Business enterprises.*
2. Small business — Canada. I. Chiste, Katherine Beaty,
1953–   .

E78.C2A155 1996   338.6'442'08997071   C96–93 1693–3

Front cover design from original artwork by Frederick A. Lepine.

The Editor, Authors, and Publisher wish to thank Times Mirror Professional Publishing of Markham, Ontario for their kind permission to use material adapted from: D. Wesley Balderson, *Canadian Entrepreneurship and Small Business Management*, 2nd Edition (Burr Ridge, IL: Irwin). © Richard D. Irwin, Inc., 1990 and 1994.

0 9 8 7 6 5 4 3 2 1
Printed and bound in Canada

TABLE OF CONTENTS ─────────────────────────

Reference

Part 1

The Small Business Decision

The decision to start one's own business is a difficult one. It may involve leaving secure employment to face an uncertain financial future, and it may change one's relationship with family and community. But small business development offers unique opportunities for aboriginal entrepreneurs.

Chapter 1 reviews the role of small business in Canada's developing aboriginal business sector. Current trends and the probable future environment for aboriginal small business form a part of this discussion.

Chapter 2 presents characteristics of successful and unsuccessful small businesses and includes a discussion of the personal capabilities possessed by a majority of successful entrepreneurs. The chapter also reviews the potential advantages and disadvantages of operating one's own business, in aboriginal communities or elsewhere.

After an individual understands the relative merits of starting a small business and feels suited for such a career, he or she can take several steps to pursue the establishment of the business. Potential aboriginal entrepreneurs can obtain a considerable amount of information to help them evaluate business opportunities. Chapter 3 of this section will present ideas that can improve information collection and analysis skills that will help the entrepreneur decide which opportunities to pursue.

C H A P T E R   1

The Aboriginal Small Business Community

Katherine Beaty Chiste

CHAPTER OBJECTIVES

☐ To discuss the evidence of increased interest and activity in aboriginal small business.

☐ To review common methods of defining small business and to explain why a definition is important.

☐ To understand the current extent of small business in Canada.

☐ To discuss the positive benefits of the growing aboriginal business sector in Canada.

☐ To explain the probable future environment for the aboriginal small business community.

SMALL BUSINESS PROFILE
Rodney & Colleen Parenteau
Saskatoon Berry Choclates

A unique product and a unique company, Parenteau's Saskatoon Berry Chocolates Inc. is owned and operated by Rodney and Colleen Parenteau of Langham, Saskatchewan.

The Parenteaus purchased their berry farm back in 1987, without any expectation that they would get involved with product diversification. But soon they found that customers also wanted trees, and that is where their company began. The Parenteaus sold trees to customers who were interested in starting an orchard. Later they began marketing Saskatoon berry jams and spreads, but they realized that these products consumed most of their limited supply of berries. They needed to find a product that would stretch out their supply.

In 1990 they decided on a market niche — the now famous "Saskatoon Berry Chocolate." The product was unique, the first Saskatoon berry chocolate in Canada. As the Parenteaus weren't really chocolatiers, there was a lot of trial and error, determination, and persistence that led to their success.

The Parenteaus perform the entire production process by hand. They grow the Saskatoon trees which produce the berries, they make the chocolate molds, fill the chocolates, wrap them, package them and then shrink-wrap them — all by hand.

Not wanting to extend themselves beyond their limits, they are controlling the growth of the company but still venturing into new product markets. Because of their success they have expanded into jams, spreads, syrup, honey, tea, and, recently, a Saskatoon wine which has won provincial and national prizes. The Saskatoon Berry Chocolate has proven to be a distinctive product for a distinctive company.

SOURCE: Speech from Rodney Parenteau, "Sharing the Harvest: The Road to Self-Reliance," *Report of the Round Table on Aboriginal Economic Development*, Royal Commission on Aboriginal Peoples, 1993; and "The Spirit Lives: Aboriginal Entrepreneurs in Canada," The Canadian Foundation for Economic Education in association with Kwakiutl District Council and Wawatay Native Communications Society Inc., 1995.

INCIDENT 1.1
The Emergence of Aboriginal Business in Canada

As aboriginal people, we hold a vision of a fully functioning and sustainable aboriginal economy, one that is interactive with the economies of Canada and the world. We want to build a prosperous future as equal and accountable partners within a new confederation that respects our history, languages, cultures, values and diversities.

For this vision to be achieved, all Canadians must recognize and build on the momentum being generated across the country by a new generation of aboriginal entrepreneurs. I say *all Canadians*, because it will not be only aboriginal individuals and communities that will drive the process. The challenge will be for non-aboriginal business investors to take advantage of the opportunity to form exciting and profitable partnerships with us.

Aboriginal people have always been traders and are no strangers to the world of commerce. Today in Canada there is a re-emergence of interest in these endeavours. According to the 1991 Post-Censal Survey conducted by Statistics Canada, at least 18,000 aboriginal people owned a business and another 34,000 indicated that they intended to become business owners or operators within two years. These are very encouraging numbers.

Another study, one commissioned by Industry Canada and conducted by an independent firm in June 1993, looked into the performance of some 300 aboriginal firms that, over a two-year period, had used the department's Aboriginal Economic Programs branch. The study reported that these businesses were performing at rates comparable to or even slightly better than the Canadian average for small businesses. The findings also showed that aboriginal businesses were excellent generators of employment for aboriginal and non-aboriginal people, particularly in rural or remote areas.

From my perspective and that of a growing number of banks and investors, there exists a critical mass of aboriginal entrepreneurs — some working together, many independently. There are opportunities to build on this base and encourage further success.

SOURCE: Kenneth C. Thomas, *Canadian Business Review*, Summer 1994, p. 12.

THE ENTREPRENEURIAL REVOLUTION

The 1980s and 90s have seen a reawakening of interest in small business, both in North America and abroad. The dream of starting out with a modest idea and then developing a successful business, as did Rodney and Colleen Parenteau, is shared by many. On the other hand, many individuals have become successful entrepreneurs out of economic necessity.

Increasingly, aboriginal people in Canada are finding entrepreneurship to be a route to empowering themselves as individuals, as families, and as communities. Northern researcher Wanda Wuttunee (Incident 1.2) sees small business development as a way to achieve aboriginal self-determination in a culturally appropriate manner. Others, such as Garry Oker of the Northern Shadow Dancers, see entrepreneurship itself as inherently aboriginal; Oker calls aboriginal entrepreneurs the new "economic warriors" who are creating their own economic future.[1]

Realization of the value and importance of the entrepreneurial and small business sector of Canadian society is now stronger than at any time since the turn of the century. Moreover,

---

1 "The Spirit Lives: Aboriginal Entrepreneurs in Canada," Sponsored by the Aboriginal Women's Council with support from Aboriginal Business Canada, Industry Canada, Coordinated by the Canadian Foundation for Economic Education; produced by Lang & Ackroyd Productions Inc., 1995.

the general interest in entrepreneurship is occurring at a time when socio-political changes in Canada are increasing the capacities of and resources controlled by aboriginal communities. As Wanda Wuttunee points out below, tremendous opportunities are opening up for aboriginal entrepreneurs.

INCIDENT 1.2
Northern Successes Chronicled by Author

Anyone can be a success in business, claims Wanda Wuttunee, and she has written a book to prove it. Wuttunee promotes "sustainable economic development" combined with diversity as a means to promote the small business industry of the North.

The diversity of the north is ripe for small businesses, explains Wuttunee, who was born in Regina and raised in Calgary. "Mega projects are not the only answer for the north. Small business is doing well. It is a significant proportion of the payroll," she adds.

"Small business is a wonderful way to be empowered, to have a say in how you run your own life. I think native people are looking for things like that. We need to take advantage from the people who have done it and pick up the best and then make it culturally appropriate."

And that is what Wuttunee hopes will be provided through her book, an insight into the experiences and successes of small businesses of the North. "It's the best time to be native. You have to stand up and do a good job. You are only limited by your own creativity and imagination."

SOURCE: Angela Simmons, *Windspeaker*, Canada's National Aboriginal News Publication, 9 November 1992, p. 8.

Since the Second World War the philosophy in many circles has been that bigger is better in both business and government. However, in the mid-1970s the critics of "bigness" gathered more support as big government and big business failed to provide the predicted panacea to society's social and economic problems. In the 1990s, governments and corporations across Canada are "downsizing" at record rates. The result is that more people and more governments are looking to small business to provide a catalyst.

Although the rapid growth which was characteristic of small business in the 1980s is unlikely to be sustained throughout the 1990s, small business will still provide a major benefit to the Canadian economy. Moreover, small business is an area of endeavour which is increasingly attracting aboriginal entrepreneurs. The following indicators suggest that an "entrepreneurial revolution" is taking place in Canada.

Increases in the Number of Business Establishments

Figure 1.1 illustrates the increasing number of business start-ups in recent years in Canada. As can be seen, the number of net start-ups increased by 34% for the years 1979–1989, despite the beginning of the recession in 1989. Regardless of which indicators are used, (such as tax returns, phone hookups, new incorporations, and business registrations), it is evident that in recent years increases in new businesses have occurred at the rate of between 5 and 12% per year.[2] Evidence shows that the majority of these new business formations are small

---

2 "The Entrepreneurial Numbers Game," *Inc.*, May 1986, 31–36.

FIGURE 1.1   Business* Start-ups and Exits, 1979–1989**

	Start-ups	Exits	Net Increase
1979–80	127,015	92,816	34,289
1980–81	134,769	95,996	38,773
1881–82	119,126	106,653	12,473
1982–83	145,154	102,251	42,903
1983–84	138,547	117,371	21,176
1984–85	152,213	110,520	41,693
1985–86	152,472	122,828	29,644
1986–87	161,285	127,085	34,200
1987–88	161,931	135,394	26,537
1988–89	165,980	140,054	25,926

* Excludes public administration; ** SOURCE: ESBO, Statistics Canada.
SOURCE: Excerpt from Small Business in Canada, Industry, Science and Technology, Canada, 1991.

businesses. For example, from 1978 to 1989 the number of Canadian companies with fewer than 50 employees grew from 582,000 to 906,592.[3]

Increases in the Number of People Employed in Small Businesses   A significant and growing proportion of Canadians have been employed in small businesses compared to larger ones in recent years. The employment trend between 1979 and 1989 for small business shows significant increase. See Figure 1.2. At the same time, employment levels in large businesses have remained the same or decreased over the same period. Clearly there appears to be a shift in the trend of employment in Canada from larger organizations to smaller ones.

Increases in the Number of Aboriginal Businesses   In 1989, a study prepared for the Canadian Chamber of Commerce found that there were 5,549 aboriginally owned businesses in Canada: 3,866 in the service industry, 632 in transport, 560 in resources, 424 in manufacturing and 67 "other" businesses.[4] The 1989 stats showed that 56% of aboriginal businesses were less than five years old, and they employed an average of six people.[5]

A 1991 Statistics Canada survey found 32,680 aboriginal people who had once owned or operated a business; 18,625 of those said they were still actively involved.[6] In the same 1991 Aboriginal Peoples Survey, 34,105 individuals reported that they planned to go into business in the next two years.[7]

---

3   *Small Business in Canada* (Ottawa: Industry, Science and Technology Canada, 1991), p. 3.
4   "New directions: federal support for Aboriginal businesses," *Aboriginal Business*, July/August 1994, 12–13.
5   *Ibid.*
6   Rudy Platiel, "Natives take to business with zeal," *Globe and Mail*, July 4, 1994.
7   *Ibid.*

FIGURE 1.2   Small Business Share of Employment,* 1979 & 1989

< 50 employees	
1979	1989
34%	39.8%

< 100 employees	
1979	1989
40.8%	47.1%

* Includes self-employed; excludes public administration.
SOURCE: Entrepreneurship and Small Business Office, Industry, Science and Technology, Canada.

Increases in Government Interest and Programs   A variety of government programs are available to aboriginal entrepreneurs. Many of them are now grouped under one heading, Aboriginal Business Canada, which has eight regional offices across the country (see Information Resources section on page 317). Ken Thomas describes the possibilities:

"The numbers show that there is a real spirit of enterprise growing in aboriginal communities. Government support should help us to build on the momentum that is growing every day... I'm talking about a rebirth of the aboriginal economy — about rediscovering our roots and traditions as people adept at trade and commerce, about innovating and building on our strengths and values, and emerging as full and independent partners in the Canadian economic federation. Such a future is within our grasp. And I think that Aboriginal Business Canada can help bring that future a little bit closer."[8]

As Thomas suggests, many aboriginal leaders now recognize the potential of small business in the growing aboriginal business sector, and governments are beginning to respond with various financial and other programs to assist the aboriginal small business owner. A current list of these programs appears in Chapter 14.

Some of these efforts have been more successful than others. The Indian Economic Development Fund of the 1970s and mid-1980s funded businesses to the tune of $150 million, a sum which could not meet the growing demand. Under the Native Economic Development Program (NEDP), the focus shifted from individual businesses to tribal and regional programs. $345 million was allocated; however the results were problematic as few band councils were able to meet the requirements of market research, infrastructure provision, and equity investment.[9]

In 1989, the Canadian Aboriginal Economic Development Strategy (CAEDS) replaced the NEDP, and the focus once again returned to individual entrepreneurship rather than community-based employment generation.[10] $874 million dollars were budgeted for a five year period, although $900 million were spent in the first four years. A 1994 Auditor General report criticized the lack of direction, coordination and accountability within CAEDS, and called for

---

8   "New directions," 12–13.
9   Ian Getty, "Recent Strategies for Socio-Economic Development," in Duane Champagne, editor, *Native North American Almanac* (Detroit: Gale Research Inc., 1994), 978.
10   *Ibid.*

project funding criteria to take greater account of the variable situations of individual aboriginal communities.[11]

In December 1994, the federal government announced a new "procurement" initiative which would steer up to $1.5 billion in government contracts to small and aboriginal businesses in Canada. Under this program aboriginal companies would be favoured for all purchases or work destined for aboriginal populations; eligible companies would have an aboriginal workforce of 35% or more and would have a majority aboriginal ownership. Canadian defenders of the initiative, which has come under criticism from a variety of directions, hope that the program will avoid the kind of abuse and corruption which have characterized a similar procurement program in the United States.[12]

At the present time in Canada there is also an Entrepreneur and Small Business office in the Department of Industry, Science and Technology which coordinates and administers programs designed to aid small business at the federal government level. The provinces likewise have departments that perform the same function for small businesses within their jurisdictions. A listing of these agencies is found in the Information Resources section beginning on page 317.

Increases in the Number of Small Business Management Entrepreneurship Courses at Colleges and Universities

The level of interest in entrepreneurial courses at Canadian colleges and universities has risen dramatically in the past few years. Moreover, a number of institutions have programs in aboriginal management, including courses directly focussed on aboriginal business development (See Incident 1.3).

INCIDENT 1.3
Demand Grows for Aboriginal Managers

The move to self-government and self-sufficiency among Canada's First Nations is creating a demand for aboriginal managers and administrators. As a result, a growing number of Canadian universities and colleges are setting up native business programs.

The University of Lethbridge's aboriginal management degree program is more than a decade old, and it helped pioneer the field. While students take such standard business courses as accounting with other students in the Faculty of Management, they also take 14 courses aimed specifically at aboriginal needs. These cover topics such as raising capital in aboriginal communities and alternative justice systems.

"We don't see this as a separate program," says Kate Chiste, who runs the program and is one of its professors. "It's an academic program within the Faculty of Management. Doing business with aboriginal people is a part of doing Canadian business, period."

Chiste says the four-year program is best suited to students who plan to work in native communities or in mainstream business in areas with a high aboriginal population. The program has 75 aboriginal students, and a placement rate of 100% for 1994 graduates.

SOURCE: Louise Kinross, *The Financial Post*, April 25, 1995, p. 21.

---

11 "Auditor-General Finds Substantial Shortcomings in CAEDS Program," *Native Issues Monthly*, February 1994, 24–25.

12 Michael Smith, "Aboriginal business may profit from new procurement program," *The First Perspective*, February 1994.

WHAT IS SMALL BUSINESS? ————————————————————

What size of business qualifies as a small business? This is not an easy question to answer as most organizations and agencies concerned with small businesses have different definitions. Knowing how various government departments define a small business is helpful in taking advantage of the tax incentives and other government assistance programs that are designed for small business. Also, a small business can benefit by knowing the size of business allowed by lenders to take advantage of small business provisions in their lending programs. These programs are available to small businesses from the Federal Business Development Bank (FBDB), provincial government lending agencies, and the chartered banks.

In view of the foregoing, it is useful to understand the criteria commonly used to distinguish a small business from a large one. There are at least four criteria that are used to make this distinction:

1. Number of Employees   Some government departments, such as the Federal Department of Regional Industrial Expansion, use the number of employees as their criteria. The Department of Industry, Trade & Commerce identifies a small business as one that employs under 100 people in a manufacturing industry and under 50 employees in a non-manufacturing industry. The Ministry of State for Small Business also uses the guide of 50 employees, while the Federal Business Development Bank considers a business that employs fewer than 75 as eligible for its Small Business Counselling Assistance. Other agencies, such as Statistics Canada and the Small Business Administration in the United States, consider small businesses to be much larger, ranging from 250 to 1,500 employees depending on the industry.

2. Gross Sales   Although the limits vary by industry, gross sales is a common method of defining small business. The Ministry of State for Small Business uses $2 million in sales, and the Small Business Loans Act in Canada is available to firms whose sales are less than $2 million. The Small Business Administration in the United States uses the following gross sales guidelines:

- Retailing: $3.5 million to $13.5 million
- Services: $3.5 million to $14.5 million
- Construction: $7 million to $17 million

3. Profits   Revenue Canada uses operating profits as its guideline for defining which businesses qualify for the "Small Business Deduction." This special deduction allows a reduced tax rate; (the tax situation of aboriginal businesses will be discussed in Chapter 11). This limit is presently set at a net operating profit of $200,000.

4. Type of Management-Ownership Structure   Another criteria used to define small business is the degree to which the owner is also the day-to-day manager of the business. Although there are exceptions, the majority of small business owners are also the managers. Because of the differences between industries and agencies, the Committee for Economic Development in the United States utilizes a slightly different and less specific approach to defining a small business. According to its definition, if any two of the following characteristics are evident, then the business may be classed as a small business.

1. Independent management (i.e., owner is the manager).
2. Owner-supplied capital.

3. Local area of operations.
4. Relatively small size within its industry.

As can be seen, it is no easy task to define the size of a small business; the definition used will depend upon the purpose and the agency or program concerned. Still, as earlier statistics suggested, most Canadian aboriginal businesses fall within most definitions of "small business".

Young Entrepreneurs

In addition to the large general increases in the number of small businesses since 1974, two additional trends are worth noting. The number of small businesses owned by people under the age of 30 has been increasing. According to Statistics Canada, over 38,000 business owners across Canada were under the age of 25 in 1986. In addition, almost 200,000 business owners were in the 25 to 34 year age bracket, making up 24% of the total number of business owners. As a result almost one third of the entire business population is under 35 years of age, showing that business ownership is an attractive career option for many younger Canadians.

This trend is of relevance to aboriginal communities, which are younger than the rest of the Canadian population. For example, in 1991, 42% of the aboriginal population were under the age of 25.[13] In some areas, as described in Incident 1.4 below, aboriginal youth are being specifically targeted by entrepreneurship training programs.

INCIDENT 1.4
Aboriginal Students Succeed as Entrepreneurs

Arctic, a Winnipeg T-shirt company, will cease operation this month after less than a year in business. The company is not a casualty of the recession, but rather a successful project undertaken by students from the Children of the Earth High School participating in the Junior Achievement program.

They created and sold T-shirts which feature a strikingly beautiful original Aboriginal artwork printed on the front. Neville Trevenen, program teacher, said he was impressed by the students' involvement and enthusiasm, which contributed greatly to the success of the project.

The Children of the Earth students received advice and guidance from their sponsor, the Royal Bank of Canada, and about nine other business people. Trevenen said this was a positive experience for the students because the advisors dealt with their questions and opinions seriously on an adult level.

SOURCE: Mike Smith, *The First Perspective*, July 1994.

Female Entrepreneurs

A second general trend is the increasingly important role which women are playing in entrepreneurial activity in Canada. In 1988 small businesses owned by women were 23.7% of the total, up from 21.3% in 1981. This trend parallels the general increase in employment for women in Canadian society. The growth of women entrepreneurs is increasing at a more rapid rate than any other ownership factor. In addition, almost one third of the young entrepreneur group is made up of women.

Data are scarce on the participation by aboriginal women in entrepreneurial activities, but several surveys suggest that aboriginal women constitute a growing percentage of all aboriginal entrepreneurs. The first survey on aboriginal women in service sector small business was published in 1991. This survey found that 37% of aboriginal businesses were operated by women.[14]

An earlier study found that aboriginal businesswomen tend to be "social entrepreneurs, meaning that they start businesses not to make a profit or to become independent, but to create jobs for kin and friends and to provide local goods and services."[15] Some aboriginal business programs, such as the Calmeadow Foundation, target aboriginal women in particular.

CONTRIBUTIONS OF SMALL BUSINESS

The small business sector is important to aboriginal communities and Canadian society in a variety of ways.

Labour Intensity

Small businesses are generally conceded to be more labour intensive than large companies. This means that they typically employ more people than a larger business to produce a certain level of output, and therefore have a particular attractiveness for communities, such as many aboriginal ones, which for various structural reasons have low levels of employment. In addition small firms have accounted for most of the new jobs created in Canada between 1979 and 1989.[16] It is estimated that this sector will have produced another one million new jobs and virtually 100% of net job creation[17] between 1980 and 1990.[18] In this era of general concern over employment levels, it is not surprising that current government policy includes incentives to promote the establishment of small business. Not only does small business provide significant contributions to employment, but recent research indicates employees feel that small companies are better places to work than large ones.[19]

Productivity and Profitability

Since the turn of the century, the conventional wisdom concerning productivity in organizations was that larger organizations offered a greater opportunity for *productivity* and *profitability*. As a result both business and government have tended to increase in size. However, the validity of this thinking has been seriously questioned in recent years and has been shown to be empirically weak. Figure 1.3 shows that small businesses score substantially higher than

---

14 Economic Development for Canadian Aboriginal Women, Inc. *Aboriginal Women's Success in Business; 1982–1991.* Ottawa: EDCAW, 1993, 6.
15 *Ibid.*
16 *Statistical Profile of Small Business in Canada,* 1983 (Small Business Secretariat, quoted from report of Department of Regional Economic Expansion).
17 "Canada's Entrepreneurial Revolution Advances," *Small Business,* June 1988, 24.
18 Canadian Federation of Independent Business, projection made at the International Council of Independent Business Conference, Toronto, May 1984.
19 Robert Levering, Milton Moscowitz, and Michael Katz, *The 100 Best Companies to Work for in America, 1984* (Scarborough, N.Y.: New American Library, 1985).

FIGURE 1.3   Return on Sales for Selected Industry Groups, Canada 1990 (%)

INDUSTRY GROUP	SMALL BUSINESSES Sales Levels		ALL BUSINESSES
	100K–499,999	500K–2,000K	
Manufacturing	3.8%	4.9%	4.0%
Construction	6.9	6.7	2.3
Wholesale	4.6	3.9	1.8
Retail	2.5	2.9	3.4
Services	13.7	7.8	6.3

SOURCES: *Statistical Profile of Small Business in Canada* (Statistics Canada), 1987; *Corporate Financial Statistics* (Statistics Canada), 1987; and *Key Business Ratios*, 1987, Dun & Bradstreet, Canada Ltd.

all businesses in most industries in return on sales (profit to sales), a standard measure of profitability.

Moreover, of the eight attributes of success listed by Peters and Waterman in their study of successful corporations,[20] no fewer than six are characteristics commonly found in small businesses:

1. Bias for Action   Preferring to do something, anything, rather than sending an idea through endless cycles of analyses and committee reports has been found by these organizations to encourage new ideas and creativity. This principle seems to be typical of most successful businesses.

2. Staying Close to the Customer   Learning customer preferences and catering to them. Small business is generally closer to and has more contact with the consumer. The larger organizations spend considerable amounts of money to maintain this closeness; businesses in small interrelated aboriginal communities have this kind of closeness naturally.

3. Autonomy and Entrepreneurship   Breaking the corporation into small companies and encouraging them to think independently and competitively has become a part of many large businesses. Both individual and group autonomy are a traditional social value of many aboriginal cultures, and the possibility of working on their own as a "jack or jill of all trades" is an attractive one for many aboriginal entrepreneurs.

4. Productivity through People   Creating in all employees the awareness that their best efforts are essential and that they will share in the rewards of the company's success seems to be a major goal of the successful companies. In the small business, the owner and employees typically share in the rewards of success and the disappointments of failure of their efforts. A successful business in an aboriginal community can offer tangible benefits for members of that community.

---

20 Peters and Waterman, *In Search of Excellence*.

5. Hands-On Value Driven   Insisting that executives keep in touch with the firm's essential business and promote a strong corporate culture is another attribute of success. A recently popular method of management known as Management by Walking Around is evidence of the realization of the need for management to be familiar with the employees and the operation of the business. This is once again something that the successful owner-manager does faithfully.

6. Simple Form Lean Staff   Few administrative layers, with few people at the upper levels, are characteristic of many of these successful businesses. In most small businesses, employees have a direct line of access to the owner-manager. This situation can increase the flexibility of the organization as well as employee morale.

Flexibility

Small business is generally able to respond more quickly than large business to changes in the economy, to government policies, and to competition. In addition to this, many markets, such as relatively remote reserve communities, can only be served by small business because they may be too small or too localized for a large company to service profitably. This situation alone presents countless opportunities for aboriginal entrepreneurs.

Social Contributions

Small business owners often seem to have a long-term interest in the communities in which their businesses operate. As a result, they appear to contribute to those communities in non-business ways to a greater extent than an employee of a large corporation might do.[21] For the aboriginal small business owner, the "social" aspects of entrepreneurship are often a key reason for going into business in the first place.

SMALL BUSINESS AND THE FUTURE

Canada is now in a period of rapid change, and this trend is expected to continue. Aboriginal communities in particular are in a period of transition as they assume increasing responsibilities and gain increasing control over resources. This means that aboriginal businesses will face a significantly different environment as the 21st century begins. Small business flexibility will continue to be a competitive strength for the aboriginal entrepreneur, as changes occur in technology, consumer demographics and buying patterns, and in the competitive aspects of markets.

Technology

Technology has revolutionized the business activities of both small and large businesses. The ability of the entrepreneur to manage large amounts of information through computers as effectively as the larger business has signalled significant small business opportunities. Technological capacity can be of special advantage to small businesses in remote aboriginal

---

21 Nelson A. Riis, Commons Debate, February 7, 1985, Ottawa, 2120.

communities, helping close the knowledge gap between themselves and businesses with larger infrastructures.

Financial management and accounting, marketing research and planning, promotion and consulting are all areas where small businesses, many of which are home based, have been successful. As the cost of computer technology decreases, more small businesses will take advantage of computer applications in these areas.

New technology has also allowed small businesses to subcontract many services from larger businesses and government organizations which do not have the interest or ability to carry out these activities themselves. The general devolution of responsibility from the Canadian government to aboriginal communities presents a wide field of opportunity. Small businesses, however, must be prepared to intelligently embrace new technology or face the possibility of obsolescence and lack of competitiveness. There are few sectors where lack of knowledge about technological change will not adversely affect performance.

Consumer Demographics and Buying Patterns

Aboriginal entrepreneurs will want to consider Canada-wide demographic trends as well as the demographics of their own communities. Aboriginal communities themselves are getting younger. But Canadian consumers as a whole are aging. Of particular interest to most businesses is the "baby boom" consumer, born between 1946 and 1964. These people are the largest and most significant demographic group, comprising close to one third of the Canadian population. This group is currently entering its highest income earning period, resulting in large expenditures for certain types of goods and services.

Canadian seniors, while small in number, hold close to 80% of personal wealth and are big spenders on travel, health and fitness products and various services. The high incidence of working women has created greater economic clout for women as well as a greater demand for time-saving products and convenience. All demographic groups in Canada have a concern for the environment and a demand for quality products at a reasonable price.

Each of these demographic and demand trends represents opportunities for entrepreneurs. Many examples of how entrepreneurs are responding to these trends are presented in the profiles and incidents in this text. Markets will become further fragmented as businesses attempt to satisfy consumer wants and needs. This increase in segmentation should favour small businesses that cater to these smaller, more specialized markets.

Competitive Aspects of Markets

There have been three major occurrences in the past few years which have had an impact upon the already competitive situation most small businesses face. The first is the Free Trade Agreements which will liberalize trade among Canada, the United States, and Mexico. Second, there is a worldwide movement to global markets which has been augmented by recent developments in Eastern Europe. Third is the response to the growth of the small business sector by large business.

The Free Trade Agreements

The Canada-U.S. agreement will gradually remove trade barriers between the two countries, but it will also remove protection for certain industries. In general, Canadian small business has been in favour of the agreement because of the large consumer market to the south.

Some Canadian entrepreneurs have already found success in this market. Many have found, however, that there are still other difficulties to be overcome before they can effectively compete. Examples are such factors as higher Canadian taxes and distribution costs.

Free trade with the United States has also increased the competition from U.S. firms expanding into Canada. This has been most noticeable in the retailing industry. Although there will likely be adjustments in particular industries in the short term, the overall competitiveness of the affected industries is expected to improve. Similar consequences to the first agreement are expected as a result of the North American Free Trade Agreement (NAFTA) with the U.S. and Mexico.

Global Markets

The world is currently experiencing a major shift to the globalization of markets. This will mean that many small businesses will eventually include an international aspect to their operations. Canadian small businesses will find increased access to export markets as trade barriers are removed. Current GATT (General Agreement on Tariffs and Trade) talks suggest that this might occur.

Although the trend towards trade liberalization has been occurring gradually over a number or years, the recent decline of communism in the eastern bloc has signalled a number of opportunities for entrepreneurs. Consumers in these countries have an insatiable demand for western products and services, and as remaining barriers and purchasing power problems are overcome these areas represent huge untapped markets. In addition, many European consumers have a pre-existing interest in North American aboriginal culture, which may lead to business opportunities in areas such as aboriginal tourism. Aboriginal Business Canada has recently announced a program to take advantage of the export potential of aboriginal businesses (Incident 1.5 below).

INCIDENT 1.5
Aboriginal Business Announces Export Program

Aboriginal Business Canada (ABC), a division of Industry Canada, has announced a program intended to assist aboriginal businesses to develop export capabilities and markets. ABC has assigned trade specialists in its offices across Canada to help aboriginal clients access the broad range of export-assistance services available; provide financial support for marketing planning, trade missions and export promotion activities; and participate in special sectoral and advocacy initiatives sponsored by Aboriginal Business Canada.

According to ABC, aboriginal businesses have particular export potential in the areas of traditional aboriginal food products, in authentic tourism destinations and products and in "indigenous-to-indigenous" trade opportunities with First Peoples in other countries.

SOURCE: *Native Issues Monthly*, February 1995, p. 22.

Large Business Response

Small businesses have always had difficulty competing with large businesses, particularly for capital, raw materials, and labour. This situation is not expected to change appreciably in some industries. Financing problems continue to plague small businesses, and business financing has traditionally been problematic for aboriginal businesses. Despite new programs, influence over suppliers by large businesses is strong, and wage rates paid by larger organizations and government are often too high for the smaller business to compete. However, many aboriginal businesses are drawing from a different labour market than large mainstream corporations.

In addition to the difficulty of matching wage rates, the 1990s and beyond are expected to produce labour shortages, which will increase the competition for competent employees even more. Small businesses will need to find ways of retaining top employees through nonfinancial methods. In small communities such as many aboriginal ones, the human resource pool is already limited. On the other hand, the overall youth of the aboriginal population means that they will be entering the workforce in increasing numbers.

One positive aspect is that many large businesses and government agencies are subcontracting the purchase of products and services to small business, and as mentioned earlier a federal procurement program is on stream which would send contracts towards aboriginal businesses. There is also evidence that many small businesses are joining together through such means as industry associations in an attempt to be more competitive. Here again, the opportunity for aboriginal business networks is clear; the Northeastern Alberta Aboriginal Business Association is one example (Small Business Profile, Chapter 2).

ECONOMY

The performance of many small businesses is directly related to the Canadian economy. During the recession of 1981–82, net increases in the number of small businesses decreased (see Figure 1.1). This reflects the fact that it is harder for businesses to become established during such times; also, the number of failures is higher because of lower revenues. The recession of the early 1990s has had a similar effect on the performance of the small business sector. There is evidence, however, that those businesses which do start during a recession have a greater chance of survival than those started during expansionary periods.[22] Incident 1.6 illustrates what entrepreneurs will need to do to cope with difficult times in the economy.

INCIDENT 1.6
The New Challenge of the 90s

Entrepreneurs will be talking about the 1990–91 recession long after the red ink flows back again. Panellists at the Future Watch Roundtable agree this recession has reshaped the economy. "In southwestern Ontario, it's been the worst recession since the '30s and it's taken a real toll," says John Cowperthwaite, national director of entrepreneurial services for Ernst & Young.

The economy is changing. But *Profit's* panellists, a stellar lineup of innovative and award-winning entrepreneurs, believe those who adapt and become tougher competitors will survive and prosper in the upswing. "You can bitch and yell about it, but the world is becoming more competitive," says Conald Ziraldo, president of Inniskillin Wines Inc. of Niagara-on-the-Lake, Ontario. "If you want to stick around, you've got to join in." Our panellists suggest a three-step process to competing in the new '90s.

1. Get to know your market better, and deliver what your customers want.
2. Motivate your work force and reassess operations to produce the best products you can.

---

22 Cathy Hilborn, "Recession Startups Not So Risky Business," *Profit Magazine*, July–August 1991, 8.

3. Look to export markets for future growth and diversification.

SOURCE: Cathy Hilborn, "The New Challenge of the '90s," *Profit Magazine*, December 1991, p. 26.

POLITICAL CLIMATE

During the 1980s and early 1990s, the political climate for small business ownership seemed to be improving. This was evidenced by attempts to reduce the burdens of paperwork and provide tax incentives to small businesses. The political climate for aboriginal business ownership is also improving. Land claims settlements, the move towards devolution from and dismantlement of the Department of Indian Affairs, and the push for aboriginal self-government have drawn attention to the tremendous potential capacities of aboriginal communities and aboriginal entrepreneurs.

Although there is considerable interest in government circles in reducing government involvement in business and encouraging entrepreneurial activity, as was shown by recent government consultations,[23] most small business proponents are still waiting for significant action to take place. In fact, the enactment of the Goods and Services Tax (GST) has had a much more severe effect on small business than on larger businesses. More will be said about the GST and its applicability to aboriginal businesses in Chapter 11.

Continued collective lobbying efforts through organizations such as the Federation of Independent Business are required to achieve a political environment which is more conducive to the establishment and successful operation of the small business. In addition to those general efforts, aboriginal organizations such as the Canadian Council for Aboriginal Business are active proponents of the aboriginal small business sector.

SOCIAL CLIMATE

Canadian society looks quite favourably upon small business and entrepreneurial activities as a way of making a living, and in many small communities entrepreneurship and micro-enterprise are one of the most promising forms of economic development. Although this trend is expected to continue, adequate preparation and planning will be increasingly required to achieve success following this route.

The challenge is for entrepreneurs as prospective owner-managers to sharpen their skills in this competitive and rapidly changing society. An entrepreneur in today's world cannot survive on guesswork. The remaining chapters in this book will cover the critical skill areas a prospective entrepreneur will benefit from in starting and operating a successful small business.

SUMMARY

1. Many countries are turning to small business and private initiative to assist in their economic growth, and in Canada the developing aboriginal business sector includes increasing numbers of successful aboriginal entrepreneurs.

---

23 *The White Paper — Recent Cross Canada Consultations Inviting Submissions from Small Businesses* (Government of Canada, Ministry of State for Small Business).

2. The entrepreneurial revolution is evidenced by increases in business establishments, employees in small businesses, government small business programs, and college and university small business courses.
3. Although defining a small business is difficult, a definition is useful in comparing and evaluating small businesses as well as taking advantage of various lending and assistance programs.
4. Some of the common criteria in defining small business are gross sales, number of employees, profitability, and type of management structure.
5. A majority of aboriginal businesses fall within the definition of a small business.
6. In recent years there has been an increase in small businesses established by young people and in the percentage of small businesses started by women.
7. Small businesses can provide jobs, innovations, high productivity, and flexibility for owners and employees.
8. Aboriginal small businesses are a way in which individual entrepreneurs can make social and economic contributions to their communities.
9. The climate for starting a small business in the future should improve; however, there will continue to be competitive disadvantages that entrepreneurs will have to overcome.

DISCUSSION QUESTIONS

1. Why do you think there has been an increase in entrepreneurial activity in aboriginal communities? Do you think these trends will continue? Why?
2. What do you think the greatest opportunities are for the developing aboriginal business sector in Canada?
3. What is meant by the statement "Small business is the backbone of the Canadian Economic System"? Give evidence to support this statement.
4. What are the particular appeals of entrepreneurship for aboriginal women and aboriginal youth?
5. Ask three small business owners about their projections for the future of small business. What problems and opportunities do they foresee?

SUGGESTED READINGS

Aboriginal Law and Business. Toronto: Insight Press, 1993.

Bulloch, John F. "Competing in the Global Economy." *Journal of Small Business and Entrepreneurship*. July–September 1991.

Casson, M. *Entrepreneurship*. Brookfield: Elgar Publishing, 1990.

Coates, Ken. "Aboriginal Economic Activity in Canada." In Duane Champange, ed. *The Native North American Almanac: A Reference Work on Native North Americans in the United States and Canada*. Detroit: Gale Research, 1994, 958–69.

Danco, Leon A. *Beyond Survival: A Guide for the Business Owner and His Family*. New York: Centre for Entrepreneurial Management, 1986.

Drucker, Peter F. *Innovation and Entrepreneurship*. New York: Harper & Row, 1993.

Gasse, Yvon and Harold Bherer, eds. *Native Entrepreneurship: The Key to Autonomy*. Proceedings of the National Conference on Native Entrepreneurship. Beaupré, Québec, August 1990.

Getty, Ian. "An Overview of Economic Development History on Canadian Native Reserves." In Duane Champange, ed. *The Native North American Almanac: A Reference Work on Native North Americans in the United States and Canada* (Detroit: Gale Research, 1994), 969–83.

Grossman, G. and Helpman, E. *Innovation and Growth in the Global Economy*. Cambridge, Mass.: MIT Press, 1991.

Hosmer, LaRue. *The Ethics of Management*. Burr Ridge, IL: Irwin Inc., 1991.

Hosmer, LaRue. *Moral Leadership in Business*. Burr Ridge, IL: Irwin Inc., 1993.

Kretchman, L., L. Cranson and B. Jenning. *Entrepreneurship: Creating a Venture*. Toronto, Ontario: Harcourt Brace Jovanovick, 1991.

Liepner, M. and J. Herve. *The Entrepreneurial Spirit*. Toronto, Ontario: McGraw-Hill Ryerson, 1991.

Mancuso, J. *Mid Career Entrepreneur: How to Start a Business and Be Your Own Boss*. Chicago: Dearborn Finan., 1993.

Scherer, F. and M. Perlman. *Entrepreneurship, Technological Innovation, and Economic Growth*. University of Michigan Press, 1992.

Small Business in Canada, 1991. Industry, Science and Technology Canada 1991. Government of Canada.

Thompson, Pat. "Characteristics of the Small Business Entrepreneur in Canada." *Journal of Small Business and Entrepreneurship* 4:3, Winter (1986–1987), 5–11.

Trosper, Ronald L. "Traditional American Indian Economic Policy." *American Indian Culture and Research Journal* 19:1 (1995), 65–95.

C H A P T E R   2

The Small Business Decision

Katherine Beaty Chiste

CHAPTER OBJECTIVES

☐ To discuss the advantages and disadvantages of small business ownership for aboriginal entrepreneurs and communities.

☐ To review the personal attributes typical of a successful small business owner.

☐ To explain the common reasons why some businesses fail and others succeed.

☐ To assist in evaluating the small business decision from an organizational point of view.

☐ To discuss the types of business environments that foster small business success.

☐ To investigate the differences between entrepreneurs and managers.

SMALL BUSINESS PROFILE
Dave Tuccaro
Neegan Development Corporation Ltd.

Dave Tuccaro, a Treaty Indian from the Mikisew Cree Band in Fort Chipewyan, Alberta, was hired as general manager of Neegan Development Corporation in 1991. At that time Neegan was a heavy equipment company owned by four Indian bands in Northern Alberta. It had been experiencing serious financial difficulties, and Tuccaro was called in to turn the company around. Due to his extensive business experience in band management and economic development, his perseverance in putting in gruelling 14 hour days, and the assistance of the banks and Syncrude, Dave Tuccaro was able to return Neegan to profitability in two years.

This success has earned him a nomination as Canada's Turn-Around Entrepreneur of the Year Award and in 1995 the Regional Aboriginal Recognition Award. While he was managing Neegan, Dave recognized the long-term potential of the business and decided to purchase it in 1994. Currently, Neegan services Syncrude Canada at Fort McMurray, Alberta as well as other customers. With Tuccaro's able management it has been successful at securing and maintaining a substantial portion of the business in its market area.

Through Neegan, Tuccaro has been successful at putting many aboriginal people to work and encouraging others to start their own businesses. His desire to help his people is evidenced by his position as President of the Northeastern Alberta Aboriginal Business Association, a group committed to strengthening the ties that aboriginal business has to corporate Canada. Dave Tuccaro's experience is a good example of the persistence which successful entrepreneurs possess. Says Tuccaro, "If they can do it, so can I."

SOURCE: Used with permission of Dave Tuccaro.

THE SMALL BUSINESS DECISION: PERSONAL EVALUATION

When thinking about starting their own business, potential business people may want to consider the consequences of such a move, both on themselves and on their families and communities. Failure to do so can lead to disillusionment, frustration, and an unsuccessful attempt to capitalize on a viable business opportunity. A good way to begin this personal evaluation is to become aware of the potential advantages and disadvantages of starting and operating one's own business.

ADVANTAGES OF SMALL BUSINESS OWNERSHIP

There are some unique advantages to running one's own business as opposed to being an employee. The more common ones are listed below.

More Personal Contacts with People   Running a small business usually means making contact with a large number of people, including customers, suppliers, and employees. Those who enjoy working with people and are skilled at it find this aspect of their business to be most rewarding. Those who want to remain in a familiar community rather than relocate to pursue employment may also find small business an appealing option.

Independence   Often independence is the primary reason for going into business for oneself. This includes the freedom to make one's own decisions without having to account to a superior for one's actions. A recent study of successful entrepreneurs indicated that the majority started their business to "control their own life" or to "be their own boss."[1] Entrepreneurs should realize, however, that even though they own their own business, they still must answer to customers, suppliers, key employees, and creditors.

Skill Development   Abilities in many functional areas of management are necessary and can be developed when running a small business. Communities in which people are raised to be "jills and jacks of all trades" may have a number of members well suited to small business.

Possible Financial Rewards   Because of the higher risk associated with operating a small business, there is also the possibility of obtaining a higher financial return. Many small businesses are very profitable, providing for their owner's financial independence. It should be noted, however, that the promise of financial gain is seldom the motivation for successful entrepreneurs in starting their business.[2] Therefore while the possibility of financial reward is present, it is seldom the sole motivating force behind a small business start-up.

Challenge   Many people today start small businesses because of the challenge and feeling of personal accomplishment. Archie Gladhue of Lasso Contracting, profiled in Incident 2.2, says, "One of my favourite accomplishments is having non-Native people recognize that we can do the job. I'd like to convince more Native people to get into business. It's been a challenge for me. It's been an experience. And it has been worthwhile."[3]

---

1   "Inc. and U.S.A. Today Survey of 500 Fastest Growing Private Companies," *Inc.*, June 1986, 48.
2   *Ibid.*
3   "Self-employment way to create challenges," *Windspeaker*, 18 January 1993, 7.

Enjoyment   Most successful entrepreneurs enjoy what they do. In fact entrepreneurs tend to get their best ideas from their hobbies.[4] Mary Coyle of Calmeadow Foundation, which lends money to "borrowers' circles" of First Nations people, says, "Where we saw people a number of years ago considering what they were doing as a hobby, particularly the smaller home-based activities, now they see themselves as entrepreneurs who are self-employed and providing work for others in the community out of choice."[5]

The fact that entrepreneurs enjoy their work explains in part the reason why financial rewards are not necessarily their prime motivation in establishing their businesses. It also explains to a certain extent the large amount of time they spend with their businesses. An indication of the level of enjoyment that entrepreneurs get from running their own businesses is the fact that over 90% of Canadian entrepreneurs said that they would start their own business again.[6]

DISADVANTAGES OF SMALL BUSINESS OWNERSHIP

While there are many advantages in owning and operating a small business, there are disadvantages as well. Some of these are described below.

Risk   The failure rate of small business is very high. It has been estimated that four out of every five small businesses will fail within the first few years. Although there are many reasons for these failures, the major causes appear to be inexperience or unbalanced management.[7] Still, aboriginal small businesses have been found to survive at rates equivalent to or greater than other businesses, with aboriginal businesses in the construction and retail trade being especially successful.[8]

Stress   Studies show that small business owners have high stress levels, high incidence of heart trouble, and a high rate of divorce — owing to the increased pressures of managing their own businesses.[9] In owning a business, it is difficult, if not impossible, to confine concerns about the business to the workplace. Typically these pressures will affect one's personal life and family situation.

Many Abilities Required   The acquisition of the required skills such as accounting, finance, marketing, and personnel management can be a difficult task that many owner-managers never master. This is particularly true for the countless businesses that start as micro-enterprises. In these situations the entrepreneur generally cannot afford to hire professionals in these areas. As an article from *Windspeaker* suggests (Incident 2.1), "being your own boss" can be a tough job.

---

4   Karl Vesper, "Freedom and Power: What Every Entrepreneur Craves," *Success*, May 1988, 48.
5   Quoted in Rudy Platiel, "Natives take to business with zeal," *Globe and Mail*, 4 July 1994.
6   Pat Thompson, "Characteristics of the Small Business Entrepreneur in Canada," *Journal of Small Business and Entrepreneurship* 4:3, Winter 1986–87, 5.
7   *The Canadian Business Failure Record, 1984*, (New York: Dun and Bradstreet, 1984), 1–19.
8   Goss Gilroy Inc., *Financial Performance and Employment Creation Relating to Firms Assisted by ABDP (Aboriginal Business Development, Industry, Science and Technology Canada* (Ottawa: Goss Gilroy Inc.), June 1993, vi.
9   David P. Boyd and David E. Gumpert, "Coping with Entrepreneurial Stress," *Harvard Business Review*, March–April 1983, 44–64.

INCIDENT 2.1
Being Boss a Tough Job

Working for yourself is such a wonderful dream! No one to boss you around. Start when you want, finish when you want. And the money will just roll in.

Sad to say, this is a dream. Being your own boss means that you have many bosses — like your customers, creditors, the government and employees. Here is a sobering fact. Businesses can fail because of many reasons, and 40–80% of all new businesses fail within the first year. Let's look at some of the pitfalls.

- 97 percent of all business failures are the result of poor management:
  - ☐ no skills in that area
  - ☐ improper knowledge of the market
  - ☐ poor price setting
  - ☐ incorrect sales forecast
  - ☐ weak or non-existent business plans
  - ☐ poor self-discipline
  - ☐ poor bookkeeping
  - ☐ got into business too fast, didn't think the idea through

- In many cases a business person has to do a number of distasteful things like:
  - ☐ collecting unpaid bills
  - ☐ listening to customers' complaints
  - ☐ settling employee disputes
  - ☐ firing poor employees
  - ☐ keeping things on schedule
  - ☐ doing the books, filing and cleaning up

- To sum it all up, running a successful business is a blend of many skills:
  - ☐ good salesmanship
  - ☐ understanding economics, bookkeeping, financial management
  - ☐ knowing the marketplace, the customer, the competition
  - ☐ getting along well with people
  - ☐ planning

Where do you fit into this dream? You may have some of these skills and are not afraid to tackle the ones you don't have. That's an entrepreneur's spirit you have, and don't let go!

SOURCE: Heather Halpenny, "Being Boss a Tough Job," *Windspeaker*, Canada's National Aboriginal News Publication, June 30–July 3, 1994, p. 8.

Financial Rewards   Although the possibility of making a large income does exist, there are relatively few small business millionaires. It is typical, especially during the first few years of a business, for the financial rewards to be meagre. This situation applies even for those businesses that are growing rapidly; these businesses are not necessarily profitable.

People Conflicts   Because owning a small business tends to require more contact with people, the potential arises for more conflicts with employees, suppliers, and customers. Also, in an interrelated community, issues such as extension of credit or employee discipline may be a special source of conflict. Thus, what is often thought of as an advantage can turn into both a disadvantage and a frustration of small business ownership.

Time Demands   Almost all small businesses, at least initially, require long hours of work. The hours an entrepreneur works may be much longer than if she or he was working for someone else. A recent study of small business owners indicates that almost half work over 50 hours per week, and 86% say they work on weekends.[10] As Archie Gladhue points out, family support is crucial (Incident 2.2).

INCIDENT 2.2
Self-Employment Way to Create Challenges

If there is a secret to building a successful business, it boils down to careful planning, good management and support from the family, says Archie Gladue, whose family is tied to the Janvier Reserve in northern Alberta.

"I would say do a good study on what you are going to get into. Make sure that the families are aware they will need to give their support because it takes a lot of hours and a lot of stress," says the man at the helm of Lasso Contracting.

For the last 15 years, Gladue has been applying his simple philosophy of hard work and good management to his group of Fort McMurray-based companies. The result has been the creation of a thriving business, offering jobs to the region's communities, and the satisfaction of a job well done.

"For me it has been self-rewarding," Gladue says. He hopes other young people growing up in the communities will make entrepreneurial career choices. It's a good way to make a living, according to Gladue, as well as one that offers more than just financial rewards.

SOURCE: *Windspeaker*, Canada's National Aboriginal News Publication, January 18, 1993, p. 7.

PERSONALITY CHARACTERISTICS TYPICAL OF A SUCCESSFUL OWNER-MANAGER

What are the personality traits of successful owner-managers like Archie Gladue? Charles A. Garfield, in his book *Peak Performers*, estimates that 70% of the 1,500 peak performers he studied were entrepreneurs.[11] These individuals exhibited some common characteristics. However, entrepreneurs, aboriginal and others, are a diverse group, and different skills may be needed at different stages of business development. The aboriginal entrepreneur may also benefit from an entrepreneurial zest within his or her own community. Patrick Lavelle of the Canadian Council for Aboriginal Business says, "Aboriginal communities are by and large more entrepreneurial than non-native communities — they're prepared to try almost anything."[12]

Achievement Orientation   Mainstream business wisdom places a high value on achievement, competition, aggressiveness, and hard work as the ideal characteristics of owner-managers. In this view, entrepreneurs tend to be disciplined goal setters and to have a bias for action; they also tend to have above average focus and drive as well as the initiative to make things happen. Because they are hard workers, they generally possess good health to maintain this high level of energy.

---

10 Small Business Survey, Ronm Rotenberg, Brock University, 1989.
11 Charles A. Garfield, *Peak Performers* (New York: William Morrow, 1985).
12 "The Evolution of Aboriginal Business," *Financial Post*, April 9, 1994, C1.

Risk Taking   The very nature of small business, as previously described, illustrates that entrepreneurs are risk takers, although they often do not think of themselves as such. Evidence shows, however, that successful entrepreneurs usually do take calculated risks. They do not fear failure but use it as a source of motivation.

Independence   Entrepreneurs have a tendency to resent authority and to want to take credit or discredit for their own actions. Karl Vesper, the well-known spokesman for entrepreneurship, states in his book *New Venture Strategies* that "the entrepreneur...has a basic human appetite to crave for freedom and power over his/her circumstances." Strongly correlated with independence are self-confidence and self-assurance. Often these traits are acquired through parents who were also small business owners. A recent study found that 35% of Canadian entrepreneurs had parents who owned businesses.[13]

Creativity   Successful entrepreneurs tend to be creative and are willing to try new ideas. They are not afraid to evaluate an idea in a non-traditional way and to ask questions such as "Why not?" Such entrepreneurs are sensitive to new trends in society and potential opportunities that develop as a result of such trends.

Strong Verbal and Numeric Skills   Successful small business owners have an ability to communicate their thoughts well and have numeric skills that aid them in solving many of the problems that arise in operating a small business. Although they may not have achieved a high formal education, successful entrepreneurs have usually acquired the necessary skills and knowledge from various life experiences.

Most successful entrepreneurs also have above average marketing and selling skills. Not only are these skills helpful in promoting the business to customers, but they are also essential in obtaining debt or equity capital, in securing suppliers, and maintaining employer loyalty. They are also valuable in establishing networking contacts or sources of assistance to their operations.

Problem-Solving Abilities   Entrepreneurs identify problems quickly and can respond with effective solutions. Typically they rank above average at sorting through the irrelevant and getting to the heart of a problem.

Strategic Planning   Successful small business owners tend to be excellent at setting business objectives and developing different ways of achieving them. They adapt to change easily and know their industry and product thoroughly.

Perseverance   Because of the difficulties in starting and operating a small business, those that are successful tend to have perseverance. They do not quit amidst adversity. Dave Tuccaro, profiled at the beginning of this chapter, has persevered to turn around Neegan Development Corporation and secure and maintain a substantial portion of business in northern Alberta.

In order to assess the suitability of one's personality for starting a small business, the entrepreneur can evaluate his or her own capabilities in the above areas. An example of a mainstream business checklist is found in Figure 2.1.

---

13 "A Nation of Entrepreneurs," *Report on Business Magazine*, October 1988, 62.

FIGURE 2.1 Personality Characteristic Checklist

If the statement is only rarely or slightly descriptive of your behaviour, score 1.
If the statement is applicable under some circumstances, but only partially true,
score 2. If the statement describes you perfectly, score 3.

Score

 1. I relish competing with others. _____
 2. I compete intensely to win regardless of the rewards. _____
 3. I compete with some caution, but will often bluff. _____
 4. I do not hesitate to take a calculated risk for future gain. _____
 5. I do a job so effectively that I get a feeling of accomplishment. _____
 6. I want to be tops in whatever I elect to do. _____
 7. I am not bound by tradition. _____
 8. I am inclined to forge ahead and discuss later. _____
 9. Reward or praise means less to me than a job well done. _____
10. I usually go my own way regardless of others' opinions. _____
11. I find it difficult to admit error or defeat. _____
12. I am a self-starter; I need little urging from others. _____
13. I am not easily discouraged. _____
14. I work out my own answers to problems. _____
15. I am inquisitive. _____
16. I am not patient with interference from others. _____
17. I have an aversion to taking orders from others. _____
18. I can take criticism without hurt feelings. _____
19. I insist on seeing a job through to the finish. _____
20. I expect associates to work as hard as I do. _____
21. I read to improve my knowledge in all business activities. _____

A score of 63 is perfect; 52 to 62 is good; 42 to 51 is fair; and under 42,
poor. Obviously scoring high here is not a guarantee of becoming a successful
small business owner, since many other personal qualities must also be rated.
But it should encourage you to pursue the matter further.

THE SMALL BUSINESS DECISION: ORGANIZATIONAL EVALUATION ———

It is useful not only to evaluate one's personal capabilities to operate a small business
successfully but also to investigate what it is that makes some businesses successes and
others failures. The following discussion may help the potential small business owner incorporate those things successful businesses do right while avoiding the mistakes that other
businesses have made.

SMALL BUSINESS SUCCESSES

Despite the high risk associated with starting a small business, many successful aboriginal small businesses are in operation today. Numerous examples of these are given throughout this book by way of the Incidents and Profiles. Listed below is a review of the characteristics of such successful small businesses.

Alertness to Change   Those businesses that are flexible and plan ahead are able to adapt to changing environmental conditions quickly and, in many cases, more effectively than can larger businesses. The success of many small computer software companies is a good example. This industry is changing very rapidly, and thus there are opportunities for small business to service various aspects of it. The ability of an entrepreneur such as Roland Bellerose (Incident 2.4) to recognize a need and respond to it contributed to his success.

Ability to Attract and to Hold Competent Employees   Small business tends to be labour intensive, and thus the value of its employees cannot be overstated. Being able to attract and retain good employees in small or remote communities can be a particular challenge. On the other hand, in a small interrelated community, aboriginal entrepreneurs will have a great deal of "on-the-ground" knowledge to help them evaluate potential employees and their life circumstances. An example of one aboriginal business which has successfully attracted employees in a local community is given in Incident 2.3.

INCIDENT 2.3
Local Business Provides Training and Employment Opportunities

> On a remote coastal lake on the east side of Victoria Island, which lies 200 miles north of the Arctic Circle, brothers George and Gary Angohiotok operate a fishing camp. They are majority partners in Northern Emak Outfitting, "emak" being the Inuit word for "waters". The camp offers fishermen from around the world the opportunity to catch arctic char in Char Lake. Bill Tait, who operates Adventure North Explorations in Yellowknife, and Jerome Knapp, a journalist, are the other partners.
>
> Each season Northern Emak employs about seven guides and a cook. The company plays an active role in providing training and employment opportunities for people in the community. Both George and Gary are certified guides. Although the two do not require certification from their employees, they are encouraged to seek certification since it will improve their employability. Through their work with Northern Emak, the young guides are able to develop invaluable "people skills". Bill notes, "There's a multiplier effect with a business. Skills and dollars stay in the community and multiply."
>
> SOURCE: Wanda Wuttunee, "Northern Emak Outfitting Inc.," Centre for Aboriginal Management, University of Lethbridge, 1991.

Closeness to Consumer   Businesses that have a good knowledge of consumers' wants and needs and are able to incorporate these into the operations of their companies tend to be more successful. This involves a constant monitoring of and response to the market.

Thoroughness with Operating Details   Successful businesses operate under detailed and controlled operating plans, whether it be in the plant or out in the market. Goals, reports, and constant evaluation and adjustment are used constantly.

Ability to Obtain Needed Capital   A possible constraint to the operation and growth of any business is the lack of funds. Successful businesses, however, often seem to have little difficulty obtaining start-up and operating capital. They are aware of the sources of available financing and are able to make an acceptable presentation of their requirements to both equity or debt sources as the situation requires. Roland Bellerose, for example, turned to Peace Hills Trust to help finance his graphics and photography business (Incident 2.4).

INCIDENT 2.4
Use Both Worlds to Your Advantage

>   Roland Bellerose is a successful entrepreneur. He is the owner of a fast-growing graphics and photography business called Clicks & Bits in Calgary, Alberta. He is also a Cree. Those two facts put him on the cutting edge of a profound change. A growing number of natives are starting their own businesses. Indian and Northern Affairs estimates 6,000 businesses are owned by First Nations people across Canada. And those figures don't include firms run by non-status natives like Bellerose.
>   Being a native has been both a blessing and a handicap to Bellerose's business career. His culture gave him a sense of values that has contributed to the success of his business. "I grew up in a culture where giving back is valued very highly. I think that's why I harp so much on quality." Additionally, being a native helped him win orders from many of the bands located around Calgary. But when he started out four years ago, it was hard to get financing. In the end he turned to Peace Hills Trust, a company set up by the Sampson Band in Alberta. "I didn't have to put up with a lot of stereotyping that I did with the other financial institutions," he says.
>   "A smart businessman will use both worlds to his advantage," according to Roland Bellerose. That's why this entrepreneur is successful.
>
> SOURCE: Paul Rodgers, "Natives find focus," *Calgary Sun*, June 27, 1993. Reprinted with permission of the *Calgary Sun*.

Effective Handling of Government Laws, Rules, and Regulations   Successful small businesses keep up-to-date with legislation and programs that may affect and benefit their operations. They realize that ignorance of certain regulations can cost the organization not only in a direct financial way but also, perhaps more importantly, in the loss of a reputation or an opportunity. Developing aboriginal tax law is one area with which aboriginal entrepreneurs may wish to keep current.

Environments Conducive to Small Business Success

In addition to the foregoing internal characteristics of successful small businesses, there are some important environmental situations in which small businesses may have a competitive edge. Some of these conditions are:

1. Where personal attention to daily operations by the owner is essential to success, such as a service business. In this type of business, the expertise of the owner-manager is a major component in generating revenue.
2. Where owner contact with the employees is important to the motivation of staff and the quality of work done. Specialized or custom-made manufacturing processes, service businesses, and other businesses in which employees have direct contact with the customer might fit into this category.

3. Where the business is more labour and less capital intensive. A business that relies heavily on people as opposed to machines to provide its product or service may be easier to manage if small in size. The retail industry is one case in point.
4. Where flexibility is required. This is indicative of industries with high growth rates, erratic demand, or perishable products.
5. Where demand is small or local, and thus large businesses are generally less interested in pursuing them.
6. Where governments offer considerable encouragement in the form of financial, tax, and counselling assistance. Much of this assistance is directed at smaller businesses in the manufacturing, processing, and exporting industries. Such industries represent potential opportunities for small businesses.

An aboriginal entrepreneur thinking about whether to start a small business could investigate whether his or her business opportunity is affected by any of these environmental conditions.

SMALL BUSINESS FAILURES

Operating one's own business, while holding considerable appeal for many, can be disappointing as well. In this section some of the causes of small business failure will be discussed with the purpose of helping prospective entrepreneurs avoid making these mistakes when they start their own businesses.

INCIDENT 2.5
Ray and Ruby

On July 4, 1995 Harold Gray, Business Development Supervisor for the Alberta Indian Investment Corporation (AIIC) was about to leave his Edmonton office for the day when his secretary buzzed him over the intercom: "Ray and Ruby are here to see you." "Send them right in," Harold replied. "Just the people I've been waiting for," he thought to himself.

Ray and Ruby, a married couple in their late thirties who both had experience in the restaurant business, had approached AIIC with a business plan to purchase and operate a restaurant in a Calgary suburb. When their loan application was approved, Harold had spent many hours with the couple to make sure they understood what was required of them. He believed that Ray and Ruby were committed to the venture and had the potential to succeed.

But the couple soon found themselves working very long hours, and some unsuccessful changes they made to the restaurant's operations were an added source of stress. They decided to take a four week holiday without notifying AIIC, leaving a friend in charge, and by the time they came back the landlord had closed the doors of the restaurant.

When Ruby and Ray arrived at Harold's office, it took them only a few minutes to let him know their intention to walk away from the restaurant and declare personal bankruptcy. Ray said, "Harold, here are the keys to the restaurant, our house, and our three vehicles. We are quitting the business. We cannot go on, it is just too hard for us."

SOURCE: "Ray and Ruby," Centre for Aboriginal Management, University of Lethbridge, 1991.

The situation described in Incident 2.5 has not been uncommon in recent years as many Canadian small businesses have failed. This is evidenced by the number of business bankruptcies in Canada, which has been steadily climbing in recent years. Bankruptcy figures alone, however, do not give a complete picture of business failures as many businesses are placed in receivership, and other business owners simply close the doors and walk away, as did "Ray and Ruby".[14] Estimates indicate that in 1989, while there were about 10,000 bankruptcies, close to 140,000 businesses in Canada actually ceased operations.[15]

Businesses follow much the same life cycle as products in that both have start-up, growth, maturity, and decline phases (see Chapter 7). The majority of businesses that fail pass completely through this life cycle within five years of start-up. Therefore, a small business owner has little time to remedy serious mistakes. A review of Statistics Canada information reveals that only 55–60% of businesses are still operating three years after they were established.[16]

It can be valuable for entrepreneurs to understand the reasons why businesses fail so that they can avoid a similar occurrence. As Figure 2.2 illustrates, 97.1% of business failures are related to inexperience or incompetence in management skills. More specifically, some of the types of management weaknesses typical of failing small businesses are the following: budgeting problems, receivables and payables management, inventory management, fixed-asset administration, high debt load, and marketing problems. The second half of this text is devoted to discussing these principles of management, the lack of which seems to contribute to difficulties arising in unsuccessful firms.

ENTREPRENEURSHIP AND SMALL BUSINESS MANAGEMENT

Is there a difference between entrepreneurship and small business management? Up to this point in the text, the two terms have been used interchangeably; however, a distinction will now be made. Though different, both entrepreneurship and small business management skills may be necessary at different stages during the life cycle of a business.

Entrepreneurial Skills

Entrepreneurial skills are required to start or expand a business. The specific traits describing entrepreneurship are creativity, flexibility, innovativeness, risk-taking, and independence. Entrepreneurs tend to be idea-oriented. The genuine entrepreneur has a high tolerance for ambiguity and change, and he or she thinks and plans for the long term.

Managerial Skills

The skills of a manager are useful in maintaining and solidifying an already existing product, service or business. The effective manager knows how to develop strategy, set organizational goals, and develop methods by which these goals can be attained. Managers require skill and

---

14 The Canadian Business Failure Record, 1984.
15 *Small Business and Special Surveys* (August 17, 1989), Statistics Canada.
16 Jeffrey A. Timmons, Leonard E. Smollen, and Alexander L.M. Dingee, *New Venture Creation: A Guide to Entrepreneurship* (Homewood, IL: Richard D. Irwin, 1985), 28.

FIGURE 2.2   Classification of Causes of Business Failure in Canada
Total year, 1983

#	%			
31	1.5	**Neglect**	due to:	Bad habits Poor health Marital difficulties Death Other
10	0.5	**Fraud**	on the part of the principals, reflected by:	Misleading name False financial statement Premeditated overbuy Irregular disposal of assets Other
220	10.7	**Lack of experience in the line**	evidenced by an inability to avoid conditions which result in:	Inadequate sales Heavy operating expenses
339	16.4	**Lack of managerial experience**		Receivables difficulties Inventory difficulties Excessive fixed assets Poor location Competitive weakness Other
517	25.1	**Unbalanced experience**	some of which could have been provided against through insurance:	Fire, flood Burglary Strike
925	44.9	**Incompetence**		
18	0.9	**Disaster**		Employee fraud Other
2,060	100.0	**TOTAL**		

Management Skills 97.1%

SOURCE: Adapted from *The Canadian Business Failure Record* (Toronto, Ont.: Dun & Bradstreet, Canada Ltd., 1984), pp. 1–19.

knowledge in functional areas such as finance, marketing, personnel, and operations. Such skills are most valuable after a business has been established.

The skills possessed by the entrepreneur and the manager, while distinct, are both essential for long run success of a business. Entrepreneurial skills help get the business started while

FIGURE 2.3 Small Business Skills

Type	Characteristics	Appropriate Situations
Entrepreneurial	• creativity and innovativeness • risk taking • idea-oriented	• generating ideas or solutions to problems • independence • starting new business • expanding or adding new products
Managerial	• strategy development and goal-setting • prefers to know outcomes of operations • team player • works through others • skills in finance, marketing, personnel, operations	• reaching performance objectives • maintaining control of actions or activities

managerial skills ensure that the business continues to operate successfully. Later, entrepreneurial skills may once again be necessary to secure growth of the business.

A major problem for many small businesses is that it is rare to find an individual who has strengths in both of these areas. As most small businesses are started and operated by the same person, some skills or characteristics must be hired or acquired. Failure to do so may mean a lack of success for the venture. Figure 2.3 summarizes the distinction between the two types of skills and their appropriate situations. Part Two of this text discusses essential considerations in starting a business (the entrepreneurial side), and in these chapters reference will be made to this individual as the *entrepreneur*. Part Three of the text covers the management skills required for the already established enterprise (the management side), and the individual is referred to as the *owner-manager* or the *small business manager* in those chapters.

SUMMARY

1. The major causes of small business failure are generally related to inexperienced or incompetent management. Some of the specific areas where difficulties are found are budgeting, receivable and payable management, inventory management, fixed-asset administration, debt management, personnel handling, and marketing problems.
2. Situations where small businesses can be successful have the following characteristics: good owner-manager rapport with employees, high labour intensity, personal attention to daily operations by the owner, markets requiring flexibility, and markets where demand is local.

3. There are both advantages and disadvantages to owning a small business. Some of the most common advantages are frequent contacts with people, independence, skill development in many areas, and possibility of financial rewards. The disadvantages include high risk, time demands, high stress levels, conflicts with people, multiple skill demands, and possibly meagre financial rewards.

4. Mainstream business wisdom suggests that there are certain personality characteristics required to be a successful owner-manager. This list includes achievement orientation, risk taking, independence, innovativeness, strong verbal and numerical skills, problem-solving ability, strategic planning ability, and perseverance.

5. For long-term success, the small business owner will need to develop managerial as well as entrepreneurial skills.

DISCUSSION QUESTIONS

1. What do you think are the most common reasons for the failure of aboriginal small businesses? Investigate the causes of failure for a small business you are familiar with.

2. Which of the characteristics of successful small business owners do you feel is the most important? Why? Do you think any of these characteristics conflict with traditional aboriginal values?

3. How do managerial skills differ from entrepreneurial skills? When would an entrepreneur's skills be more useful than a manager's? Why?

4. What characteristics did Dave Tuccaro in the Small Business Profile have? Were they managerial or entrepreneurial? Explain.

5. Interview a small business owner and determine what he or she feels are the advantages and disadvantages of small business ownership.

SUGGESTED READINGS

Bedard, George. "Telltale Signs of Trouble." *Small Business Magazine*. March 1987, 38.

Burch, John G. "Profiling the Entrepreneur." *Business Horizons*. September–October 1986, 13–16.

The Canadian Business Failure Record Book. Toronto: Dun & Bradstreet, of Canada Ltd., 1992.

Cook, James R. *The Start-up Entrepreneur*. New York, NY: Harper Collins Publishing, 1987.

Drucker, Peter F. *Innovation and Entrepreneurship: Practice and Principles*. New York, Harper and Row, 1993.

Garfield, Charles A. *Peak Performers*. New York: Warner Books, 1989.

Gould, Allan. *The New Entrepreneurs: 80 Canadian Success Stories*. Toronto: McClelland & Stewart Bantam, Ltd., 1991.

Kao, Raymond W.Y. *Entrepreneurship and Enterprise Development*. Holt, Rinehart & Wilson, Toronto, 1989.

McMullan, W., Ed & Wayne Long. *Developing New Adventures*. Toronto: HBJ Publishers, 1990.

Rumball, Donald. The Entrepreneurial Edge, Key Porter Books, Toronto, 1989.

Vesper, Karl H. *New Venture Strategies*. Prentice Hall, Toronto, 1990.

CHAPTER 3

Business Opportunities for Aboriginal Entrepreneurs

— D. Wesley Balderson

CHAPTER OBJECTIVES

☐ To review the non-quantitative aspects of evaluating business opportunities.

☐ To assess the attributes of aboriginal communities which are conducive to small business success.

☐ To introduce the methods by which an aboriginal entrepreneur can enter a market with a product or service.

☐ To discuss the types of information available to assist in the selection of a small business and illustrate how that information can be utilized.

☐ To provide a systematic way to assess an industry quantitatively and evaluate the financial feasibility of a specific small business opportunity.

SMALL BUSINESS PROFILE
Kaaydah Schatten Forrest
Ceiling Doctor International Inc.

Kaaydah Schatten is an entrepreneur who has turned a small cleaning business into a rapidly growing international franchise system. A once abandoned child from the Campbell River Reserve in British Columbia, Kaaydah determined early in life that she would rise above the poverty she was raised in while maintaining her native roots. She learned as much as she could about business and law at college, and also on her own.

Having a keen interest in land and building development, she gained valuable experience in the real estate industry by offering to work for a successful realtor for free. While doing this she not only was hired permanently and promoted to senior accounting assistant, but she also learned much about consumer needs which could be turned into successful business ventures. One consumer need that she learned about was the problem of soiled ceilings. Many renovations to buildings were carried out because the ceilings were dirty. Kaaydah launched a ceiling tile cleaning service which would clean tiles in place, with no removal necessary.

"I've developed a service that people wanted and needed, a service that fulfilled a basic need in society," says Kaaydah of her ceiling cleaning service. She researched the market and could see that this need would translate into a viable business opportunity if she had the right system and product to deliver the service. "We've developed a way of removing dirt from ceilings in buildings using an ecological product and special equipment." Ceiling Doctor capitalized on this method to expand operations rapidly. Ceiling Doctor sold 33 North American franchises from 1983 to 1986 and has now expanded to many countries throughout the world. In addition, Ceiling Doctor has consistently been ranked as one of the top franchise opportunities in the world.

Kaaydah has some advice for aboriginal people who are in the process of selecting business opportunities. "There are a lot of natural resources on the reserves. For example, on the West coast, we supply Chinese chopsticks on the international market. If you have fewer resources in your community, take stock overall of what you could export."

Kaaydah includes in her activities fundraising for native organizations such as the Canadian Council for Native Business and the Canadian Native Arts Foundation. Although she is very successful today, Kaaydah also experienced financial difficulties partly due to the recession in the early 1980s. She advises aboriginal entrepreneurs to be persistent even when things don't go well: "I lost money before I earned any. Money is only a kind of energy form, unlimited and endless." Kaaydah Schatten's hard work, persistence, and willingness to put in an effort before receiving a reward has contributed to her success as an entrepreneur.

SOURCE: Used with permission of Kaaydah Schatten Forrest.

EVALUATION OF BUSINESS OPPORTUNITIES

Chapter 2 discussed ways to evaluate one's personal suitability for small business ownership. Much of this chapter deals with the evaluation of the opportunity itself. There are five areas for the aboriginal entrepreneur to evaluate. First, non-quantitative factors should be assessed and related to the personal circumstances of the entrepreneur. Second, if the business is to be established in an aboriginal community, the community itself should be evaluated. Third, the decision about how to break into the market needs to be made. Fourth, information should be collected and fifth, a quantitative assessment should be carried out. Each of these steps will be discussed in detail in this chapter.

NON-QUANTITATIVE ASSESSMENT OF BUSINESS OPPORTUNITIES

Goals   The individual should examine his or her personal goals regarding income earned from the business, and ask the following questions: How well will this type of business allow me to achieve not only financial and occupational status goals, but also any social goals I may have to help develop my community?

Content of Work   The individual should assess his or her suitability for the business's working conditions. What type of work will the business involve? Will the business require hard physical work or considerable contact with people?

Lifestyle   What type of lifestyle will the business allow? Will the hours be long, or concentrated in the evenings or on weekends, or require attention during particular seasons of the year? Will the business allow family members to be involved? Remember that most small businesses take much more time to operate than the owner anticipates prior to start-up.

Capabilities   In addition to the personal characteristics needed to run a small business that were discussed in Chapter 2, at least three other capabilities are required.

The first requirement is good health. As mentioned earlier, managing a small business usually involves long hours and is often physically and mentally stressful. One will need good physical health and stamina as well as the ability to withstand high levels of stress.

The second requirement is expertise in the fundamentals of management, including administration, marketing, and finance. While formal management courses can provide valuable training, many successful small business managers have acquired expertise in these areas through self-education.

The third requirement is a sound financial base. Although some types of service businesses may require only a minimum capital investment, it may be difficult to start other businesses with less than $10,000 to $50,000. This amount may, in fact, be only the equity portion which qualifies a business to acquire the necessary capital. Start-up funding may be available for aboriginal entrepreneurs through various government programs. See Chapter 6 for details.

Experience   As the data in Figure 2.2 (page 33) illustrate, lack of experience or unbalanced experience are two major causes of business failure. One of the best preparations prospective small operators can make is to acquire work experience in the type of business or industry they plan to go into. An example of such an approach is found in Incident 3.1. In this example the entrepreneur had some well-defined career goals and had extensive experience in the field prior to establishing his business. Another benefit of experience is the personal contacts acquired while working in a particular industry. For many entrepreneurs, assistance from such sources can be invaluable in successfully establishing their business.

INCIDENT 3.1
Guide Finds True Peace in the Bush

Ken Steinhauer spent 20 years in the big city, but his heart is in the bush. Raised on the Saddle Lake Reserve, Steinhauer is hoping his two-year-old, Edmonton-based company will help native people stay on the land. Now 46, Steinhauer has been a guide for the past 20 years, taking out friends and visitors to enjoy the bush.

Alberta Native Guide Services was born out of frustration. When the provincial government began to auction hunting tags a few years ago, Steinhauer was convinced it would hurt native guides who didn't have the money to bid. He decided to start a company that would buy tags and hire natives to take out-of-province hunters into the woods.

"There's got to be an avenue for people who want to get back to the land," says Steinhauer. "We have to hold on to some of the vestiges of the past."

Today, Steinhauer is working with two native guides in the Slave Lake area showing Americans the lay of the land during hunting season. The company's reputation has grown by word-of-mouth, and demand for its services has increased.

Steinhauer foresees a government ban on hunting by non-Canadians. As a substitute for this important source of income, he wants a network of well-trained native guides to be in place to take tourists on traplines for nature experiences. Steinhauer insists there must be a way to help native people make a living while staying close to the land.

SOURCE: *Windspeaker*, Canada's National Aboriginal News Publication, July 5, 1991, p. 19.

Many entrepreneurs establish their businesses and work in them part-time while holding another job. This is an excellent way to gain experience and minimize risk. Although such an approach is not possible in some situations, many successful businesses originated from a part-time job.

ATTRIBUTES OF ABORIGINAL COMMUNITIES

Prior to making a decision about the type of small business to establish, it is important that the aboriginal entrepreneur who hopes to establish a business in an aboriginal community evaluate the community realistically. It may possess certain characteristics or resources which will contribute positively to the success of his or her venture. On the other hand, constraints may also exist which will make success difficult to obtain. Some of the areas which should be evaluated are:

Political Sovereignty   Research has shown that bands which have control over decision making and the use of resources tend to be most successful in generating small business success.[1] These same studies show that as sovereignty of band decision making rises, so do

---

[1]   Stephen Cornell and Joseph P. Kalt. "Reloading the Dice: Improving the Chances for Economic Development on American Indian Reservations," Harvard Project on American Indian Economic Development, March 1992, 13–14.

the chances of successful business development. The same principle seems to apply to the individual entrepreneur, that is, the less interference an entrepreneur receives from the band the greater are the chances of success. In view of the above, the aboriginal entrepreneur should investigate whether a community can make its economic development decisions free from internal and external interference, and also whether the community allows its entrepreneurs the same privilege.

Financial Capital Access   Notwithstanding the above caution, the aboriginal entrepreneur should also evaluate the community's willingness to assist, encourage, and provide financial capital to the entrepreneur.

Location and Size of the Community   The aboriginal entrepreneur should observe whether a business located in an aboriginal community is disadvantaged because of distances to suppliers or the market. The population of the community as a potential market should also be evaluated. While a method of doing this will be discussed later in this chapter, it should be noted that many reserves in Canada are too small to provide a market for a viable business. In these cases the off-reserve market will need to be developed if the business is to be successful.

Natural Resources   As Kaaydah Schatten noted, many aboriginal communities in Canada contain a high level of natural resources which may provide numerous business opportunities. The entrepreneur should take an inventory of such resources and an investigation of the ability and willingness of the community to develop them as a guide for opportunities for successful businesses. Examples of such development include fishing, forestry, mining, agriculture, and tourism. An example of using the strengths of the reserve in a business project is shown in Incident 3.2.

INCIDENT 3.2
Blood Reserve Planning Major Tourism Project

Plans to build a major tourism-recreation facility on southern Alberta's Blood reserve are about to become a reality. The proposed tourist facility is the dream of a group of local farmers and business people, who established the Niitsitapi Society to create employment and business opportunities on the reserve. Organizers have estimated the cultural centre could provide several hundred new positions for the job-starved band.

The cultural centre is designed to be an educational and recreational shop for tourists, built along the lines of the Polynesian Cultural Centre on the island of Oahu, in Hawaii. It will feature historical displays and cultural exhibits from North American Plains Indians as well as 11 other aboriginal cultures, including some from South America, the Pacific islands, Australia and New Zealand.

"The three major things that bring tourists to Alberta are dinosaurs, the mountains and Indians." says Louis Dardon, Niitsitapi's operations manager. "People don't really know anything about native culture except what they see in the movies."

Initial plans call for each culture to be represented as a mini-village, demonstrating lifestyles, legends and language. Visitors will be able to participate in native sports, purchase native handicrafts and eat native foods. Longer range plans will see the addition of an amusement park, swimming pool and mini-golf course, as well as other recreational facilities.

SOURCE: *Windspeaker*, Canada's National Aboriginal News Publication, April 13, 1992, p. 18.

Human Capital   If the aboriginal entrepreneur will require employees, an assessment should be made of the availability and capability of the workforce in a community. Generally workers are available as the unemployment levels in many aboriginal communities are quite high. Depending on the business, finding employees with the required levels of expertise may be more difficult.

Culture   A very important consideration of a community's potential for successful small business development relates to the culture. The success of small enterprises seems to be higher in communities where cultural norms support individual accumulations of at least modest wealth, where individual achievement is honoured and not cause for personal rejection, where commercialization is accepted, where interaction with non-natives is supported, and where people's political allegiances may not be fixed on central tribal authorities.[2] A major question arises regarding the merging of capitalism and traditional aboriginal values. Incident 3.3 illustrates how capitalism is operating in Canada's Arctic.

INCIDENT 3.3
Capitalism in Nunavik Unique Blend of Traditional, Modern Economies

During the Makivik Annual General Meeting in Kuujjuaq last spring, Charlie Watt said the market economy was spreading to more countries, with the downfall of communism in the former Soviet Union and the East Bloc countries, and to a certain extent in China. Watt mentioned these events to explain the economic change that is occurring in Nunavik with the creation of more sophisticated businesses, including the imminent marketing of wild meats.

While some aspects of the capitalist economy are evident, such as the existence of businesses, factories, banks, stock markets, and the ability to own private property, some are invisible. The invisible parts are those forces of the market economy that dictate how supply will meet demand, how prices will change as a result of competition, and a variety of other factors. Clearly one of the questions that has to be asked is whether Inuit are trading their traditional values for capitalist ones, or making the capitalist economy conform to traditional Inuit values. The research suggests that there is considerable evidence that the latter is taking place, and the emergence of a group of Inuit business leaders provides some support for this view.

One of the more interesting aspects of the capitalist system is that it creates an environment whereby certain individuals will become entrepreneurs. Within the last five years, there is measurable growth in this activity, and stories to tell in each community about people who are going through the initial stages of creating small businesses. There are some fundamental differences, but the start-up process appears to be similar to that experienced by small businesses anywhere in Canada.

SOURCE: *Windspeaker*, Canada's National Aboriginal News Publication, Aug. 30–Sept. 10, 1993, p. 10.

Consideration of the above criteria and conditions may not only help an entrepreneur to evaluate the potential success for a business opportunity but may also suggest which types of businesses may be more appropriate for certain communities.

---

2 *Ibid.*, p. 46.

BREAKING INTO THE MARKET

Aboriginal entrepreneurs have essentially three ways to enter a market by establishing a new business. The first is to offer a totally new product to the market. This involves "inventing" a product that meets a need not currently being fulfilled. Thousands of successful products have resulted from an individual's dissatisfaction with existing or lack of existing products. Many fad or novelty types of products fit into this category. The needs these types of products satisfy are often emotional or subjective rather than rational. Products such as pet rocks and mood jewellery fit this description.

A second approach is to offer an existing product to a different market or industry. Phillip Kives, founder of K-Tel International, was the master of this type of approach. His company achieved success by acquiring products currently sold abroad and marketing them in North America. Another form of this approach is to offer an existing product or service in the same geographical market, but to a different age or income group.

The third way to enter the market is to offer a product or service similar to those already existing in the same market. In this case, the prospective small business owner attempts to obtain some competitive advantage over the existing products or businesses in the industry to maintain viability. Perhaps the market is large enough to accommodate an additional business, or the level of satisfaction with existing businesses or products in the industry is low. An example of this type of business establishment is given in Incident 3.4.

A firm may also break into the marketplace through "ideological marketing," one example being "green" firms who attempt to capitalize on their environmental correctness. Aboriginally owned and operated businesses also have an opportunity to distinguish themselves from competitors through their aboriginal corporate identity. For example, large corporations which operate in aboriginal territory, such as Syncrude, may seek out small aboriginal businesses to support their operations.

Regardless of the approach used, it is important to look at the growth trends within the industry, the number of competitors, and their relative market share, as well as their strengths and weaknesses prior to entering the market.

INCIDENT 3.4
Russell Roundpoint

> When Russell Roundpoint took up golf a few years ago, business was the furthest thing from his mind. But as his game improved, he began to see that golf offered a lot more than recreation.
>
> "I did some research, and I found that golf is the fastest growing game in the world," says Roundpoint, who was recently elected Grand Chief of the Mohawk Council of Akwasasne. "There's a new golf course opening each day somewhere in the world."
>
> Since quality golf equipment is traditionally sold at a high markup in exclusive pro shops, Roundpoint saw an opportunity for a discount operation. Using his own capital and a loan, he opened International Discount Golf in August 1993, at the Peace Tree Trade Centre in Akwasasne, near Cornwall, Ontario.
>
> "There was a void in the market and we took advantage of it," he says. "We were able to get professional level equipment and, through volume, sell it at discount prices."
>
> The store's sales have grown steadily as it has established a reputation as a credible source of top-quality equipment for all skill levels. In addition to low retail prices made

possible by volume buying, International offers additional tax savings because of its location at Akwasasne.

SOURCE: *mawiO'mi*, 1994, p. 12.

COLLECTION OF INFORMATION

The key to making a wise decision regarding which industry to enter and the type of business to start is the gathering and analysis of information. The more relevant the information, the greater the reduction of uncertainty about the results of this decision. Recent studies show that the overwhelming majority of small business owners do no formal marketing research, although many do informal, unsystematic information gathering.[3]

Some of the reasons entrepreneurs commonly cite for lack of research and investigation are that it is too time consuming, too expensive, too complicated, and irrelevant. Some aboriginal entrepreneurs may feel that they know the market in their area well enough that information collection is not necessary. However, there are some simple, inexpensive, and effective methods of collecting and analysing data available to any entrepreneur.

Sources of Information

The first thing entrepreneurs should be aware of is the many sources of information that are available to assist them in their investigations. Two general types of information can aid prospective small business owners in selecting the right small business. The first, secondary data, consists of data previously published by another organization. The second, primary data, is data collected by the entrepreneur.

Secondary Data

Secondary data takes the form of reports, studies, and statistics that another organization has already compiled. There is no shortage of secondary data to aid the entrepreneur. A major problem, however, is finding information relevant to one's own situation. This may be particularly true in the case of aboriginal entrepreneurs who elect to start a business on a reserve and have trouble doing research due to insufficient information being available for the reserve. In addition, the secondary data available may be too general or may not be relevant to the type of business being established. Also, some reports are out of date and thus will need to be adjusted to make them useful. Such data can be updated by projecting past trends.

Secondary information is inexpensive, which makes it very attractive to the prospective small business owner. Much of the secondary information available in Canada is provided by the federal provincial, and territorial governments. However, valuable secondary information is also available from private and semi-private sources. A local economic development department may also be a source of secondary data for the aboriginal entrepreneur. A complete listing of those sources most relevant for aboriginal small businesses is presented in the Information Resources section beginning on page 314. Figure 3.1 gives an example of using secondary data to begin the feasibility analysis for a small business. This example uses Statistics Canada

---

3   Raymond Kao, "Market Research and Small New-Venture Start-Up Strategy," *Journal of Small Business and Entrepreneurship*, Spring 1986, p. 36.

FIGURE 3.1 Assessing Market Feasibility Using Secondary Data Opening a Florist Shop in Chateauguay, Quebec

Problem: To estimate the size of the market for a florist shop in Chateauguay.

Step 1: Determine the population in Chateauguay using Statistics Canada reports.

Area	Population
Census Metropolitan Area of Chateauguay	38,000

Step 2: Determine the total retail sales for florist shops in Canada.

Retail Shop	Sales
Florist	$444,600,000 (1987)

Update sales figure to present year by increasing it by the inflation rate (2%) for each year the statistics are out of date. Assuming present year is 1991 — 4 years out of date — then add 4 × $8,892,000 = $35,568,000). The 1991 projection would therefore be $480,168,000.

Step 3: Calculate per capita sales for florist shops in Canada:

= (florist sales — 1991 projection / Canadian population — 1991 census)
 = 480,168,000 / 27,296,859
= $17.59

Step 4: Apply the per capita projection to the Chateauguay market:

= $17.59 (per capita sales) × 38,000 (pop. of Chateauguay)
= $668,420

This shows that almost $670,000 could be expected to be spent in Chateauguay area florist shops.

SOURCES: 1987 Statistics Canada, 1991 Census — Statistics Canada, 1992 Market Research Handbook — Statistics Canada.

reports to estimate market potential for a florist shop in Chateauguay, located near the Kahnawake Reserve in Quebec.

In addition to obtaining published secondary information, entrepreneurs can consult various agencies for counselling about both starting up a business and continuing ongoing operations. The most inexpensive and often most valuable source is the counselling provided to entrepreneurs by federal, provincial, and local governments. Aboriginal Business Canada provides assistance with feasibility studies, business planning, establishing or expanding business operations, and marketing. In addition the Federal Business Development Bank can provide start-up counselling as well as analysis of an already operating business. This latter service is offered through the Counselling Assistance for Small Enterprises program (CASE). The

CASE program is available to businesses employing fewer than 75 employees and uses retired business people as consultants. Many aboriginal communities and entrepreneurs have also received assistance from CESO (Canadian Executive Services Overseas), which has assisted over 20,000 First Nations projects since 1968. Incident 3.5 describes this type of service.

INCIDENT 3.5
Native Entrepreneurs Count on CESO Volunteers

Getting practical advice from an expert CESO volunteer who has time-proven experience upon which to draw makes good business sense. That's the clear conclusion of many First Nation businesses and organizations across Manitoba, northwestern Ontario and the rest of the country who use CESO volunteer advisors time and time again for their professional, business and technical expertise.

Take the case of CESO and Irene Maningway's flower and gift shop on the Peguis Reserve. From the start, Irene's shop had all the makings of success. It is located in a busy mall that also houses a grocery store, a restaurant and the First Nation's offices. Irene, who had prior retail experience, keeps her store open long hours, seven days a week, with part-time help from her daughter. Yet despite her efforts and strong sales, Irene was operating at a deficit. Recognizing that she needed solid practical advice on how to balance her books, she called on experts from CESO.

Volunteer Fred Tippen and Assistant Regional Manager Ron Scanlan helped Irene turn her business around. They set up a small business accounting program for her which made tracking sales and expenses easy. "We started from the ground up," says Fred. "Now the business is being well managed and we turned it from a deficit to a positive cash flow position."

SOURCE: *First Perspective*, May 14, 1993.

Most provincial governments also employ small business consultants to assist the small business (see page 317 of the Information Resources section for the addresses of these agencies in each province). Many provincial agencies provide start-up and business plan preparation assistance.

Another potentially valuable source of assistance comes from universities and colleges. Many universities have student consulting programs designed to aid the small business owner. Using the expertise of graduating or graduate students, these programs can assist in preparing feasibility analyses or evaluating a business problem for a minimal fee, usually the cost of materials used (page 318 of the Information Resources section lists universities in Canada that have such programs; several colleges also offer similar services).

Other potential counselling sources are local band or settlement economic development officers or consultants provided by the band. Such professionals as lawyers, accountants, and bankers, although more expensive, may also be helpful.

In addition to the types of assistance just described, a new concept appears to promise considerable help in establishing new enterprises: the incubation centre. The incubation centre consists of an organization, usually a municipal or provincial agency, that provides essential services for new small businesses, either free or at minimal cost. Office space, secretarial services, computer capabilities, and financial and business counselling are examples of these services. In 1992, approximately 500 incubators were operating in North America including more than 1,000 incubator tenants, and estimates indicate that new incubators are opening at a rate of one per week.[4]

Primary Data

Primary data is information collected through one's own research. Although usually more costly to obtain than secondary data, it can also be more current and relevant. Primary research is essential if secondary sources do not provide information required for the feasibility analysis. It may also be beneficial to supplement information obtained from secondary sources. Despite these advantages, small business owners have traditionally hesitated to do much primary research because of their lack of knowledge about how to do it and its relatively high cost.

Some research methods, however, are not complicated and can be of great value to the entrepreneur in evaluating the feasibility of a potential business opportunity. Three general methods can be used to collect information through primary research: observation, surveys, and experiments.

Observation   Observation involves monitoring the who, what, where, when, and how relating to market conditions. For the small business, this method might involve observing auto and pedestrian traffic levels, or customer reactions to a product, service, or promotion. It may also entail simply observing sales or expenditure levels. The observation method may be expensive, as it requires that time be spent in monitoring events as they occur. Moreover, an entrepreneur from a remote community may find it costly to observe any potential urban market. Another limitation of observation research is that it only allows one to make inferences about the reasons people respond in certain ways; there is no two-way interaction with potential customers that might shed light on their motivations.

Surveys   To obtain more detailed information from potential consumers and to better understand their motivations in purchasing a product or service, an entrepreneur can carry out a survey. He or she should clearly define the objectives of the research prior to questionnaire construction, and ensure that each question addresses one of the objectives. Usually it is not possible to survey every potential customer or the total market; therefore, only a part of the market is surveyed. It is essential, however, that the responses obtained be representative of the total market.

Three types of surveys are used to collect market information: mail surveys, telephone surveys, and personal interviews.

■ Mail Surveys
Mail surveys are most appropriate when:

* Only a small amount of information is required.
* Questions can be answered with "yes-no," "check the box" answers, or brief responses.
* A picture of the product may be required.
* An immediate response is not required.
* Potential customers can easily be reached through the mail.
* If an non-aboriginal language is used most people in the community can read and write it.

One problem with mail surveys is their poor response rate, typically under 50%, and the lack of control over who fills out the questionnaire. Also the preparer needs to make sure

---

4   "Incubator Update," *Inc.*, January 1993, p. 49.

that the mail survey is not too long or too complicated. Figure 3.2 shows a simple mail survey carried out for a small business to assess initial demand for an aboriginal restaurant.

■ Telephone Surveys

Telephone surveying has become the most popular survey method in recent years, most likely because of its low cost and quick response time. However, it is even more restricted than a mail survey in the amount and detail of information one can obtain. The telephone interviewer should follow a survey guide to ensure consistency; Figure 3.3 offers an example of a typical phone survey guide. However, in communities where few people have telephones or party lines are common, telephone surveys may be problematic.

FIGURE 3.2   Mail Questionnaire: Aboriginal Family Restaurant

1. Approximately how often does your family eat at a restaurant or dining lounge in the town of Peterborough?*
    a. Less than once per month
    b. Once per month
    c. Once every two weeks
    d. Once per week
    e. Two to three times per week
    f. More than three times per week

2. Approximately how much do you normally spend when you eat out at a restaurant or dining lounge?
    a. $10 and under
    b. $11–$15
    c. $16–$20
    d. $21–$25
    e. Over $25

3. Are you familiar with the unique aspects of aboriginal cooking?
    ❑ Yes   ❑ No

4. If a family restaurant specializing in aboriginal cuisine was opened in Peterborough would you...
    a. Probably never go
    b. Definitely try it
    c. Patronize it regularly if food, service, etc., were adequate

5. Where would you prefer such a facility to be located?
    a. Downtown
    b. West Peterborough
    c. South Peterborough
    d. North Peterborough
    e. Does not matter

Thank you very much for your time and cooperation.

* Name of the city has been changed.
SOURCE: Academy Management Services, Lethbridge, Alberta.

FIGURE 3.3   Telephone Questionnaire Guide: Sporting Goods Rental Store

A sporting goods store, located in a city of approximately 58,000 people, wanted to start renting summer sports equipment. The following survey was designed to determine consumer demand for such a rental business.

Survey number: _____

Phone number: _____

Hi, my name is _____. I am presently conducting a survey to determine people's summertime leisure activities in the city. A few moments of your time to answer the questions would be greatly appreciated.

1. Can you tell me if you participate in any of the following activities during the summer?

   [List the equipment...and the responses]

2. A lot of people ski in the winter because ski equipment can be rented at a fraction of its retail price. Are there any summer activities you would participate in if the equipment was available on a similar basis?
   a. _____
   b. _____

3. Are you older than 18 years of age?
   ❑ Yes   ❑ No (If no, record and terminate)

4. Would you consider renting the following equipment if available at reasonable prices? Please indicate if you already have the item.

   [List equipment]

5. (Fill in for all respondents)
   ❑ Male   ❑ Female

6. Age:
   ❑ 18–25   ❑ 26–35   ❑ 36–50   ❑ over 50

7. Income:
   ❑ under $12,500   ❑ $12,501–$20,000   ❑ $20,001–$30,000   ❑ over $30,000

Thank you very much for participating in this survey.

SOURCE: Student Consulting Project, University of Lethbridge.

■ Personal Interviews

The most expensive type of survey is the personal interview. While this method generally costs more and requires greater expertise, it is the best approach for obtaining more detailed information and opinion-oriented responses. As the number of people surveyed typically is smaller than in mail or phone surveys, this method is more suitable for interviewing knowledgeable people in an industry as opposed to surveying a cross section of potential consumers.

It may involve surveying one individual at a time or, as many large companies do, surveying several people together in what is called a focus group. The personal interview may be used for such purposes as testing a new product concept or advertisement, or evaluating a company's image. Entrepreneurs may want to take advantage of gatherings such as tribal council meetings, trade shows or pow-wows if they are targeting aboriginal consumers in particular.

Entrepreneurs are often unsure about what types of questions to use in a survey. Some of the areas in which information should be obtained are the following:

- Respondents' reaction to the product or service.
- The price respondents are willing to pay for the product or service.
- Respondents' willingness to purchase the product or service (usually answers to such questions are overly positive and should be adjusted downward by as much as 20%).
- Frequency of purchase.
- Level of satisfaction with current product or service.
- Demographic characteristics of the respondents.

Experiments   An experiment involves an attempt to simulate an actual market situation. For an inventor, it may mean letting a number of people try out a new product and then finding out their reactions. For a business, it may mean marketing a product on a limited basis and observing sales levels, or surveying to find out the level of satisfaction with the product or service. This method is costly in that the product must be developed and marketed, albeit on a limited basis. The main advantage of experimental research, or test marketing, is that it measures what people actually do, not just what they say they will do, concerning a product. Small businesses have successfully used this method in taking prototype products to trade shows, exhibitions, or potential customers to assess potential acceptance.

The proper collection of secondary and primary data can be invaluable to entrepreneurs as they assess business opportunities. It can provide a base of data that, if analysed correctly, may allow the capitalization on a successful opportunity on the one hand or the avoidance of a disaster on the other. The types of market research just described require an investment in time and money, but many successful entrepreneurs are convinced they are a worthwhile investment.

Although owner-managers often use these information collection methods prior to starting their businesses, they can and should utilize them on an ongoing basis after the businesses have been established to stay abreast of changes in market conditions. Many successfully established businesses have eventually failed because they lost touch with consumers and/or the market conditions. To avoid this, the small business should set aside the effort and money required to regularly collect and use relevant market information. Chapter 7 discusses this subject further.

QUANTITATIVE ASSESSMENT OF BUSINESS OPPORTUNITIES ⸺⸺⸺⸺

Preparing the Feasibility Analysis

Once the entrepreneur has collected the relevant information about the market, the next step is to use this information as quantitatively as possible to assess the financial feasibility of the proposed venture. The purpose of this assessment is to determine if the business will earn the amount of income that the entrepreneur desires. The financial feasibility analysis as described in this section is most appropriate for starting a new business from scratch, but much of it could be applied to the purchase of an existing business or the operation of a franchise.

There are three steps in estimating the financial feasibility of a proposed business venture. The first step is the determination of potential revenue (demand) for the total market. The second is to estimate the share of total market revenue that the new business might obtain. The third is to subtract the associated expenses from the revenue estimate to arrive at a projected estimated net income for the business. A more detailed explanation of the steps in calculating a feasibility analysis is presented next. A detailed example of such an analysis is given in Figure 3.4, beginning on page 55.

Step 1: Calculate Market Potential

The purpose of this step is to arrive at a dollar or unit sales figure for the total market. It may involve three substeps:

1. Determine the market area and its population.   Identify the geographic area or target market the business will serve. This can be done by obtaining a map and marking off the size of the market. Then estimate the population (numbers) within that market that might conceivably purchase the type of product or service to be offered. This process yields an estimate of the size of the target market.

2. Obtain revenue (sales) statistics for this market area for the product type or service.   Usually federal, provincial, or municipal governments have this information for many standard types of products or businesses. For example, Statistics Canada publishes retail expenditure and manufacturing data for many products and services. If total revenue or sales figures are not available for the proposed type of business or product, but per capita or per family expenditures are obtainable, simply multiply this figure by the population estimate that has already been obtained in substep 1 (population of market × per capita expenditures).

If the product or service is new and no secondary data are available, use secondary data for a similar product. If there is no similar product, primary research in the form of a survey may be used to assess consumer acceptance of the concept. If the results of such a survey indicate a certain percentage of the market shows a purchase interest, multiply that percentage by the size of the market to obtain the market potential estimate.

3. Adjust the market potential total as necessary.   If one is able to obtain actual revenue statistics for the market, usually the only adjustment needed is to update the data. As mentioned previously, secondary data are typically a year or two out of date. A simple way to update sales and expenditure data is to increase the amount of sales by the annual rate of inflation for the years involved. This might also include a forecast of trends that will affect demand in the future. Such trends could be included in the estimate.

If national averages of per capita expenditures are used, adjustments for local shopping patterns must be made. A common adjustment in this regard is to adjust for those living in the market area who purchase outside the market, and vice versa. For example, if it is estimated that 20% of the market buys the product or service outside of the market area, reduce the market potential by 20%. When assessing the market potential of isolated communities, entrepreneurs should also consider the number of people who go into larger centres to shop (rather than purchasing locally) simply because "people go into town because people like to go into town."

Projections should include one-year and five-year estimates to reflect trends that may exist in the industry. Projections should also include trends with respect to growth of the competition that might affect future market share.

Step 2: Calculate Market Share

The purpose of this step is to estimate the percentage of the total market potential that the proposed business will obtain. Because the method of calculating market share differs significantly depending on the type of business, market share calculations for retail, manufacturing, and service firms are illustrated separately.

Retail Firm

1. Estimate the total amount of selling space in the market devoted to the merchandise the new business will sell (usually in square feet or metres). This involves taking an inventory of space of competing stores (specialty and department stores) devoted to this product. This estimate may be obtained informally by observation or by asking the owners. In some areas, secondary information about retail selling space may be available through the municipal or city government or department.

2. Estimate the size of proposed store (in square feet or square metres). The entrepreneur will probably have a good idea of the size of the proposed store. The actual size, of course, may depend upon availability of outlets.

3. Calculate the market share based on selling space as follows: The information collected in steps 1 and 2 are now integrated in the following formula:

$$\frac{\text{Proposed store selling space}}{\substack{\text{Total market selling space} \\ \text{(including proposed store)}}} = \text{Percent market share}$$

4. Make adjustments to reflect competitive strengths and weaknesses regarding the proposed store. Typical adjustments might include the following: (a) Decrease percentage share if the competition has a better location, is larger in size, or has considerable customer loyalty. A decrease in the percentage should also be made because the proposed store is new and will take time to build customer loyalty. (b) Increase percentage share if the proposed store offers unique products, service, location, advertising, or other advantages over the competition.

   The amount of the adjustments may be arbitrary and somewhat subjective, but typically they are fractions of a percentage of the market share.

5. Multiply the revised market share percentage by the market potential estimate obtained in step 1. The result is a dollar revenue estimate for the proposed business for the first year of operations. By applying market trends to this figure, a one- to five-year estimate can be obtained if required.

Manufacturing Firm

1. Estimate the total productive capacity in the market for the product to be manufactured. Typically this will be calculated in units but it may be in dollars. This will involve

estimating the production size of competitors (both domestic and foreign). If the product is new and no competition exists, market share is the same as the market potential calculated previously.

2. Estimate the productive capacity of the proposed manufacturing operation.

3. Calculate the market share based on productive capacity. The information obtained in steps 1 and 2 are integrated into the following formula:

$$\frac{\text{Production capacity of proposed business}}{\text{Total production capacity (including proposed business)}} = \text{Percent market share}$$

4. Make adjustments to reflect competitive strengths and weaknesses the proposed plant may possess. The market share percentage estimated in step 3 will likely need to be adjusted. The strengths and weaknesses of competitors should be determined and compared with the proposed business. Often primary research may be required to obtain this type of information.

   Generally a higher market share can be obtained in industries in which competitors are smaller in size, the product can be differentiated from the competitor's products, and primary research shows a particular dissatisfaction with existing products.

   Market share will tend to be smaller if the industry is made up of a few large and powerful competitors who hold key contracts, or where consumer satisfaction with the existing product is determined to be high.

   Even though the existing market may look formidable, some sectors of the economy look favourably on purchases from small business and from aboriginal small businesses in particular. The federal, provincial and territorial governments, aboriginal government administrations, and corporations who do a lot of business in aboriginal communities are excellent potential purchasers. These types of markets are discussed in Chapter 7. For a manufacturing firm, success at obtaining key contracts may provide the certainty required to calculate the market share and bypass some of these calculations.

5. Multiply the estimated market share percentage by the market potential estimate obtained in step 1. This figure projects estimated dollar sales for the first year of operations. As in the retail example, industry trends can assist in estimating this figure for more than one year.

Service Firm

1. Estimate the total capacity of the service available in the market area. The base used to calculate capacity will vary depending upon the type of service being offered. For example, restaurant capacity may be measured by number of seats, tables, or square footage; motel capacity by number of rooms or beds; and beauty salon capacity by number of employees or number of work stations. It is important to determine which base most accurately reflects the service capacity. This estimate can be obtained by observing existing businesses or talking to their owners.

2. Estimate service capacity of proposed business. This involves projecting the size of the proposed business in terms of service capacity.

3. Calculate share based on capacity base. The information obtained in steps 1 and 2 is integrated into the following formula:

$$\frac{\text{Proposed business service capacity}}{\begin{array}{c}\text{Total market service capacity}\\\text{(including proposed business}\\\text{service capacity)}\end{array}} = \text{Percent market share}$$

4. Make adjustments similar to those made for a retail store. The adjustments in the service industry tend to be more significant than in retailing. The opportunity to differentiate from competitors in the service industry is much greater than in retailing which tends to deal with more standardized products. Therefore, the percentage adjustments may be larger for service industry market share calculations.

Step 3: Calculate Net Income and Cash Flow

1. Using the market share revenue figure obtained in step 2 as the starting point, calculate the expenses expected to be incurred for the business. Most of these figures should be obtained by checking with suppliers and other similar businesses. However, some secondary sources, such as those provided by Statistics Canada, provide typical operating statements for many types of small business. Often these statements express expenses as a percentage of revenue and thus can be easily adapted to the proposed business.

   Some of the more important required expenses are:

   ■ Cost of goods sold and gross profit percentages.
   These can be obtained from secondary data but should be confirmed with suppliers.

   ■ Cash operating expenses such as rent, wages, utilities, repairs, advertising, and insurance.
   These expenses can also be obtained from secondary sources, but should be verified by checking with vendors of these services as they may differ for the market area of the proposed business.

   ■ Interest and depreciation.
   A list of the cost of capital items (i.e., building and equipment) and total start-up costs will need to be made so that yearly depreciation and interest expenses can be calculated. Chapter 6 presents information on determining start-up costs and subsequent interest calculation.

   One should remember that only the portion of these assets estimated to be used during that period should be included as the depreciated expenses. Using these start-up costs as a basis, an estimate of the amount of debt and annual interest costs using current rates should be determined.

2. Subtract expenses from revenue to determine the projected net income from the proposed business in the first year and subsequent years if required. Once a projected income figure is calculated, the prospective entrepreneur is in a position to evaluate and compare this result with other types of available investments. Return (income) as a percentage of investment (funds put into venture) can be compared to other types of businesses or "safe" uses of money, such as the return obtained by putting the funds into a bank. The

rate of return of the business should be higher than bank interest, however, to compensate for the risk factor that accompanies a new business.

It is conceivable and not uncommon for the projected income for the new business to be negative, at least in the first few years of operation. Usually the entrepreneur is taking a long-term view of the business, and thus long-term projections may be required to evaluate financial feasibility. It could also be that the main goal of the business is to provide more employment for the entrepreneur's community. In such a case the financial feasibility of the business should still be estimated to determine the overall cost of providing this employment.

In addition to a net income projection, many feasibility analyses include a projected cash flow statement. This document is of particular interest to potential lenders and investors. The cash flow simply describes the cash in minus the cash out on a chronological basis. Usually cash flow statements are shown monthly (see Chapter 6). The sample cash flow in Figure 3.4 is shown on a yearly basis for simplicity.

A quantitative financial feasibility analysis for a small aboriginal business is presented in Figure 3.4. This example illustrates the steps described in the preceding sections.

Another potentially important part of the feasibility analysis, for the manufacturing firm, is to estimate the level of production and sales required to break even financially. A detailed discussion of break-even analysis is included in Chapter 8.

Once the feasibility analysis is completed, the prospective aboriginal entrepreneur should have enough information to decide whether or not to pursue a particular business opportunity. The areas covered up to this point can be used to make this decision. Figure 3.5 (on page 58) presents a checklist for personal and opportunity evaluation.

FIGURE 3.4 Feasibility Analysis for a Sporting Goods Store in
The Pas, Manitoba

STEP ONE: CALCULATE MARKET POTENTIAL

1. **Market Area**. The market area is the population of The Pas plus outlying regions. The primary market for this region includes towns within a 10-mile radius of The Pas which includes The Pas Band Reserve and Carrot Valley. The secondary market includes the population within a 50-mile radius. The total population of the primary market is 9000, and the total for the secondary market is 1500.

2. **Sales for Market Area**. The per capita sales for sporting goods stores in the market area can be determined through two sources. First, the actual sales figures may be published and available from the municipality concerned. Second, if that information is not available, find the per capita sales by taking Canadian or provincial sales of sporting goods stores divided by the respective population. This information is available from Statistics Canada.

Figure 3.4 continued...

$$\frac{\text{Sporting Goods Stores Sales —}}{\text{Population — Canada (1991)}} = \text{Per Capita Sales}$$

$$\frac{\$2,360,000,000}{27,000,000} = \$87.40$$

* SOURCE: Statistics Canada.

Once per capita sales have been determined, this number can be applied to the market area population.

Primary Market = Population × Per Capita Sales
= 9000 × $87.40
= $786,600

Secondary Market = Population × Per Capita Sales
= 1500 × $87.40 × .5
= $65,550

(It is estimated that only 50% of people in the secondary market will make their purchases in The Pas. Therefore multiply the secondary market by .5.)

Market Potential = 786,600 + 65,550
= $852,150

3. **Adjustments**. Typical adjustments might include updating secondary information regarding population and purchases by applying past trends.

STEP TWO: CALCULATE MARKET SHARE

1. **Estimate Selling Space in the Market**. There are 3 other sporting goods stores in The Pas with a total estimated size of 900 sq. meters. (Primary research collected by observation)

2. **Size of Proposed Store**. The size of the proposed store is 400 sq. meters.

3. **Calculation of Market Share**. Percentage share of the market:

$$\frac{\text{Proposed Store Selling Space}}{\text{Total market selling space (including proposed store)}} = \frac{400 \text{ m.}^2}{1300 \text{ m.}^2} = 30.7\%$$

4. **Adjustments**. The percentage of market share would probably have to be decreased slightly, because the proposed store is new and would not have built up clientele and the reputation of an existing store. Based on these factors market share has been reduced to 25%.

5. **Multiply Market Share Percentage by Market Potential**.

Market Share × Market Potential = Estimated Market Share
25% × $852,150 = $213,037

Therefore market share is approximately $210,000.

Figure 3.4 continued...

STEP THREE: CALCULATION OF NET INCOME AND CASH FLOW

The Pas Sporting Goods
Projected Income Statement

Item	Amount	Percent of sales	Source of Information
Sales	$210,000	100	Step 2
Less: Cost of Goods Sold	136,500	65	Stats Canada
Gross Margin	73,500	35	Stats Canada
Expenses:			
Manager Salary	20,000		Primary info
Employee Wages	20,000		Schedule 1
Rent	24,000		Primary Info
Utilities/Phone	6,500		Primary Info
Professional Fees	800		Primary Info
Insurance	500		Primary Info
Repairs and Maintenance	1,000	0.7	Stats Canada
Advertising	2,000	1	Stats Canada
Misc. Supplies	500	0.2	Stats Canada
License/Tax	100		Primary Info
Depreciation	2,000		Schedule 2
Interest	3,500		Schedule 3
Total Expenses	80,900		
Net Income (loss) before tax	$(7,400)		

Schedule 1 (obtained through primary research)

Employee Wages
1 full time employee $15,000
1 part time employee $ 5,000
Total $20,000

Schedule 2

Depreciation schedule
Equipment cost = $10,000 (primary information-suppliers)
Capital Cost Allowance (CCA) = 20% (Master Tax Guide)
Depreciation = $10,000 × .20 = $2,000 in year one

Schedule 3

Interest schedule
Amount borrowed = 35,000
Interest Rate = 10%
Interest in year one = 3,500

Figure 3.4 continued...

Schedule 4

Calculation of Cash Flow

The Pas Sporting Goods
Projected Cash Flow for Year One

Cash Inflow	
Beginning Cash	$ 20,000
Bank Loan	35,000
Sales	210,000
Total Cash Inflow	$265,000
Cash Outflow	
Start-up Costs	10,000
Merchandise purchases	160,000
Manager Salary	20,000
Employee wages	20,000
Rent	24,000
Utilities/Phone	6,500
Professional Fees	800
Insurance	500
Repairs/Maintenance	1,000
Advertising	2,000
Misc. Supplies	500
License/Tax	100
Interest & Loan Payment	10,500
Total Cash Outflow	255,900
NET CASH FLOW	$ 9,100

SOURCE: Eric Bignell, Small Business Project, University of Lethbridge.

FIGURE 3.5 Self-Assessment for a Small Business Opportunity

PERSONALITY — Do I possess most of the personality characteristics of successful entrepreneurs introduced in Chapter 2?

NATURE — Does this business opportunity meet my occupational and lifestyle goals and interests? Will it make the hoped for contribution to my community?

ABILITIES — Do I have expertise in the fundamentals (financial, marketing, personnel, production) needed to manage this business opportunity? If I do not, am I able and willing to acquire or hire such expertise?

EXPERIENCE — Do I have experience with the business or industry? If not, am I able and willing to get it or find someone who can assist me to get started?

FINANCIAL BASE — Do I currently have or can I obtain the necessary funds to finance the venture?

COMMUNITY CAPABILITIES — If I intend to start the business in an aboriginal community, is it a community which seems conducive to success?

FEASIBILITY — Does the financial feasibility of the business opportunity meet my expectations and financial goals?

SUMMARY

1. Before deciding which small business opportunity to pursue, the aboriginal entrepreneur should consider non-quantitative factors such as his or her goals, the content of the work, the lifestyle the business offers, and the individual's capabilities and experience.

2. In targeting an aboriginal community as a market, the entrepreneur should evaluate community attributes which may contribute to the success of the venture. Such attributes include community and entrepreneurial autonomy, access to financial capital, location and size of the community, natural resources, access to human capital, and cultural attitudes to entrepreneurship.

3. There are three ways to enter a market with a new product or service. The first method is to offer a totally new product. The second is to offer an existing product to a different market or industry. The third is to offer a product or service similar to those that already exist in the same market.

4. Two general types of information are available to aid a potential aboriginal small business owner in identifying a business opportunity. The first and most inexpensive method is to collect secondary information about a potential market. Government documents and other sources can provide valuable secondary data. When few current secondary data are available, prospective small business owners can collect primary data to help determine the feasibility of their business idea.

5. Primary data is information collected through one's own research. Although usually more costly than secondary data, it can be more relevant and current to the analysis. Three general methods of doing primary research include observation, surveys, and experiments. Surveying usually is the most effective method for a small businesses.

6. The purpose of an incubation centre is to provide otherwise costly services to many small businesses at minimal cost. Office space, secretarial services, computer capabilities, and financial and business counselling are examples of such services.

7. There are three steps in estimating the financial feasibility of a proposed business venture. The first step is to determine potential revenues for the total market. The second step is to estimate the proposed business share of that total market. The third step is to subtract the associated expenses from the revenue estimate to determine an estimated net income for the prospective business.

DISCUSSION QUESTIONS AND CHAPTER PROBLEMS

1. Briefly explain the three ways of entering a market. List examples that fit these methods other than those mentioned in the text.

2. John Bird is thinking of developing a new coin laundry on the reserve. He first needs to do some market research to determine the demand for the product. What kind of information should he collect?

3. What could Ken Steinhauer (Incident 3.1) have done to develop a financial feasibility analysis for the guide business?

4. Why is it important to make adjustments in market potential and market share figures?

5. For a small business opportunity of your choice, show how you would evaluate the non-quantitative factors such as goals, experience, lifestyle, and content of work. How well does the business fit with these factors?

6. Design a simple mail questionnaire to assess demand for a taxi service in your community.

7. From Dun & Bradstreet, "Key Business Ratios", find the "Return on Sales, Gross Profit, and Current Ratios" for a jewellery store, a clothing manufacturer, and a grocery store.

8. Using secondary research, develop a market potential analysis for a bakery in your area.
9. The new bakery has a proposed selling space of 500 square feet. The total amount of selling space devoted to bakery products in your market is 8,400 square feet. From the market potential estimated in Problem 8, what would be the market share in dollars for this new bakery?
10. Evaluate the attributes for small business success or ideological marketing for your own community.
11. Evaluate the following personal interview survey* intended to indicate opportunities for new businesses on the Blood Reserve in southern Alberta. The survey was randomly administered to 362 of the 5,000 residents of the reserve. The survey respondents were of varying ages, from several communities on the Blood Reserve.

Question one — How often do you come to Standoff per week?

    Never   Once   Twice   Three times   Four times   Five times   Over five times

Question two — How often do you go to Standoff to do your shopping?

    Never   Once   Twice   Three times   Four times   Five times   Over five times

Question three — How often do you shop outside of Standoff per week?

    Never   Once   Twice   Three times   Four times   Five times   Over five times

Question four — Where do you do the majority of your shopping outside of the reserve?

    Cardston   Lethbridge   Fort Macleod   Other

Question five — Please indicate the two most important considerations when purchasing the following items:

Item	Location	Credit Service	Quality	Price
Groceries				
Eating Places				
Bakery Items				
Snack Food				

* Used with permission.

SUGGESTED READINGS

Barnes, Kenneth and Everett Banning. *Money Makers*. Toronto: McLelland and Stewart, 1985.

Bodell, R., G. Rabblor and L. Smith. *Entrepreneurship: The Spirit of Adventure*. Toronto: Harcourt Brace Jovanovick, 1991–92.

Cornell, Stephen and Joseph P. Kalt. "Reloading the Dice: Improving the Chances for Economic Development on American Indian Reservations". Harvard Project on American Indian Economic Development, March 1992.

Federal Business Development Bank. *Developing a Financial Forecast*. Montreal, 1991.

Federal Business Development Bank. *How to Prepare a Market Study*. Montreal, 1989.

Gray, Douglas A. and Diane L. Gray. *The Complete Canadian Small Business Guide*. McGraw Hill, Toronto, 1988.

Kahn, Sharon. *101 Best Businesses to Start*. New York: Doubleday, 1988.

McDaniel, W., and A. Parasuraman. "Practical Guidelines for Small Business Marketing Research." *Journal of Small Business Management*, January 1986.

OECD. *Implementing Chance: Entrepreneurship and Local Incentive*. Paris: OECD, 1990.

Part 2 | Preparing for Small Business Ownership

Once an entrepreneur has assessed an opportunity, the next important consideration is selecting from three methods of assuming ownership of the business: organizing a business from scratch, buying an existing business, or signing a franchise contract. Chapters 4 and 5 provide information to help evaluate each of these methods.

The last, but equally important, start-up consideration is obtaining financing. Chapter 6 discusses the critical factors the entrepreneur should consider in obtaining financing to establish and operate his or her venture.

C H A P T E R   4

Organizing a Business

————————————————————— D. Wesley Balderson

CHAPTER OBJECTIVES

☐ To describe the advantages and disadvantages of organizing a business from scratch, purchasing a business, and becoming a franchisee.

☐ To discuss the importance of formulating and following a business plan.

☐ To review the essential components of a small business plan.

☐ To consider the different legal structures through which an aboriginal business might operate.

SMALL BUSINESS PROFILE
Leighton Wensley & Brent Ballard
Aboriginal Business Magazine

Leighton Wensley and Brent Ballard frequently discussed the benefits of high levels of entrepreneurial activity with aboriginal bands. One of their concerns, however, was that there seemed to be little in the way of resources and encouragement specifically tailored towards the aboriginal entrepreneur. Ballard was a graduate of the University of Saskatchewan in business and had experience teaching Indian and Métis post-secondary business students. Wensley, a Cree, also graduated from the U. of S. as well as the Gabriel Dumont Institute in the business administration program. Wensley and Ballard spent about a year researching the idea of an aboriginal business magazine, after they noticed that there was no magazine which related to the aboriginal entrepreneur.

Based on this information, they decided to pursue the opportunity. They organized their business with Wensley in charge of sales and marketing and Ballard handling the business aspects. They recruited journalist Jeff Campbell to be the editor of the new magazine. Campbell was a journalism graduate of the University of Regina with related experience in both Alberta and Saskatchewan.

In addition to a well developed business plan, *Aboriginal Business Magazine* established three specific objectives. The first was to facilitate communication between aboriginal entrepreneurs and business owners. Secondly, they intended to educate aboriginal and non-aboriginal people alike about the issues and ideas surrounding aboriginal business. The last objective was to bring credibility and legitimacy to aboriginal business to further economic development geared to aboriginal self-government.

The first issue of 5,000 copies of *Aboriginal Business Magazine* was launched in June of 1994, and it was well received by the aboriginal and non-aboriginal community alike. *Aboriginal Business Magazine* should be a valuable resource for the over 3,000 aboriginal businesses in Canada, and its establishment illustrates the value of a clear strategy and business plan in starting a business.

SOURCES: *Windspeaker*, Canada's National Aboriginal News Publication, May 23–June 5, 1994, p. 11; *Aboriginal Business Magazine*, June 1994, pp. 8–10.

GETTING STARTED: ESTABLISHING THE BUSINESS ————————————

Once the aboriginal entrepreneur has assessed the feasibility of a business opportunity and found it to be favourable, the next step is to select a method of establishing the business. There are three methods: the first is to organize a business from scratch; the second is to purchase an existing business; and the third is to become a franchisee. This chapter discusses the essential steps in organizing a business from scratch, and details the steps of a business plan. Chapter 5 deals with purchasing an existing business and franchising. Many aspects of business plan preparation covered in this chapter are also applicable to the methods of business establishment discussed in Chapter 5.

In making a decision to organize a business from scratch, the entrepreneur opts for greater independence in establishment and operation of the business. Figure 4.1 illustrates this concept. The option of organizing a business is often chosen by an entrepreneur who wants the satisfaction of creating the business and adding his or her own personal touch to all its aspects. It may also be the preferred route in a community where few suitable businesses are for sale or when there is little chance of obtaining a franchise for the market area. Although there is an increase in purchasing and franchising opportunities for aboriginal people, the majority of aboriginal small businesses currently start from scratch. Therefore, the aboriginal entrepreneur should be aware of the advantages of organizing a business from the ground up as well as the potential drawbacks.

Advantages of Organizing a Small Business from Scratch

Organizing a small business from scratch offers several advantages. First, this option allows the small business owner to define the nature of the business, the competitive environment in which to operate, the market to reach, and the size and extent of operations to set up. In the business profile that opens this chapter, Leighton Wensley and Brent Ballard were free to select each of these aspects for their new business.

Second, the owner can obtain the exact types of physical facilities (building, equipment, and location) preferred. Buildings and equipment can be tailored to meet his or her requirements precisely. The owner can also choose the most appropriate location for the market, an important competitive tool in retailing.

Third, the owner can obtain fresh inventory tailored to the target market. Thus, the risk of products becoming obsolete or difficult to sell is minimized.

Fourth, the owner can personally select and train the employees for the business rather than having to rely on the existing personnel of an established business.

FIGURE 4.1 Methods of Establishing a Small Business

Method of Establishment	Organizing	Buying	Franchising
Level of independence	Higher	Medium	Lower
Level of risk	Higher	Medium	Lower

Finally, the owner can develop his or her own information systems such as bookkeeping and methods of evaluating the operation. The owner can also take advantage of the latest technology in equipment and materials.

Disadvantages of Organizing a Small Business from Scratch

Starting one's own business also carries some substantial risks. First, the owner lacks historical information on which to base future plans. This can be a drawback if uncertainty of market demand, supplies, and operations exists. It is also generally more difficult to obtain financing if projections are based on estimates rather than on an extension of trends from existing operations.

Second, the advantage of personally assembling physical facilities can become a liability because of the time required. In some industrial situations where prompt establishment is critical, one of the other methods of small business establishment (purchasing a business or signing a franchise contract) may be more advisable.

Third, a new business always has start-up problems or things that have to be worked out. Incident 4.1 illustrates some of the surprises two aboriginal entrepreneurs encountered in attempting to establish their business.

Fourth, establishing outside relationships with financial institutions, suppliers, and other key professionals is often time consuming. For example, new small businesses typically are not granted initial trade credit, whereas an existing business or franchise has far less difficulty. The savings in interest costs can be substantial.

Finally, the owner faces the risk that there will be insufficient demand for the product or service. Even if a feasibility analysis is carried out prior to business start-up, some uncertainty regarding the extent of the market may remain.

INCIDENT 4.1
Family Partnership Offers Freedom, Cooperation

Clifford Atkinson and Juanita Hoflin joined together in a brother-sister partnership to own and operate Triangle Greenhouses Ltd. in St. Paul, Alberta. Hoflin's hands-on experience in the greenhouse business was just the background she needed to get her own business started. They shared the work and day-to-day operations of the greenhouse, and they discovered they had interests in different areas of the business.

Like any business start-up, Hoflin and Atkinson had a number of problems to overcome. The season started off with a break-in and many unforeseen expenses. Some immediate renovations were needed to improve the customer service area. Equipment broke down and needed to be replaced. The previous owner went to work for the competition and took some of her customers with her.

They get a lot of support from their families, and the partnership arrangement means that Atkinson can spend time with his wife and Hoflin can be with her husband. The partnership gives them someone to work business problems out with.

Hoflin has some advice for anyone considering going into business for themselves: "Figure out how much this is all going to cost you and expect to spend twice as much time and money. Don't give up. Anything worth doing takes time and effort, which is something you can have lots of even if you are broke. Expect to work even longer hours than before but remember they are for you, not for someone else."

SOURCE: *Windspeaker*, Canada's National Aboriginal News Publication, Feb. 1995, p. 25.

THE SMALL BUSINESS PLAN ———————————————————

"The data points to the crucial need for entrepreneurs to formulate business plans, not just for raising capital, but for organization and classification of long and short-term goals. A business plan is a vital tool for the entrepreneur, a blueprint to be referred to again and again to keep business growth on course." (Joe Mancuso, President of the Centre for Entrepreneurial Management)

The use of business plans by Canadian entrepreneurs is increasing. A recent study of 100 successful Canadian small business owners found that 53% utilized full-scale plans, 91% of which had a time frame and 98% of which were written down. On the other hand, only 4% did not prepare a plan.[1]

One aboriginal entrepreneur who relied on a business plan is Kevin Greyeyes, who runs Saskatoon's R.R. Northcote, a river cruise which is one of the city's best known tourist attractions. Greyeyes says, "Try to stay with a plan. If you fail to plan, you're planning to fail. That's what I heard from some profound and deep guy, but that's basically what I found out. I tried to deviate from the plan and do things my own way, but it wasn't working and I had to jump back on course."[2]

To organize a business efficiently, the entrepreneur should follow a step-by-step plan. A systematic plan is essential not only in establishing the business but, as Dr. Mancuso indicates, also in obtaining required funding and in running the business's ongoing operations. Incident 4.2 illustrates the value of the business plan for one small firm. The basic steps in preparing a business plan are as follows:

- Establish business objectives.
- Plan the marketing approach.
- Select the location.
- Determine the physical facilities.
- Plan the financing.
- Plan the personnel.
- Investigate the legal requirements.

This chapter gives a brief overview of these steps. Chapters 7 through 10 discuss the operating aspects of these areas in more detail and should be consulted before beginning preparation of a business plan. A checklist for a small business plan, and an actual business plan following this format for a landscaping business on Alberta's Blood Reserve, are presented in the Checklists and Examples section on pages 278 and 279 respectively. Note that a business plan may also be necessary when purchasing a business, obtaining a franchise, acquiring financing, and performing other essential activities.

Establish Business Objectives

The first step in preparing a business plan is to have clearly thought-out and formally written objectives for the business. To be effective, an objective must be specific. Specific and quantitative objectives allow meaningful evaluation of the business's performance. Objectives can be set in the following areas for the initial year and for a few years following start-up.

---

1   Donald Rumball, *The Entrepreneurial Edge*, (Toronto: Key Porter Books, 1989), 225–33.
2   *Aboriginal Business*, July/August 1994, 20–22.

1. *Business size*: This includes size of the physical facilities, financial commitments, and number of employees.
2. *Production levels*: The plan should include the number of products and product lines and unit production anticipated.
3. *Performance levels*: Sales, market share, and profit level should all be estimated and may form part of the plan.

Planning the Market Approach

The second step in the business plan is to develop a marketing plan. Information regarding the calculation of market potential and market share, both essential parts of the marketing plan, was provided in Chapter 3. The following additional key aspects of a marketing plan should be investigated prior to starting the business. Incident 4.2 illustrates how a business plan can assist in obtaining needed financing.

INCIDENT 4.2

Business Plan Key to Obtaining Financing

Oil giant Shell Canada has a reputation for being a good corporate citizen. But if Greg Favelle has his way, they'll soon be good corporate partners too, as far as the native business community is concerned.

Favelle, a member of the Gitksan Wet'suwet'en Nation in northwestern B.C., is currently working in Shell's products division as an advisor on strategic development and business operations. He is working on a project which may see Shell enter a full working partnership with John McDougall and Darrel and Lionel Crowshoe, owners of Napi's Place service station on the Peigan Reserve in southern Alberta. The project will re-develop the service station, with Shell as the supplier.

Because of fiscal restraint by Shell, who normally would build the infrastructure for such a project and lease it back to its owners, the financing will come from both native and non-native resources, but not from Shell itself. "Shell's precise role will have to be negotiated, but their contribution will be as a supplier and advisor. They'd provide training and promotional support, and set the standards for the development," says Favelle.

Favelle's first job is to come up with a good financial plan; then he'll seek approval from Shell, the Peigan Band administration and the partners. "We're going to have to do some number crunching and then come up with a business plan...I want to have everything firmly in place before I talk to the potential investors about financing."

SOURCE: *Windspeaker*, Canada's National Aboriginal News Publication, Feb. 4–27, 1994.

Have a Clear Concept of the Target Market   It is important that the prospective aboriginal small business owner have a clear idea of who the target customer is and prepare a well-developed customer profile. This profile should include such demographic information as age, income, occupation, and social class in addition to certain personality and lifestyle characteristics.

After identifying a target market, the owner can follow the steps discussed in Chapter 3, such as determining market area, market area population, market potential, and market share. Sometimes this information can be obtained through secondary data, but often some primary research will be required. Chapter 7 illustrates a more detailed target market profile.

CHAPTER 4: ORGANIZING A BUSINESS   /69

Understand the Target Market's Needs, Wants, and Purchasing Habits   Understanding the target market's needs, wants, and purchasing habits is essential in formulating a marketing strategy. Answers to the following questions may prove valuable:

- Where does or where will the target customers purchase the product or service?
- When do or where will they purchase it?
- What product or service attributes influence the purchase decision?
- In what quantities will purchases be made?
- Most important, why do customers, or why will they, purchase the product or service?

Once again, the answers to some of these questions may be obtained using secondary data, but primary research may also be required.

Be Aware of any Uncontrollable Factors that Might Affect the Marketing of the Product or Service   Several factors external to the business can affect the marketing plan and should be investigated including the following:

■ Existing or Pending Legislation Relevant to the Business

New laws relating to marketing practices such as advertising, pricing, and manufacturing can have a significant impact on the business and cannot be ignored. This information may be obtained from an office of Consumer and Corporate Affairs Canada or the equivalent provincial agency. Additionally, changes to regulations and policies in the administration of aboriginal communities may be relevant to the aboriginal entrepreneur. The local aboriginal community office, economic development office or Federal Department of Indian Affairs — or other aboriginal entrepreneurs — can be consulted regarding such changes.

■ State of the Economy in the Market

The prospective small business owner should investigate whether the state of the economy relating to the market is in a recovery or recessionary period. This also can influence the effectiveness of the marketing plan. Various sources such as Statistics Canada can provide this information.

■ Extent and Strategies of the Competition

Attempts should be made to evaluate the competition and to look for competitive strengths for the prospective business. A recent study of Canadian entrepreneurs found that 33% omit this important aspect from their business plans.[3]

■ Cultural Norms of the Market

The entrepreneur should ensure that a new business conforms to the social and cultural norms of the market. The attitude of some aboriginal communities towards business and the accumulation of individual wealth may be less than positive, and the entrepreneur may want to make a special effort to garner community support. It is also important to assess the cultural norms of the target market. This is critical to success for the exporter and for companies moving into new markets.

---

3   Jerry White, "Canada's Free Trade Winners," *Small Business Magazine*, July–August 1990, 38.

■ New Technology that Might Affect the Business

New technology should be reviewed and monitored regularly as it can represent either opportunities or challenges for the business. Trade magazines and competitor strategies are good sources of information concerning new technology.

Plan the Marketing Program   After collecting the above information, the entrepreneur can formulate his or her marketing program. The essential aspects of the marketing program are as follows:

■ The Product or Service

This includes such information as how the product or service will be developed, sources of material, level of quality, variety, and packaging.

■ The Distribution System

This includes determining the path the product or service will take to reach the consumer and may involve selection of wholesalers and retailers.

■ Promotion

This involves decisions regarding promotion budgets, advertising versus personal selling, and developing appropriate communications.

■ Pricing

The development of pricing policies, including the calculation of specific price levels, should be planned.

These elements of the marketing program are discussed in more detail in Chapter 7.

Selecting the Location

The third component of a business plan is selecting a location for the business. Entrepreneurs from remote communities may face restricted market possibilities in terms of access to large markets in their home locale. On the other hand, "remote" locations may offer a distinct advantage for some businesses such as the fishing camp Northern Emak Outfitting (Incident 10.4). In setting up a new business, the prospective owner needs to determine the general trading area in which to locate, then select a specific site within the trading area.

The Trading Area   Several criteria are used to select the trading area. Choosing the general trade area is often more critical for manufacturers than for retailers or service firms, whereas the selection of a specific site within the trade area is more important for the retailer.

Economic Base   Information on population, employment levels, income levels, retail sales, and house values within the trading area may be helpful. These elements assist the small manufacturer to determine the availability of employees and expected pay scales. For retail or service firms, they indicate the potential for future retail sales. One should also examine the trends relating to these key indicators. Most of this information may be obtained from secondary data such as the government sources listed in the Information Resources section at the end of this book.

Many aboriginal entrepreneurs find that the economic potential of their own community is not sufficient to support the type of business they desire to establish. In such cases it is necessary that an expanded market including off-reserve consumers be developed for the business to be viable. More will be discussed about this in chapter 7.

Attitude of Trading Area toward New Businesses   Many aboriginal communities are eager to attract new industry and offer various kinds of incentives for new businesses. While this benefit is usually more important for manufacturers, any small business owner should contact the local band administration if the business is to be located on the reserve or city administration or Chamber of Commerce for off-reserve businesses. Often these agencies are aware of specific types of businesses their communities hope to attract.

Competition   Competitive firms in a trading area should be noted. A retail or service firm with a fixed geographic market should evaluate various trading areas on the basis of saturation levels for the type of outlet it will establish. There are many methods of calculating the saturation index. A method commonly used in the retail industry is to divide retail sales of all competitors by the selling space of the trading area.

Saturation = Competing retail sales / Competing retail space

The saturation index can be compared to the index of other trading areas or industry norms. The higher the index, the more attractive the opportunity. The statistics needed to compute a saturation index can be obtained from the city and provincial license and tax records, Dun & Bradstreet reference books, or personal visits.

Costs   A key consideration in selecting a trading area is the cost of land and buildings. Another is the cost of required services and expenses once the business is operating. These include such items as utilities, business taxes, and insurance.

The trading area decision can be quantified to allow evaluation among several alternatives. Figure 4.2 shows an example of such a calculation.

FIGURE 4.2 Evaluation of a Trading Area

1 = Poor; 5 = Excellent

Criteria	Trading Area A	Trading Area B
Economic base		
Attitude		
Competition		
Costs		
Other		
Total		

The Site   After selecting the trading area, the prospective owner should investigate the following items in selecting the specific site, primarily for manufacturing and retailing small businesses.

■ Accessibility

For the manufacturer, this means accessibility of transportation services for incoming supplies and materials, as well as ease of shipping the finished product. It might also include the site's accessibility to employees of the business, community infrastructure, and protection services such as a fire department.

For the retailer in a town or city, proximity to major arteries and transit lines and availability of parking are important to ensure maximum customer traffic. Assessing traffic patterns (both pedestrian and vehicular) may be critical to success, especially for retailers of certain types of merchandise (Chapter 7 further discusses the location considerations of retail goods). Often, a local Chamber of Commerce can provide information on traffic flows.

■ Site Costs

The cost of sites within a community vary considerably. Generally, the higher traffic areas are more expensive to buy or lease. Entrepreneurs should also investigate other costs such as utilities, taxes, and licenses.

■ Restrictions

When evaluating a site, any restrictive ordinances, for example band by-laws regarding zoning, should be investigated. Such restrictions may hinder current operation as well as future expansion.

■ Site History

The prospective owner should find out if a site has had several tenants or owners over the years. If this is the case, he or she should investigate the reasons for the turnover before proceeding to purchase or lease the site.

■ Proximity to Other Businesses

Will the surrounding businesses have a positive or negative influence on the business? Levels of competitiveness and complementarity are two significant factors. Figure 4.3 gives examples of the positive and negative effects of these factors for both non-competitive and competitive businesses.

■ Physical Characteristics

Size, frontal footage, external facade, contour, and shape are all important considerations in site selection. A business should blend in with its environment, while maintaining its distinctiveness.

The evaluation form shown in Figure 4.4, similar to the trading area analysis, might be used in making the site selection decision.

The Buy or Lease Decision   In selecting a site, one major consideration is whether to own or lease the premises. Because ownership is generally more expensive, most small businesses find that to reduce the already high risk at the initial stages, leasing is the more attractive option. There are several factors to look into before signing a lease contract.

■ Cost of the Lease

The owner-manager should investigate the cost of the lease, how rent is calculated, when the payments are due, and what taxes and utilities apply. Most leases are calculated on a

FIGURE 4.3 Influence from Neighbouring Businesses

Positive	*Negative*
Complementary businesses, e.g., a pharmacy by a doctor's office.	**Uncomplementary** businesses, e.g., a mortuary, tavern, or factory.
Competitive, e.g., could be positive for shopping goods such as clothing, automobiles, and motels.	**Competitive**, e.g., for non-shopping goods such as convenience stores.

FIGURE 4.4 Evaluation of the Actual Site

1 = Poor; 5 = Excellent

Criteria	*Actual Site A*	*Actual Site B*
Accessibility		
Costs		
Restrictions		
History		
Effect of other businesses		
Physical characteristics		
Other		
Total		

per-square-footage basis. In retailing, a percentage of gross sales is often added to the cost of the lease in the form of royalties.

■ Length of Lease

Questions concerning the length of the lease include: How long is the contract for? Is there a provision for renewal at that time? What notice is required for renewal, termination, or rent increases?

■ Restrictions

Potential restrictions on the use of the property should be investigated. Can the site be subleased to someone else? Does anyone have the right to use a part of the property? Is there any reason to expect "political interference" with leasing decisions in a community? Are there certain services or products that cannot be sold or manufactured at the site?

■ Repairs and Improvements

Who is responsible for any repairs and improvements required? When the lease expires, who will own such improvements?

■ Insurance Coverage

What insurance does the lessor have on the property? What about liability insurance coverage? What insurance coverage will be required by the lessee?

Running the Business from One's Home   The final consideration in site selection is the possibility of operating the business out of one's own home. Some situations are particularly suitable for a home-based business. First, if the business is started on a part-time basis, as many are, the costs associated with establishing a home office are minimal. Second, the lower costs associated with starting a business in one's home reduce the financial risks of a venture that may already carry a high degree of risk. Thus, a home office can serve as a temporary office until the business is more firmly established. Third, a home office is suitable for many businesses for which location is of minimal importance or where the business person does not wish to relocate out of his or her community. Many service and some small manufacturing businesses fit into this category. Fourth, locating a business in the home offers several tax-related advantages which may be applicable to off-reserve businesses.

Determining the Physical Facilities

By preparing the feasibility analysis outlined in Chapter 3, the entrepreneur will already have a detailed estimate of the total capital needed to acquire the building, equipment, furniture, fixtures, and possibly the initial inventory. The investment in buildings and equipment is typically larger for a manufacturing firm, while the investment in inventory tends to be larger for the retail firm.

Prior to construction of buildings and purchasing equipment, the relevant building codes and construction standards should be investigated and required permits obtained.

In addition to these capital requirements and standards, a plan should be made of the operations flow within the business. "Operations" includes such functions as purchasing, inventory control, the production, layout, and distribution of the finished product. Chapter 9 discusses all of these items in detail.

Insurance   One item that should be obtained prior to start-up is insurance coverage. Insurance is a method of transferring some of the risks associated with operating a business to another party, the insurance company. The entrepreneur should ensure that adequate insurance coverage is obtained prior to establishing a business. Choice of the right company and agent can be critical to success of the insurance decision. Care should also be taken to ensure that coverage is current. As replacement costs rise, the level of coverage should increase.

■ Types of Insurance

Common insurable risks for a small business include the following:

- *Loss or Damage of Property*: This type of coverage protects the business in case of fire, theft, and similar occurrences.
- *Business Interruption*: If one of the above problems occurs, this type of insurance protects the earning power lost due to the occurrence for a short period of time.
- *Liability and Disability*: This coverage includes bodily injury of employees or customers.

- *Life Insurance*: This insurance is usually bought in the form of a group insurance plan or occasionally key employee life insurance. Partners of a business may also desire to purchase life insurance for the other partner(s).

Planning the Finances of the Business

Four major financial aspects of the new business should be planned in advance of the start of operations:

Establish Capital Requirements and Make Feasibility Projections   As indicated previously, these calculations are made when preparing a feasibility analysis. The results of these calculations form an integral part of the projected income statement for at least the first year of operations, and in some cases five years into the future. In conjunction with the income statement projection, enough information would likely have been obtained to prepare a projected balance sheet and cash flow statement. The fundamentals of these statements are described in Chapter 8. It may be advisable to enlist the services of an accountant in completing these financial statements. Proper preparation of these financial data is key to obtaining funding from investors and lenders.

Determine Sources of Funding   The projections discussed above provide an estimate of the funds required to get started and to operate the business. After calculating the required funds, the owner will need to determine a balance between his or her funds (equity) and borrowed funds (debt). Because raising funds is such a critical area for the aboriginal small business, Chapter 6 is devoted entirely to the types of funds required, sources of funding for the small business, and methods of evaluating these sources.

Plan the Accounting and Bookkeeping Systems   An essential part of any business is record keeping. Bookkeeping is the recording and classifying of the internal and external transactions of the business. This may be an area that requires professional advice. Chapter 8 reviews the types of financial records kept and the different types of bookkeeping systems used by small business.

Determine Financial Evaluation Measures   One area crucial to the success of the small business is the financial evaluation of operations. To perform this evaluation, the owner should identify the key indicators of the financial health of the business. These indicators include profit margins, return on investment, and inventory turnover. The owner should also set up a system of regular monitoring and reporting of these areas. This will be discussed in detail in Chapter 8.

Planning the Personnel

Chapter 10 discusses the operating details of personnel administration for a small business. Following are the major considerations in organizing for the management of personnel:

Administrative Structure   This involves setting up the responsibility and reporting procedure for all employees of the business. If there are only two owners, the administrative structure takes the form of a clear division of responsibilities. A business with several employees might require setting up an organizational chart.

Employee Recruitment and Training   The plan for hiring, training, and managing those who will work in the business should be determined. The aboriginal entrepreneur may want to think in advance about his or her position on hiring community or family members preferentially.

Personnel Policies   Operating policies affecting employees should be stated explicitly and be formally prepared prior to the time the business begins operations.

Investigating the Legal Requirements

An aboriginal business can be significantly affected by the legal environment in which it operates. Typical areas covered are advertising and promotion, credit, sales contracts, pricing, distribution channels, personnel, and financial relationships. Legislation pertaining to each of these aspects of managing an ongoing business will be covered in later chapters.

This section discusses the legal requirements relating to establishment of the business that should be included in the business plan. Some of the most important aspects are selecting a legal structure and investigating which licenses are required. The legal information provided here and in later chapters is intended not to replace the advice and direction of a lawyer but merely to provide a background so the entrepreneur can work with such professionals more knowledgeably.

Legal Structure   The owner must decide under which legal structure the business will operate. Five types of legal structures can be used for the aboriginal business:

1. Sole Proprietorship
2. Partnership
3. Cooperative
4. Corporation
5. Joint Ventures

■ Sole Proprietorship

In the sole proprietorship, the business is owned by a single individual. Registration with the provincial government is normally required and can help protect the name of the business. Figure 4.5 lists the advantages and disadvantages of a sole proprietorship. It is important to note that the legal and tax benefits of the various forms of business organization (see Chapter 11) vary depending on whether or not the business is located on reserve by status Indians.

■ Partnership

In most ways, partnerships are similar to sole proprietorships except that partnerships include two or more partners. Partnerships typically provide increased resources, but they also increase the possibility of conflict; a partnership agreement can be drawn up to minimize such problems. This was done in the business described in Incident 4.1. There are two kinds of partnership a small business might use:

Limited partnership: In a limited partnership, one or more partners obtains limited liability in exchange for not taking an active part in the day-to-day management of the business or acting on behalf of the company. These partners, often called silent partners, usually provide only the financial investment as their part of the ownership interest. Small businesses are increasingly using this form of ownership because silent partners constitute an important source of equity funding. In addition, limited partnerships allow some tax advantages for the silent partner while retaining the positive aspects of sole proprietorship for the entrepreneur.

General partnership: In a general partnership unlimited liability applies to all partners. Figure 4.6 lists the advantages and disadvantages of partnerships. A rather complicated aspect of the legal and tax position of partnerships is the case of a status Indian joining in a partnership with a non-aboriginal person for an on-reserve business. The previous protections are available for the aboriginal partner but not for the non-aboriginal party. More will be discussed about this in Chapter 11.

FIGURE 4.5 Sole Proprietorship

Advantages	Disadvantages
1. Simple and inexpensive to start.	1. Unlimited liability (for off reserve assets only).
2. Offers individual control over operations, profits, etc.	2. Often more difficult to obtain financing.
3. Fewer forms and reports to fill out.	3. The personal tax rate may be higher than the corporate rate.
4. Some tax advantages.	4. The life of the business (off reserve only) terminates on owner's death.

FIGURE 4.6 Advantages and Disadvantages of a Partnership

Advantages	Disadvantages
1. Simple and inexpensive to start.	1. Unlimited liability. For partner also (off reserve only).
2. Pooling of financial and skill resources.	2. Death of a partner terminates the partnership unless a provision to the contrary is specified in the partnership agreement.
3. Tax advantages (i.e., income splitting).	3. Greater (for off reserve business) possibility for disagreements (buy-sell agreements should be drawn up in event of partner(s) wanting to leave the business).
	4. Difficulties of finding non-aboriginal partners because of collateral problem.

■ Cooperative

This form of business has been used frequently by aboriginal entrepreneurs, particularly in the North. In many respects a cooperative's strengths and weaknesses are similar to those of a corporation (see Figure 4.7). The distinguishing feature is that in a cooperative (which needs a minimum of six members) each member has only one vote, whereas in a corporation each voting share has a vote. Some organizations such as Bridgehead (the trading arm of Oxfam Canada) look to become marketing agents for aboriginal cooperatives which produce traditional crafts and food products.

Cooperatives have a history in Canada's north dating back to 1959, and continue to be a preferred business structure. The coop philosophy of sharing of resources finds a resonance in traditional aboriginal values. Arctic Co-operatives Limited was established in 1972; today it boasts about 10,000 Inuit and Dene members in 38 northern communities.[4] Next to the federal government Arctic Co-op is the largest employer in the north, and the only central organization for any group of aboriginal businesses in Canada.[5]

FIGURE 4.7 Advantages and Disadvantages of Incorporation

Advantages	Disadvantages
1. The continuity of the business exists even if owner dies.	1. The cost to incorporate generally ranges from $500 to $1,000.
2. The owners have limited liability.	2. There is greater reporting requirement to government.
3. May have a manager with professional training or expertise.	3. Flexibility may be reduced because of the binding provisions of the corporate charter.
4. Easier to raise funds as lending and equity investors usually look more favourably to incorporate companies.	4. Losses cannot be deducted from other personal income of the owner (off reserve).
5. The corporate tax rate on small businesses (see table on page 311) can be lower than one's personal rate (off reserve).	5. Lenders often require a personal guarantee (relevant for off reserve assets).
6. Incorporation can assist in establishing commercial credibility.	6. Corporate income subject to income tax.
7. Liability insurance may be less expensive (can be circumvented by paying income in the form of salary to on reserve status residents).	

4   *Aboriginal Business*, July/August 1994.
5   *Ibid.*

■ Corporation

The corporation or limited company is becoming an increasingly popular form of structuring a small business. The corporation is a legal entity that is separate and distinct from the shareholders of the business. Because a corporation has a separate identity, it becomes subject to tax, and assets owned by the corporation on a reserve are subject to seizure. This generally increases the availability of financing.

The day-to-day operations of a corporation are handled by a manager who is appointed by and reports to a board of directors. The board of directors is elected by the shareholders. Often in very small businesses the manager, director, and major shareholder can be the same person. Some businesses find it valuable to enlist the services of lawyers, accountants, and other non-competing business people to serve on their boards of directors.

The vast majority of incorporated small businesses are private companies. For a business to qualify as a private company the following conditions must exist:

• The right to transfer shares is restricted, usually requiring the approval of the board of directors.
• The number of shareholders is limited to 50. The company cannot sell new shares publicly.

See Figure 4.8 for a list of steps involved with incorporating a business.

■ Joint Ventures

A joint venture is an agreement between one or more sole proprietors, partnerships, or corporations to participate in a business venture. Although similar to a partnership in many ways, this increasingly popular form of business allows for individual ownership of assets in the venture. Such items as capital cost allowance can be used by either party,

---

FIGURE 4.8 Steps in Incorporation

Most entrepreneurs regard incorporation as a complex process that requires a lawyer's assistance. While it is advisable for the small business to enlist the services of a lawyer to assist in incorporating the business, some entrepreneurs with relatively uncomplicated businesses have incorporated their businesses successfully on their own. Incorporating a business has four steps:

1. Selection of a name for the business. This name must be submitted to and approved by the provincial government department that handles incorporations (see page 321 of the Information Resources section). The selection is facilitated by having a computer search done to ensure that no similar names are currently being used.

2. Development of the share structure, directors, and restrictions on share transfers, etc. The owner must determine the number of shares to authorize, the number of shares to issue, the number of directors, the timing of meetings, and approvals required for shares to be bought or sold.

3. A description of company operations. This section describes what the business can and cannot do.

4. Acquiring the necessary supplies. This includes such items as the corporate stamp, the minute book, and the necessary journals and ledgers.

depending on the need. Other advantages and disadvantages are similar to those of a partnership (see Figure 4.6). Joint ventures are becoming increasingly popular between aboriginal entrepreneurs and communities and non-aboriginal companies (see Incident 7.7). Careful planning may allow this form of business organization to be successful for aboriginal business interests.

Licences and Taxes   Prior to starting a business, the prospective owner should investigate the required licences and taxes that may be payable to the government. Licences and taxes can be levied by federal, provincial, and municipal governments, and these requirements differ for various industries. Failure to note such regulations can lead to additional start-up time, extra costs, and potential negative sentiment towards the business. Incident 4.3 describes the steps one aboriginal community took to ensure that these problems didn't occur.

INCIDENT 4.3
Big Buck Bingo Set for Reserve

The Tsuu T'ina Nation, on Calgary's western limits, hopes to attract 2,000 bingo aficionados when it opens its doors next month to the largest bingo in Calgary's history. Organizers guarantee a $100,000 payout on regular games, a hefty prize compared with the $15,000 maximum payouts on usual bingos. Additional prize payouts of $50,000 to $100,000 for bonanzas and special games also will be offered.

The super bingo is one of about 10 the Alberta Gaming Commission is licensing "to test the market," commission executive director Ian Taylor said Friday. The first super bingo was held in April on the Alexander First Nation north of Edmonton. It was so successful in attracting players from as far away as the Northwest Territories that the band is holding another one next month.

"This is another plank in our whole platform for economic stability and self sufficiency," said Peter Manywounds, the band's economic development officer. In the last two years, unemployment among the band's 900 members has dropped from 52% to 8% because of expansion within such band projects as construction of a commercial centre and new school, along with Redwood Meadows — its golf course and housing development arm.

Gambling on Indian reserves has become controversial, with some bands arguing provinces do not have jurisdiction to control reserve gambling without provincial licences. In 1985, the Tsuu T'ina Nation — then known as the Sarcee Reserve — was investigated by the RCMP for holding a bingo without a licence. But this time, said Manywounds, the band is working closely with the commission, and also with the RCMP, to keep out organized crime.

SOURCE: *Calgary Herald*, July 24, 1993, p. B1.

The following are the most common licences and taxes that apply to the small business. For a more detailed listing see page 297 of the Information Resources section.

■ Federal Government

1. **Income tax**: The income tax is a tax on incorporated companies and aboriginal individuals earning income from a business operating off a reserve in Canada. The rates vary by province and by industry (see Chapter 11). Although income tax payments are made to the federal government, part of this amount is transferred to the province or territory in which the business earns income. Some provinces now collect their own business income tax.

2. **Goods and Services Tax**: The Goods and Services Tax (GST) is a value added tax levied on many sellers' goods and services by the federal government. As with income tax, status Indians on the reserve are exempt from paying the GST. An aboriginal business is required to charge the GST, however, to non-aboriginal customers who purchase the product on the reserve. The tax, which currently is 7% of the sales price, is collected from the purchaser by the seller and remitted to the government on a quarterly basis.

3. **Excise tax**: The excise tax is an extra tax imposed on certain goods sold in Canada. Payment is made by the manufacturer and is a hidden component in the cost of purchasing these goods.

■ Provincial Government

1. **Income tax**: A percentage of federal income tax payable is assessed by the provinces for those liable for income taxes (corporations and off-reserve businesses). Some provinces (Ontario, Quebec, Alberta) collect this tax. In other provinces the federal government collects the tax and remits the provincial portion to the province. Provincial policy regarding aboriginal tax issues is not uniform in Canada (see Chapter 11).

2. **Licenses**: Many types of businesses require a provincial or territorial licence to operate. Some of these businesses may also require bonding.

3. **Sales tax**: Most provinces levy retail sales taxes on tangible property sold or imported. This tax is collected by the retailer from the purchaser at the time of the sale and is remitted to the government in much the same manner as the Goods and Services Tax. Many businesses have found the administration of the provincial sales tax more difficult since the introduction of the GST. Status Indians are not required to pay provincial sales taxes.

■ Municipal Government

1. **Licenses**: Municipalities are authorized to licence all businesses operating within their boundaries. A recent court decision found one aboriginal band to be operating as the equivalent of a municipality.

2. **Property taxes**: Municipalities are also authorized to levy property taxes on the real estate on which a business operates. No taxes, however, are levied on property owned by aboriginal individuals on reserves.

3. **Business taxes**: Other taxes levied on businesses by a municipality might be for water use or other services.

SUMMARY

1. Organizing one's own business has both advantages and disadvantages. The advantages of having a hand in determining the type of business, equipment, employees, inventory, and market are balanced against the disadvantages of uncertainty concerning demand, unforseen problems, and time required to establish the business.

2. The basic steps in preparing a business plan are establishing business objectives, planning the market approach, selecting the location, determining the physical facilities, planning the financing, planning the personnel, and researching the legal requirements.

3. Several criteria are used to select a trading area, including its economic base, the attitude of the trading area toward new businesses, the competition, and the costs involved in setting up.

4. Once a trading area is chosen, the owner selects an actual site. Criteria in site selection are accessibility, site cost, legal restrictions, site history, proximity to other businesses, and physical characteristics of the site.
5. Because purchasing a site is generally more expensive, most small businesses find that to reduce the already high risk at the initial stages of the business, leasing is an attractive option.
6. Prior to construction of buildings and purchase of equipment, the relevant building codes and construction standards should be investigated and the required permits obtained.
7. Insurance transfers some of the risks associated with operating a business to another party. The common insurable risks for small business include loss or damage of property, business interruption, liability and disability, and life insurance.
8. Four major financial aspects of the new business should be planned in advance: the capital requirements and feasibility projections, sources of funding, the accounting and bookkeeping systems, and financial and evaluative measures.
9. The aboriginal small business owner must decide under which legal structure a business will operate. The five types of structures that can be used are sole proprietorship, partnership, cooperative, corporation, and joint venture.
10. The advantages of incorporation are continuity, limited liability, professional management, and ease in raising funds. The disadvantages are the high cost of incorporating, increased reporting requirements, reduced flexibility, and some tax disincentives.
11. Provincial and municipal governments require business licences for most businesses operating in their jurisdiction.
12. The federal government levies income tax on incorporated and off-reserve businesses. Provincial governments also impose income and sales taxes, and municipalities levy property and business taxes.

CHAPTER PROBLEMS AND DISCUSSION QUESTIONS

1. Investigate a small business that is for sale. What are the advantages and disadvantages to you of buying this business as opposed to starting a similar one from scratch?
2. You are thinking of opening up a small business consulting company. What possible uncontrollable factors might affect your decision? Explain.
3. The saturation index is useful to a prospective small business owner in selecting a trading area.
    a. Using the information in the following table, which trading area would you recommend to the prospective owner?

	Location		
	1	2	3
Number of customers for the store	100,000	50,000	25,000
Average purchase per customer	$5	$7	$9
Total square footage of the drugstore (including the proposed store)	20,000	15,000	10,000

    b. If you exclude the proposed store (3,000 square feet), which area would you select?

c. Which index of saturation is more accurate — the calculation with the proposed store square footage or without? Why?

4. Which variables are important in site location for a drugstore? Note: In answering the question, take into consideration the variables in the text (Figure 4.4) and rank them from 5 (most important) to 1 (least important). Justify your ranking on each variable.

5. Interview an aboriginal small business owner about the details of his or her start-up plan. Find out what aspects were deleted from the plan that should have been included.

6. Choose a specific type of small business and obtain advice from an insurance agent on the types of insurance needed and the precise costs. Write a short report on your findings.

SUGGESTED READINGS

Gray, Douglas A. and Diana L. Gray. *The Complete Small Business Guide*. Toronto: McGraw Hill, 1988.

Halpenny, Heather. "Business Structure A Matter Of Choice", *Windspeaker*, Dec. 20, 1993, p. 8.

Kahn, Sharon. *101 Best Businesses to Start*. New York: Doubleday, 1988.

Mancuso, Joseph R. *How to Start, Finance, and Manage Your Own Small Business*. Englewood Cliffs, NJ: Prentice Hall, 1990.

Timmons, Jeffrey A. *New Venture Creation — A Guide to Entrepreneurship*. Burr Ridge, IL: Irwin Inc., 1994.

C H A P T E R   5

Acquiring a Business: Buying and Franchising

D. Wesley Balderson

CHAPTER OBJECTIVES

☐ To review the advantages and disadvantages of purchasing an ongoing business compared to the other methods of small business acquisition.

☐ To explain how to evaluate a business that is for sale.

☐ To review the methods used in determining the price to pay for a business.

☐ To discuss the significance of franchising in the Canadian economy.

☐ To describe the types of franchises that are available for the aboriginal entrepreneur.

☐ To list relative strengths and weaknesses of franchising as a method of starting a small business.

☐ To explain how to evaluate a franchise opportunity and organize a franchising system.

SMALL BUSINESS PROFILE
Joseph Etienne
Mr. Mike's Restaurant

Aboriginal franchise owners are relatively rare in Canada, says the Canadian Council for Aboriginal Business. Joseph Etienne, however, is one aboriginal person who feels that there is tremendous potential in this form of business. Etienne is a 49 year old Mohawk, originally from Oka, Quebec, but he has been out west working for a number of years. Originally he was a hard rock miner, but for the last eleven years he has been associated with Mr. Mike's franchise restaurant chain in a number of capacities including managing one of their outlets in Campbell River, British Columbia.

Recently Etienne acquired the rights to open a franchise outlet of Mr. Mike's in Penticton, B.C., a resort town on the south end of Okanagan Lake. Although he didn't have a lot of educational training to run a franchise, he spent considerable time researching the pros and cons of franchising versus other forms of business ownership. This included an investigation of different franchise organizations and talking with current franchisees to find out what their experience with the franchiser was. Etienne is of the opinion that owning a franchise outlet offers the advantages of entrepreneurship and also provides for some assistance from the franchiser. "You are doing something productive for yourself and your family. The money is there, and there's the feeling you are in business for yourself," says Etienne.

On the other hand, Joseph Etienne thinks that being a franchisee "gives you about 70 to 80% more chance to succeed than if you were an independent." He has found that Mr. Mike's provides corporate advertising, buying, training, financing and other types of assistance. This is invaluable for an individual who doesn't possess years of education or experience in the business.

Joseph has some advice for would-be entrepreneurs in the restaurant industry: "You have to have a commitment because unless you deal with your customers properly the first time, you won't be dealing with them again. You have to be there when you're needed. It's a 24 hour commitment."

Used with permission of Joseph Etienne.

ACQUIRING A BUSINESS

Two alternatives to organizing a business from scratch are purchasing an existing business and signing a franchise contract. Many entrepreneurs prefer these methods of becoming small business owners, or their situation may suggest that one of these methods will be more effective than starting from scratch. Each of these two options and their applicability to aboriginal entrepreneurs will be discussed in this chapter.

PURCHASING AN EXISTING BUSINESS

While there may not be a large number of businesses available for purchase in Canadian aboriginal communities, many off-reserve businesses could be successful enterprises if evaluated and managed correctly; an example appears in Incident 5.1. Before making the decision to buy a business, the aboriginal entrepreneur should be aware of the advantages and disadvantages of buying as compared to starting completely from scratch.

Advantages of Purchasing an Existing Business

The following are some reasons why buying a business may be an attractive alternative:

■ Reduction of Risk

Chapter 2 mentioned that there is high risk associated with starting a small business. Much of this risk can be reduced by purchasing an existing business. Uncertainty about the extent of consumer demand can be eliminated to a certain degree by examining the track record of an existing business. Therefore, with proper investigation the risk associated with a purchased small business should be less than with one that is organized from scratch. Incident 5.1 illustrates how one aboriginal entrepreneur recognized the potential of the business he was working for and decided to purchase it himself.

INCIDENT 5.1
Taking Success One Step at a Time

> No matter how a person measures success, Dave Tuccaro of Neegan Development Corporation in Fort McMurray lives up to the standards in full. Neegan started in 1980 as a company owned and operated by four Fort McMurray area First Nations and Native Venture Capital Company, a group that offers both help in acquiring business funds and advice in business management.
>
> After ten years in operation, Neegan's bumpy course threatened to be the company's undoing. Tuccaro was brought on-line as the general manager and was expected to steer Neegan through the storm. After two years of 14-hour days, seven-days-a-week work on Neegan's problems, Tuccaro could see the potential in the company. It was through the Royal Bank, a shareholder in Native Venture Capital, that Tuccaro's vision for owning the company took shape.
>
> In 1993, Tuccaro bought out the four bands' shares in the company; then in 1994, he completed the buy-out with the purchase of shares from Native Venture Capital.
>
> SOURCE: *Windspeaker*, Canada's National Aboriginal News Publication, Sept. 12, 1994, p. R12.

■ Reduction of Time and Set-Up Expense

In an existing business, physical facilities such as buildings and equipment are in place, and the product or service is already being produced and distributed. Financial relationships and other important contacts have also been established. Each of these areas not only takes time to plan and organize but also can be costly if unforeseen circumstances arise. Examples of such circumstances include lack of demand for the product or service, construction problems, production difficulties, and legal complications. Purchasing a business can minimize these potential problems. An example of a successful purchase by an aboriginal community is found in Incident 5.2.

INCIDENT 5.2
Mill to Reopen

> The reopening of a mill in Chatham could be the beginning of a new investment plan for the Miramichi region, says the chairman for the Micmac-Maliseet Development Corporation. Chief Roger Augustine, of the Eel Ground Indian Band, announced the company's intention of buying 34% of a new $60 million oriented strand board plant to be built at former Norboard plant in Chatham.
>
> The majority of the timber culled for the plant will be harvested from a 32,000 hectare area of Crown land in Kent County, south of the mill. Dividends on the plant's profits will be paid equally to the shareholders. In the case of the Micmac-Maliseet Development Corporation, dividends will be paid to the fifteen bands forming the corporation.
>
> And the bands closest to the mill will benefit directly from its reopening, predicted Stewart. "There will be 100 jobs opened in the mill, and 20 in management. There will also be 100 to 200 jobs related to the mill opening," he said. A training program for native applicants is planned.
>
> SOURCE: *Windspeaker*, Canada's National Aboriginal News Publication, July 19, 1993, p. R2.

■ Reduction of Competition

Purchasing an existing business can eliminate a potential competitor. This is an especially important consideration in fairly stable and small markets, where there may be only a few well-established competitors. Breaking into such a market with a totally new business is difficult, and the potential small business owner should investigate the possibility of purchasing rather than organizing.

■ Capitalization on Business Strength

Often a business for sale may have a competitive strength that would be difficult to duplicate with a new firm. For example, the location of the business, an important consideration in the retail and some service industries, may be excellent. Personnel, technology, or even the physical facilities of the business may be superior to those of competing firms. Key contracts or relationships with customers may be another advantage of purchasing a business; this was illustrated in Incident 5.1. In such situations, buying a business with these advantages may be an attractive alternative to organizing from scratch.

■ Possible Assistance from the Previous Owner

The previous owner may be willing to work for the purchaser of the business or at least to provide assistance for a short period of time following the purchase. This type of help can be invaluable to the new owner.

■ Easier Planning

Financial and market planning for a business is much easier when historical records are available. This information is not available for a start-up business. When approaching lenders or investors, projections from actual results of an existing business may generate more confidence than untested estimates.

Disadvantages of Purchasing an Existing Business

A prospective purchaser should also be aware of the potential disadvantages of purchasing a business. Many of these problems concern the condition of the assets and other aspects of the business.

■ Physical Facilities

The building and equipment may be old, obsolete, or below current standards. In addition, they may not be completely paid for or there may be charges or liens against them. If the prospective buyer is unfamiliar with how to evaluate the condition of such facilities, he or she may enlist the services of a professional appraiser.

■ Personnel

The business's employees may be incompetent or unmotivated. They may also resist the new ownership and reduce their productivity or even quit once the transfer of ownership is completed. The potential buyer is well advised to visit with current employees to ascertain their attitude towards change.

■ Inventory

The inventory may be obsolete or hard to sell. This factor may be especially critical in a retail store or high-technology firm. Age of inventory can often be determined through internal records or by price tag coding.

■ Accounts Receivable

The outstanding accounts may be uncollectible or costly and time-consuming to collect. An evaluation of the length of time these accounts have been outstanding can be helpful in evaluating this potential problem.

■ Financial Condition

The financial health of the business may be deteriorating or less positive than it appears in the financial statements. An in-depth evaluation of the financial condition should always be conducted prior to the purchase of a business.

■ Market

The market for the business's product or service may be deteriorating, or a strong, new competitor may be about to enter the market. In addition, such factors as the overall state of the economy, interest rates, or government policy could adversely affect the market.

■ Deciding on the Price

The prospective owner may have difficulty negotiating a price to pay for the business or evaluating the fairness of the listed price.

Many of the problems associated with buying a business can be uncovered with a detailed investigation of the operations of the business prior to purchase. Some of the key evaluation areas will be discussed in the next section. The entrepreneur can access the following information sources to identify businesses which are for sale: classified ads, government departments, local government administrations, real estate brokers, and professionals such as accountants, lawyers, or bankers. These sources may also be helpful in obtaining information with which to evaluate the business opportunity.

EVALUATING A BUSINESS FOR SALE

A wise purchase decision requires considerable investigation. The prospective buyer should look into several key areas of a business before making a decision to purchase.

Industry Analysis

The aboriginal entrepreneur should be well informed about the industry in which the business operates. Ideally this information should come from an extensive background or experience in that industry. In addition to experience, some specific areas to investigate are the following:

* Sales and profit trends of the industry.
* The degree of competition, number of competitors entering or leaving the industry, and the nature of competitors' strategies.
* The state of the economy in the market area and the extent to which the industry is affected by changes in the economy.
* Legal restrictions currently affecting the operations of the business, as well as relevant pending legislation or political pressure.
* Social and ideological concerns that may adversely affect the industry in the future.

One or more of these areas could be significant in determining the future success of the proposed purchase. As a result, they should be thoroughly investigated unless the buyer has considerable experience in the industry.

The Previous Owner

The entrepreneur should ask the following questions about the previous owner of the business:

* Why is the previous owner selling the business? The often advertised reason, "because of poor health," may refer to financial rather than physical health.
* Is the previous owner a well-known and respected member of the community? Has this reputation contributed significantly to the success of the business? Will this success continue once that individual is no longer associated with the business?
* Will the previous owner be available, temporarily at least, to provide assistance and advice to the new owner? This help can be invaluable, especially to a purchaser who lacks experience in the industry or market.
* Is the previous owner willing to finance the purchase by spreading it over a number of years? This may be helpful to the purchaser and also advantageous to the seller.
* What will the owner do after he or she sells the business? To guard against the owner starting a similar business in the same market area, the prospective purchaser might insist that a non-competition clause be included in the sales agreement.

Financial Condition of the Business

The financial condition of a prospective business is perhaps the most important area to evaluate. Care should be taken to evaluate the financial statements and assess their validity. It is advisable to review not only the most recent year's financial statements, but also those for past years. This process can reveal any trends or extraordinary circumstances. For instance, a general negative trend in profits during the past several years might suggest a lower value for the business or at least the need for more investigation on the part of the prospective buyer.

If the prospective buyer lacks a basic knowledge of accounting and an understanding of financial statements, it would be wise to enlist an accountant, if feasible, to assist in this financial evaluation. Some specific items to investigate either by oneself or with the help of an accountant are the following:

■ Validity of the Financial Statements

Since some flexibility is allowed in preparing financial statements and a wide range of bookkeepers and accountants might be preparing them, one should assess the validity of the financial information obtained from the business. This can be done by insisting on audited statements and reviewing the methods used in recording items such as depreciation, inventory value, extraordinary items, repairs, owner's salary, and the treatment and terms of debt.

The prospective buyer should also investigate whether any potential hidden liabilities, such as liens or lawsuits, exist. Some industry experts recommend that if there is a possibility of such a liability but the amount is unknown, the purchaser should buy only the assets of the business. By doing this the potential liability would accrue to the business itself rather than to the new owner.

Another task in assessing the validity of the statements is to review the income tax returns (where applicable) and bank deposits of the business. In addition, many prospective purchasers insist that the financial statements be audited to ensure their accuracy.

■ Evaluation of the Financial Statements

Once the prospective buyer is satisfied that the financial statements are complete and they accurately portray the operations of the business, he or she can evaluate the performance of the business as described in these statements. Sales, expenses, profit levels, assets, liabilities, and the cash flow position are important items. Application of various financial ratios can help in comparing the performance of the business to other firms in the industry. Chapter 8 gives a detailed discussion of ratio analysis and other financial evaluation measurements. For an illustration of the financial evaluation of a small business, see page 307 of the Checklists and Examples section.

Naturally, one would hope the business is strong financially and profitable in its operations. In some situations, however, a business may be a good purchase even if it is unprofitable at the time of evaluation. Such situations might be the following:

- The current owner lacks competence, or knowledge about the industry, but the purchaser has the competence and knowledge to turn the business around.
- The industry is, or will shortly be, in a growth position that might improve the firm's profitability and/or resale value.
- The major contributor to the firm's unprofitability is lack of capital leading to high interest costs, and the purchaser has the needed capital to inject into the business.

Condition of the Assets

The assets in a business may require thorough inspection and, for non-liquid assets, possibly an appraisal by an independent appraiser. The fee for this service is usually reasonable and may be well worth the cost. Assets to value in this manner are the following:

■ Liquid Assets (Cash, Investments)

An important question to a prospective purchaser concerns how easily the liquid assets can be converted to cash. There may be special terms or conditions with respect to these assets, for example, the time period on a term deposit.

■ Accounts Receivable

Have accounts receivable been aged? How many may be uncollectible? (Accounts receivable ageing is discussed in more detail in Chapter 8.) Enlisting the services of a professional accountant to assist in this regard may be well worth the cost.

■ Inventory

Is any of the inventory old, obsolete, or damaged? A detailed evaluation should be done by someone with knowledge and experience in this area.

■ Building and Equipment

Are the buildings and equipment old or obsolete? Are they comparable to competitors' facilities? Are there any liens against them?

■ Real Estate

What are the land taxes and service costs? If the premises are leased, is the lease transferable? What are the terms and conditions of the lease? Has the location experienced a high turnover of businesses in the past?

■ Goodwill

Goodwill is an intangible value that is added to the price of a business because of its positive reputation, customer acceptance, and experience. What value does the owner place on goodwill? Is this value realistic and reasonable? Generally, goodwill costs should not exceed 20% of the cost of the assets, even for well-established businesses.

Quality of Personnel

The purchaser of a business should evaluate the efficiency of the business's personnel. How do they compare to employees in other, similar businesses? An important factor is personnel reaction to the new owner after the purchase. It may be wise for the buyer to meet key personnel to better evaluate their reaction to the sale of the business.

External Relationships of the Business

The investigation should include a review of those organizations or agencies currently essential to the operations of the business. Will these relationships continue, and if so, under what terms or conditions? Some organizations to contact include suppliers, financial institutions, and key customers. If a business is operating in an aboriginal community, a prospective purchaser might consider the local government's relationships to businesses within its jurisdiction. The purchaser could also investigate whether there is any "aboriginal business network" in the area.

Condition of the Records

Other records to review are credit files, personnel files, sales reports, contracts, and consumer lists. These items can be valuable to the operations of the business and should be included with the business when it is purchased.

For a comprehensive checklist of the considerations in purchasing a business, see page 298 of the Checklists and Examples section.

DETERMINING THE PRICE OR VALUE OF A BUSINESS

If the preceding evaluation of the business shows positive results and the prospective purchaser decides to buy the business, he or she must make a decision concerning the price to pay for it. Is the asking price reasonable? Should a lower counter-offer be made?

Several methods can be used to arrive at a price to pay for a business. In a free market the right price is that which purchaser and seller agree upon, or where demand and supply meet. When applied to a business purchase, this price is called the market value. To use the market value method effectively, the prospective purchaser must collect data on the market values of similar businesses. In most markets the number of sales transactions of similar businesses is fairly small; thus few data may be available.

There are three other useful approaches to valuing a business. The first relies heavily on asset value. The second uses the earnings potential of the business as a basis for determining value. The third uses a combination of asset value and earnings potential. Each method can help the entrepreneur make a general estimate of the purchase price. It should be kept in mind, however, that the buyer, the seller, or the business may possess unique characteristics that cannot be incorporated into a formula. Such situations will require adjustments to a formula-determined price.

Asset Value

There are two approaches to valuing a business using the value of assets as a base: book value and replacement value.

Book Value   The book value method lists the business at the net balance sheet value of its assets minus the value of its liabilities. Chapter 8 provides the fundamentals of balance sheet assets and liabilities. This method generally understates the value of the business by a significant amount. For this reason the book value price may form a lower limit to determining the price of the business.

Replacement Value   The replacement value method lists the replacement cost of the assets as their value. Because the assets of an existing business typically are not new, the replacement value method tends to overstate the value of the business. When coupled with the liability side of the balance sheet, the replacement cost method may result in an upper limit to the price to pay for the business.

Earnings Value

The prospective purchaser is interested not only in asset value but also in how the business will perform in the future. Therefore, earnings potential is another factor that should be taken into account in setting the price of a business. Pre-tax earnings or income should be used, as the tax rates vary by province and industry, and may not even apply in the case of some aboriginal businesses.

It is also important to use average earnings in calculating earnings potential rather than just the most recent year's net income figure. Many analysts will use the previous five years' average of earnings. If earnings appear to be unstable from year to year, a weighted-average calculation might be used. The determination of average earnings using the weighted-average approach is shown in Figure 5.1. This method gives a greater weight to the most recent years' earnings in arriving at average earnings.

There are two specific methods of estimating the purchase value of the business using earnings as a base: capitalizing earnings and times earnings method.

Capitalizing Earnings   This method is commonly used to arrive at a quick estimate of the price of a business. The capitalized value is found by dividing average earnings of the business by a specified rate of return expressed as a decimal. This specified rate of return figure can be obtained by using bank interest (a risk factor of a few percentage points should be added) or another required rate of return percentage for the investment. It can also be obtained by using average return on tangible net worth statistics from such sources as Dun & Bradstreet or Statistics Canada. Figure 5.2 illustrates the capitalization earnings formula.

Times Earnings Method   This method arbitrarily multiplies average earnings by a number between 1 and 10, based on past sales and industry experience, to arrive at a price for the business. Small businesses are usually sold at between four and five times earnings, according to the Small Business Administration in the United States. This number could vary significantly for very small businesses; therefore, the advice of an experienced business broker or accountant valuator should be sought.

Combination Methods

Because both the asset value and the earnings value are important components of the price of a business, some methods combine both values. Figure 5.3 shows a combination method sometimes used. This method is tailored to the unique characteristics of each industry and is based on past experience.

As mentioned previously, determining the price of a business by using a formula may provide a good estimate of a business's worth, but the unique characteristics of each situation may alter the price actually offered and/or paid for the business.

THE PURCHASE TRANSACTION

Once a purchase price and other terms and conditions have been agreed upon, the buyer should consider enlisting the services of a lawyer to draw up the purchase agreement and close the transaction. This helps ensure that clear title to the business is transferred and that post-purchase difficulties are minimized. The purchase agreement should cover the following areas:

- The purchase price, including principal and interest amounts.
- Payment date(s), when and to whom payments are to be made.
- A detailed list of all assets to be included in the purchase.

FIGURE 5.1   Calculating Weighted Average Earnings for a Business

	Earnings	(Earnings × Weight factor)		Weighted Average Earnings
Last year	$ 5,000	5,000 × 5	=	25,000
Two years ago	7,000	7,000 × 4	=	28,000
Three years ago	4,000	4,000 × 3	=	12,000
Four years ago	10,000	10,000 × 2	=	20,000
Five years ago	14,000	14,000 × 1	=	14,000
	$40,000	15		99,000

Average earnings = $40,000 / 5 years = $8,000
Weighted average earnings = $99,000 / 15 = $6,600

FIGURE 5.2   Capitalization of Earnings Formula

$$\frac{\text{Average Earnings}}{\text{Predetermined interest rate or rate of return required for investment}} = \text{Capitalized Value}$$

FIGURE 5.3   Combination Methods for Pricing a Business

Type of Business	Price Offering Range
Apparel Shops	.75 to 1.5 times net + equipment + inventory
Beauty Salons	.25 to .75 times gross + equipment + inventory
Fast-food Stores	1 to 1.25 times net
Grocery Stores	.25 to .33 times gross, including equipment
Insurance Agency	1 to 1 times renewal commissions
Manufacturers	1.5 to 2.5 times net, including equipment + inventory
Restaurants	.25 to .50 times gross, including equipment
Retail Stores	.75 to 1.5 times net + equipment + inventory
Travel Agencies	.04 to .10 times gross, including equipment
Video Store	1 to 2 times net + equipment

Source: Gustav Belle, *The Small Business Information Handbook* (New York: John Wiley & Son, 1990), pp. 30–32.

- Conditions of the purchase: what non-financial requirements, if any, are part of the purchase? Many purchase contracts are signed subject to the purchaser obtaining suitable financing.
- Provisions for noncompliance with conditions, including penalties for breaches of the contract.
- Collateral or security pledged in the transaction (if the seller is financing the sale).

Negotiating the Deal

In purchasing a business, the first formal step is to make the offer to purchase. The offer may be made directly by the buyer or through a realtor or lawyer. In either case, the offer to purchase is best made after consulting a lawyer and accountant. As part of the negotiating strategy concerning price, the potential buyer should have calculated (preferably financially) the maximum amount he or she can offer for the business. This value is generally somewhat higher than the original purchase offer. As negotiations continue, the purchase price or other aspects of the agreement may have to be altered.

The buyer is normally required to make a deposit of 5 to 10% of the purchase price as a show of good faith. This amount should be minimized at least until the seller has met the conditions of the agreement.

ACQUIRING A FRANCHISE

Franchising is becoming an increasingly popular method of establishing and operating a small business. Many entrepreneurs find the opportunity to operate their own business with slightly less risk an attractive option (see Figure 4.1). Others enter franchising out of necessity, having lost jobs with larger organizations. Franchising now occurs in most industries and is experiencing rapid growth in the service sector. Although franchises have not seen widespread growth on reserves in Canada or by aboriginal entrepreneurs in the past, it is expected their use will increase in the future.

From the franchiser's point of view, franchising provides a source of capital and a stable and motivated work force, thus usually leading to higher performance. For the franchisee, franchising offers a turn-key operation with valuable assistance from the franchiser.

One dilemma the entrepreneur often faces is that as the business grows, funds are needed for expansion. In addition, expansion of a business usually requires the addition of new employees. The new employees often lack the same incentive as the owner to make the business succeed. Again, franchising has been the answer for many.

Although the concept has been around for decades, franchising has experienced its most rapid growth in North America only since the 1950s. Franchises exist in almost all industries today. A major reason for the large recent increase in the number of franchises is expansion into the service sector, which is the fastest growing sector in the Canadian economy. The profile at the beginning of this chapter exemplifies this trend. Figure 5.4 lists the largest franchises in Canada today.

WHAT IS FRANCHISING?

A common definition for a franchise arrangement is a patent or trademark licence entitling the holder to market particular products or services under a brand or trademark according to pre-arranged terms or conditions.

FIGURE 5.4   Canada's Leading Franchising Companies

Franchise	Gross Revenue	Parent	Type of Business
Canadian Tire	$2,986,900	Billes	Family Retail Hardware
Shoppers Drug Mart	2,843,600	Imasco	Retail Pharmacies
McDonalds Restaurants of Canada	1,357,300	McDonalds Corp.	Fast Food
Marlin Travel Group Ltd.	723,200	Several	Travel Agency

Today many applications of this definition translate into a broad range of franchising relationships. The various types of franchises can be grouped into three categories:

1. **Manufacturer-Directed Franchises**: In this type of franchise the manufacturer of a product grants the right to a dealer to sell the product. This right, which tends to be geographically exclusive, often requires no initial fee. Manufacturer-directed franchising is common in such industries as automobile sales, gasoline distributorships such as Napi's Place (Incident 4.2), and farm implement dealerships. This type of franchising is successful only when the manufacturer has an established name, a solid reputation, and considerable consumer loyalty.
2. **Wholesaler-Retailer Directed Franchises**: In this arrangement one member of the distribution channel, such as the wholesaler or retailer, initiates the organization of the franchise. The primary purpose of such an organization is generally to centralize many management and operational functions and to take advantage of volume buying for a group of sellers. As with the manufacturer-owned franchise, there is usually not an initial fee, but an equity investment in the franchise may be required.
3. **Franchising Company**: This type of franchise usually involves a company that sells a product or service in exchange for an initial predetermined fee and an ongoing royalty. The franchisee gains the right to sell under the franchiser's name and receives the franchiser's assistance and management expertise. Franchising companies are commonly found in the retail and service industries. In recent years many companies utilizing this method of franchising to expand their operations have experienced rapid growth.

ADVANTAGES OF FRANCHISING

Compared to the other two methods of starting a small business, (organizing and buying), franchising offers many specific advantages:

■ Proven Market for the Product or Service
Except for newly established franchises, a known market exists for the franchiser's product or service. Information about the performance of existing franchises is normally supplied or

can be obtained by the franchisee. Such a track record makes it much easier to make projections for future operations.

This instant pulling power of the product also greatly helps the small business owner shorten the duration of the initial stage of the business when the market is being developed and resulting revenues are low.

■ Services that the Franchiser May Provide

A franchising company typically provides many valuable services to a franchisee. A description of some of these franchiser services follows:

■ Selection of Location

Assistance in selecting the location can be very important, especially if location is critical to the success of the business, such as off-reserve businesses in retailing and in the service industry. Often a franchiser has considerable site selection expertise that can be used in establishing a business.

■ Purchase or Construction of Site, Buildings, and Equipment

The franchiser's experience and financial resources in this area may mean considerable savings of time and money. In addition to providing expertise, the franchiser may even purchase or construct the facilities for the franchisee.

■ Provision of Financing

Some franchisers will provide financing for franchisees, and their association with the franchisees often helps obtain financing. For example, the Royal Bank, through its Franchise Assistance Program, allows favourable interest rates on franchisee loans because of a franchisee's association with a well-known franchiser. A franchise organization may also successfully deal with the financing difficulties experienced by aboriginal businesses located on reserves.

■ Standardized Methods of Operating

Standard operating procedures and manuals are often part of the service the franchiser provides in the areas of cost accounting, control systems, and customer service standards. Such methods can result in considerable savings for the small business. Incident 5.3 illustrates how this service benefits franchisees in the fast-food industry.

■ Advertising

Most franchisers will provide national advertising that may benefit the franchisee. Such a level of promotion may be difficult and costly for the franchisee to develop unassisted. As Incident 5.3 illustrates, group advertising brings greater consumer awareness.

INCIDENT 5.3
Franchise Performance

Why do franchises enjoy healthier sales figures? Buying into a system helps franchisees avoid many of the common mistakes made by new businesses. In the fast food industry, for example, poor inventory control can result in spoilage or not having enough food on hand. To help its franchisees, Toronto-based Mr. Submarine provides procedure manuals that cover everything from inventory control to a list of product shelf lives. "We cover all aspects of the business," says franchising director Thanos Dimitrakopoulos, up to and including "when to clean tables and take out the garbage."

Equally important are the economies of scale franchises enjoy in purchasing and advertising. With group advertising, for example, comes greater consumer awareness.

"A typical single-unit store might spend 2 to 5% of gross revenues on advertising," says Stanley Brown, a franchise consultant with Laventhol & Horwath in Toronto. To get the same impact as a franchise organization with 18 stores, says Brown, an independent business would have to spend much more. Dimitrakopoulos agrees: "Every time we open a new location, it's an advertisement for the other 325."

SOURCE: Gordon Brockhouse, *Profit Magazine*, July\Aug, 1990, p. 48.

■ Purchasing Advantages

Because the franchising company purchases large volumes of inventories for its franchisees, it can pass resulting cost savings on to the franchisees on purchases made from the franchiser.

■ Training

Most franchisers provide training to new franchisees. This may take the form of an instruction manual or thorough training at a franchiser's school. A McDonald's franchisee, for example, receives training at Hamburger University and can even receive a bachelor's degree in Hamburger-ology! Because of the extra training provided, franchising (as opposed to organizing or buying) may be suited to someone who lacks experience in the industry. The profile at the beginning of this chapter illustrates the help that Joseph Etienne received from his franchising company.

Because of these advantages, a franchisee's chance of success in the business is higher than that of an entrepreneur who organizes or buys his or her small business. The franchising industry advertises a failure rate from only 4 to 8%, which is much lower than the rate for non-franchised businesses.[1]

POTENTIAL DISADVANTAGES OF FRANCHISING ───────────

Because of the apparent advantages just discussed, many individuals have signed franchise contracts. However, some suffered disillusionment and failure a short while later. It is critical that the prospective franchisee be aware of the potential difficulties that can arise when one enters the world of franchising. The following are some of the more common dangers:

■ Lack of Independence

In signing a franchise contract the franchisee can expect to receive a certain amount of assistance from the franchiser. The franchiser will monitor the business, however, to ensure that the conditions of the contract are being met. This condition restricts the franchisee's freedom and independence.

■ Cost of the Franchise

Most franchises have a price consisting of an initial fee and continuing royalties based on operations. To enter most franchise organizations, individuals will have to accumulate a certain amount of capital to either pay the fee or provide the facilities. The table on page 299 of the Checklists and Examples section provides details on this subject, including the financial requirements of some of the better-known franchises in Canada.

---

1   Faye Rice, "How to Succeed at Cloning a Small Business," *Fortune*, October 28, 1985, 60.

■ Promises not Fulfilled

Most franchising companies indicate they will provide such services as training and advertising. In some cases, however, this assistance does not materialize or is inadequate.

■ Restrictions of the Contract

The franchise contract may contain some restrictions that inhibit a franchisee's freedom. Such restrictions include the following:

- *Product or Service Offered*: The franchisee may not be allowed to offer for sale any products not procured by the franchiser.
- *Line Forcing*: The franchisee may be required to offer the franchiser's complete line of products for sale, even if some are not profitable in his or her market area.
- *Termination*: The franchisee may not be able to terminate the franchise contract without incurring a penalty. The franchisee may be prohibited from selling the business or passing it on to family members.
- *Saturation of the Market*: In some industries franchising companies have allowed over saturation to occur in a particular geographic market. This puts financial pressure on those franchisees operating within that market. If a franchiser has a large initial fee and no royalties, its major concern may be the selling of franchises rather than the ongoing success of individual franchises.
- *Lack of Security*: A franchiser may elect not to renew a franchise contract once it has expired or may terminate a contract prior to its expiry if the franchisee has violated the terms or conditions.
- *Cost of Merchandise*: The cost of merchandise purchased from the franchiser may exceed the price that the franchisee can obtain elsewhere. However, the contract may require the franchisee to purchase from the franchiser.
- *Effectiveness of Promotion*: Most franchisers provide promotion and advertising for their franchisees. In some situations, however, the promotion is not effective for the franchisee's market and may be time-consuming and costly for the franchisee to participate in. Often a franchisee does not wish to participate in these programs but is required by the contract to do so. Some franchisers may also be unfamiliar with aboriginal markets.

■ Exaggeration of Financial Success

Most franchising companies provide promotional literature for prospective franchisees. This information generally contains financial statements for the typical franchisee. In some cases these estimates have been overly optimistic, and the actual results for the franchisee are disappointing.

EVALUATION OF A FRANCHISE OPPORTUNITY ———————

In view of these potential disadvantages, it is critical that a thorough investigation of the prospective franchise be made before signing the contract. Several key areas should be examined in evaluating a franchise. Information to assist in this decision can be obtained from several sources including those covered below.

Industry Associations   Organizations such as the Canadian Franchise Association (Toronto), the local Chamber of Commerce, and various other industry associations may provide valuable information about a franchiser's history, reputation, operations, size, and number of operating franchises. Page 322 of the Information Resources section lists several agencies that can provide assistance. Various publications also offer assistance, including the *Franchise Annual*, published by the Canadian Franchise Association in St. Catherine's, Ontario; *Franchise Yearbook*, published by *Entrepreneur Magazine*; and the *InfoFranchise Newsletter*, published by Info Press in St. Catherine's, Ontario.

Professionals   A prospective franchisee is well advised to enlist an accountant or economic development officer to review the financial side of the franchise to ensure that the information provided is accurate. Often financial statements do not conform to Generally Accepted Accounting Principles (GAAP) or are unrealistic.

A lawyer's expertise can also be used in reviewing the terms and conditions of the contract. Because the franchising industry is becoming so specialized, it may be worthwhile to enlist a lawyer who is knowledgeable or experienced about franchise issues. The franchisee should ensure that his or her rights are protected and that there is a clear understanding of both franchisee and franchiser responsibilities regarding the following items:

- Initial fee. How much and when paid?
- Royalties. How much and when paid?
- Additional costs for training, and management assistance.
- The total investment required, and how the balance will be financed.
- Assistance offered by franchiser.
- Product pricing fees.
- Termination conditions. Are they specific and realistic?
- Advertising provided.
- Do any merchandise requirements and/or restrictions exist?
- Liability insurance. Who carries it, and what is covered?
- Geographic territory. What is the geographic territory of the franchise, and is it exclusive?

Other Franchisees   One of the most valuable sources of information for the prospective franchisee is communication with other franchisees from the same organization. Has the franchisee been happy in his or her association with the franchiser? Has the franchiser lived up to the promises made? How does the franchiser resolve difficulties that have arisen?

Government Agencies   The Consumer and Corporate Affairs departments or their equivalents at the federal and provincial levels of government may also provide information about the practices of franchisers. In addition, the provinces of Alberta and Quebec require franchisers to register and provide disclosure of information that could be helpful to the franchisee in this investigation. The industry division of Statistics Canada can also provide a fraud checklist for potential investors.

Checking with the above sources can provide much valuable information to aid in the franchise decision. However, some final and critical questions remain. How much drawing power does the franchise name and product or service have? Is the franchise fee worth the drawing power and services provided? The latter may not be a critical question for the well-established franchises such as McDonald's or Dairy Queen, but it may be very important for the lesser-known franchise. Market research obtained through secondary sources or even collected by the prospective franchisee might provide enough information to evaluate the strength of the franchiser's drawing power upon which to base an investment decision. Specific areas to investigate include industry trends, consumer acceptance of the concept, and franchisability of the concept.

Because the signing of a franchise contract is a major step for an entrepreneur, the investigation should be thorough. A comprehensive checklist for the prospective franchisee to use in this evaluation can be found beginning on page 300 of the Checklists and Examples section.

THE ENTREPRENEUR AS A FRANCHISER

An increasingly popular method of entrepreneurship in franchising is not being the franchisee, but selling franchises and becoming the franchiser. One example of an aboriginal entrepreneur who has become a successful franchiser is Kaaydah Schatten Forrest, who was featured in the aboriginal entrepreneur profile at the beginning of Chapter 3. Her Ceiling Doctor franchising company is one of the most successful service-maintenance franchises in the world.

Before a prospective franchiser attempts to sell franchises, several requirements must be met: Is the type of business franchisable? What information is required? How much capital is needed? All of these questions should be addressed in the process of becoming a franchiser.

What Businesses Can Be Franchised?

Franchises abound in many industries today, but a franchise business must have a sound concept. The franchise should be distinct, be practical, and fill a need. It must also be easy to teach and clearly communicate to others. It must be capable of being replicated and transferred to other geographical areas. Suzy Okun, a co-founder of the franchise Treats (which specializes in desserts) elaborates on this idea: "We sell a concept," says Suzy. "We take what the palate already knows, and we make it electric! We take what the customer has already seen and do it differently".[2]

How Do You Become a Franchiser?

Once the franchiser is satisfied a business is franchisable, he or she must take several essential steps to developing the franchise. Some of the most important are the following:

1. **Establish a Prototype**: The franchiser should set up and operate a prototype business long enough to iron out the bugs and get a clear picture of market demand. This business can also serve as a reference point for prospective franchisees to use in their evaluations. To be useful, the prototype should be making a consistent profit.
2. **Prepare the Necessary Information**: Information prospective franchisees will require includes promotional literature regarding the franchise and detailed financial data not only for the company but also for a typical franchise. A prospective franchisee requires information on capital needed, potential income, cash flow projections, and future trends in the industry to make an informed decision. It is recommended that someone with accounting expertise be retained to assist in preparing this information.

---

2   Kenneth Barnes and Everett Banning, *Money Makers: The Secrets of Canada's Most Successful Entrepreneurs* (Toronto: McClelland & Stewart, 1985), 84.

3. **Investigate the Legal Requirements**: The franchiser should investigate the legal requirements in setting up a franchising company. Some of these requirements might be:
   - Registration and disclosure with government agencies. As mentioned earlier, some provinces require detailed information before franchising can begin.
   - The required business licenses and incorporations.
   - Other laws regulating the operations of franchises.

   In addition to the above, the franchise contract should be drawn up by someone with legal expertise to ensure that the rights of both parties are protected. The legal operations of the franchise and the responsibilities of both franchiser and franchisee are formalized in the franchise contract. The franchiser needs to decide which services and what assistance to provide, what restrictions to impose, and what to require from the franchisee in return. A more detailed listing of the typical contract provisions appears in the checklist on page 300 of the Checklists and Examples section.

4. **Develop a Planned and Standardized Program of Operations**: Standardization of procedures is an essential part of a successful franchise and enables the franchiser to monitor operations more easily. An operations manual is generally developed using the experience of the prototype business. As mentioned above, the methods or "system" that is used is typically the "service" that is franchised. The franchiser must ensure that the operations manual is understandable and easy to integrate into franchisee operations.

5. **Obtain Adequate Financing**: To franchise successfully, the franchiser will need capital to set up the prototype business, do the necessary market research, prepare the promotional literature and financial estimates, and develop the system of operations. A rapid expansion program may even require outside equity financing from a venture capital company or other financial institution.

SUMMARY

1. The potential advantages of buying a small business include the reduction of risk, time, set-up expense, and competition; capitalization of business strength; possible assistance from the previous owner; and easier planning. Potential disadvantages include problems with physical facilities, personnel, inventory, and accounts receivable; deterioration of the business's financial condition or market; and difficulty in negotiating a purchase price.

2. The key areas an entrepreneur should investigate in carrying out an industry analysis are sales and profit trends, degree of competition, state of the economy in the market area, legal restrictions, and social and ideological concerns that may have an adverse impact on the industry in the future.

3. Before making a purchase decision it is important to understand the effect of the previous owner's reputation on the success of the business. It is also important to find out why the owner is selling the business.

4. To determine the financial viability of a business, one should analyse the validity of the financial statements, evaluate those statements, review the condition of the assets, consider the personnel, study the external relationships of the business, and look at existing records.

5. In some situations a business may be a good purchase even if it is unprofitable at the time of evaluation. This may be the case if the current owner lacks competence or knowledge about the industry, if the industry is or will shortly be in a growth position, and if the main reason for the company's lack of profitability is the lack of capital. In

each case, if the potential owner can correct or improve the situation, the struggling business may be a wise purchase.

6. There are three general approaches to valuing a business. The first method uses the asset value. The second uses the earnings of the business, and the third uses a combination of assets and earnings to determine the price.

7. When developing a purchase agreement, make certain that the purchase price, payment date(s), conditions of purchase, and any provisions for noncompliance with terms are included.

8. Franchising has enjoyed phenomenal growth in recent years and is showing signs of increased use by aboriginal entrepreneurs. One reason franchising is popular is the increased incentive for franchisees. Franchising continues to allow many organizations with a proven concept or product to expand more rapidly to meet demand.

9. The three types of franchises are (a) the manufacturer-directed franchise, in which the manufacturer of a product grants the right to a dealer to sell the product; (b) the wholesaler-retailer directed franchise, in which one member of the distribution channel, such as the wholesaler or retailer, initiates the organization of the franchise; and (c) the franchise company, which involves a company selling a product, service, or system in exchange for an initial predetermined fee and an ongoing royalty.

10. Franchising offers the following advantages over the other two methods of starting a small business: a proven market, services such as selection of location, purchase or construction of site, financing, standardized methods of operating, advertising, volume purchasing, and training. The potential disadvantages of franchising are lack of independence, cost of the franchise, unfulfilled promises, restrictions of the contract, saturation of the market, lack of security, cost of merchandise, and possible exaggeration of financial success.

11. Several key areas should be examined in evaluating a franchise. Information can be obtained from several sources to assist in this decision, including the Association of Canadian Franchisers, professionals such as lawyers and accountants, other franchisees, and government agencies.

12. Becoming a successful franchiser yourself entails five steps. The first step is to develop a franchise prototype to iron out any difficulties. The second is to prepare the necessary information for the prospective franchisee. The third is to investigate the legal requirements of setting up a franchise company. The fourth is to plan and standardize the program of operation to facilitate the monitoring of operations. The last step is to ensure you have adequate financial capacity to keep up with possible rapid expansion.

CHAPTER PROBLEMS AND DISCUSSION QUESTIONS

1. Your brother George Alook wants to own his own business. His area of expertise is the sporting goods market. He has checked into opening his own store or purchasing an existing shop in the downtown areas of the city adjacent to your reserve. The existing store is a seven-year-old proprietorship with sagging sales. There are four main sporting goods shops in the city (60,000 people). The existing business is in a prime location, and the market and product line are well established. The financial condition, however, includes a large amount of accounts receivable. With this information George turns to you as a consultant. What advice would you give George on whether to purchase the existing business or start his own? What additional factors should he take into consideration? Justify your answer.

2. Your band's development corporation is investigating the purchase of a fertilizer manufacturing plant. The results of your analysis of the firm are extremely positive except for an unidentifiable annual payment of $100,000. With further investigation you learn that the $100,000 is being paid in fines for dumping toxic waste. The previous owner has determined that it costs less to pay the fines than it would to properly dispose of the waste by deep well injection. In light of recent government actions, and your community's own feelings and relationship with their traditional land base, how does this affect your decision to purchase? Explain.

3. Sally's Bar and Grill is available for purchase. Sally's earnings for the past five years have been:

       Last year — $50,000
       Two years ago — $60,000
       Three years ago — $30,000
       Four years ago — $40,000
       Five years ago — $25,000

   Determine the value of the business using the following methods (use current bank interest rates).
   a. Capitalized earnings value
   b. Times earnings value

4. Do an industry analysis for the existing grocery stores in your area. Complete your analysis using all the areas mentioned in the text.

5. From an advertisement in the paper, contact the seller of a business. Find out the price and other information pertinent to the sale. Does the asking price seem reasonable? Check with industry averages to evaluate the performance of the business.

6. Contact a franchiser and obtain information about becoming a franchisee. Using the procedures discussed in this chapter, evaluate the attractiveness of this opportunity.

7. What possible advantages did Ceiling Doctor Inc. (Profile, Chapter 3) realize in franchising their outlets instead of expanding through chain operations?

8. Discuss in detail the steps you would follow in developing a maid cleaning franchise system.

9. Visit a local franchise in your city and ask the manager what he or she thinks are the advantages and disadvantages of franchising.

10. Using the same franchise as in question 7, gather information from government agencies and other sources about that franchise. From your collected information and the results of question four, would you invest in a franchise of this company? Justify your answer.

11. Review the checklist of considerations beginning on page 298 of the Checklists and Examples section. Are there any special considerations you would add for purchase of a business in an aboriginal community?

SUGGESTED READINGS

Bunn, Verna A., and C.R. Steedman. *How to Buy and Sell a Small Business*. Toronto: Checkerbooks, 1987.

Coltman, Michael M. *Buying and Selling a Small Business*. Washington, DC: Self Counsel Press, 1991.

Franchising in the Economy, 1990–92. Canadian Franchise Association and Price Waterhouse. Toronto: 1992.

Jones, Constance, and the Philip Lief Group Inc. *The 220 Best Franchises to Buy*. New York: Bantam, 1993.

Kingston, John P. and P.E. McQuillan. *Valuation of Businesses: A Practical Guide*. Toronto: CCH Canadian Ltd., 1986.

Walton, Ennis J. and Michael J. Roberts. "Purchasing a Business: The Search Process." Boston: Harvard Business School, 1989.

Zaid, Frank and Jerry White. *The Canadian Franchise Guide*. Richard De Boo Publishers, 1986.

C H A P T E R   6

Financing Aboriginal Small Businesses

Patricia Elemans

CHAPTER OBJECTIVES

- ☐ To discuss the importance of outside funds to an aboriginal small business.

- ☐ To illustrate a method for determining the amount of capital required.

- ☐ To identify the sources of equity and debt funds that are available to start and operate a small aboriginal business.

- ☐ To explain the considerations involved in obtaining equity or debt financing.

- ☐ To discuss how to prepare a proposal to obtain financing for the small business.

SMALL BUSINESS PROFILE
Rhonda Longboat
Walpole Island Reserve

Rhonda Longboat had a dream. She wanted to start a small business that she and her husband could run on their southern Ontario farm. What she had in mind was a stable of horses for riding lessons and trail riding in the summer; when winter drifted over the Walpole Island Reserve near Lake St. Clair in southwestern Ontario, she proposed to give hayrides for neighbours and other members of the Walpole Island Indian Band

It was a modest dream by conventional business standards, but unusually difficult to realize. Like most new entrepreneurs, Longboat needed start-up capital to get her business off the ground: about $27,000 for horses, improvements to her barn, and fence posts and wire to enclose paddocks.

Under ordinary circumstances the numbers and intangibles would have looked good to a bank manager. But the circumstances were not ordinary. Longboat is a status Indian, part Mohawk and part Cayuga, living on a reserve. In the eyes of the business loan divisions of Canada's major banks, those facts have traditionally added up to a losing combination.

Longboat eventually got the money she needed. And at least a portion of it came from The Bank of Nova Scotia, thanks to one of several initiatives sponsored by Canada's financial community so that aboriginal entrepreneurs can realize their dreams.

Rhonda received her loan through a borrowing circle. She built her paddocks, fattened up her six horses, cut trails, developed her riding courses and planned a grand opening party. In the summer of 1994 she served over 1,500 individuals. She is hoping that the summer of 1995 will be even better.

SOURCE: Richard Wright, "Financing Native dreams," *Windspeaker*, Canada's National Aboriginal News Publication, March 14–24, 1994, pp. 12–15.

SMALL BUSINESS FINANCING

The inability to obtain adequate funding has often been cited as a major small business frustration and a primary cause of some small business failures by non-aboriginal people. For aboriginal people the problem is magnified ten-fold. Paradoxically, the very law that was intended to protect First Nations people, Section 89 of the Indian Act, has proven to be the strongest obstacle to obtaining financing for new and ongoing ventures. Section 89 prohibits the seizure and mortgage of real and personal property of an aboriginal person living on a reserve by anyone other than another aboriginal person. This prevents aboriginal people living on reserves from using land and assets as collateral — a must for most traditional lending institutions.

However, it appears that this situation is slowly improving as is evident in Incident 6.1. Banks, government, and other lending institutions are realizing the size of the emerging aboriginal market and business community. Banks are beginning to tailor their services and use creative practices to get around section 89 of the Indian Act in an effort to service this growing market. Some banks are, among other initiatives, establishing branches on reserves and developing Aboriginal Banking Service divisions. This, combined with the ingenuity and initiative of aboriginal business people and leaders, is gradually making it easier for aboriginal entrepreneurs to access capital. Incident 6.2 and the profile at the beginning of the chapter illustrate that new methods to raise funds and new sources of funds are emerging for aboriginal entrepreneurs.

INCIDENT 6.1
Partnership Possible because of Changes to Small Business Loans Act

Management consultant Matt Vickers has dissolved his firm in order to form a partnership with his artist brother, Roy Henry Vickers.

To finance the new venture, called Eagle Dancer Enterprises, the two borrowed money through the Bank of Montreal under the previously inaccessible Small Business Loans Act.

Legislation, which has been in place since 1961, states that every Canadian citizen shall be able to participate in this program, except for Indians living on reserves. The Bank of Montreal started negotiations with Industry Canada to get around the act. Finally, the federal government agreed to loan Indians money for equipment, but not for real estate, because equipment can be used as collateral.

SOURCE: Linda Caldwell, *Windspeaker*, Canada's National Aboriginal News Publication, July 18–July 31, 1994, p. 8.

INCIDENT 6.2
Mortgages Made Available for Properties on Reserve

A new program developed by the Bank of Montreal will help aboriginal people access mortgages to build houses on their reserves, a first in Canada.

Previously, banks did not make real estate loans for buildings on reserves because they could not foreclose on the property, since land cannot be owned by anyone other than a member of that community. Because the bank had no security they would not make a loan.

The way around this is to appoint three trustees, all highly respected members of the community. Ownership of the real estate is transferred to the trustee, who arranges the mortgage with the bank.

If the borrower meets the loan obligations and pays the mortgage off, ownership of the land and housing is transferred back to him.

If the borrower defaults on the mortgage, the trustees can sell the land and building to another member of the community. The property does not leave the ownership of the reserve members.

SOURCE: Linda Caldwell, *Windspeaker*, Canada's National Aboriginal News Publication, July 18–July 31, 1994, p. 8.

Although many small businesses have experienced difficulties due to their inability to obtain needed funds, statistics show that financing woes are often a symptom of other management problems.[1] Lack of management competence and experience can result in the following specific financial problems:

- Underestimating financial requirements.
- Lack of knowledge of sources of equity and debt capital leading to either the inability to obtain funds or the failure to obtain them at the lowest cost.
- Lack of skills in preparing and presenting a proposal for financing to a lender or investor.
- Failure to plan in advance for future needs, resulting in last-minute financial crises.
- Poor financial control of operations leading to failure in payment of loan obligations.

This chapter will discuss each of these important areas to assist the aboriginal entrepreneur in obtaining financing for establishing his or her business.

DETERMINING THE AMOUNT OF FUNDS NEEDED

The first step in securing capital (funds) for the business is to determine the amount of money needed. Any lender or investor, whether it is a bank, trust company, band, settlement, capital corporation, private lender, or government organization, will want to see evidence of a systematic and thoroughly prepared statement of fund requirements. In this regard, it is helpful to divide required funding into two categories: start-up costs and ongoing operating requirements. The entrepreneur's own funds available for the venture can then be subtracted from the projected required amounts to obtain the capital needed from outside sources, as is shown in the following formula:

$$\text{Capital requirements} = \frac{\text{Start-up costs} + \text{Operating requirements} - \text{Owner funds}}{\text{available for investment}}$$

Start-Up Costs

Capital will be required to finance land, buildings, equipment, inventory, raw materials and other items needed to start up a business. The owner should obtain and verify quotes from sellers of these assets and owners of existing similar businesses. A contingency factor for potential price increases during the planning and start-up phase should be added. For example, all estimates should be increased by a certain percentage to build in financial flexibility in case there are price increases or unknown additional costs. Incident 6.3 is an example of a company that used financial planning for a successful start-up.

---

1 *The Canadian Business Failure Record, 1984* (Toronto: Dun & Bradstreet Business Education Division, 1983).

INCIDENT 6.3
Keep Costs to a Minimum

Planning, minimizing expenses, operating a pilot project and setting clear policies for clients were key to getting Northern Emak off to a successful beginning.

Northern Emak Outfitting Ltd. is located on a remote coastal lake on the east side of Victoria Island, which lies 200 miles north of the Arctic Circle. George and Gary Angohiotok are two of the partners who operate the successful fishing camp. The other two partners are Bill Tait, who runs Adventure North Expeditions Ltd. and Jerome Knapp, a well-known journalist.

One of the important reasons for the success of the fishing camp is the policy of minimizing the initial outlay of expenses. The owners do not believe in having high capital expenses. When they started they bought all of the equipment at a minimum cost. Bill points out, "We didn't want to invest a lot of money in the thing, so if the fishing business goes downhill we've cut the risks... The Government would like us to invest a million dollars in a business and have a big opening — cut ribbons and have Ministers there. What we have here is the bare bones operation that just tries to make money and hopefully will survive."

In addition to minimizing expenses, another successful element in the start-up phase was the pilot project. It was an inexpensive way to assess whether or not a demand for a fishing camp existed and could be met properly. According to Bill, "The main thing is that if you've got to walk a thousand miles, the first mile is the hardest. With the pilot project George and Gary travelled the first mile, just to get the kinks out, and then we let it roll."

Once a business concept has been identified and seems to be feasible, then time should be spent planning the venture in detail. Financial planning was very important for George. Determining that the required services are available at a reasonable cost prevented problems. In this case, there are unemployed people in Cambridge Bay with the necessary skills to operate a fishing camp, and planes are available for charter to take clients to and from the camp.

SOURCE: Wanda Wuttunee, "Northern Emak Outfitting Inc.," The Centre for Aboriginal Management, Faculty of Management, The University of Lethbridge, 1991.

Start-up capital will also be required to finance some of the operating costs during this period. Usually a delay in sales revenues occurs for a start-up business, but many operating expenses are incurred before the business begins operating. Incident 6.4 is an example of how one creative entrepreneur overcame this hurdle.

INCIDENT 6.4
Altruism Motivates Fort McMurray Entrepreneur

Doreen Janvier, a 29-year-old former resident of the Janvier reserve, south of Fort McMurray, launched DMJ Enterprises in 1990. The company supplies workers for the oilsands giant Syncrude's heavy equipment wash bays. The company started with 14 employees, all from Janvier, but now has an all-native, 25 member staff hired out of Janvier and Fort McMurray.

Doreen started DMJ Enterprises with a $10,000 investment from her own savings. But she needed another $30,000 to make the payroll during her first three months while waiting out Syncrude's standard 90-day delay on paying invoices. To get over this first hump she put up her house, truck and skidoo for collateral to ensure help from the banks.

SOURCE: *Windspeaker*, Canada's National Aboriginal News Publication, January 4, 1993, p. 9.

The entrepreneur will need to make estimates of these types of expenses and should include them in the capital requirements. Following are costs that often fit into this category:

- Initial inventory
- First few months' payroll, including owner's salary
- First few months' utilities
- First few months' rent
- Initial advertising
- Prepaid items such as utility and rent deposits, and insurance
- Remodelling costs and the cost of furniture and fixtures
- Legal and professional fees
- Licenses and permits
- Any other operating costs that need to be paid before revenues are generated.

Start-up costs may be difficult to project. Figure 6.1 illustrates a start-up cost projection. Note the sources of information accessed to prepare this statement.

FIGURE 6.1   Start-up Cost Schedule

Item	Cost	Source
Land and Buildings	0	Leased from band; if purchased, a similar business or quotes from suppliers
Equipment	$ 34,000	Other similar businesses or quotes from suppliers
Initial Inventory	70,000	Other similar businesses or quotes from suppliers; use the formula: Inventory = Projected sales ÷ Inventory Turnover (300,000 ÷ 4.3)
Wages (first two months)	6,000	Other similar businesses or current wage rates
Utilities and telephone		
Deposit	100	Quotes from provider
First 2 months	680	Quotes from provider
Rent (deposit)	500	Quotes from lessor
First 2 months	3,000	Quotes from lessor
Advertising	960	Quotes from advertising agency or media
Insurance (prepaid)	975	Quotes from insurer
Licences and permits	200	Quotes from municipal agency
Other prepaids	285	Other similar businesses
TOTAL START-UP REQUIREMENTS	$116,700	

Ongoing Operating Costs

The entrepreneur should prepare a cash flow statement to calculate financial operating requirements after the start-up period. A **cash flow statement**, explained in more detail in Chapter 8, is simply a record of all projected cash inflows and outflows. An example of such a statement appears in Figure 6.2. In this monthly cash flow, for a hypothetical business, it has been calculated that up to $65,285 may be needed to finance operations. This occurs in the first month. If debt financing were used, the entrepreneur would most likely attempt to arrange a $66,000 line of credit (operating loan) with a lender to cover this amount when required. Such a method of financing would allow the business to withdraw and deposit funds on an ongoing basis as long as the total amount withdrawn at any point in time did not exceed $66,000.

The Owner's Net Worth

After estimating start-up and operating capital requirements, the owner should prepare a personal net worth and capability statement. Preparing this statement will not only help determine the amount of the owner's funds to invest in the business, but will probably be required by a lender if the owner needs to borrow the necessary capital. The essentials of the personal net worth statement are the same as for a business's balance sheet. An example of a net worth statement appears in Figure 6.3.

DETERMINING TYPES OF FINANCING

Two general sources of funds can be used to finance a small business. The first is **equity** or **ownership financing**. The second is funds obtained from borrowing, usually referred to as **debt financing** (including trade credit). Many small businesses use both forms of financing to get established. Entrepreneurs can obtain funding from lending institutions, bands, settlements, territorial governments, family members, external private investors, retail companies, friends and from government agencies. Each of these types of financing will be discussed in this chapter.

Equity Financing

Equity financing involves giving up ownership of the business in return for capital. The sources of equity financing are private investors, corporate investors, government, bands and settlements.

Private Investors   This source includes obtaining funds from friends, relatives, or private investors in exchange for selling shares in an incorporated company or for a percentage of ownership in a sole proprietorship. It is especially critical from an investor's point of view that there be a clear understanding of conditions, authority, and responsibilities of all of the investors under such an arrangement. The investor's degree of involvement can vary greatly. Some investors expect only a reasonable return on their investment, while others expect to be full operating partners in the business in addition to receiving a return on their capital.

An increasingly popular form of private financing is to sell ownership interest to the employees of the business. Many companies have noticed that in addition to obtaining funds, this method of financing results in dramatic increases in productivity.

FIGURE 6.2 Sample Cash Flow Statement

	Feb	Mar	Apr	May	Jun	Jul	Aug	Sep	Oct	Nov	Dec	Jan
Opening Balance	$ 0	$-65,285	$-48,595	$-31,905	$-55,173	$-34,871	$-14,569	$-36,839	$-17,289	$ 2,261	$-19,811	$ 1,967
Bank Loan	35,000	0	0	0	0	0	0	0	0	0	0	0
Sales												
Cash	12,000	12,000	12,000	13,750	13,750	13,750	13,750	13,750	13,750	14,250	14,250	14,250
Credit	0	12,000	12,000	12,000	13,750	13,750	13,750	13,750	13,750	13,750	14,250	14,250
Total Receipts	47,000	-41,285	-24,595	-6,155	-27,673	-7,371	12,931	-9,339	10,211	30,261	8,689	30,467
Disbursements												
Furniture and Fixtures	34,000	0	0	0	0	0	0	0	0	0	0	0
Rent	1,500	1,500	1,500	1,500	1,500	1,500	1,500	1,500	1,500	1,500	1,500	1,500
Utilities	200	200	200	200	200	200	200	200	200	200	200	200
Promotion (2% of Sales)	480	480	480	550	550	550	550	550	550	570	570	570
Telephone	140	140	140	140	140	140	140	140	140	140	140	140
Wages & Salaries	3,000	3,000	3,000	3,000	3,000	3,000	3,000	3,000	3,000	3,000	3,000	3,000
Inventory	70,000	0	0	41,820	0	0	41,820	0	0	43,350	0	0
Maintenance & Repairs	240	240	240	270	270	270	270	270	270	270	270	290
Professional Fees	330	330	330	330	330	330	330	330	330	330	330	330
Insurance	975	0	0	0	0	0	0	0	0	0	0	0
Interest & Bank Charges	1,420	1,420	1,420	1,208	1,208	1,208	1,960	1,960	1,960	712	712	712
Loan Repayment	0	0	0	0	0	0	0	0	0	0	0	35,000
Total Disbursements	112,285	7,310	7,310	49,018	7,198	7,198	49,770	7,950	7,950	50,072	6,722	41,742
CASH (+/-)	$-65,285	$-48,595	$-31,905	$-55,173	$-34,871	$-14,569	$-36,839	$-17,289	$ 2,261	$-19,811	$ 1,967	$-11,275

NOTE: 50% of monthly sales are cash and 50% are credit. The credit sales are collected in the next month.

FIGURE 6.3   Suggested Format for a Personal Net Worth Statement

Personal Net Worth Statement For: _____

As of _____, 19___.

Assets		Liabilities	
Cash on hand and in banks	$ _____	Outstanding debts	$ _____
Savings account in banks	_____	Owing to banks	_____
Canada savings bonds	_____	Monthly payments (auto)	_____
Automobile	_____	Other	_____
Other property	_____	Net Worth	_____
Other assets	_____		
Total	$ _____	Total	$ _____

Another form of private equity investment is to sell shares in the business to anyone who is interested. This is known as **going public**, wherein shares in the company are sold at a public stock exchange. This form of financing was discussed in detail in Chapter 4. Generally, small businesses are not large enough to seek public equity for the business startup.

Corporate Investors   Many companies are interested in investing in a small business in the hope that the value of their investment will increase over time. Often they then sell their ownership interest back to the original owners when the owners are in a better position to finance the business independently.

Companies whose major activity is investing in smaller and medium sized businesses are called **venture capital companies**. These companies use highly sophisticated evaluation techniques and accept only a small percentage of applications.[2] A venture capital company typically looks for a business within a high growth industry, with sound management and the possibility for a return on investment of between 20 and 40%. Generally they are not long-term investors. An entrepreneur seeking venture capital assistance should be aware of the areas of the business to which investors will pay specific attention. Normally such factors as the abilities and expertise of the management team, the level of development of the product or service, and industry trends are key elements in this evaluation.[3]

Government   Traditionally the government has been hesitant to provide equity investment to small business. However, programs have been developed in recent years that permit gov-

---

2   "Venture Capital: More Money, Still Choosy," *The Magazine That's All about Small Business*, May 1984, 49.
3   Stanley Rich and David E. Gumpert, "Business Plans That Win $$$: Lessons from the MIT Enterprise Forum," *Venture*, June 1985, 72.

ernment funding and incentives for venture capital firms, allow for direct equity investment by government in the business and provide grants to businesses. Incident 6.5 highlights several businesses that benefitted from government sponsored programs. Some of these programs and agencies are described next.

INCIDENT 6.5
Eight Native-Run Businesses Receive Federal Contributions

Eight native-run Alberta businesses received a total of about $230,000 in contributions from Industry, Science and Technology Canada.

Tom Hockin, federal minister of state responsible for small businesses and tourism, made the announcement in conjunction with Small Business Week. The contributions are being made through Ottawa's Aboriginal Business Development Program. The businesses included two restaurants and a taxi business. "The diversity, adaptability and skill evident in these examples of aboriginal entrepreneurship are sure signs that aboriginal business is alive and well in Canada," Hockin said in announcing the contributions.

SOURCE: *Calgary Herald*, October 26, 1991.

Aboriginal Business Canada (ABC)   ABC provides direct-funding and non-funded business assistance to aboriginal businesses in Canada. In addition, it supports the network of Aboriginal Capital Corporations across the country. A description of Aboriginal Business Canada, the types of services offered, and the locations of offices are presented beginning on page 323 of the Information Resources section. Incident 6.6 profiles a company that benefited from this program.

INCIDENT 6.6
Wickaninnish Gallery

If you're looking to buy aboriginal art in Vancouver you'll probably want to spend some time at the Wickaninnish Gallery. The gallery specializes in original art, jewellery, clothing featuring traditional designs, and gifts — all purchased directly from aboriginal artists in British Columbia.

The Wickaninnish Gallery is co-owned by Patricia Rivard and her husband Jean. "Wickaninnish" is the name of Patricia's great-grandfather — a statesman of the Nuu Chah Nulth Nation. Patricia carries the Indian name "Hai Na Kuu Kwa Hy Ne Coo Qua," which means "bearer of the light," and reveals her honoured status as the one who performs the "Dance of Light" to open a "Potlatch" or gathering of tribes.

The gallery is one of the attractions on Granville Island, a trendy shopping destination in Vancouver. Started in 1987, with a grant of $50,000 from the NEDP (now Aboriginal Business Canada), the store has seen sales increase from $150,000 in its first year of operations to over $500,000 annually. In 1993 Patricia established Wickaninnish Wholesale to service the growing demand for aboriginal art from corporate and overseas clients. She is now developing a strong clientele base in the U.S., Japan and Europe.

With Patricia's and Jean's combined dedication to quality, and their ability to seek out new opportunities, the upcoming years for Wickaninnish Gallery and Wickaninnish Wholesale look bright.

SOURCE: Joe Courchene, Tale'awtxw Aboriginal Capital Corporation.

Aboriginal Capital Corporations (ACCs)   These corporations, funded by Industry Canada, are owned by native people and provide loans to native businesses. There are 33 ACCs in Canada.[4] Although required to follow certain guidelines, ACCs have the ability to tailor loans and loan provisions to the specific needs of their clientele. Not only do they provide funding to aboriginal ventures, they also provide assistance in all aspects of starting and managing an enterprise. An example of one such corporation is the Tale'awtxw Aboriginal Capital Corporation in British Columbia. Its services and requirements are outlined on page 329 of the Information Resources section. Most capital corporations have similar guidelines. The process that applicants must go through to obtain funding through a capital corporation and what the corporations look for in an applicant's proposal are outlined in Incident 6.7.

INCIDENT 6.7

Tale'awtxw Aboriginal Capital Corporation

Joe Courchene is an Ojibwa Indian from the Sagkeeng First Nation, located 130 km. northeast of Winnipeg. Joe graduated from the University of Manitoba in 1985 with a Diploma in Agriculture. Since that time he has been active in the aboriginal economy throughout western Canada.

Joe's experience includes working at the University of Lethbridge in their Aboriginal Management Program, numerous positions as an Economic Development Officer (EDO) and, most recently, as a development officer with the Tale'awtxw Aboriginal Capital Corporation in North Vancouver, B.C.

As an EDO he had the opportunity to manage restaurants, construction companies, fire-fighting companies, and general contracting businesses as well as establishing development corporations. Joe says, "It was not always easy to work as an EDO/manager of the different businesses. When organizations are looking for new EDOs they are generally already having problems. My responsibility was to provide direction and expertise to the employers to keep the businesses operating or, in some cases, to help them establish a new business." In all of these activities, securing financing and turning the business around was the major responsibility. A business plan was always required to illustrate the objectives of the business, identify the market potential and, most importantly, determine if the business would capture its fair market share. Financiers also wanted to know the location of the business, capital assets the business had or required, whether it was a new or existing business, historical and projected financial statements and a repayment schedule for the requested financing.

As a development officer for Tale'awtxw Joe was responsible for assisting clients in developing their businesses and securing financing from the capital corporation, chartered banks or Aboriginal Business Canada. He outlines the following steps that an applicant must go through in order to receive financing.

1. **Complete a statement of intent**. This provides information on the individual and what they are proposing to achieve. The client must provide documentation to show they are Aboriginal, Status, Inuit or Métis. The development officer then reviews the statement and interviews the client to assess the merits of the proposed venture. Five areas are then evaluated.
   i. *Management experience and capabilities of the client*: They look for a minimum of two years experience in the proposed industry. A resume should be included with the statement of intent to demonstrate this experience.

---

4   Calvin Helin, Sources of Capital, *Mawio'mi Journal*, Summer 1994, Number 3, 9–12.

    ii. *Market*: What is the condition of the market? Does the applicant have a contract to provide services or is the client going to be competing against other established businesses? Who are its competitors?

    iii. *Financing*:   What is the individual's credit history and what needs to be financed? When an individual signs the statement of intent, they give Tale'awtxw the right to conduct a credit check. The types of assets that require financing are assessed. For example, hard assets such as trucks are more securable than leasehold improvements. Is the individual prepared to risk his or her own assets, including cash, to establish the venture? It is generally expected that the client risk at least 10–20% cash to establish the proposed venture.

    iv. *Profitability of the proposed venture*: Is it going to be financially feasible?

    v. *Feasibility and benefits*: Is it feasible and who will benefit from the business? If the above items prove satisfactory the proposal is moved to the feasibility study/ business planning stage.

2. **Feasibility Analysis**. The client must submit a feasibility analysis to demonstrate that the venture is feasible. This analysis includes a report on the market potential, market share and projected financial statements of the business. The study is assessed by a development officer such as Joe, and if it appears viable the project is moved to the business planning stage.

3. **Business Plan**. At this stage the business objectives, management team, location, physical facilities, capital requirements, proposed financing, projected financial statements, personnel policies, and legal structure must be detailed. All areas, including the entrepreneur, are then reviewed in greater detail. The plan is compared to existing businesses, assessed relative to the market, and judged for potential risk.

SOURCE: Joe Courchene.

Federal Business Development Bank (FBDB)   As part of their mandate the FBDB will participate with other investors as a principal in the provision of investment capital in businesses it views as promising. Generally the purpose of such financing is to provide an adequate equity base to allow the firm to receive funding from additional sources.

Provincial Programs   Provincial governments have provided incentives for the formation of small business investment companies, which act similarly to venture capital companies. The various Provinces and Territories have different loan fund programs. A brief listing of current provincial government equity capital programs appears on page 325 of the Information Resources section.

Bands, Settlements and Territorial Governments   Bands, Settlements and Territorial Governments may provide equity, debt, or grants to entrepreneurs establishing new businesses and those requiring financing for expansion. Funding is generally done through local Economic Development Corporations located in Economic Development offices. Like other lending institutions, most will require evidence from the would-be small business owner that the business is viable, and that the owner is committed to ensuring the survival of the enterprise — they will want to see that the applicant has committed some of his or her own funds to the prospective venture. They will also want to see that the business is good for the community, that it provides needed services and/or creates employment. Specific terms and conditions need to be worked out with individual communities or First Nations' governments.

Advantages and Disadvantages of Equity Financing   Before proceeding to obtain equity capital, the entrepreneur should be familiar with the advantages and disadvantages of equity financing versus debt financing. Equity financing offers the following advantages:

1. There is no obligation to pay dividends or interest. This flexibility allows a firm to invest earnings back into the business in its early years when these funds are usually needed most.
2. Often the original owner benefits from the expertise the investor brings to the business in addition to the financial assistance.
3. Equity capital expands the borrowing power of the business. Most lenders require a certain percentage of equity investment by the owners before they will provide debt financing. Thus, the more equity a business has, the greater its ability to obtain debt financing.
4. Equity financing spreads the risk of failure of the business to others.
5. Many organizations that provide equity funding also provide other services to the entrepreneur. Examples include continued training in management, seminars and workshops, contacts, assistance in preparing business plans and marketing proposals, and information on how to access export markets and technology.

Disadvantages of equity financing include the following:

1. Equity financing dilutes the ownership interest of the original owner and leads to decreased independence. Because of this drawback, many owner-managers are hesitant to follow this route in obtaining capital.
2. With others sharing the ownership interest, the possibility of disagreement and lack of coordination in the operations of the business increases.
3. A legal cost may be associated with issuance of the ownership interest.

Debt Financing

Few small businesses are able to get established and continue operations without some sort of debt financing. About 30% of the $70 billion loaned to business in Canada is held by small business.[5] Because of the high possibility that debt financing will be required, it is essential that the entrepreneur be aware of the attractions, and dangers, of using it. It is also important that he or she have an understanding of the sources of debt capital and the characteristics and requirements of the various financial lenders.

Advantages and Disadvantages of Debt Financing   Some of the positive benefits of using debt are as follows:

1. It is possible to obtain a higher return on investment by using debt. If borrowed funds earn a higher return than the associated interest cost, it is possible to increase the overall return on investment for a business through debt financing. Figure 6.4 illustrates this concept. The $10,000 investment could be any productive asset or change in the business.
2. Interest costs in a business are tax-deductible expenses (assuming the business is not on a reserve) whereas dividends paid as a result of equity ownership are not tax deductible.
3. Debt financing may allow more flexibility in that there is no loss of ownership control.

---

5   *Small Business Views the Banks* (Toronto: Canadian Federation of Independent Business, 1988).

FIGURE 6.4 Debt Financing and Return on Investment

Basic Information:
Amount to invest = $10,000
Interest rate = 16%
Investment cost = $10,000
Estimated return per year = $2,500

Calculation of percentage return after one year:
1. If no debt was used:

$$\frac{\text{Return}}{\text{Investment}} = \frac{\$2,500}{\$10,000} = 25\%$$

2. If debt was used (assuming only $2,000 was invested, $8,000 was borrowed to purchase the investment, and the interest on $8,000 is $1,280):

$$\frac{\text{Return}}{\text{Investment}} = \frac{(\$2,500-1,280)}{\$2,000} = \frac{(\$1,220)}{\$2,000} = 61\% \text{ return}$$

Note: The potential investment income that could be earned on the $8,000 not invested in the project could be added to this amount.

---

4. Some organizations that provide debt financing also provide the same support as those providing equity financing (refer to point 5 under the advantages of equity financing).

Some of the potential negative aspects of debt financing are as follows:

1. Interest must be paid on borrowed money. Interest costs can be high, and high interest expenses are a common problem in many failing businesses. During the period from 1975 to 1985, interest rates in Canada were extremely high. This caused serious hardship to many small businesses, and the inability to pay interest costs resulted in the foreclosure and/or bankruptcy of many businesses.
2. Debt financing creates additional paperwork requirements for the entrepreneur, and the lender may monitor the business.
3. When using debt financing, the total risk of the venture lies squarely on the owner's shoulders. There are no other partners or shareholders to assume some of this risk.

Sources of Debt Financing   Several sources of debt financing are available to small businesses, including private lenders, corporate lenders, private lending institutions, bands, settlements, territorial governments, and government agencies.

■ Private Lenders
One increasingly common source of debt capital for small business is the borrowing of funds from the owners of the business. These funds are called **shareholders' loans,** and they offer some unique advantages. While the interest paid is a tax-deductible expense for the business, the repayment terms are often flexible. In addition, lenders often view share-

holders' loans as equity as long as these funds are left in the company. Some believe this method combines the advantages of equity and debt financing.

Another source of private debt is borrowing from other individuals such as friends or relatives. As with shareholders' loans, it may be possible to structure flexible repayment terms.

■ Corporate Lenders

In some circumstances other companies may lend funds to a small business. Often these are larger firms that have established some connection or working relationship with the small business. One example of such funding would be the granting of trade credit by a company to a small business that purchases merchandise from that company. Most small businesses use this source of financing wherever possible. Trade credit for inventory is normally financed for 30, 60, or 90 days, with discounts for prompt payment. Equipment is usually financed for up to five years, with a 20 to 30% down payment required.

Another type of lender associated with accounts receivable is a factor. Factor companies purchase accounts receivable from a business at a discount. The business obtains needed cash, and the factor collects the accounts receivable. An increasing number of businesses in Canada are enlisting factoring companies to obtain short-term financing.

The sale and leaseback is another form of financing involving other businesses. In this arrangement, the business sells an asset to another company, which in turn leases it back to the seller. The advantage of the sale and leaseback is that the seller not only has the use of the funds of the sale but also may benefit from the tax deductibility of the lease payments.

■ Regular Private Lending Institutions

This category includes those companies whose major purpose is the lending of funds. The most common of these are the following:

- *Trust Companies*: Trust companies are geared primarily for mortgages on long-term capital assets such as land, buildings, and equipment. An example of a Trust Company that focuses on servicing First Nations People and businesses is profiled in Incident 6.8.
- *Credit Unions*: Credit unions are usually locally owned. They tend to be concerned primarily with personal loans, but in some communities they also provide significant financing to small businesses.
- *Finance Companies*: These are high-risk lenders charging a higher rate of interest than other agencies. As with credit unions, the majority of their loans are personal loans.
- *Chartered Banks*: By far the largest source of small business financing is Canada's chartered banks.

INCIDENT 6.8
Peace Hills Trust a Success Story

> As First Nations' activity in the Canadian economy continues to grow at an unprecedented rate, Peace Hills Trust continues to generate steady progress as the financial institution of choice for Canada's First Nations.
>
> Peace Hills Trust has become a leader in native economic development since the company began a concerted effort to increase its profile nationally. The company has been managing First Nations owned trust funds for more than a decade. Funds belonging to native bands, organizations and individuals account for a large share of the company's business. The bulk of the company's loan portfolio is made up of reserve projects such as house construction, arenas, schools, shopping centres and band administration offices.

The company's understanding of financing on-reserve projects and its ability to structure alternative types of debt servicing packages are its major strengths.

SOURCE: *Windspeaker*, Canada's National Aboriginal News Publication, March 14–27, 1994, p. 16.

■ Government

As was discussed earlier, First Nation, territorial, provincial and federal governments have established programs that provide both debt and equity financing. Federal programs are administered through a variety of avenues that include Industry, Science and Technology; Aboriginal Business Canada; and Indian and Northern Affairs. Band, settlement, and territorial government programs are generally administered through community economic development offices.

Unique Problems in Obtaining Debt or Equity Financing

Many aboriginal people face unique problems when trying to access either debt or equity funding. These are briefly outlined as follows:

- Because lenders cannot seize assets of aboriginal people living on reserves these assets can not be used as collateral for loans, making lenders reluctant to provide debt for on-reserve businesses.
- In order to receive loans, lending institutions will consider the education and business experience of the applicant. Although this is an area of increasing strength among First Nations people, "Statistics show that native entrepreneurs are less likely than other Canadians to have accumulated business experience and are less prepared by the Canadian school system to make a go of a new business, even if they can get started."[6]
- Lenders generally require that the owner contribute personal funds and equity to the business. Aboriginal people are less likely to have accumulated savings and access to "love money" — equity financing from private sources. Aboriginal incomes are on average 25% less than the Canadian average so there is less family money available to help capitalize the start-up.[7]
- Many First Nations communities are in "remote" locations. This makes it difficult for bankers and lenders to monitor the business closely, making them more reluctant to lend to such businesses. In some of these communities banks, trust companies, and credit unions do not have branches, making it difficult for would-be entrepreneurs to access them.[8]

As discussed at the beginning of the chapter these difficulties are slowly being overcome. As was seen in Incident 6.8 there are now trust companies geared directly to First Nations' People and their needs, and as Incident 6.9 shows there are now aboriginal investment corporations that are owned and operated by First Nations people. Additionally, regular private lending institutions are beginning to tailor their services to aboriginal people and businesses. Some of Canada's largest banks have appointed senior V.P.s in charge of aboriginal banking

6   Richard Wright, "Financing Native Dreams," *Windspeaker*, March 14–27, 1994, 12.
7   *Ibid.*
8   Jim Bell, "The Cashless Society: Will Credit Unions Take Hold in the NWT?," *Arctic Circle*, November/December 1990, 47–49.

and are doing whatever they can to "go over, under and around section 89 of the Indian Act."[9] Incident 6.10 explains several ways the Act can be circumvented.

INCIDENT 6.9
Investment Firm Launched

Canada's first aboriginally controlled global investment corporation was launched by the Inuvialuit Regional Corporation. The Aboriginal Global Investment Corporation will provide investment management for aboriginal funds, including funds from land claim settlements.

The investment corporation offers diversified and balanced exposure to investment markets in Canada, the United States, Europe, Asia and the Pacific Rim.

The corporation draws on 10 years' experience from the Inuvialuit Regional Corporation in managing the first major land claims settlement in Canada. The Inuvialuit are Inuit from the Northwest Territories and number 5,000.

SOURCE: *Windspeaker*, Canada's National Aboriginal News Publication, Oct. 11–24, 1993, p. 12.

INCIDENT 6.10
Financing Native Dreams

Ron Jamieson, a Six Nations Mohawk and Vice President of Aboriginal Banking for the Bank of Montreal, explains that there are several ways to circumvent section 89 of the Indian Act.

1. Take a partial government guarantee to the capital markets and raise money against a guaranteed instrument, and then deliver it to on-reserve organizations. This still involves heavy government involvement, but it provides capital for businesses and development.

2. The Kamloops Amendment. The Kamloops Amendment, passed in 1988, allows Indian bands to designate a portion of reserve lands for commercial development. In effect, the band returns the land to the Crown and leases it back. The land is therefore no longer subject to the Act, so the band can then offer it as security by way of a mortgage or leasehold interest for a number of years.

3. Appoint native trustees in the community to act as bank agents. "Status Indians on a reserve can take the security of other status Indians." (Highlighted in Incident 6.2).

SOURCE: Richard Wright, *Windspeaker*, Canada's National Aboriginal News Publication, March 14–27, 1994, pp. 12-14.

Of the methods outlined in Incident 6.10 the most applicable to the small business owner would be the third. The others are geared to projects that require significant funding, for example, establishing manufacturing facilities or large scale tourism facilities.

Government Lenders   Government agencies at both federal and provincial levels lend money, provide grants, and give counselling assistance to small businesses. At the federal level, the major small business lender is the Federal Business Development Bank (FBDB) and Aboriginal Business Canada for aboriginal businesses. Initially government lending agencies

9   Richard Wright, 12.

were established to assist those small businesses unable to obtain financing from conventional sources because of high risk. In recent years, however, they have relaxed this attitude somewhat and have become more similar to other lending institutions.

The potential advantages of approaching a government agency are the following:

1. The agency can finance high-risk or low-equity ventures which characterize many small businesses.
2. Government lenders may be more willing to rewrite loan terms and conditions if the business gets into trouble. They also tend to be less quick to foreclose on a failing business.
3. Government agencies may provide a lower interest rate than the chartered banks. Many provincial government lenders fall into this category. FBDB rates, which are adjusted periodically, are usually similar to chartered bank rates.
4. Some government lenders and programs have been set up specifically to target aboriginal entrepreneurs.
5. Government lenders may provide some equity capital in the form of temporary ownership or grants, depending upon the type of business and its location.
6. Government lenders may provide management counselling along with funding to assist the business.
7. Government lenders may provide grants that cover a minimum percentage of costs but enough to attract regular bank financing to cover remaining costs.
8. Government agencies may provide loan guarantees to provide security for traditional lending institutions.

Although these advantages may make borrowing from government agencies attractive, there are potential disadvantages of which the small business owner should also be aware:

1. A government agency usually requires more information to review a loan application than other lending institutions do.
2. The time period required for approval of a loan tends to be longer than with private lending institutions.
3. Most government agencies exert more monitoring and control over the businesses they lend to and often require regular reports on operations.
4. Some government programs are only available to a narrowly defined segment of the aboriginal population.

In addition to the government agencies established to provide both debt and equity financing, several federal government programs also provide financial help for the small business. The table beginning on page 326 of the Information Resources section briefly reviews government programs that are most helpful for small businesses.

Most provinces also have various programs designed to provide financial assistance to the small business community. Some of these and other programs are reviewed starting on page 333 of the Information Resources section.

Historically the federal and provincial governments have been the primary source of funding for aboriginal businesses; however, with increasing fiscal restraint in Canada, budgets for aboriginal and other programs have been cut and are likely to see further reductions. This will increase the pressure on small business owners to seek funding from alternate sources.

DETERMINING THE TERMS OF FINANCING

The small business owner should carefully evaluate the characteristics of the sources of financing to ensure their suitability to the needs of the business. The length of term and type of financing required may assist in making the decision among lenders, as Figure 6.5 shows. The length of the term allowed by a lender is normally equivalent to the useful life of the asset, except in the case of land, which is often carried on a 20-year term.

An often costly mistake made by some owner-managers is to use funds obtained for long-term purposes to get them through short-term crises. Inevitably this creates a more serious financial crisis a short while later. If capital requirements were underestimated, the owner should approach the lender again with this information and attempt to have the lender adjust the funds provided.

FIGURE 6.5 Matching Financing to Assets

Type of Loan	Sources	Use	Security	Loan Characteristics
Short-term (demand) loans	Banks, private sources, factoring houses, confirming houses	Receivables inventory (working capital items)	Assignment of receiveables and inventory, personal guarantees, assignment of life insurance	Can be withdrawn on short notice; no fixed payment terms; interest, principal rates fluctuate
Medium-term (3–10 year) loans	Banks, term lenders, financial houses, leasing companies, foreign banks, private sources, government programs	Equipment, furnishings, vehicles, leaseholds, new business investments	Chattel mortgages, conditional sales contracts, or assignment of equipment insurance	Specific repayment terms; interest either fixed or floating with prime rate
Long-term (15–25 year) mortgages, bonds, debentures	Trust companies, foreign banks, private sources	Property, land, and buildings, new business investments	Collateral mortgages, assignment of property insurance	Fixed repayment terms; fixed interest rates

SOURCE: Geoffery Brooks, "Matching Your Financing to Your Assets," *Small Business Magazine*, September 1983, p. 38.

FINANCING MICRO-ENTERPRISES

Many entrepreneurs begin their ventures as micro-enterprises. Such enterprises are usually started as home-based businesses and do not have significant start-up capital requirements. Owners may only require $1,000 to $3,000 to begin operations. Home craft businesses and home maintenance and service businesses are examples. Frequently such entrepreneurs do not have business plans, personal equity, or collateral that can be used to obtain loans from traditional lending sources. In an effort to overcome this difficulty several micro-funding programs have been established.

Peer Lending

One financing option open to many micro-businesses is "Peer Lending."[10] Programs such as the First Peoples' Fund (refer to the list beginning on page 333) specialize in providing small loans to micro-enterprises. With such a program borrowers take responsibility for one another's loans instead of using collateral. Funding is generally provided by financial institutions with backing from non-profit organizations, communities, or corporations. Incident 6.11 explains how the program originated and how one "borrower-circle" got established.

INCIDENT 6.11
Unique Loan Program Helps Fund Micro-Enterprises

The Oss-gob-weh-tod-win ("mutual assistance" in the Ojibway language) Loan Fund is a joint project between the Calmeadow Foundation and the Wikwemikong Development Commission (WDC).

Wikwemikong is home to the Indian tribes of the Odawa, Ojibway and Pottawatomi. It is located on the eastern side of Manitoulin Island in Ontario. Chartered in 1973 as a non-profit corporation, the WDC's goal is to improve life for reserve members through economic development activities. Although the WDC is essentially the economic arm of the Wikwemikong people, it is a separate entity from the Band Council, with its own directors appointed from the reserve population at large.

Founded in 1983 by Martin Connell, the Calmeadow Foundation is a non-profit organization dedicated to encouraging the economic self-reliance of disadvantaged people in Canada and the Third World. The programs supported by the Foundation provide credit at market terms to enable micro-entrepreneurs to increase employment, income and productivity, and to improve the quality of life of the borrowers and their families.

The goal of the Native Self-Employment Loan Program (NSELP) was to "develop a replicable and institutionally acceptable model of appropriate, efficient and cost-effective credit delivery to native people involved in the micro-enterprise sector." Recognizing that conditions were worse for native women, the program focused on their participation.

The program was set up so that individual borrowers formed borrower circles. These are groups of four to seven micro-entrepreneurs who meet regularly to submit loan repayments and act as support groups. The loan of any one group member was guaranteed (in relation to WDC) by the group as a whole.

---

10 Paul Waldie, "Peer Loans Find Ready Niche: Would-be Small Businesses Need Neither Plan nor Collateral," *The Financial Post*, May 14/16, 1994, S32–33.

Through the efforts of Calmeadow, the Toronto Dominion Bank entered into a tri-partite agreement with Calmeadow and WDC. This allowed a WDC Community Advisory Committee to approve the formation of groups and submit loan requests to the TD bank for quick automatic processing. Commercial rates of interest were applied to loans, and these were guaranteed to the bank by Calmeadow. Circle meetings were used in part to collect payments which would be passed on to the WDC. The latter acted as an administrative intermediary between the circles and the TD bank, recording and forwarding payments and promoting and monitoring the Loan Fund in the community.

It was up to a borrower circle to decide who would receive the first two loans. Initial loans were capped at $1,000 and as satisfactory repayment patterns were established loans could go as high as $3,000. The chairperson of each new borrower circle joined appointed members on the Community Advisory Committee.

In early 1988 Kettle Point Reserve in Southwestern Ontario was added as the second pilot project community and in July Sachigo Lake, a reserve in Northwestern Ontario, had joined as the third and final pilot project community.

A November 1988 interim evaluation report indicated that in total 63 people were participating in the loan program, 23 of whom were women. The types of businesses supported ranged from commercial retail, foods processing, trapping and personal services to forest products and recreation. The success of the program suggests that the Oss-gob-weh-tod-win name was appropriately chosen.

SOURCE: "Oss-gob-weh-tod-win Loan Fund," The Centre for Aboriginal Management, Faculty of Management, The University of Lethbridge, 1991.

The focus of the Calmeadow Foundation is to serve individuals, especially women, who have the most difficulty accessing credit but are determined to start their own micro-enterprises.[11] The Calmeadow philosophy is "firmly grounded in the belief that tiny amounts of money can change people's lives," and they specialize in lending money to those who have no credit history or collateral.[12] Programs such as this give entrepreneurs the opportunity to get their ventures started, learn from a network of peers and experienced professionals, gain experience in business, establish a track record, develop a credit rating and gain confidence in their abilities and their ventures. All of these factors make it easier to approach banks and other financial institutions for funds to expand their enterprises or to start new ventures.

Local Governments

Another potential source of funding for micro-enterprises is aboriginal governments. Through Community Economic Development Organizations many First Nations' governments can provide seed money to those looking to start small ventures.

Federal Business Development Bank

The FBDB also has a micro-loan program. These loans are available to businesses that are in the start-up or early growth stages. Owners must have completed a Training and Counselling program from the FBDB that is designed to help entrepreneurs develop their business plans.

---

11 "Investing in People," *Calmeadow Annual Report*, Oct. 31, 1994.
12 Isabel Vincent, "No-collateral lender helps fledgling firms," *Globe and Mail*, April 25, 1996, A6.

PREPARING A PROPOSAL TO OBTAIN FINANCING ———————

In attempting to obtain financing, a small business owner should be aware of those areas about which the lender requires information. In addition to completing the loan application, the owner should include financial projections. A detailed and well-prepared loan proposal will go a long way toward ensuring the approval of a loan application.

Criteria Used in the Loan Decision

Most lenders make the loan decision by evaluating the following three criteria:

1. **The Applicant's Management Ability:** The lender will want to be sure the applicant has the skills, experience, and ability to make the business succeed. To evaluate the applicant's managerial ability, the lender will specifically want to know the following.
   - *How Much the Applicant Knows about the Business:* The lender will probably ask questions about the business or industry to ascertain the applicant's level of knowledge. The lender will also be interested in any previous experience the applicant has had that relates to the proposed business.
   - *How Much Care was Taken in Preparing the Proposal:* The lender will want to see a detailed plan of what the loan is for as well as a listing of the other sources of financing for the project. The steps of a business plan, outlined in detail in Chapter 4, should provide the basis for the financing proposal. Several statements will be required, and it is important that the applicant document the source of the information in those statements. The first statement is the lending proposal, which typically follows the format shown in Figure 6.6.

     In addition to the lending proposal, the lender will probably want to see a proposed income and cash flow statement for at least the first year of operations, and probably longer. A balance sheet may also be required. These statements should be carefully prepared following the format discussed in Chapters 3 and 8. As mentioned above, each item on the statement should be well researched and documented. The lender will want to know what provision has been made for the owner's salary and for potential contingencies. An entrepreneur is well advised to enlist an accountant or the services of local organizations such as Community Futures Programs or Economic Development Offices if he or she is weak in financial statement preparation.

2. **The Proposal:** Obviously the lender will assess the idea or proposal itself. Using the income statement and cash flow projections, the lender will assess the chances of repayment

FIGURE 6.6 Loan Proposal and Format

Program		*Financing*	
Land	$20,000	Bank loan	$60,000
Building	50,000	Own funds	20,000
Equipment	10,000		
Total	$80,000	Total	$80,000

of the loan. The lender will evaluate not only the specific business but also industry trends, including the extent of competition and experiences of similar businesses. The lender may also check with experts in the industry. Many chartered banks now have industry specialists on staff to assist in this type of evaluation.

Some of the specific types of evaluation used in the lending industry are:

- *Level of working capital* — the dollar difference between current assets and current liabilities. Working capital should be sufficient to meet current obligations as they become due and finance delays in revenue caused by such items as accounts receivables.
- *Current ratio* — current assets compared to current liabilities. A healthy current ratio, or rule of thumb, is 2:1.
- *Quick ratio* — current assets less inventories compared to liabilities. A healthy ratio is 1:1.
- *Debt-to-equity ratio* — percent of owner's equity compared to debt. A minimum debt-to-equity ratio is 4:1 (25% equity). For smaller businesses, most lenders prefer to see 50% equity.

Chapter 8 discusses each of these ratios in greater detail.

The lenders will also want to see projections for the basic financial statements such as the balance sheet and income statement. The fundamentals of these statements are covered in Chapter 8.

Because of the security position on the loan, the lender will want to know if the business will be established on or off a reserve and whether another lender is also providing funding for the project and, if so, what collateral it has taken as security for the loan. The lender will also want to ensure that the funds loaned will be secured by some form of saleable collateral. On capital assets, a lender generally allows only about 80% of the market value of the assets as security. The reason is that if the lender needs to realize (repossess) on the security, obsolescence, selling, and administration costs will reduce its value.

3. **Applicant's Background and Creditworthiness**: In addition to the project itself and the applicant's management ability, the lender will require some additional information in judging the applicant's creditworthiness.

- *Personal Information*: In filling out a loan application, an applicant is usually required to file information typical to a personal résumé — items such as age, marital status, education, and work experience. When applying for funding from programs or organizations aimed at aboriginal entrepreneurs, applicants will also be asked whether they are Status, non-Status, Métis, or Inuit. An example of a Personal Data Sheet and Loan Application for an Aboriginal Capital Corporation is shown on page 331 of the Information Resources section.

- *Present Debt and Past Lending History*: The lender will want a list of the current state of any loans outstanding and may require information about the applicant's past loan history as well. Most lenders are members of credit bureaus that provide a complete credit history of the applicant. Lenders will generally use this source to verify the information provided by the applicant.

   If an applicant is just starting out and does not have a credit history, lenders will place more emphasis on other aspects of the proposal. For example, more consideration will be placed on the business plan, the viability and potential profitability of the business, as well as the personal character of the person applying for the loan.

- *Amount of Equity the Applicant has Invested*: All lenders will want to know the amount of the applicant's personal funds going into the project. Usually cash equity is required, but occasionally capital assets or even "sweat equity" may be acceptable. The amount of equity funds required varies depending upon the risk associated with the project, but as mentioned above, few lenders will provide financing if the applicant has less than 20 to 25% equity to invest in the business.
- *Will the Applicant be Banking with the Lender?* Many lenders will request that the applicant's business accounts be transferred or opened at the lending bank. They may also require that a compensating balance be held in account as collateral.

Lender Relations

Once financing has been obtained, it is important that the business provide up-to-date information to the lender regarding current operations and future plans. Regular financial statements and lease contracts can help establish trust between the banker and the owner-manager. Some organizations, such as Aboriginal Business Canada and Aboriginal Capital Corporations, require that businesses provide regular and up-to-date financial information as a condition of a loan and/or the letter of offer. Many businesses have found that maintaining a close working relationship with lenders helps ensure adequate levels of financing in the long run.

What do entrepreneurs do if they have investigated both equity and debt sources and are unable to obtain the needed capital? Probably the first thing to do is find out the reasons for refusal and possibly reword the proposal to bring it more in line with the lender's requirements.

Changes may be necessary to make the proposed business more attractive to lenders and/or investors. One option that is increasingly being used to reduce the amount of funds required for capital purchases is to consider leasing or renting an asset. Leasing the asset generally does not require a down payment. The ability to obtain a lease is usually based more on the earning power of the asset and the business than on the background of the owner. Later, when a company is in a more stable condition, the owner may succeed in obtaining funds to make a purchase if he or she desires. Specific conditions of leases are discussed in Chapter 4.

SUMMARY ——————————————————————————————

1. Lack of managerial competence and experience can often result in such financing problems as underestimating financial requirements, lack of knowledge of sources of capital, lack of skills in preparing and presenting a proposal for financing to a lender, failure to plan in advance for future needs, and poor financial control in payment of loan obligations.
2. Start-up capital includes initial inventory, deposits and first months' payment for payroll, utilities, rent, advertising, insurance, licenses and permits, cost of renovations, furniture and fixtures, and legal fees. Accounts receivable and any other operating cost that needs to be paid before revenues are generated should also be planned for.
3. An essential step in determining the amount of capital needed is to determine the owner's net worth. This helps determine the amount of funds the owner(s) has to invest in the company and will probably be required by a lending institution.

4. General sources of equity financing are private investors, corporate investors, government programs, and aboriginal and non-aboriginal governments.

5. The advantages of equity capital as compared to debt financing include no interest obligation, expertise of the investor(s), expanded borrowing power, and spreading of risk. The disadvantages include dilution of ownership, increased potential for disagreements, and the cost incurred in the issuance of the ownership interest.

6. The potential advantages of debt financing over equity capital are a possible higher return on investment, tax deductibility of interest, flexibility, and ease of approval. The disadvantages include interest expense, additional paperwork, and the lack of diversification of risk to other investors.

7. Sources of debt financing include owners of the business, corporate lenders, regular lending institutions, aboriginal governments, and government agencies.

8. Government agencies at both federal and provincial levels lend money, provide grants, and offer counselling assistance to small businesses. These agencies are more willing to finance higher-risk businesses, may be more willing to rewrite loan terms and conditions, often provide lower interest rates, and may provide equity capital. On the other hand, government agencies usually require more information, tend to take longer to approve loans, may require more collateral, and usually exert more monitoring and control over the businesses to which they lend.

9. Sources of funding for micro-enterprises include Peer Lending, Community Economic Development Offices, and the Federal Business Development Bank.

10. Criteria most lenders use in making loan decisions are the applicant's managerial ability, the proposal itself, the amount of money the applicant is investing in the business, available collateral, and the applicant's background, personal character, and creditworthiness.

11. If the entrepreneur cannot obtain financing, he or she should reevaluate the proposal and make any changes necessary to make the proposal more attractive to potential lenders or investors. The entrepreneur can also consider leasing instead of purchasing to reduce the amount of funds required.

CHAPTER PROBLEMS AND DISCUSSION QUESTIONS

1. Indicate whether each of the following is a start-up cost (S), an ongoing operating cost (O), or both (B).
   a. $1,000 for first month's rent
   b. $25,000 for store fixtures
   c. $1,000 for third month's rent
   d. Weekly cleaning fee of $250
   e. Purchase of $50,000 inventory
   f. Payroll expense
   g. $1,000 for advertising in *Windspeaker*
   h. Prepaid insurance
   i. Delivery expense
   j. Purchase of hide for tanning

2. Imagine you are preparing a business plan for a small manufacturing firm in your community. Using the Information Resources beginning on pages 323, 326, 329, and 333, determine what programs are available for possible assistance? How could each program help your business?

3. a. Using Figure 6.5 as a reference, match the following list of assets to the type of financing, source, and loan characteristics needed:
      i. Capital for building of manufacturing plant
      ii. Bus to transport tourists
      iii. Inventory purchase
      iv. Equipment (life expectancy two-three years)
    b. Why is it important to match financing to your assets?
4. Interview an employee at one of the government agencies that offers equity or debt financing to small businesses. Determine the purpose, the merits, and the weaknesses of that program.
5. Interview a loans officer in an Aboriginal Capital Corporation to determine what he or she looks for in a loan application.
6. Using Figure 6.3, calculate your personal net worth.

SUGGESTED READINGS

Assistance to Business in Canada (ABC) 1986. Montreal: Federal Business Development Bank; 1986.

Gray, Douglas A. and Diana L. Gray. *The Complete Canadian Small Business Guide.* Toronto: McGraw Hill, 1988, pp. 145–63.

Knight, Russell M. "An Evaluation of Venture Capital Rejections and Their Subsequent Performances." *Journal of Small Business and Entrepreneurship,* Fall 1985.

Mancuso, Joseph R. *How to Start, Finance, and Manage Your Own Business.* New York: Englewood Cliffs, NJ: Prentice Hall, 1990.

Mancuso, Joseph R. *How to Get a Business Loan without Signing Your Life Away.* New York: Managing Your Money Software, 1993.

Mason, Scott P. and Susan L. Roth. "Note on Bank Loans." Boston: Harvard Business School, 1991.

Presenting Your Case for a Loan. Toronto: Thorne Ridell, Chartered Accountants. 1987.

Small Business in Canada. Industry, Science and Technology Canada, 1991, pp. 57–69.

Sources of Venture Capital in Canada. Ottawa: Department of Industry, Trade and Commerce, Government of Canada, 1987.

Part 3

Managing the Aboriginal Small Business

Part Two of this text dealt with issues relating to the organization and establishment of a small business. Once the business has been established, various management fundamentals should be followed to ensure that the business stays viable and competitive.

Part Three discusses five of these management areas. Chapter 7 focuses on the marketing principles that are essential in understanding the market and getting the product or service to the consumer. Chapter 8 covers the recording and controlling of the financial aspects of the business. Both marketing and finance are areas in which aboriginal entrepreneurs are increasingly gaining training and competence. Chapter 9 discusses some fundamental components of the internal operations or production aspects of the business. Chapter 10 includes a review of the principles of personnel management applicable to the small organization. Chapter 11 presents a brief review of the most relevant tax considerations for the aboriginal small business.

C H A P T E R   7

Marketing Management

——————————————————————————— *D. Wesley Balderson*

CHAPTER OBJECTIVES

☐ To describe the role of the marketing function of an aboriginal business enterprise.

☐ To discuss the importance of identifying and satisfying consumer needs.

☐ To explain the critical need for continual information gathering to ensure long-run viability of the business.

☐ To discuss the components of a marketing program: product, price, distribution, and promotion.

SMALL BUSINESS PROFILE
Laurie & Francine Deer
Tentsations

In 1987 Laurie and Francine Deer spotted an opportunity for a new business renting circus-type tents to the public for special occasions. They had difficulty finding such a tent at a reasonable price for Francine's wedding and wondered if this product could develop into a feasible business.

Although Laurie and Francine are Mohawks from the Kahnawake Reserve in Quebec, they noticed that these type of tents were being used for much more than pow-wows and celebrations on the reserve. The use of tents was increasing in retail markets, business events and festivals, concerts, sports events, weddings and even backyard family barbecues.

Laurie and Francine were careful to research their market thoroughly, however, before they established Tentsations. They researched suppliers and markets, and drew up a business plan with the assistance of Concordia University's Small Business Consulting Bureau. Once completed, they invested their savings, purchased 17 tents, and began selling the idea through word of mouth. Although they did not have a lot of money to spend on advertising they were able to use publicity through a news story that was aired about their business because of its uniqueness.

Tentsations has expanded rapidly outside of the native community with near capacity usage during the summer months; these two entrepreneurs are now looking at possibilities for the winter months and the opening of an outlet in the U.S.

As William Brooks, an instructor at Lower Canada College in Montreal, puts it "The real key to success in Tentsations and small companies like it is the irrepressible spirit of enterprise. Laurie and Francine have followed a classic business start up formula mixed with the right amount of their own personalities for a successful initiative."

SOURCE: Used with permission of Laurie and Francine Deer.

THE ROLE OF MARKETING MANAGEMENT IN ─────── THE SMALL ABORIGINAL BUSINESS

Marketing activities are often overlooked by new owner-managers after the business has been established. Some of the possible reasons this happens are: (1) Owner-managers do not understand fully what marketing is; (2) owner-managers may not think marketing is necessary, that is, they may believe that if they have a good enough product it will sell itself; or (3) owner-managers tend to be so busy with the day-to-day activities and problems of the business they do not take the time to assess the market and develop a marketing plan.

Regardless of these "causes" of failure in applying marketing principles in the small business, it is critical that the owner-manager understand them. Even though some marketing expertise is available through government, band, or tribal council sources, it is unlikely that the small business can afford to hire a specialist in marketing in the long term. Therefore, the owner-manager requires some knowledge of marketing principles. The aboriginal owner-manager will have to do a considerable amount of marketing, not only to potential customers, but also to suppliers, employees, lenders, government agencies, and perhaps even community members.

The major purpose of this chapter, then, is to acquaint the aboriginal owner-manager or manager of a band-owned enterprise with fundamentals of marketing that can aid in sustaining the growth of the business. Some of the principles also apply to establishing a business, and were mentioned briefly in Chapter 3. Other marketing principles form an important part of a business plan and were discussed in Chapter 4.

An owner-manager may become involved in the following marketing activities:

- Defining the target customer, target customer characteristics, and information concerning their product/service wants and needs.
- Understanding those influences outside of the business that will affect its operations.
- Developing the product or service.
- Developing the channel(s) of distribution.
- Setting price levels for the product or service.
- Providing information or promoting the product or service to those who are influential in the purchase.

This chapter will discuss relevant aspects of each of these components of marketing separately. It is important to note, however, that these components need to be coordinated and managed together as a system to be most effective.

THE TARGET CUSTOMER ───────────────

In preparing the feasibility analysis in Chapter 3, we stressed the need to define the target customer. The ability of the entrepreneur to clearly identify a specific market is critical to success, as the Small Business Profile that opens this chapter shows. This is important in making a quantitative estimate of the size of the market. The small business owner might attempt to reach and collect information about the following target markets:

1. The consumer market.
2. The industrial market.
3. The export market.

Each of these markets has unique characteristics that must be taken into account in developing the marketing program.

The Consumer Market

The aboriginal owner-manager can obtain information about various characteristics of the consumer market. Some characteristics that may be most helpful in developing the marketing program are the following:

1. *Demographic characteristics*: These include items such as age, income, education, occupation, and location of residence.
2. *Lifestyle characteristics*: Lifestyle characteristics include such things as activities, interests, opinions, media habits, and personalities of target market individuals.
3. *Purchase characteristics*: This includes what, when, where, and how much of the product or service the consumer purchases.
4. *Purchase motivations*: This is one of the most important items of information. It explains the reasons behind consumer purchases. In addition to understanding the "why" of the purchase, the entrepreneur should attempt to understand other factors that might influence the purchase. Common sources of influence are members of the consumer's cultural group, social class, and family.

Once this type of information has been obtained, the development of the marketing program — including product characteristics, pricing strategy, distribution channels, and method of promotion — becomes much easier, and the program is usually more effective.

Much of the above information about the target customer can be obtained through primary research or secondary data, as discussed in Chapter 3. It is important for the small business owner to realize that collecting information about the target consumer is not a one-time event. Such information should be used continuously to help the owner stay responsive to changes in consumer needs and wants.

Most successful companies, whether large or small, stay that way because they are close to the consumer and incorporate consumer wants and needs into their marketing program. This philosophy, called the **marketing concept**, has been taught in introductory marketing courses for a number of years. Many small businesses are successful initially because they fill a consumer need, but as they grow sometimes they fall out of touch with their customers. This situation usually leads to difficulties, particularly in competitive markets.

Other companies define their consumer markets too broadly. As a result, their marketing programs may fail to meet the needs of any one group in the market. The marketing practice of tailoring the marketing program to each specific market is known as **market segmentation**. Figure 7.1 illustrates the target market information for a distinct market segment for an aboriginal clothing manufacturer. In this example the owner-manager has selected a specific group of consumers toward which to direct her marketing strategy.

The demographic information needed to prepare quantitative estimates of feasibility (see Chapter 3) can be obtained from such secondary sources as government census reports. The information on lifestyles, purchase characteristics, and motivations may be available from industry marketing research reports; on the other hand, the owner-manager may need to collect this data herself or himself. This thorough consumer profile allows the clothing manufacturer (Figure 7.1) to develop a market strategy that responds to the consumers' characteristics and needs. For instance, a high-quality, distinctly aboriginal garment might be desirable. Higher prices reflecting this level of quality would probably not affect demand negatively. Advertising

FIGURE 7.1   Target Market Profile for an Aboriginal Clothing Manufacturer

The typical consumer has the following characteristics:

Demographics

Sex:	Female
Age:	20–49
Income:	higher than average for women
Occupation:	employed, many professionally
Education:	high school and college graduates
Lifestyle:	Activities: exercise and participation in sports, high social interaction; husband and wife both work, enjoy the outdoors, attend cultural events
Interests:	appearance, health, fashion
Opinions:	conservative economically, liberal on social issues, feel strongly about advancing aboriginal interests
Personality:	achievement-oriented, outgoing, independent

Purchase Characteristics

What:	higher quality and higher price clothing with aboriginal identity
Where:	mail order or specialty store
When:	spring and fall
How much:	spend more than the national average on clothing

Motivations

Benefits sought:	superior quality and distinct aboriginal characteristics
Influencers:	reference groups and social class are the main influencers in choice of clothing, through word of mouth and some direct mail advertising utilizing testimonials

showing young, socially active, and successful models might be effective. Testimonial endorsements may also have some influence. Incident 7.1 illustrates the importance of understanding consumer needs.

INCIDENT 7.1
Understanding Customer's Needs is Key

Percy Darnaby knows the importance of providing a product that meets the customer's needs. Percy, a member of the Eel Ground First Nation in New Brunswick, is president of Abenaki Associates, a company that specializes in providing computer-based services and training to aboriginal clients. A federally incorporated company, Abenaki Associates has offices in Hobbema, Alberta and in Ottawa. Abenaki Housing Inventory Management Systems is one of the company's brainchildren and has been selected as the winner in the Process and Management category of Canada Mortgage and Housing Corporation's (CMHC) 1994 Housing Awards.

Having worked with First Nations Housing as a federal government employee, Percy knew firsthand how crucial the need is for accurate information about housing on reserves. Keeping tabs on the condition of housing under their management has often meant a mammoth undertaking for First Nations. However, with Abenaki's extremely easy-to-use software program, First Nation communities can produce accurate and up-to-date assessments of their housing situation with just a few touches to the computer keyboard. The beauty of the Abenaki Housing Inventory Management System is that it both reports and analyses. The system not only provides an effective means to gather complete information on all housing units, but also produces analytic reports that can help communities plan future approaches to funding requirements.

Since the software was first introduced into the market in the spring of 1993, approximately 100 First Nations, tribal councils and housing agencies have purchased the program. Abenaki Associates pays close attention to what its customers want. The company maintains a database of comments and suggestions made by clients at training sessions and through follow-ups with customers. This continued consultation with aboriginal users contributed to the company receiving the CMHC award and is key to their success.

SOURCE: *Windspeaker*, Canada's National Aboriginal News Publication, Feb. 1995, p. 25.

The Industrial Market

The second type of market the aboriginal small business might attempt to reach is the industrial market. This market includes companies, institutions, or even individuals who purchase a product to assist in the manufacture of other products. Many companies which operate on or close to aboriginal communities have developed policies of targeting aboriginal businesses to provide goods and services for their operations. Syncrude Canada is one company with such a policy (Incident 7.2).

INCIDENT 7.2 ───
Syncrude and Aboriginal People: Policy Statement

Since 1984, Syncrude has purchased over $120 million worth of goods and services from native-run businesses. There are 20 active aboriginal contractors servicing Syncrude, representing 20% of all contractors working at the Syncrude site. These aboriginal companies are encouraged by Syncrude to hire aboriginal people. Many of these contractors compete successfully for open bidding contracts.

Our commitment to encouraging aboriginal businesses has been maintained through such strategies as sole sourcing-contracts and restricting bids, on occasion, to aboriginal suppliers and contractors. In addition, Syncrude has advanced funds to some aboriginal contractors to assist with short-term cash flow problems. Syncrude also encourages aboriginal employees to set up their own businesses.

SOURCE: A Report On The Relationship Between Syncrude Canada Ltd. and the Aboriginal People of Northeastern Alberta, 1995, p. 19.

Government purchases, an ever-increasing market for small business, might also be classed as an industrial market. Incident 7.3 illustrates how government purchasers are becoming increasingly popular customers for aboriginal businesses.

INCIDENT 7.3
Inuvialuit Company Wins Two Contracts

The Department of National Defence is proving to be a lucrative ally to a native-owned company in the North. The Inuvialuit Development Corporation recently won two separate contracts with the DND, one to fly helicopters and the other to guard fighter jets.

IDC won a $350,000 contract to provide helicopter services to the DND's North Warning System in the Inuvialuit Settlement Region of the northwestern NWT, company president David Connelly announced in February. And on March 3rd, the company announced it had secured a second contract, valued at $170,000, to provide security and facility maintenance to the DND's CF–18 Forward Operating Locations at Inuvik Airport.

The benefits of the CF–18 contract will be widely felt throughout the community, IDC chairman Eddie Dillon said. IDC was able to underbid the second lowest contract by 12%. "The benefits and potential future opportunities that the contract will bring to the community are what made this contract so attractive," according to Dillon.

SOURCE: *Windspeaker*, Canada's National Aboriginal News Publication, March 14–27, 1994, p. 15.

In consumer markets, buying influences include emotional motivations as well as rational ones. Industrial goods, on the other hand, are purchased primarily for rational reasons. Such characteristics as price, quality, dependability of supply, capability to manufacture to specification, speed of manufacture and delivery, and services offered are commonly considered in making industrial purchases. The purchasers, often acting as a committee, are well informed about the product category and are also aware of competitive offerings. Generally the information required by the purchaser is of a technical nature, calling for a well-trained and knowledgeable sales staff on the part of small business.

In attempting to reach the industrial market, the following areas should be investigated: (1) which companies and government agencies purchase from small businesses, (2) the influences on industrial demand, and (3) how the bidding-tendering process works.

Companies and Government Agencies that Purchase from
Small Business   A large number of purchases by some organizations are made from small businesses in Canada. Many of these organizations purposely look to small business to fill their product and service needs.

Influences on Industrial Demand   Demand for industrial goods is derived from demand for the final product. Because of this relatively delayed response, industrial demand changes can be easier to predict than consumer demand changes. Some of the key indicators to industrial demand changes are:

- The state of the economy and its effect on the purchase of the end product.
- Government legislation or regulations.
- Potential competition for the purchasing company.
- Specific bodies or agencies that exert influence on the purchases.

The Bidding-Tendering Process   The aboriginal small business owner should be aware of how a purchase decision is made and which criteria or specifications are used to make the decision in the industrial market. Because many industrial goods, particularly those bought by the government, are purchased on a tender-bid basis, it is essential that the small business owner be skilled in preparing and submitting bids within such a system.

The Export Market

Canada has always been known as a trading nation. In recent years the value of exports has contributed an estimated 20% of Canada's employment and 30% of GNP.[1] Export sales increased from $40 billion in 1977 to $157.5 billion in 1992.[2] In the past, a large portion of exports came from primary and resource industries which consisted of large companies and government agencies. Recently, however, many small businesses have been successful at exporting manufactured goods to foreign countries. Because of both the vast potential in these foreign markets and the considerable encouragement and assistance provided by the government, this is an option the aboriginal small business owner should not overlook. Incident 6.9, on the Inuvialuit Regional Corporation, demonstrates this potential for aboriginal entrepreneurs.

The recently signed Free Trade Agreement between Canada, the United States, and Mexico is rapidly opening up new markets for Canadian small businesses. Similar agreements with other Latin American countries, currently being negotiated, may provide additional markets for aboriginal goods and services, and the potential exists for an "indigenous people's business network" to develop in North and South America.

The small business owner who plans to export needs to investigate (1) the forms of government assistance available for exporting, (2) the unique characteristics of the foreign market, and (3) the mechanisms of exporting.

Government Assistance Available for Exporting   Many government programs are designed to encourage and assist the entrepreneur who desires to export a product or service to another country. Some of the more active agencies and programs are listed on page 339 of the Information Resources section.

Export Clubs   Many cities have established export clubs which meet regularly to exchange ideas and information about exporting.

Other Aboriginal Agencies and Programs   There are other programs and agencies which can assist the aboriginal entrepreneur develop export markets. These are described in the Information Resources section, on pages 314, 317, and 318.

Provincial and Territorial Government Programs   Most provincial and territorial governments are very active in encouraging exports and may have specific incentive programs to assist in this regard. The Department of Industry, Trade, and Commerce or the equivalent in each province can provide information about their programs.

1   John Meyer, "Canada's Exports Reach Record High — Total Sales Top $90 Billion Mark," *Export Opportunity*, March 31, 1984, 1.
2   Report on Business, *Globe & Mail*, Feb. 19, 1993, as reported by Statistics Canada for 1992.

As can be seen, considerable assistance is available for a prospective exporter. Specific addresses for the relevant agencies are found on page 339 of the Information Resources section.

Unique Characteristics of the Foreign Market

A second requirement for success in exporting is to understand the peculiarities of the foreign market. Many companies have experienced difficulties in marketing internationally because they have failed to obtain enough information about the various markets. Several of the agencies mentioned above can provide answers to the questions listed in Figure 7.2.

Incident 7.4 provides an example of one aboriginal entrepreneur who was successful in understanding foreign consumer demand.

INCIDENT 7.4
Aboriginal Products Find Overseas Niche

If the tourist can't come to the gift store, then the gift store will go to the tourist. This has increasingly become the philosophy for many aboriginal business owners who sell either traditional or modern aboriginal merchandise, and have found eager markets overseas.

Just ask Mark Bernard, owner of the six month-old Mystic Wolf Native World Trading, located among the trendy shops of Winnipeg's Corydon Avenue. Bernard collects authentic native artifacts like dreamcatchers, medicine wheels, mandelas and spirit shields from reserves throughout midwestern Canada, the United States, and even Latin America. Bernard also sells art from such well-known native artists as Sydney Kirkness, Jeff Monias and Dave Morriseau.

It was while he was travelling through Europe in 1989 that he discovered the fascination that Europeans have for aboriginal culture. "Europeans have more respect and knowledge for the native culture than North Americans. They understand the history and have a real feel for it," says Bernard, who is of Sioux and Cree origin.

FIGURE 7.2 Key Areas for Developing a Foreign Marketing Strategy

1. What needs does the product fill in this culture?
2. What products (if any) are currently meeting these needs?
3. What differences are there in the way the product is used (consumed)?
4. What are the characteristics of the consumers who will buy the product?
5. Can the consumers afford to purchase the product?
6. What are the political or legal restrictions to marketing the product?
7. What are the distribution and media capabilities in the culture?
8. What language differences exist?
9. What nonverbal communications should be noted?
10. What information collecting restrictions might there be?

Bernard, who exports to France, the Netherlands, England, and Germany, expects these markets to grow as Mystic Wolf grows. "Right now it's about 50–50 (domestic and foreign sales), but I foresee it being much more than that. I'm in the infancy stage right now and as I grow my markets will grow."

SOURCE: *The First Perspective*, May 1995, p. 10.

Mechanisms of Exporting   Information about the mechanics of exporting can also be provided by the agencies discussed earlier. Some of the essential features of an exporting arrangement are as follows:

■ Documentation

Contracts, invoices, permits, insurance, and bills of lading must be drafted or obtained.

■ Methods of Credit Offered

Letters of credit, accounts receivable, and consignment sales are often a part of the process.

■ Physical Distribution

The type of shipment, transfer of title, and inspection points will have to be determined.

■ Channel of Distribution

Sales representatives, government agencies, export agents, and trading houses will need to be identified and contacted.

■ Security

Export insurance and guarantees must be obtained.

Because many of these items are complex, it is recommended that the entrepreneur seek assistance from the agencies mentioned earlier to ensure that safe and proper procedures are followed in carrying out the mechanics of exporting. Many Canadian exporters have found that one of the most effective ways of doing business abroad is to strike a partnership with firms in the country they are targeting.

Even trade within the NAFTA trade zone can be highly complex. Many First Nations have traditional territories which span the more recent "international boundaries" between Canada, the United States, and Mexico and argue that they are exempt from non-aboriginal trade regulations. Aboriginal entrepreneurs can also be caught in mainstream trade disputes. For example, Ken Dillen, originally from an Ontario First Nation and proprietor of Just Like Mom's Bannock, recently had 250 bushels of Canadian wheat confiscated by Canada Customs on the grounds that he lacked a proper export permit.[3]

EXTERNAL INFLUENCES ON THE MARKET

In any market, conditions exist that may have a significant impact on the small business but are outside of the control of its owner. Nevertheless, the owner-manager can make an effort to respond effectively to these external influences:

• Identify which external conditions are affecting the business.

---

3   "Export rules stifle bannock maker," *Lethbridge Herald*, September 12, 1995.

- Set up a system to continually monitor the relevant external influences. For the owner-manager, this might mean regularly obtaining reports, newsletters, and studies that contain up-to-date information on these conditions.
- Adjust internal operations to respond to changes in these external influences most effectively.

Some of the most common external influences that could affect the aboriginal business are the economy, the competition, financial and legal restrictions, and the social and cultural environment.

The Economy   The state of the economy in the market area is a critical external condition. For most products and services, market demand is directly related to upturns and downturns in the economy. The small business is often able to react more quickly than large businesses to such changes.

Competition   As mentioned in Chapter 1, a small business usually finds itself competing against larger firms over which it has no control. New technology used by competitors is another factor in assessing competition, especially in growth industries. In some cases a small business may have a competitive advantage because of its size. The Free Trade Agreement between Canada, the United States, and Mexico not only opens up new markets for Canadian entrepreneurs, but also increases competition for Canadian businesses as U.S. and Mexican companies enter Canadian markets. The trend toward free trade throughout the hemisphere is likely to increase competition. These situations were discussed in Chapter 2.

Financing   One of the constraints that many aboriginal entrepreneurs face is the limited amount of financial capital available to them. For reserve residents this is primarily due to the reluctance of conventional lenders to provide financing to aboriginal people because of their inability to obtain security for assets located on the reserve. However, there are various sources of financing for aboriginal people, and creative programs are being developed to solve this problem (see Chapter 6). Incident 7.5 illustrates that the government is recognizing this need.

INCIDENT 7.5

Money, Technology and Exports Answer to Economic Woes

Native people need better access to financing, technology and export opportunities if they are to achieve economic prosperity, says a report by a federal advisory committee on the economy. "Severe economic and social obstacles have restricted the ability of aboriginal peoples to participate in Canada's economy," the report said. The report pointed out five key areas that could improve economic conditions for First Nations. The recommendations include planning between banks and Native economic development groups to help get investment capital into communities, the development of new training programs and encouraging Native business participation in international trade fairs.

SOURCE: *Windspeaker*, Canada's National Aboriginal News Publication, November 9, 1992.

Legal Restrictions   This influence includes the laws and regulations with which the business is required to comply. The owner-manager should keep up to date with any legislation that might affect business operations. Additionally, aboriginal businesses may be affected by political influences in their bands, reserves, and communities. The owner-manager should consider such pressures in establishing the business. For band-owned businesses, independence from the politics of the band appears to be related to the commercial success of the venture. This will be discussed in more detail in Chapter 12.

Social and Cultural Influences   This factor encompasses trends in the culture in which the business operates that may affect demand. The culture may dictate norms the population is generally hesitant to violate, or suggest new growth industries that can be attractive opportunities. One cultural constraint which aboriginal businesses face comes from aboriginal communities themselves. Success at business management and the resulting accumulation of capital is looked upon unfavourably by some aboriginal people, and there is vigorous philosophical debate over the appropriate goals and ethics of aboriginal business people and the nature of "competition" itself. This condition may be another barrier to ensuring the cooperation and support of aboriginal governments and members alike. The aboriginal entrepreneur may be required to promote the benefits of a successful business internally before it is promoted to the actual market.

Figure 7.3 illustrates how a small business can work with these uncontrollable conditions.

FIGURE 7.3   Working with External Influences

External Influence	Indicator	System to Monitor	Possible Internal Adjustment
Economy	Inflation rate Unemployment level	Collect relevant government and industry reports regularly on retail sales	Drop prices Increase advertising
Competition	Define who competition is Define strengths and weaknesses of competitors Competitor's use of new technology	Own evaluation Competitor's new products Competitor's reaction to your strategies	Product or service changes New target markets
Legal	What laws affect your business What changes in laws are pending	Regular receipt of legislative changes from government documents and industry reports	Product or service alterations Promotional changes
Social and Cultural	Lifestyle trends Demographics Purchase patterns	Industry and government reports regarding social statistics and purchases	New products or services Channel changes Promotional themes and levels

DEVELOPING THE PRODUCT OR SERVICE

As we mentioned at the beginning of this chapter, the product or service to be offered should be designed to meet a target market demand. To ensure responsiveness to consumer demand, the owner-manager should think of the product or service in terms of how it satisfies consumer needs. A prototype of the product should be prepared and tested with a representative sample of the market. This type of information should be collected prior to finalizing the production decision.

Some major decision areas which the small business owner should be familiar with when developing a product strategy are discussed next.

Develop Product or Service Policies   Product policies should cover such items as quality level, product or service depth and width, packaging, branding, level of service, and warranties.

Decide How the Product will be Manufactured   For many small businesses, contracting with another firm to manufacture a product is advantageous. This may be an especially viable alternative during the early stages of a business, when the risk is higher. Once the product has achieved market acceptance and the volume of production has increased, it may be more cost effective to acquire the manufacturing capability.

Understand the Product Life Cycle   All products or services have a life cycle, as Figure 7.4 shows. As the product moves from the introduction to the decline stage in its life cycle, the marketing strategy for the product and even for the business may also change. This means changes may be required in pricing, in distribution, in promotion, and even in the product or service. Knowing that the product or service has a life cycle helps the owner-manager plan for any necessary adjustments to the marketing strategy when the maturity

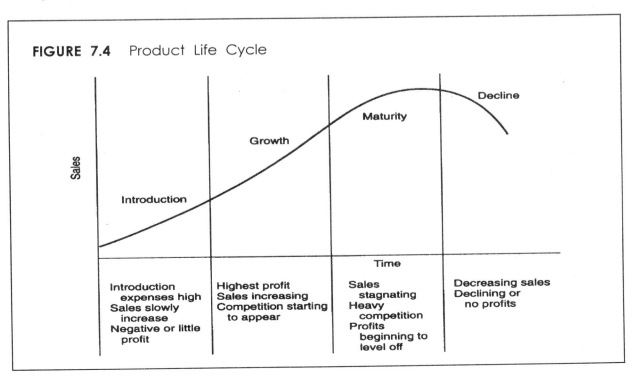

FIGURE 7.4 Product Life Cycle

stage is reached. Such modifications can help prolong the life cycle of the product or service. Strategies include the following:

- Appealing to a new target market.
- Adjusting the product or service to meet changes in customer needs.
- Increasing promotion to enhance frequency of purchases.
- Emphasizing different uses or characteristics of the product or service.
- Offering a new product or service.

Determine Factors that may Accelerate Product or Service Adoption

Research has shown that people in a market generally adopt new products or services at different rates. Those who purchase first are the innovators or **early adopters** and often are the opinion leaders in a social group. The innovators and early adopters typically make up about 15% of the market but have a far greater influence because the rest of the market usually looks to this group before purchasing.[4]

After the small business owner has identified the innovators and early adopters within the target market, every attempt should be made to test market the product or service to that group first. If the early adopters accept the product or service, they may even do much of the initial promotion simply because of their use of the product. Early adopters and opinion leaders tend to be vocal about the products and services they try and use. In addition, they tend to have higher income and education levels, be more socially active, be more willing to take risks, and have greater exposure to printed media.

In addition to understanding the characteristics of innovators and early adopters, the small business owner should be aware of the factors that can speed up product adoption and attempt to capitalize on them. Following are some of the more important factors:

■ Relative Advantage

If the product or service appears to have a significant advantage over existing ones and if this advantage can be communicated effectively, it is more likely to have a faster adoption.

■ Complexity

If the product is difficult to understand, the adoption rate is typically longer. In such a case promotion should have an informational or educational content.

■ Divisibility

A product or service that can be purchased in small amounts with a minimum of social or financial risk usually has a quicker adoption rate.

■ Communicability of Results

If the results of using the product or service are quickly evident and easily communicated to others, its adoption rate will be more rapid.

In summary, the less risk associated with the purchase decision, the more rapid the adoption rate. The owner-manager, therefore, should do whatever possible to reduce such risk when introducing a new product or service. Providing information and offering a guarantee or warranty as part of the purchase are commonly used methods for reducing risk.

---

4   Everett M. Rogers with F. Floyd Schoemaker, *Communication of Innovation* (New York: Free Press, 1971), 270.

Understanding How the Consumer Classifies the Product
or Service   Marketers use a standard classification system for categorizing consumer goods. This system can be valuable in developing the marketing strategy for the small business. The classifications are as follows:

■ Convenience Goods

Convenience goods are purchased with minimal effort. They may be necessities, unplanned purchases, or emergency goods.

■ Shopping Goods

Shopping goods are purchased only after comparison with similar products. Comparisons may be made on the basis of price if competing products are viewed as similar or in terms of quality or style if competing products differ.

■ Specialty Goods

Consumers have substantial brand or product loyalty with specialty products or services. As a result they are willing to spend considerable effort to locate and purchase the brands and products they desire.

Figure 7.5 illustrates strategy implications for each of these classifications. The focus of the marketing strategy is determined by how the target consumer classifies the product or service.

FIGURE 7.5   Strategy Implications for Good Classifications

Type of Good	Price	Distribution	Promotion
Convenience	While usually lower priced goods, the markups tend to be high	Within a certain range price is not important to consumer; Located close to consumers, either in relation to where they live or within the store	Availability important to customer; Promote availability; Point-of-purchase displays for impulse goods
Shopping	For similar products the price must be competitive as consumers are price sensitive; For dissimilar products that are still competitive price is not as important to the consumer	Located close to competing products to aid comparison	Promote price advantage for similar products or quality/style advantage for dissimilar products
Specialty	Within a certain range price is not important to customer	Location not important to customer	Promote which outlet carries the product or brand

DEVELOPING THE DISTRIBUTION SYSTEM

Many entrepreneurs develop an excellent product but lack knowledge about the best way to get it to the consumer. An effective distribution system should provide the product or service to the right consumer, at the right place, at the right time, and in the right quantity. An example of an aboriginal entrepreneur who has recognized the importance of timely distribution is given in Incident 7.6.

INCIDENT 7.6
Flooring, Appliance Store can Meet Every Need

Frank Deshane has a good sense of humour, and it will come in handy considering the business he's in. Keshane sells carpets and appliances from his store in Saskatoon. Keshane said he saw a need for a native business to offer housing material at better prices than what other companies were offering.

Keshane knows his clientele, especially people living on reserves. "Almost every band in Canada is building houses right now and we can serve their every need. I always promise my customers we can deliver anywhere in Canada in 24 hours. If they called today from the Yukon, their material would be on their front door the very next day. And if a customer wants us to come to their reserve to talk about prices, our delivery service or simply to choose carpets, we'll bring the store to them. We do presentations of our product," explains Keshane.

It's First Nations Flooring's goal to expand across the country. "We can't look back now. I just hope native people do business with us. We're here to offer them the best service possible and the lowest prices," he adds.

SOURCE: *Windspeaker*, Canada's National Aboriginal News Publication, April 12, 1991, p. 26.

The **distribution channel** is the path that a product or service follows from the producer to the consumer. It includes the different organizations or individuals who will assist in this movement toward consumption.

The small business owner needs to address three main distribution decision areas: the type of channel to use, the length of the channel, and the number of distributors authorized to sell the product.

Channel Options

A small business can follow two basic channel paths, although various combinations of these types of channels are possible.

Manufacturer to Consumer (Short-Direct Channel)   This type of channel involves distributing the product or service directly to the consumer. The transportation and selling functions are carried out by the owner-manager or the sales staff. Often small businesses lack the financial capacity or expertise to hire and train their own sales forces.

Manufacturer to Wholesaler/Retailer to Consumer (Long-Indirect Channel)   In this type of distribution channel the wholesaler or retailer purchases the product and resells it to another channel member or the consumer. The manufacturer assumes less risk with this method but generally has less control over the distribution as well as a lower profit margin. The small business may utilize this type of distribution channel by going to a retailer or wholesaler directly or visiting a trade show attended by these intermediaries. Many products receive their initial start from successful trade show experience.

Another consideration in choosing the channel option is to investigate the type of organization which will be distributing the product. Care should be taken to ensure that this distributor has the expertise, resources, and dependability. An example of an aboriginal company that has ensured its success by choosing its distributors wisely is shown in Incident 7.7.

INCIDENT 7.7
Osoyoos Indian Band

> The Osoyoos Indian Band runs Inkameep Vineyards of Oliver, British Columbia. This is the largest wine-grape vineyard in Canada and the first that is 100% aboriginally owned and managed. Inkameep supplies grapes to wineries throughout British Columbia, contributing to several award winning wines. Two of the vineyard's major alliances are with Gehringer Brothers Estate Winery and Summerhill Estate Winery. According to owner and wine maker Walter Gehringer, the native-run business is looking for long-term relationships, loyalty and a common vision. He finds the Inkameep staff approachable and willing to listen. "It's an educational process both ways," says Gehringer. "We're both interested in quality." The proprietor of Summerhill, Steve Cipes, also sees having a common vision as a critical reason for the success of his company's joint venture with Inkameep. As he notes, Summerhill and Inkameep are determined to make a product of which they are both proud.

> SOURCE: *Canadian Business Review*, Summer 1994, p. 13.

Channel Length

The decision regarding length will depend on the concerns of the manufacturer mentioned above. It also involves examining the product and market characteristics identified in Figure 7.6.

Channel Intensity

Another channel decision is how many distributors/dealers will be allowed to sell a product. Generally speaking, products that require greater selling effort, seller knowledge, and sales expertise are best distributed through a more exclusive type of arrangement. Standardized or convenience-type products usually call for a more intensive channel system. Because product availability is important in such a system, many dealers are allowed to carry the product.

SETTING THE PRICE FOR THE PRODUCT OR SERVICE

Another marketing strategy variable within the control of the owner-manager is the setting of price for the product or service. Pricing is a critical part of the marketing strategy: the small business cannot afford to make a pricing mistake in a competitive industry. To approach price-setting effectively, one must understand the factors that affect price. These factors can be classified as either external or internal.

External influences, as discussed earlier, include the state of the economy in the market area, the extent of competition, possible legal restrictions, cultural or societal attitudes toward certain price levels, and target market demand. Typical internal influences on pricing

FIGURE 7.6   Deciding Channel Length

DIRECT/SHORT CHANNEL (Manufacturer to consumer)	INDIRECT/LONG CHANNEL (Manufacturer to wholesaler/agent to retailer to consumer)
Implication to Manufacturer	
• More expensive to set up	• Cheaper to set up
• Greater potential return	• Least return
• More risk	• Less risk
• More expertise needed	• Less expertise needed
Product Characteristics	
• Perishable	• Standardized
• Technical	• Inexpensive
• Large, bulky	• Proven demand
• Expensive	
Market Characteristics	
• Geographically concentrated	• Geographically dispersed
• Product awareness low	• Awareness high
• Sales effort required	• Less sales effort required

policy are internal costs, the firm's long-term objectives, and pricing policies as set by the owner-manager.

In setting price levels for a product or service, the entrepreneur may find that some of these factors are more influential than others. As a result, businesses use three general bases for price setting that take these influences into account: cost, demand, and competition.

Cost-Based Pricing

In **cost-based pricing** the major influence is the cost of producing a product for the manufacturer, of purchasing and selling the product for the retailer, and of providing the service for the service firm (internal influences). Figure 7.7 illustrates the use of cost-based pricing in each of these types of businesses.

Once the costs have been determined, a percentage mark-up is added to reflect the profit objective of the firm. The owner-manager should realize, however, that initial mark-up is seldom achieved. Markdowns and inventory shrinkage should be estimated (see Figure 7.7) and built into the mark-up calculation.

Demand-Based Pricing

Demand-based pricing uses consumer sensitivity to price as the major factor in arriving at the final price (external influences). Usually primary research in the form of surveying will be required to assess acceptable prices for new products. Figure 7.8 illustrates the results of

FIGURE 7.7   Cost-Based Pricing Methods

Manufacturing Firm

Direct material cost per unit	$ 18.00
Direct labour cost per unit	21.00
Variable overhead (manufacturing)	10.00
Fixed overhead (factory)	30.00
Total manufacturing cost per unit	79.00
Selling costs per unit	3.00
General overhead (allocated per unit)	5.00
Total cost per unit	87.00
Desired profit	13.00
Selling price	$100.00

Retail Firm

Cost of merchandise	$ 50.00
Selling and storage (estimated)	20.00
Estimated markdowns	5.00
Desired profit	25.00
Selling price	$100.00

In retailing, the difference between the price and the cost of inventory is known as markup. In this example it is $50 and is usually expressed as a percentage in the following manner:

Percentage = (100–50) ÷ 100 = 50%

Service Firm

Estimated cost of providing service per customer	$ 60.00
Estimated overhead costs per customer	20.00
Desired profit per customer	20.00
Selling price	$100.00

such a survey incorporated into a demand curve. Each point on the line shows the quantity demanded at the related price. For example, at a price of $30 demand would be 10 units; at $20 demand increases to slightly more than 15 units. In this example the total revenue at the $30 price is $300 (30 × 10), whereas at $20 the total revenue is $320 (20 × 16). This situation can be described as price elastic. In **price-elastic** situations, price increases result in a negative effect on demand. For some types of products (convenience and specialty) and some industries (those with little direct competition) price may be less important to the purchaser, and thus a change in price may not significantly affect demand. If this condition exists, it means the business has much more freedom and flexibility in setting prices than it would in a more competitive and price-sensitive situation.

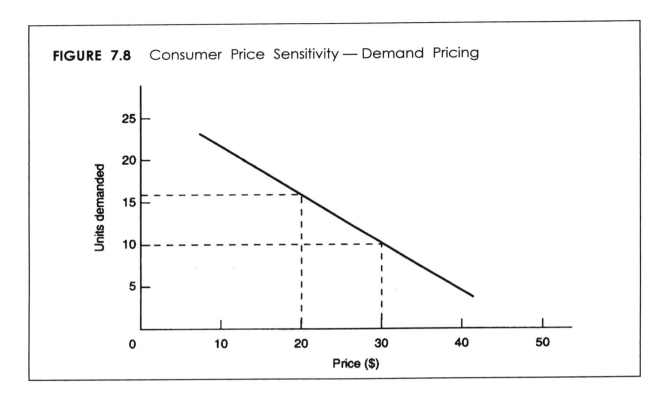

FIGURE 7.8 Consumer Price Sensitivity — Demand Pricing

For products and services already on the market, existing price levels and industry experts may provide valuable information to assist in setting demand-based prices.

Competition-Based Pricing

Firms in a growing number of industries are using **competitive pricing,** in which the major consideration in setting prices is the price levels and policies of the competitors (external influences). Many firms conduct ongoing price checks on the competition to guide their own pricing. The small firm may wish to set prices at a fixed percentage above, equal to, or below the competitors' price.

The small business owner should not rely too heavily on only one of the above methods of pricing. All these methods are important in most industries, and each should be taken into account when setting the final price for a product or service.

PROMOTION

Today most businesses must actively promote their products or services and provide specific information to the purchaser. An aboriginal entrepreneur can use four methods to provide information about his or her product or service: advertising, sales promotions, public relations, and personal selling.

Advertising   Advertising is a non-personal form of promotion. It is directed at a mass audience through various forms of media such as television, radio, newspaper, magazines, billboards, and direct mail. A small business owner should be aware of the strengths and weaknesses of each of these types of media and exactly when each is appropriate. This information is presented in Figure 7.9.

FIGURE 7.9 Advertising for Small Business

Media Type	Advantages	Disadvantages	Particular Suitability	Typical Costs
Newspapers	Flexible Timely Local market Credible source	May be expensive Short life Little "pass-along" Nonselective audience	All general retailers or for definable market areas similar to circulation	One-page ad: large market ($1,200–$1,600) small market ($500–$600) (prices dependant upon length of contract)
Television	Sight, sound, and motion Wide reach	Cost Clutter Short exposure Less selective	Definable market area surrounding the station's location for certain products	30 Seconds of prime time: large local market ($500–$700) small local market ($150–$200)
Direct Mail	Selected audience Personalization Flexible	Relatively expensive per contact High "throwout" rate	New and expanding businesses; those using coupon returns or catalogues	Approximately $1 per contact
Radio	Wide reach Segmented audience Inexpensive	Audio only Weak attention Short exposure	Business catering to identifiable groups: teens, commuters, housewives	30 seconds of prime time: large local market ($150–$200) small local market ($35–$50)
Magazines	Very segmented audience Credible source Good reproduction Long life Good "pass-along"	Inflexible Long lead times Costly	Restaurants Entertainment Identifiable target Markets Mail order Chains	Approximately $30,000 for one-page, four-colour ad in Chatelaine (French and English)
Outdoor	Flexible Repeat exposure Inexpensive	Mass market Very short exposure Brand name retailers	Amusements Tourist businesses	1 month of prime location billboard, large market ($2,000–$2,500)
Telephone Directories	Users in the market for goods or services Continuous ads Costs relatively low	Limited to active shoppers Limited visibility Not dynamic	Services Retailers of brand name items Highly specialized retailers	Inexpensive; depends on size of ad

Sales Promotions   Sales promotions are also non-personal forms of promotion but are directed at a much more restricted audience than advertising is. Examples of sales promotions are point-of-purchase displays; coupons and discounts; contests; and participation in trade shows, aboriginal activities, and exhibitions. All of these mechanisms are effective forms of advertising for the small business, and some are relatively inexpensive.

Public Relations   As Incident 7.8 illustrates, public relations, or publicity, can also be an effective form of promotion for the small business. This is particularly the case when the product or service is innovative or extraordinary in some way. This form of promotion may involve public interest news stories and forging alliances with the media. Public relations may also include sponsorship by the business of community projects such as sporting teams or events, or specialty advertising such as calendars, pens, hats, and the like. Public relations is generally inexpensive and can be helpful in promoting not only the product or service, but the business itself. Public relations also offer a business a chance to contribute something back to the community which supports it.

INCIDENT 7.8
Champions' Place Restaurant Inc.

Champions' Place Restaurant, located in Hobbema, Alberta, was run by Dick and Madeline Lightning, a couple who both had previous experience in the restaurant business. They catered to a luncheon clientele, many of them employees of the four Bands in the area. Champions' specialty was Oriental food, but they also served Western cuisine, the main fare for all other nearby restaurants.

The name "Champions'" was itself a form of promotion. The local hockey, fastball, and volleyball teams, and the cowboys who frequented the restaurant, often left their championship trophies for display.

Two years ago Champions' spent $4,900 on advertising and promotional displays, which had increased to $8,000 this past year. According to Madeline, "We donated such things as cash, horse blankets, buckles, and trophies — which don't come cheap." In retrospect she reflected, "Although we spent a lot, I don't think our methods used to promote Champions' were the most effective."

Dick believed that promotional activity was necessary, but he felt it had to be more professional: "In a small community, as a business owner, we're always hit by various groups who want us to make financial donations. We don't do that anymore. Now we give them dinner certificates instead, and this seems to be working better for us."

SOURCE: "Champions' Place Restaurant Inc.," The Centre for Aboriginal Management, Faculty of Management, University of Lethbridge, 1991.

Personal Selling   The conditions conducive to a short distribution channel or an emphasis on personal selling were discussed earlier in this chapter. Most businesses will require some personal selling as part of their marketing strategy, although the ability to "sell a product" is not something every individual possesses or every culture values. Owner-managers are often required to promote themselves, their businesses, and their products to customers, bankers, suppliers, and government agencies through personal selling. If salespeople are employed, they will need to be trained not only with respect to product or service knowledge but also in selling skills. Other aspects of training, supervision, and motivation of a sales force will be discussed in detail in Chapter 10.

STEPS IN CARRYING OUT A PROMOTIONAL CAMPAIGN ——————

How does the owner-manager prepare the promotional program for the product/service and/or the business? The following are the essential steps in carrying out a promotional program that can be used as a guide for the small business:

1. **Set Promotional Objectives**
   Specific objectives should be set prior to the promotion. Typical examples are the desired percentage increase in sales, the amount of traffic to be generated, and the percentage of awareness increase desired.

2. **Determine the Target of the Promotion**
   While in many cases the target will be the ultimate consumer, often it may be a broker in the distribution channel or another group that has considerable influence over the purchase.

3. **Understand the Target's Needs and Perceptions of the Product or Service**
   Once the target of the promotion has been determined, it is essential that information be gathered about that group with regard to their needs, media habits, and perceptions of the product category or specific product or service. This information is similar to the consumer profile discussed earlier.

4. **Develop a Relevant Theme**
   The next step is to develop a theme for the promotion that will reflect responses to target needs and perceptions and help achieve the promotional objective. It is important that only one theme be used, since too many themes or too much information can confuse the consumer and lead to unsatisfactory results.

5. **Determine the Method or Media to Use**
   The decision about which promotional type to use often depends on the relative importance of creating awareness and/or closing the sale. Figure 7.10 lists the strengths of each of the previously mentioned types of promotion with respect to these purposes. As the figure illustrates, advertising and public relations and some sales promotions tend to be more effective in creating awareness, whereas personal selling tends to work better for achieving or closing the sale.

FIGURE 7.10 Effectiveness of Promotion Types

	Personal Selling	Sales Promotions	Public Relations	Advertising
Create awareness of product or business	Weak	Weak	Strong	Strong
Develop interest in product	Weak	Medium	Weak	Strong
Increase desire to purchase product	Medium	Medium	Weak	Medium
Achieve product purchase	Strong	Medium	Weak	Weak

6. **Develop a Specific Promotional Message**

   Once the theme and medium have been determined, it is possible to develop the specific type of message to be used. As Figure 7.9 points out, some types of information are not appropriate for certain types of media.

7. **Setting the Promotional Budget**

   Once a method of promotion is determined, it is then possible to estimate the cost of the promotion. Several methods are used to determine amounts to spend on promotion. The most common approach is the percent of sales method. Standard percentages for various businesses can serve as a guide in using this method (see page 303 for examples). The percent of sales method is theoretically weak but simple to apply, which explains its high rate of use by small businesses. A business owner should remain flexible in using this method, however, as market and product conditions may necessitate a deviation from the averages.

8. **Implement the Promotional Program**

   An essential feature of implementing the program is proper timing. Certain times of the year, the week, and even the day may be inappropriate to promote the product or service to the target market.

9. **Evaluate Effectiveness of Promotion**

   The owner-manager should attempt to evaluate the promotional effectiveness to aid in future promotions. Evaluating effectiveness is made much easier if specific objectives such as those mentioned earlier are set. Observations of results and surveys may be used in this evaluation. The mechanics of using primary research methods were discussed in Chapter 3.

As this chapter illustrates, many aspects are involved in the marketing plan of a small business. Being able to integrate all of these aspects so that they comprise a clear and coordinated strategy often spells the difference between a successful and an unsuccessful business. Page 304 of the Checklists and Examples section provides an example of a marketing plan checklist.

SUMMARY

1. Marketing activities include defining t304he target customer's needs and wants, monitoring the relevant outside influences, developing the product or service, selecting the channel of distribution, setting the price, and developing the promotional program.
2. The three types of target markets a small aboriginal business may attempt to reach are consumer markets, industrial markets, and export markets.
3. Information required in exporting includes the forms of government assistance available, the peculiarities of the foreign market, and the mechanisms of exporting.
4. Some of the most common external influences affecting the small business are the economy, the competition, legal and financial restrictions, and society and culture.
5. In dealing with external influences the owner-manager must identify which external conditions have an effect on the business and then set up a system to monitor and effectively respond to changes in these influences.
6. All products or services have a life cycle in which sales and profits increase then eventually decline over time. Business strategy will change as the product or service moves through its life cycle.

7. To reduce risk in the early stages of a product life cycle, some small businesses get other companies to produce their product.

8. Speed of adoption of a new product can be increased by developing significant advantages over existing products, reducing complexity, providing for the purchase of the product in smaller amounts, and seeing that the results of using the product are quickly evident and easily communicated.

9. The classifications of consumer goods include convenience, shopping, and specialty goods. The marketing strategy will be different for each.

10. The major decision areas in distribution include being aware of the channel options, deciding on the length of the channel, and determining the channel intensity.

11. In determining length of the distribution channel, the owner-manager should examine market and product characteristics as well as the firm's capabilities.

12. An intensive channel is utilized where product availability is important. Exclusive channels are found for products that need greater sales effort and support.

13. The three methods of setting price are cost-based, demand-based, and competitive-based pricing.

14. Price-elasticity is a measure of consumer sensitivity to various price levels. The owner-manager should determine how important price is to the consumer.

15. There are four methods of providing information about a product or service. These methods are advertising, sales promotion, public relations, and personal selling.

16. The following are the essential steps in carrying out a promotional program: (1) set promotional objectives; (2) specify the target of the promotion; (3) understand the target's needs and perceptions of the product or service; (4) develop a relevant theme; (5) determine the method and/or media to use; (6) develop a specific promotional message; (7) set a promotional budget; (8) implement the promotional program; and (9) evaluate effectiveness of the promotion.

CHAPTER PROBLEMS AND DISCUSSION QUESTIONS

1. Define the target market for Abenaki Associates (Incident 7.1). What are the target market demographics, lifestyle characteristics, purchase characteristics, and purchase motivations (see Figure 7.1)?

2. Illustrate how Mystic Wolf (Incident 7.5) could successfully complete the three steps in developing an export market as outlined in the chapter. Do you see any ethical issues arising in their work?

3. Discuss the uncontrollable variables that might affect Mystic Wolf in their exporting of aboriginal artifacts and artwork.

4. Develop a marketing mix (i.e., product, promotion, price, distribution) for a bakery.

5. Where is Kellogg's Corn Flakes in the product life cycle? What has Kellogg's done to prolong the life cycle of Corn Flakes?

6. What could a new cereal company do to speed up the adoption rate of its cereals?

7. How would you classify the following products (Figure 7.6)? How would you promote and distribute these products? Explain.
   a. discount clothes
   b. works of fine art
   c. chocolate bar
   d. bread

8. Develop a distribution system for the Osoyoos Band (Incident 7.8). Which channel should the product use? What should the channel intensity be?

9. Which pricing system would you use for the following products or services? Why?
    a. a construction company on the reserve
    b. admission price to the local rodeo
    c. aboriginal clothing
    d. grocery products

10. Using a scale of –1 to +1, how would you rate the following products for elasticity, where –1 is inelastic, 0 is neutral, and 1 is elastic? Justify your answer.
    a. salt
    b. Porsche automobile
    c. Skidoos

11. You have been approached to develop an advertising campaign for a new local tourist lodge. The owners realize they need to develop awareness amongst consumers but have a limited amount of funds available for advertising. Using Figure 7.9 as a guide, decide which media type to use for the advertising campaign. Justify your decision to use or not to use each media type.

12. Review Figure 7.2 (Developing a Foreign Marketing Strategy). How would you apply this set of questions with respect to marketing in an aboriginal community?

13. Choose the promotional types (advertising, personal selling, sales promotion, and public relations) you would use for the following list of products. Explain why.
    a. arts and crafts store
    b. travel guide service
    c. financial consulting to reserve businesses
    d. hand-made moccasins
    e. participation program (government fitness program)
    f. aboriginal golf tournament

14. Interview a local aboriginal business owner and ask him or her what the business's marketing strategy is. Determine the promotional strategy. Are these strategies similar to the principles discussed in the chapter?

15. Is it appropriate for an aboriginal business person to view members of his or her community (or anyone else) as "target consumers"?

16. Is it appropriate for traditional aboriginal arts and crafts to be viewed and marketed as "products"?

SUGGESTED READINGS

Blake, Gary and Robert Bly. *How to Promote Your Own Business*. Scarborough, Ont.: Canadian Small Business Institute, 1990.

Davidson, Jeffery P. *The Marketing Source Book for Small Business*. New York: Wiley, 1989.

Dorff, Ralph. *Marketing for the Small Manufacturer*. Englewood Cliffs, NJ: Prentice Hall, 1983.

Industry, Science and Technology Canada. *Small Business in Canada, 1991*. Ottawa, 1991.

C H A P T E R   8

Financial Management

Patricia Elemans

CHAPTER OBJECTIVES

☐ To review the fundamentals of small business accounting.

☐ To discuss the various types of accounting systems that a small business can use and the situations in which one or another might be most appropriate for an aboriginal business.

☐ To describe the considerations in purchasing a computer for the small business.

☐ To show how to develop and use budgets and financial planning tools.

☐ To illustrate how to evaluate and control the financial operations of the business.

☐ To discuss the important aspects of credit management for the small business and the use of credit in aboriginal communities.

SMALL BUSINESS PROFILE
Iqaluit, NWT
Amarok Country Food Store

Amarok Country Foods seemed to be plagued with problems from day one. It is located in the town of Iqaluit, which is located at the top, northeastern end of Frobisher Bay in the south of Baffin Island, Northwest Territories. The town sits near the site of a traditional Inuit summer fishing camp, on the rocky coastline of the Canadian Shield uplands.

Amarok Country Foods was established in 1978 by the Amarok Hunters and Trappers Association in Iqaluit. The primary objective of the Board at the time was to ensure that country food would be available to Inuit people in Iqaluit who did not have someone to hunt and provide food for them. The Board wanted the store to be run as a non-profit organization, selling food as inexpensively as possible to the people who needed it.

The store's financial and managerial history is one of both successes and failures. After a rough beginning the store was successful from 1979 to 1981 but by the end of 1982 it was clear that there was great mismanagement of the store's finances. By the end of June 1982 there was a loss of $41,086 and it had current debts of over $80,000 with no money to pay them.

A new manager was hired and the store was rebuilt between 1983 and 1986. In 1983 the store had a net income of $37,175, and in 1984 total revenues increased another 15% with a net income of $45,206. By 1985 total revenues levelled off and the profit for the year was $5,346. In 1986 the previous manager-trainee took over operations. From June 1986 to August 1988 the store's operations got out of control. By the end of 1986 there was a net loss of over $45,000. The number of employees in the store increased, inventory control was poor and financial records were in disarray. An independent auditor indicated that there was no control over cash, proper financial records had not been maintained, there were no proper costing procedures on inventory, and inventory records were not kept.

A new manager was brought in in 1987 and there was a net income of $32,524. However, the store was holding a very large quantity of inventory and suffering from a severe cash flow problem.

A new manager was once again hired in January 1988. Unfortunately the manager did not have experience in retail management. Once again there was little control over the financial and other business systems. At this point the Board engaged the services of an outside bookkeeping service to take care of the financial records of the store to ensure that the records were kept in order and up to date.

SOURCE: Frederick H. Weihs, "Amarok Country Food Store, Case Study Kit," Prepared for the Native Management and Economic Development Program, Trent University, Peterborough, Ontario.

THE NEED FOR FINANCIAL RECORDS

The opening profile illustrates how financial management problems can spell disaster for a small business. Such a situation occurs often with small businesses. A recent survey found that from 24 to 45% of Canadian small business owners did not understand basic financial measurement ratios used in evaluating their businesses.[1] Failure to understand and manage the financial aspects of a business can be disastrous for the small business owner. The need for competence in this area is continually growing as new technology and greater competition in many markets require closer monitoring of operations and quicker decision making. Keeping proper records can warn the owner-manager in advance of future financial difficulties and can assist in planning the growth of the business.

If the business is situated off a reserve or if it is incorporated the owner-manager will also have to maintain proper records to satisfy government requirements. While few owner-managers are fond of Revenue Canada, the fact that this agency requires accurate record-keeping to calculate a business's tax liability may actually be a benefit for the small business.

Record-keeping is also necessary if a business is required to borrow money. Lenders, whether banks, bands, settlements, or government agencies, will require that proper record-keeping be followed to ensure that debt obligations are met.

Accurate and current records of the operations of the business are essential for the evaluation and control of business operations regardless of the type of business (service, retail, manufacturing), form of business (sole proprietorship, partnership, band or settlement owned, coop or corporation) or where it is located (on a reserve or settlement, remote community or in a city). These records guide the owner's day-to-day decision making and are critical to understanding what is going on in the business. They provide information in areas such as whether or not the business is making a profit, what the business owns and what it owes, whether there is cash available to buy supplies and inventory, the level of sales, what the cash from the business is used for, when inventory should be ordered, what type of inventory is selling, what peak sales periods are, what should be spent on items such as inventory, advertising and so on. A business owner cannot make decisions that are crucial to the survival of the business without this type of information.

Small business owners may be tempted to neglect the financial aspects of the business and devote their time to the day-to-day operational side of the business such as production, personnel management, and marketing. This often occurs because they have an incomplete understanding of how to manage the record-keeping system effectively. Understanding the management aspects of record-keeping requires the review of some basic accounting fundamentals.

THE ACCOUNTING CYCLE

Figure 8.1 illustrates, in a simplified way, the process by which transactions of the business are translated into financial statements.

1   "Small Business Magazine's First Annual Survey of Canada's Entrepreneurs," *Small Business*, June 1987, 49–53.

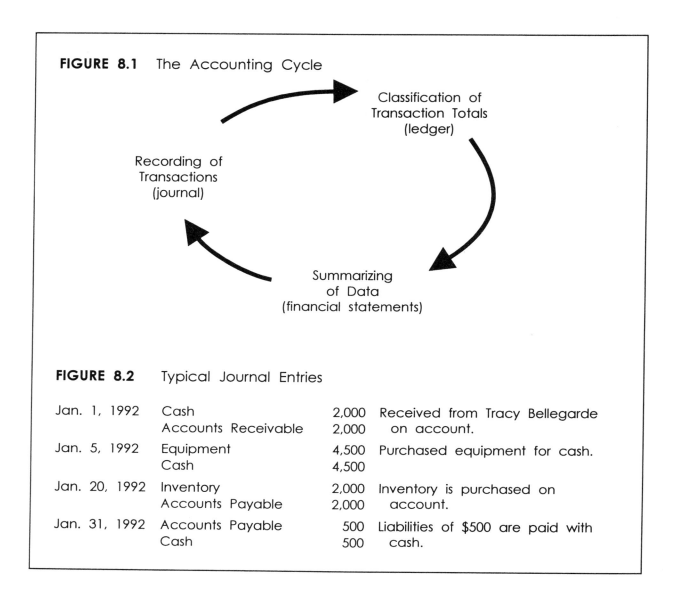

FIGURE 8.1   The Accounting Cycle

Classification of
Transaction Totals
(ledger)

Recording of
Transactions
(journal)

Summarizing
of Data
(financial statements)

FIGURE 8.2   Typical Journal Entries

Jan. 1, 1992	Cash	2,000	Received from Tracy Bellegarde
	Accounts Receivable	2,000	on account.
Jan. 5, 1992	Equipment	4,500	Purchased equipment for cash.
	Cash	4,500	
Jan. 20, 1992	Inventory	2,000	Inventory is purchased on
	Accounts Payable	2,000	account.
Jan. 31, 1992	Accounts Payable	500	Liabilities of $500 are paid with
	Cash	500	cash.

Recording Transactions

Transactions are recorded chronologically (as they occur) in a record called a **journal**. Many types of journals are used. In a business where there are few transactions, these entries may be made manually. In many retail businesses the daily cash register tape total may be used to record the revenue journal entries. The check register can be used to record payments or disbursements. In businesses having a large number of transactions, the journal may be kept mechanically through the use of a bookkeeping machine or by a computer.

In accounting, double-entry recording is used. This means that the amounts of each transaction are recorded twice. This procedure accurately reflects the fact that each transaction will affect two parts (accounts) of the business. Often a decrease in one will mean an increase in another. For example, if a snowmobile costing $3,000 is purchased for the business and paid for in cash, the amount of cash in the business decreases by $3,000, and equipment in the business increases by $3,000. The use of double-entry accounting also allows double checking the accuracy of the entries.

Figure 8.2 illustrates how some typical recording entries might appear in a small business journal. In each of these transactions, for every increase in one account there is a corresponding decrease in another account. At the end of the period, the totals of increases and decreases at the bottom of the page for a number of transactions should be equal.

Bartering

In some communities bartering may occur as a way of paying for goods and services, and often no records are kept of such transactions. However, items that are bartered can be recorded in much the same manner as other items. For example, if a customer pays for hunting supplies with meat, which the owner will consume, the transaction would be as follows. A miscellaneous asset account (**meat**) would be increased by the retail value of the hunting supplies and the **sales** account would be credited by the same amount. **Hunting supplies** (inventory) would be decreased by what they cost the small business owner and the **cost of good sold** account (an expense) would be increased. Since the owner will be consuming the meat it can be considered a form of salary. An account called **salary** (or drawings) would be increased and the miscellaneous asset account (**meat**) would be decreased.

Classifying Transaction Totals

Once the transactions have been accurately and properly recorded, the next step is to group or classify similar transactions together. These groupings or classifications are called **accounts** and are entered into a book called a **ledger**. A ledger keeps a running balance of the dollar amounts in each account so that the net totals may be known at the end of each period. As with journal entries, a ledger may be kept manually or by computer. An example of some accounts of a typical ledger for service, retail, and manufacturing firms is shown in Figure 8.3. The recording and classifying steps of the accounting cycle are usually referred to as **bookkeeping**. Many small businesses have found it valuable to hire an accountant to set up the bookkeeping system that is most appropriate for their business.

Summarizing Data

The third step in the accounting cycle involves taking the account totals from the ledger and putting them together to form the financial statements. Although this final step tends to be done by accountants their services may not always be available. In this situation it is vital for business owners to learn to prepare the statements on their own because of the importance of the information. There are numerous books available that can effectively teach the small business owner how to prepare these statements. These statements indicate the past success and current position of the business. It is important that the small business owner understand what financial statements mean and how to use them. Essentially three financial statements can be valuable to the owner of a business.

Balance Sheet (Statement of Financial Position)   This statement presents in summary form a snapshot picture of what the business owns and owes at any point in time. Those items that the business owns are termed **assets** and those owed are either **liabilities** (owed to sources outside the business), or **equity** (owed to owners). Figure 8.4 illustrates a balance sheet for a hypothetical small business. Assets and liabilities are generally listed in

FIGURE 8.3 Typical Ledger Accounts

Service Firm	For a Retail Firm add these accounts	For a Manufacturing Firm add these accounts
Sales	Sales Returns and Allowances	Machinery
Cash	Sales Discounts	Accumulated
Accounts Receivable	Furniture and Fixtures	Depreciation: Machinery
Accounts Payable	Accumulated	Cost of Goods Sold
Land	Depreciation: Furniture	Raw Materials
Building	and Fixtures	Direct Labour
Accumulated Depreciation: Building	Merchandise Inventory	Factory Overhead
Office Equipment		
Accumulated Depreciation: Office Equipment	Cost of Goods Sold	
	Purchases	
	Purchase Returns	
Office Supplies Inventory	Purchase Discounts	
Retained Earnings	Transportation In	
Salaries Expense		
Telephone Expense		
Advertising Expense		
Office Supplies Expense		
Depreciation Expense: Building		
Depreciation Expense: Equipment		
Miscellaneous Expense		
Salaries Payable		
Utilities Expense		
Licenses and Taxes Expense		
Insurance Expense		
Accounting and Legal Expense		

order of liquidity with the most liquid being first. Usually assets and liabilities are divided into current (to be consumed in one year) and non-current (more than one year).

Income Statement (Statement of Profit and Loss) This statement shows the results of the operations of the business for a given time period. This statement was introduced in Chapter 3 and is an integral part of the feasibility analysis and the business plan. The

---

FIGURE 8.4

Small Business Corporation
Balance Sheet
(as of December 31, 1995)

Assets

Current Assets:

Cash	$ 3,449	
Accounts receivable	5,944	
Inventories	12,869	
Prepaid expenses	389	
Total current assets		$22,651

Fixed Assets:

Land, buildings, and equipment cost	26,926	
Less accumulated depreciation	13,534	
Total fixed assets		13,412

Other Assets:

Investments	1,000	
		1,000
TOTAL ASSETS		$37,063

Liabilities and Shareholders' Equity

Current Liabilities:

Accounts payable	$ 6,602	
Other current liabilities	845	
Total current liabilities		$ 7,447

Other Liabilities:

Mortgage payable	3,000	
		3,000
TOTAL LIABILITIES		10,447

Shareholders' Equity:

Common stock	15,000	
Retained earnings	11,616	
Total shareholders' equity		26,616
TOTAL LIABILITIES AND SHAREHOLDERS' EQUITY		$37,063

---

profit or income is determined by taking revenue from operations and subtracting expenses incurred in earning that revenue. Figure 8.5 illustrates an income statement for a hypothetical small business.

The Cash Flow and/or Statement of Changes in Financial Position   The importance and format of the **cash flow statement** was discussed in Chapter 6. This statement is similar to the income statement except that only cash inflows and outflows are shown.

FIGURE 8.5

Small Business Corporation
Income statement
(for the Year Ended December 31, 1995)

Net Sales	197,000
Cost of goods sold	123,000
	74,000
Gross Margin on Sales	
Operating expenses:	
Selling expenses	1,200
Sales salaries expense	18,300
Depreciation expense — store equipment	2,000
Total Selling expenses	21,500
General expenses:	
Depreciation expense — building	3,000
Insurance expense	765
Miscellaneous general expenses	425
General salaries expense	7,200
Total general expenses	11,300
Total operating expenses	32,800
Net Operating Margin	41,200
Other Expenses:	
Interest expense	2,750
Net Income before interest and taxes	38,450
Income taxes	14,450
Net income	$24,400

In recent years it has been common to examine not only the cash position of a business but also all of its asset/liability accounts over time. This has led to the popularity of a statement called the **Statement of Changes in Financial Position.** As its name implies, this statement presents balance sheet account changes from one period to the next. It can be helpful in explaining why a business may have a positive net income but a decrease in cash for the same period of operation, a situation that mystifies some small business owners. As the examination of the statement of changes of financial position can be complex, an example of a cash flow statement for a small business is shown in Figure 8.6.

ACCOUNTING SYSTEMS FOR THE SMALL BUSINESS

There are several types of accounting systems used by small businesses today. Variations occur because of differences in size, type of business (retail, service, manufacturing), industry, number of transactions, and expertise of the owner. The following is a brief description of some of the more common general systems used.

FIGURE 8.6

Small Business Corporation
Cash Flow Forecast, 1995

	Jan	Feb	Mar	Apr	May	Jun
Cash Receipts						
Sales in 1995		$ 5,000	$ 7,500	$10,000	$10,000	$ 10,000
Accounts receivable for 1994	$19,000	$13,000	6,000			
Equity funding		10,000				
TOTAL CASH RECEIPTS	$19,000	$28,000	$ 13,500	$10,000	$10,000	$ 10,000
Cash Disbursements						
Cost of sales:						
Labour	$ 5,000	$ 5,000	$ 5,000	$ 7,000	$ 7,000	$ 7,000
Materials	400	800	800	$ 1,000	$ 1,100	$ 1,100
Transportation	300	400	400	500	400	400
Accounts payable from 1994	12,000	10,000	10,000	6,000		
Selling expense	400	800	800	800	800	800
Administration	250	550	550	550	550	550
Fixed-asset investment						
Long-term debt repayment			2,500			2,500
Income tax instalment			3,000			3,000
Interest on debt:						
Long-term debt			680			640
Bank loan (other cash source)	400	350	270	370	430	440
TOTAL CASH DISBURSEMENTS	$18,750	$17,900	$ 24,000	$16,220	$10,280	$ 16,430
Monthly cash surplus/deficit	$ 250	$10,100	$-10,500	$-6,220	$ -280	$ -6,430
Accumulated cash surplus/deficit for 1995	$ 250	$10,350	$ -150	$-6,370	$-6,650	$-13,080

One-Book System

This type of system is most appropriate for the very small business with few transactions. It combines the recording and classifying steps of the accounting cycle into one step and presents this information on one page in a typical columnized ledger. Figure 8.7 illustrates a typical one-book system. In this example the journal entry is recorded in columns 1 through 5 and the ledger accounts are entered in columns 6 through 10. The double-entry procedure is followed, and column totals at the end of the period are taken to prepare the financial statements.

FIGURE 8.7 Illustration of a One-Book Accounting System

			— Bank —		— Revenues —		——— Expenses ———		
1	2	3	4	5	6	7	8	9	10
Date	Description	Chq. No.	In	Out	Sales	Misc.	Wages	Advert.	Other
Sep 1/95	Wages paid for August	25		5,000			5,000		
Sep 8/95	Sales for wk. 1		8,000		8,000				
Sep 12/95	Paid utility bill	26		800					800
Sep 15/95	Sales for wk. 2		6,500		6,500				
Sep 19/95	Paid advertising bill	27		400				400	

One-Write System

A simplification of the one-book system is the one-write or "pegboard" system used by many small businesses. The format is the same as that for the one-book system. Special carbon checks are used, however, so that when a disbursement check is made out it automatically enters the name and amounts into columns 2, 3, and 4 of the journal. This eliminates one operation and reduces the potential for error in transposing the information from the check register to the journal columns. The ledger part of the entry is the same as for the one-book system. One-write systems are commercially available and are usually reasonably priced.

Multijournal System

For businesses that are larger or have a large number of similar transactions, the journal and ledger entries may be separated into two books. It is common for the business to utilize more than one journal, such as a sales journal, disbursement journal, payroll journal, and others. This can simplify the entry procedure and allow an easy transfer of the journal totals to the ledger accounts.

The multijournal system, along with the one-book and one-write system, is a manual system whose use is decreasing as more and more small businesses are adopting automated systems.

Computer Service Bureau

An attractive option for many small businesses, located in larger cities, which are not in a position to purchase their own computerized accounting systems is to make use of a computer service bureau. Most of these services are offered by accounting firms. For a monthly fee, a small business can take its journal and/or ledger totals to such a bureau and within a few days receive detailed financial statements for the period (usually monthly). Much of the bookkeeping will still need to be carried out by the business, but a good portion of steps 2 and 3 of the accounting cycle can be provided by the service bureau. The big advantage is the detail of the reports which can be valuable in operating the business.

Although computer service bureaus are generally available in larger cities they are not always available in smaller or more remote communities. In these situations is it best for owners to learn to produce and maintain their own financial records and statements. Many cities, communities, and bands have economic development offices which offer incubator and training programs for small business owners. These programs provide training on how to maintain financial records and can be of great service to those just starting out. An example of such a program is the Treaty Seven Economic Development Corporation: A Community Futures Program, located in Southern Alberta, which offers free workshops and training in bookkeeping and computer use for aboriginal small business owners in the Treaty Seven area.

Small Business Computer Systems

Many small businesses are finding that computer systems are no longer reserved solely for large companies. Many have also found great benefits from purchasing a computer, as is shown in Incidents 8.1 and 8.2. Not only has the cost of the computer come down so that it is affordable for the small business, but there is now an abundance of software programs in use that are written especially for small businesses and aboriginal needs. Incident 8.3 profiles such a system.

INCIDENT 8.1
Computer Keeps Track of Nickels and Dimes

Bill Wright, owner-manager of Georgia Straight Collision Ltd. of Courtenay, British Columbia, barely broke even, despite revenues of $730,000. He says the problem was simply an inability to keep track of the company's spending. Says Wright: "We were moving too fast to keep track of the nickels and dimes, which quickly amounted to what we should have made in profit."

Wright decided to computerize the business so that sales and expense information, which had been slipping through the cracks, could be kept and analysed. He selected a package called the Automotive Repair Management System (ARM), specifically designed for collision shops by 3M Canada Ltd., paying $12,000 for the software and $6,000 for the PC on which to run it. The system keeps track of inventory and the productivity of employees, and handles all paper work from purchase and work orders to the final customer bill.

If Wright had a reasonable handle on the business in 1984, he now has percentages down cold. The flat rates determined by the Insurance Corporation of British Columbia are stored right in the system, as are material and labour costs. Instead of relying on an annual analysis from his accountant, Wright can make most of his critical ratios appear with a couple of keystrokes.

Now approaching $1 million in revenue for 1985, with a 12% net profit margin, Georgia Straight boasts a second location and an additional line of business.

SOURCE: Randall Litchfield, *Small Business*, April 1986, p. 18.

INCIDENT 8.2
Northern Retailer Uses Computer to Manage its Inventory

In 1987, Ian Sutherland, a Winnipeg-born chartered accountant, led a group of investors in a $180-million buy-out of a division of Hudson Bay's northern retail outlets. He renamed the company North West Co. The company is now the dominant retailer in Canada's north and the largest private employer of native people in the country. The company no longer drops into northern communities as it once did, but must bargain the terms of its continued presence. For example, in December, 1992 it opened a store in Sandy Lake First Nation. The $1.5 million store is a joint venture with profits shared between the retailer and the band.

One of North West's first goals when taking over the chain was to upgrade the 17th century style inventory and distribution system. Paper invoices used to take weeks, sometimes months, to complete. Today, when a store manager in Nanisivik on Baffin Island determines how many VCRs, snowshoes or video games he needs, he punches a hand-held computer that registers the order at North West's 360,000 square-foot distribution centre in Winnipeg. A shipment schedule is drawn up instantaneously.

SOURCE: David Roberts, "41 below but getting warmer," *Globe and Mail*, February 1, 1994, p. B24.

INCIDENT 8.3
Software Tailored to Aboriginal Needs

Percy Darnaby knows the importance of providing a product that meets the customer's needs. Percy, a member of the Eel Ground First Nation in New Brunswick, is president of Abenaki Associates, a company that specializes in providing computer-based services and training to Aboriginal clients. A federally incorporated company, Abenaki Associates has offices in Hobbema, Alberta and in Ottawa.

Abenaki Housing Inventory Management Systems is one of the company's brainchilds and has been selected as the winner in the Process and Management category of Canada Mortgage and Housing Corporation's (CMHC) 1994 Housing Awards.

Having worked with First Nations Housing as a federal government employee, Percy knew first hand how crucial the need is for accurate information about housing on reserves. Keeping tabs on the condition of housing under their management has often meant a mammoth undertaking for First Nations. Now, however, with Abenaki's extremely easy-to-use software program, First Nation communities can produce accurate and up-to-date assessments of their housing situation with just a few touches to the computer keyboard. The beauty of the Abenaki Housing Inventory Management System is that it both reports and analyzes. The system not only provides an effective means to gather complete information on all housing units, but also produces analytic reports that can help communities plan future approaches to funding requirements.

Since the software was first introduced into the market in the spring of 1993, approximately 100 First Nations, tribal councils and housing agencies have purchased the program.

Abenaki Associates pays close attention to what its customers want. The company maintains a database of comments and suggestions made by clients at training sessions, and through follow-ups with customers. This continued consultation with Aboriginal users contributed to the company receiving the CMHC award and is key to their success.

SOURCE: "Software manages housing easily," *Windspeaker*, Canada's National Aboriginal News Publication, February 1995, p. 25.

Computer systems can manage several types of information requirements for a small business. Some of the more common operations normally used are the following:

- *Word processing*: This is a simplified and efficient method for any written correspondence.
- *General ledger*: Complete bookkeeping/accounting system of all business transactions.
- *Database files*: Storing, monitoring, and retrieving information on inventory, personnel, customers, and suppliers.
- *Payroll*: Simplified payroll systems including cheque writing.
- *Financial planning*: Spreadsheet packages to prepare actual and projected financial statements.
- *Capital investment decisions*: These decisions are made easier through the use of programs that calculate interest costs, payback, and present values.

In all of these functions the computer can allow for increased speed and accuracy of maintaining records, improved service to customers, improved and more timely information to managers, and reduced operating costs. Figure 8.8 reviews the specific application and strengths of computers. Note that the selection of software is the most important aspect of the computer decision. Software that will carry out the operations the small business requires should be selected first, followed by the hardware on which the software will run. This ensures that the hardware is powerful enough to handle the demands placed on the computer.

Despite the benefits, purchasing a computer does not automatically solve an owner-manager's financial problems. Many small businesses have purchased a computer only to find that

FIGURE 8.8 Some Benefits of Using a Small Business Computer

Applications	Reduce Labour Expense	Shorten Billing Cycle	Carry Less Inventory	Increase Sales	Control Costs	Manage Cash	Plan and Control Growth
Accounts payable	X				X	X	X
Accounts receivable	X	X	X	X		X	X
Business modelling				X	X	X	X
General ledger	X			X	X		X
Inventory control	X	X	X	X	X	X	X
Order entry	X	X	X	X		X	X
Payroll	X				X		X
Word processing	X			X			

SOURCE: Data General Corporation, *The Insider's Guide to Small Business Computers* (Westboro, Mass: Data General Corporation 1980), p. 8.

it was the wrong decision. It is important that the small business owner fully understand the potential pitfalls of computer ownership as well as the benefits. Some of the potential disadvantages include the following:

■ Cost

Although microcomputer costs are coming down, an adequate total system for most small businesses could still cost over $3,000.

■ Support and Servicing

For those small businesses located in remote communities it may be difficult and cost prohibitive to receive adequate support, training, and servicing for a computer system should there be problems.

■ Adequate Infrastructure

Having the proper infrastructure is important to operating a computer. For example, to function effectively and with minimal problems computers require a relatively constant and consistent supply of power. This may not always be available. Power failures and surges can cause a computer to malfunction.

■ Obsolescence

The computer industry is changing rapidly. This is resulting in very short life cycles for most computers. Often, by the time a computer is purchased and operating, new improved versions hit the market.

■ Employee Resistance

Employees within an organization, especially in communities where sophisticated technology is rare, may resist the introduction of a computer. The owner may need to involve such employees in the decision and purchase process in order to help dispel their resistance.

■ Capabilities

Many types of computers are available with different capabilities and characteristics. Some computers cannot do what the small business owner requires them to do. Thorough investigation of the business's needs and computer capabilities is required to avoid this situation. Business owners should purchase a computer with future growth and expansion in mind, recognizing the possible need to be able to add to existing capacity.

■ Set-Up Time

Installing a computer system, educating and training those who will use it, and eliminating the bugs will take time. It is recommended that the system previously used by the small business be continued for a short period of time in case such a problem arises.

■ Failure to Compensate for Poor Bookkeeping

Some small businesses purchase a computer hoping that it will clean up their bookkeeping systems. However, a computer will not help a bookkeeping system that is sloppy and inaccurate. After all, the same information that is being entered on a manual basis must be entered into the computer. A common rule of thumb used in the computer purchase decision is that if the information generated by a manual system is accurate but takes a long time to prepare and retrieve, then a computer may be of great assistance.

As the preceding discussion shows, the decision to purchase a computer is not one to be made haphazardly. It should be approached systematically and with thorough investigation.

A checklist for use in making a computer purchase decision is presented on page 304 of the Checklists and Examples section.

MANAGEMENT OF FINANCIAL INFORMATION FOR PLANNING ————

The first part of this chapter has dealt with the fundamental aspects of collecting and maintaining the financial information within the business. This information is of minimal value, however, unless it is used to monitor, evaluate, and control current operations as well as plan for the future. James Buchkowsky, writing in *Aboriginal Business*, sees three reasons why goal-setting can help with financial planning: motivation, guidance, and performance evaluation.[2] Buchkowsky suggests seven steps toward setting financial goals:

1. **Nature of the Financial Goal**
   Define your goals as specifically as possible They can be dollar amounts such as sales or a percentage return.
2. **Time Period**
   Set a time limit for your business to reach a goal. Goals that have no deadline tend to be forgotten.
3. **Quantified Goal**
   Develop three scenarios for your business. Develop one that is optimistic; when everything falls into place just right. Try to estimate the probability of it occurring. Next develop one that is pessimistic; when everything goes wrong. Again estimate the probability of it occurring. Do this same analysis for the most typical case. If possible, use experience as a guide. Now, blend these three scenarios together to form a quantified, realistic, and challenging goal.
4. **Key Business Functions**
   Determine which key business functions will help you achieve your goals i.e. marketing, production, etc.
5. **Key Personal Actions**
   Define what actions and tasks are necessary to achieve the goals. Possible actions include making decisions, purchasing, and communication.
6. **Reward for Business**
   Specific and tangible rewards should be offered for reaching a goal. For maximum effect, specify the goal and the potential reward at the same time.
7. **Reward for Self**
   Reward yourself for achieving your goals.[3]

Short-Term Financial Planning

Short-term financial planning consists of preparing an estimated future financial result of operations of the business. This kind of plan is generally referred to as a **budget** and was described in Chapter 3 in the preparation of the feasibility analysis. Although budgets can provide many benefits to an organization, relatively few small businesses prepare or work

---

2   James Buchkowsky, "Financial Goal-Tending: Seven Steps for Setting Financial Goals," *Aboriginal Business*, July/August 1994, 8.
3   *Ibid.*

with budgets. Using a budget, however, can be a very valuable financial tool within a business for the following reasons:

■ Clarification of Objectives

A budget forces an organization to anticipate future operations and set goals and procedures to accomplish them.

■ Coordination

The budgeting process draws together employees and/or departments and brings them into the planning process to input into the budget information relevant to their responsibilities.

■ Evaluation and Control

A budget allows the manager to quickly determine discrepancies that may require investigation. This is often called **variance analysis**. It also allows comparison of planned (budgeted) amounts with actual results, which can lead to improved effectiveness in the long term. Figure 8.9 shows how a budget might be established and used. After the comparison of budgeted (planned) and actual results, attempts can be made to explain the reasons for the differences. Consequently, changes might be made to correct the differences or refine the budgeting process.

Long-Term Financial Planning

Three types of long-term financial planning decisions can affect the small business: decisions regarding capital investment, capacity, and expansion.

The Capital Investment Decision   Most long-term planning will include the question of future capital purchases. This may involve the acquisition of land, buildings, equipment, or even another business. The small business owner needs to have a simple but accurate way of financially determining if the decision will be sound. Some of the more commonly used methods of estimating future return for capital investments are illustrated below.

■ Rate-of-Return Method

This method estimates the annual rate of return of the new investment. After this value has been determined it can be compared to alternative investments. Figure 8.10 shows how a rate of return for a capital asset is determined.

■ Present Value Method

This method employs the time value of money in looking at future cash inflows and outflows. Future inflows and outflows of cash are discounted because of the fact that cash held today is worth more than cash received or paid in the future. Present value rates are collected from present value tables which most accounting and finance texts provide. The rate required to equalize discounted outflows (for purchase of the assets) and discounted inflows (income from the assets) represents the discounted rate of return of the asset.

■ Payback Method

This method (which is similar to the rate of return method), estimates the number of years required for the capital investment to pay for itself. Figure 8.11 illustrates how the payback method might be used.

The Capacity Decision   Another important financial planning decision which the small business, especially the small manufacturer, must make is the size and extent of operations. Financial management techniques related to capacity help to answer such questions as how

FIGURE 8.9

Small Business Corporation
Income statement
(for the Year Ended December 31, 1995)

	Budgeted	Actual	Difference	Explanation
Net Sales	$197,000	$180,000	$17,000	
Cost of Good Sold	123,000	120,000	3,000	Material costs increase
Gross Margin on Sales	74,000	60,000	14,000	
Operating Expenses				
Selling Expenses:				
Advertising	1,200	1,200	0	
Sales salaries	18,300	18,300	0	
Total Selling Expenses	19,500	19,500	0	
General Expenses:				
Depreciation — store equipment	2,000	4,000	2,000	Additional equipment purchased
Depreciation — building	2,000	3,000	0	
Insurance	675	1,200	525	Premium increase
General salaries	7,200	7,200	0	
Miscellaneous general	425	600	175	
Total General Expenses	13,000	16,000	2,700	
Total Operating Expenses	32,800	35,500	2,700	
Net Operating Margin	41,200	24,500	16,700	
Other Expenses:				
Interest	2,750	3,200	450	Rate increase
Net Income before Income taxes	38,450	21,300	17,150	
Income taxes	14,450	7,455	6,995	Marginal rate decrease
Net Income	$ 24,000	$ 13,845	$10,155	

many units should be produced and how large the plant should be. A useful technique to help answer these questions is break-even analysis.

The **break-even point** is the point at which the level of output (in units or dollars) is equal to fixed and variable costs. By applying break-even analysis, the small business owner can determine the minimum level of operations required to financially break even. The use of break-even analysis could form an important part of the feasibility analysis which was discussed in Chapter 3.

FIGURE 8.10 Rate of Return Method

Steps	*Example*
1. Calculate total cost of investment.	$50,000
2. Estimated depreciable life of investment.	5 years
3. Calculate average value of investment over life. Beginning value ($50,000) plus end value (0) divided by 2 equals average value.	$50,000 ÷ 2 = 2.5 years
4. Estimate average annual profit over depreciable life (net of depreciation).	$10,000
5. Average profit divided by average investment.	$10,000 ÷ $25,000 = 40%

A reasonable rate of return on a capital investment is between two and three times the prime rate of interest. Using this criteria, the 40% rate of return in this example represents an attractive investment.

FIGURE 8.11 Payback Method

Steps	*Example*
1. Calculate total cost of investment.	$50,000
2. Estimate depreciable life of investment.	5 years
3. Calculate annual depreciation charge.	$10,000
4. Estimate average annual profit over depreciable life.	$10,000
5. Cost of investment divided by cash inflow (profit + depreciation).	$\dfrac{\$50,000}{(\$10,000 + \$10,000)} = 2.5$ years

The payback period for the capital investment would be 2.5 years. As this is considerably less than the depreciable life of the asset, it appears to be an attractive investment.

The formula for break-even analysis is as follows:

$$BEP = \frac{\text{Fixed costs}}{\text{Contribution per unit}} = BEP \text{ in units}$$

or

$$BEP = \frac{\text{Fixed costs}}{\text{Contribution as percent of sales}} = BEP \text{ in dollars}$$

where

Fixed Costs = Costs that will not vary as production increases (e.g., costs of plant, equipment, and some overhead expenses)

Contribution per unit = Selling price – Variable costs

The Expansion Decision   Break-even analysis can also be used to help the owner-manager decide whether to expand the scope of operations. The same formulas can be used, but only on an incremental basis as follows.

■ The Effect of Fixed Cost Adjustments

$$\text{BEP} = \frac{\text{Additional fixed costs}}{\text{Contribution per unit}} = \begin{array}{l}\text{Additional unit volume needed}\\ \text{to cover additional fixed costs}\end{array}$$

$$\text{BEP} = \frac{\text{Additional fixed costs}}{\text{Contribution as percent of sales}} = \begin{array}{l}\text{Additional sales volume needed}\\ \text{to cover additional fixed costs}\end{array}$$

■ The Effect of Variable Cost Adjustments

Another use of incremental break-even analysis is to measure the effects of changes in the components of the formula, such as variable costs. The following example illustrates this calculation:

$$\text{BEP} = \frac{\text{Fixed costs}}{\text{New contribution/unit}} - \frac{\text{Fixed costs}}{\text{Old contribution/unit}}$$

$$= \begin{array}{c}\text{Additional unit volume needed to cover}\\ \text{additional variable costs}\end{array}$$

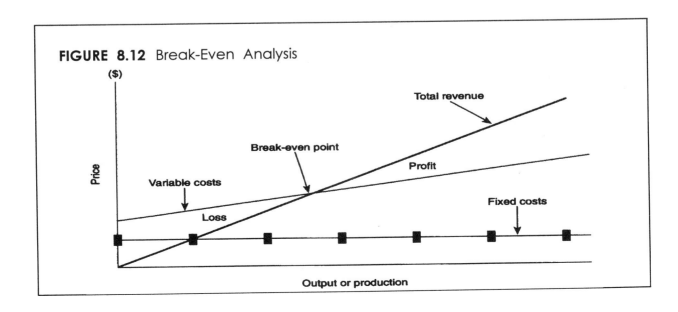

FIGURE 8.12 Break-Even Analysis

$$BEP = \frac{\text{Fixed costs}}{\substack{\text{New contribution as} \\ \text{percent of sales}}} - \frac{\text{Fixed costs}}{\substack{\text{Old contribution as} \\ \text{percent of sales}}}$$

$$= \substack{\text{Additional sales volume (in dollars) needed} \\ \text{to cover additional variable costs}}$$

EVALUATION OF FINANCIAL PERFORMANCE

Quantitative evaluation of the performance of a business is an essential management task. Because they lack a financial background, many small business owners rely on their accountants to look after the financial end of the business. An accountant may be essential for preparing year-end financial statements, but few small businesses can afford continual financial management advice from this source and many small businesses do not have access to such services. For these reasons, the small business owner is well advised to acquire a basic working knowledge of some of the key financial evaluation components of the business. This can enable the owner to monitor and control operations throughout the year, not just at the year-end.

Several measures can also be used to evaluate the results found in the financial statements. Some of the more common techniques are described next.

Management of Current Financial Position

One critical problem many small businesses face is a shortage of cash to finance operations. Some small businesses find it hard to understand that as their businesses become successful and grow, this tends to cause a strain on operating funds. Equally hard for many to understand is the situation in which the income statement shows a profit, but the cash position of the business has deteriorated.

The reason these situations occur is that most small businesses do not operate on a cash basis of accounting. (Some service businesses, farmers, and fishermen use cash basis accounting methods, however). The system used is called an **accrual-based** accounting system. With an accrual system a transaction does not need to involve a cash transfer for it to be recorded. For example, a sale of merchandise is recorded as revenue for income statement purposes whether it is paid for in cash or purchased on credit. Likewise many non-cash transactions may affect the income statement, whereas some cash transactions may not.

The above discussion illustrates the need to closely monitor the cash position of the business. As we saw, this is difficult to do by examining only the income statement. The balance sheet and cash flow statements are essential components of monitoring the cash position.

If the cash position of the business needs to be improved, an effective way to do so is to reduce the length of time from payment for inventory to receipt of payment for the inventory once it is sold. This cycle has three essential components:

1. Time taken to pay accounts payable.
2. Time taken to sell inventory.
3. Time taken to receive payment for inventory.

Figure 8.13 illustrates how to use these components in reducing this cycle for a hypothetical business.

FIGURE 8.13

Small Business Co. Ltd.
Balance Sheet

Assets		Liabilities	
Accounts receivable	$100,000	Accounts payable	$ 40,000
Inventory	50,000	Bank loans	100,000
Fixed assets	140,000	Shareholders' equity	150,000
Total assets	$290,000	Total liabilities and shareholders' equity	$290,000

Small Business Co. Ltd.
Income Statement

Sales	$750,000
Cost of goods sold	500,000
Gross profit	250,000
Expenses	200,000
Net profit	$ 50,000

1. Time taken to pay accounts:

$$\frac{\text{Accounts payable}}{\text{Cost of goods sold}} \times 365 = \frac{\$40,000}{500,000} \times 365 = 29.2 \text{ days}$$

This means that, on average, it takes 29.2 days to pay for inventory purchased.

2. Time to sell inventory:

$$\frac{\text{Inventory}}{\text{Cost of goods sold}} \times 365 = \frac{\$50,000}{500,000} \times 365 = 36.5 \text{ days}$$

This means that, on average, it takes 36.5 days to sell the inventory.

3. Time to receive payment:

$$\frac{\text{Accounts receivable}}{\text{Sales}} \times 365 = \frac{\$100,000}{750,000} \times 365 = 48.67 \text{ days}$$

This means that, on average, it takes 48.67 days to receive payment for inventory sold. The business cycle for this company is:

$$-29.2 \text{ days} + 36.5 + 48.7 = 56 \text{ days}$$

To increase the cash position, suppose the business was able to increase the accounts payable and decrease the turnover and receivable day totals for each component by five days. The result of these actions is shown below.

1. *Time taken to pay accounts*: A five-day increase substituted in the formula would increase accounts payable from $40,000 to $46,849 with a resulting in-

Figure 8.13 continued...

crease in cash of $6,849 by using the above formula. This five-day increase might have been accomplished by obtaining extensions from suppliers or simply not paying accounts payable until absolutely required.

2. *Time to sell inventory*: A five-day decrease substituted in the formula would decrease inventory from $50,000 to $43,150 with a resulting increase in cash of $6,850. Such a decrease might be as a result of increased advertising, more careful purchasing, or greater incentive to salespeople.

3. *Time taken to receive payment*: A five-day decrease substituted in the formula would decrease accounts receivable from $100,000 to $89,589 with a resulting increase in cash of $10,411. Such a decrease might be accomplished by increasing the intensity of collection procedures and/or submitting charge card receipts more often. The total effect of these measures on the cash position of the company would be $6,849 + $6,850 + $10,411 = $24,110 increase. The owner-manager, of course, would have to balance this increase in cash against the costs of accomplishing the five-day increases or decreases.

SOURCE: Adapted from *Key Business Ratios, 1990*, Dun & Bradstreet Canada.

Evaluation of Financial Statements

Once the financial statements have been prepared, several relationships between various account totals can assist in evaluating the operations of the business. This evaluation of relationships is called **ratio analysis**. It can be used to compare financial performance of the business to other similar businesses or to previous results for the same business.

Reports of financial ratios for other businesses are prepared by industry associations, Statistics Canada, and Dun & Bradstreet. These reports are collected from many businesses across the country; thus, when using them it is important to use comparable businesses from the same industry.

Financial ratios help in isolating and analysing weaknesses within the business. Four categories of ratios are commonly used in evaluating a small business. Each will be discussed next; illustrations of these ratios for a small business appear on page 305 of the Checklists and Examples section.

Liquidity Ratios Liquidity ratios assess the business's ability to meet financial obligations in the current period. Two liquidity ratios are commonly used: the current ratio and the acid test or quick ratio. The calculation for these ratios are as follows:

$$\text{Current ratio} = \frac{\text{Current assets}}{\text{Current liabilities}}$$

This figure, expressed as a ratio, should be higher than 1:1 and usually between 1:1 and 2:1.

$$\text{Acid test or quick ratio} = \frac{\text{Current assets} - \text{Inventories}}{\text{Current liabilities}}$$

The quick ratio is more suitable for businesses that have a high level of inventories. A ratio of 1:1 is considered to be healthy.

If the liquidity ratios are lower than they should be, the business may have difficulty meeting obligations within the year and will have a hard time raising further debt capital.

Productivity Ratios   Productivity ratios measure efficiency of internal management operations. They include the inventory turnover ratio and the collection period ratio.

The calculation of the inventory turnover ratio is as follows:

$$\text{Inventory turnover} = \frac{\text{Cost of goods sold}}{\text{Average inventory at average cost}}$$

or

$$\text{Inventory turnover} = \frac{\text{Sales}}{\text{Average inventory at retail price}}$$

Inventory turnover reveals the number of times in a year that the inventory is turned over (sold). Average turnover rates vary considerably by industry but usually should not be lower than two to three times. If the inventory turnover is too low, it may reflect poor inventory buying, whether in terms of being overstocked or buying low-demand inventory.

The collection period is calculated as follows:

$$\text{Collection period} = \frac{\text{Accounts receivable}}{\text{Daily credit sales}}$$

This ratio reflects the average number of days taken for purchasers to pay their accounts to the business. Normal collection periods are in the 20 to 40 day range. If the collection period is too long, it may mean that the credit-granting policy is too loose, the administration of billing is too slow, or the collection of accounts is too lax.

Profitability Ratios   Profitability ratios measure the effectiveness of operations in generating a profit. There are four ratios in this category. The first ratio is gross margin.

$$\text{Gross margin} = \text{Gross sales} - \text{Cost of goods sold}$$

This figure, usually expressed as a percentage of gross sales, can be used for comparisons. Gross margin for an individual product is calculated by subtracting cost from selling price and is commonly called **mark-up**. Average gross margins usually range from 20 to 50%. If gross margins are lower than they should be, the cause may be poor buying, failure to emphasize high-margin items, theft or spoilage, or price levels that are not current.

The profit on sales ratio measures profit as a percentage of gross sales:

$$\text{Profit on sales} = \frac{\text{Net profit (before tax)}}{\text{Gross sales}}$$

Typically the average percentages fall within 1 to 5%. A lower than average profit-to-sales percentage can reflect a problem either in pricing or with expenses. Pre-tax profits are normally used, as the tax rates may vary by province, industry or may not be applicable at all. In addition, reporting agencies publishing industry standards may use pre-tax profits as a comparison.

The third profitability ratio is the expense ratio:

$$\text{Expense ratio} = \frac{\text{Expense item}}{\text{Gross sales}}$$

Many specific expenses on the income statement may be expressed as a percentage of gross sales. These figures can then be compared to similar businesses.

The return on investment ratio reflects the profitability of the owner's investment:

$$\text{Return on investment} = \frac{\text{Net profit (before tax)}}{\text{Owner's equity}}$$

This ratio may be compared not only with those of other similar businesses but also with other alternative investments. If compared to the bank rate of interest, it is important to remember that there is risk associated with the business. Thus, the return on investment should be higher than the bank rate to compensate for this.

Debt Ratio   Finally, the debt-to-equity ratio measures the solvency of the business or the firm's ability to meet long-term debt payments.

$$\text{Debt to equity} = \frac{\text{Debt}}{\text{Owners' equity}}$$

Acceptable debt ratios vary, but generally speaking it should not be greater than 4:1. A lender normally will not provide further financing to a firm with a higher ratio.

CREDIT AND THE SMALL BUSINESS

A major decision that an owner/manager must make is whether or not to grant credit. The owner may feel a strong obligation to grant credit to friends and family, particularly in small communities. Although there are many benefits to granting credit there are also many potential problems (as outlined below). Many small businesses simply choose not to offer credit in order to avoid the personal and financial problems that it can create while others feel that a business cannot be operated effectively without it.

One aboriginal business which grants credit selectively to community members is the Stanley Mission gas bar and grocery store north of Lac La Ronge, Saskatchewan. The general manager of the store, Bob Walker, comments on the issue: "The people are so accustomed to operating and doing business with credit that it was soon apparent that we could not carry out an effective business without it." He adds of the community-owned store, "The board of directors, made up of community members, established a small line of credit for those they knew would be considered a good credit risk... Most of the people we have extended credit to keep up on their bills. They live here and they want to shop here so it's to their benefit if they keep a good record with their own store."[4]

Before deciding to grant credit an owner/manager should understand the fundamentals of credit granting and management to effectively control receivables and to minimize potential problems.

Advantages of Credit Use

The advantages of offering credit include the following:

- A credit program will undoubtedly result in increased sales and may be necessary to remain competitive.
- Credit customers are more likely to be loyal to the store or business than cash customers.
- Credit customers tend to be more concerned than cash customers with quality of service as opposed to price.
- The business can maintain a record of credit customer purchases and information about regular customers which can help in formulating future plans.
- In some instances, offering credit can assure small businesses that consumers will shop there and that payments will be made. For example, some aboriginal businesses have made arrangements with band administrations and their employees to allow employees to charge all purchases. At the end of the month the business bills the administration for goods and services provided to employees. The money due is taken directly from employees' pay cheques and sent to the business.
- Offering credit can be a service to the community. In communities where banking services do not exist the local store generally acts as an informal bank. In these situations, customers may have no alternative other than to leave their cheques with the business as a form of credit. There simply may not be enough cash available in the business to cash all community cheques.[5]

Disadvantages of Credit Use

A credit program can also create certain difficulties:

- There will generally be some bad debts when using a credit program. The number of bad debts depends in large measure on how strict the credit granting policy is and how closely accounts are monitored.
- It may be difficult to approach friends and family on outstanding debts.
- Slow payers cost the business in lost interest and capital that could be used for more productive investments. It is estimated that in many businesses losses as a result of slow payers are greater than losses from bad debts.
- There are increased bookkeeping, mailing, and collection expenses. Purchase records need to be kept, statements mailed, and accounts monitored and collected. As a result of this cost many small businesses do not offer their own credit program.

4   Vi Munroe, "Sharing Success in Stanley Mission," *Aboriginal Business*, June 1994, 20–21.
5   Jim Bell, "The Cashless Society," *Arctic Circle*, November/December, 1990, 47–49.

- It may be difficult to monitor and track bad debts in remote communities, communities where residents are on the land for a significant portion of the year, or communities with little formal infrastructure such as telephones and mailboxes.

Management of a Credit Program

If a small business owner decides to use a credit program some essential steps should be followed to ensure maximum effectiveness.

Determine Administrative Policies   This includes such things as application forms, credit limits for customers, the procedure to follow on overdue accounts, determining which records to keep, and deciding when to send statements. In communities where transfer payments account for a large percentage of income, the small business owner should establish the credit system to take into account the timing of these transfer payments. For example, bills should be received by customers near the very end or the very beginning of each month.

Set Criteria for Granting Credit   A small business may want to assess much the same areas that a lender would assess in considering a small business loan, although perhaps not in the same detail. Some of the essentials would be past credit history, other accounts held, monthly income, references, and bank used. A small business may be well advised to utilize the services of a credit bureau located in most cities or a commercial agency such as Dun & Bradstreet to evaluate customer credit-worthiness.

If commercial services are not available and customers do not have credit histories, owners may have to rely on their personal knowledge of community members.

Set Up a System to Monitor Accounts   Proper management of accounts receivable involves classifying accounts by the length of time they have been outstanding. This is called **ageing of accounts receivable**. Common categories used are under 30 days, 30 to 60 days, 60 to 90 days, and over 90 days. Experience shows that the longer an account is outstanding, the smaller the chance is of collecting it. Therefore, special attention should be paid to overdue accounts.

Establish a Procedure for Collection   A uniform procedure should be set up regarding the use of overdue notices, phone calls, credit supervision, legal action, and/or a collection agency. If these methods are not appropriate or are too costly, less extreme methods can be used. A common example of such a method is to post the name of those with overdue accounts in areas for all community members and patrons to see.

Lax supervision of accounts has led to many small business failures, so this is an area of credit management that cannot be ignored. An example of such a collection policy is shown in Figure 8.14. Another approach to credit and collection policy appears in the LRS Landscaping Plan, Section VI.5 (page 289 of the Checklists and Examples section).

One form of collection sometimes used by small businesses is a factoring company, which can also be a source of small business financing, as discussed in Chapter 6. This type of company purchases the accounts receivable for cash and attempts to collect them. In some cases, a factoring company handles the overall credit program for the business and even provides debt financing.

FIGURE 8.14 An Example of a Collection Policy

	30 days	*45 days*	*60 days*	*75 days*	*90 days*
Communication	Letter, telephone; copy of statement	Letter, telephone; copy of statement	Letter, telephone	Letter, telephone	Registered letter or lawyer's letter
Message	Overdue account, please remit	Pay in 15 days or deliveries will be stopped	Deliveries stopped; pay immediately	Pay in 15 days or account will be turned over for collection	Action is being taken
Action	None	None	Stop deliveries	None	Use collection agency or small claims court

SOURCE: "Small Business Review," pamphlet (Toronto: Thorne Riddell Chartered Accountants, April 1981), p. 5.

Use of Bank Credit Cards

Because of the high costs and risks involved in operating their own credit programs, many small businesses in cities and towns find that the most effective way to use credit is through bank credit cards such as Visa and Mastercard. The credit card companies assume the risk of bad debts and cover much of the administration costs of bookkeeping and issuing of statements in return for a fee — usually from 2 to 6% of sales, depending upon volume. Because of the high ownership of these cards by consumers today, most retail and service firms find their use essential to enhancing sales.

Some retailers are also experimenting with debit cards. Much like the bank credit card, the debit card automatically transfers the sale amount from the customer's account at the bank to the business's account. The obvious advantage of debit cards are the quick repayment and reduction of accounts receivable.

SUMMARY

1. The three-step process of the accounting cycle includes: (1) recording the transactions (journal), (2) classifying the transaction totals (ledger), and (3) summarizing the data (financial statements).

2. Three financial statements that can be valuable to the owner-manager of a small business are the balance sheet, the income statement, and the cash flow statement.

3. The common types of bookkeeping systems used by small business today are the one-book system, one-write system, manual multijournal system, bookkeeping machines, computer service bureaus, and small business computers.

4. Some of the more common operations computers can perform are word processing, general ledger, database files, payroll, financial planning, and capital investment decisions.

5. Some potential disadvantages of computer ownership are cost, lack of servicing and infrastructure in some areas, obsolescence, employee resistance, restricted capabilities, and set-up time.

6. Short-term financial planning consists of preparing an estimated future financial result, or a budget, and comparing it to actual results.

7. Three types of long-term financial planning decisions are capital investment decisions, capacity decisions, and expansion decisions.

8. Ratio analysis enables the small business owner to compare the financial performance of the company to those of other firms in the industry and to the company's own past performance.

9. Common financial ratios include liquidity ratios, productivity ratios, profitability ratios, and debt ratios.

10. The advantages of using credit are a likely increase in sales, increased store loyalty, improved information about purchases, and providing needed community service. The disadvantages of using credit are bad debts, difficulties in collection, slow payment, and administration costs.

11. Essential aspects of administering a credit program are defining administrative policies, setting up a system to monitor accounts, and setting up a procedure for collection.

CHAPTER PROBLEMS AND DISCUSSION QUESTIONS ——————————

1. For the following transactions, indicate which accounts are changed and by how much.
   a. Feb. 14, 1995 — Received $1,000 from Jenny Thunder on account.
   b. Feb. 14, 1995 — Purchased equipment for $1,500 (paid cash).
   c. Feb. 15, 1995 — Paid owner Bill Heavyhead $2,000 for January's salary.
   d. Feb. 18, 1995 — Paid telephone bill of $90.87.
   e. Feb. 19, 1995 — Bought ice cream on account, $395.00.

2. If the Board of Directors of Amarok Country Food Store (profiled at the beginning of the chapter) decided to purchase a computer, what should they do to ensure the purchase of the right computer for the business?

3. Calculate the rate of return for the following investment. The total cost of the investment is $250,000, the depreciable life of the investment is 10 years, and the annual profit (net of depreciation) is $30,000. What is the rate of return? What other considerations are there besides financial ones?

4. Assume that the annual depreciation charge for the investment in Problem 3 is $25,000; determine the payback period of the investment.

5. Determine the break-even point in dollars for an investment with fixed costs of $100,000 and an estimated contribution of 60%. How much revenue would it need to produce before you would invest?

6. a. From the balance sheet and income statement of Sam's Paint and Drywall (below) determine the following ratios:
   i. Current ratio
   ii. Inventory turnover
   iii. Profit to sales
   iv. Return on investment
   v. Debt to equity
   b. From Dun & Bradstreet's *Key Business Ratios* book on industry norms, evaluate each one of the ratios above.

Sam's Paint and Drywall
December 31, 1995
(in thousands of dollars)

Assets		Liabilities and Net Worth	
Cash	$ 12	Accounts payable	$ 15
Inventory	41	Notes payable — bank	4
Accounts receivable	18	Other	20
Total current assets	71	Total current liabilities	39
Fixed assets:		Long-term liabilities	39
Vehicles	10		
Equipment	15		
Building	22		
Land	23	Total net worth	63
Total fixed assets	70		
Total assets	$141	Total liabilities and net worth	$141

Income Statement
December 31, 1995
(in thousands of dollars)

Sales	$280
Less: cost of goods sold	186
Gross margin on sales	94
Less: operating expenses	81
Net profit	$ 13

7. Conduct an informal survey of three small businesses to find out which accounting system they use. Determine whether their systems are working effectively.
8. Why would a small gasoline retailer drop its credit program?
9. Doreen's Draperies has gross sales of $15,000 per month, half of which are on credit (paid within 30 days). Monthly expenses are as follows: wages $3,000, utilities and rent $2,000, advertising $300, miscellaneous $500. Inventory is purchased every 3 months and totals 30,000 for each order. Yearly expenses paid for in advance are insurance $1,000 and rent deposit $700. Prepare a 6 month cash flow statement for Doreen's Draperies. What advice would you give this business based on the cash flow statement?

SUGGESTED READINGS

Cornish, Clive G. *Basic Accounting for the Small Business: Simple Foolproof Techniques for Keeping Your Books and Staying Out of Trouble*. Vancouver: International Self-Counsel Press, 1992.

Cornish, Clive G. *Basic Accounting for the Small Business*. Vancouver, B.C. International Self-Counsel Press Ltd. 1985.

Fundamentals of Record Keeping and Finance for Small Business. New York: The Centre for Entrepreneurial Management, 1986.

C H A P T E R   9

Operations Management

——————————————————————————————— *Patricia Elemans*

CHAPTER OBJECTIVES

☐ To discuss management of the physical facilities of a small business.

☐ To explain the types of layouts used in small businesses.

☐ To illustrate methods of purchasing and controlling inventories in the small business.

☐ To consider the unique operations issues of aboriginal businesses such as home-based businesses and tourism ventures.

SMALL BUSINESS PROFILE
Vancouver Island
Nuu-chah-nulth Tribal Council Smokehouse

Danny Watts, Chairman of the Board of Nuu-chah-nulth Tribal Council Smokehouse Ltd., was facing a dilemma. There were a number of operational problems ongoing at the Smokehouse's plant in Port Alberni, B.C. It had become increasingly evident that the plant had not been designed to maximize the efficiency of the smoked salmon manufacturing process. Other developments, such as a projected growth in sales volume, exacerbated the situation.

N.T.C. Smokehouse produced smoked salmon of various varieties, sizes, and formats. The operation was originally designed as a small to mid-sized manufacturing/retail facility to take advantage of the excellent local supply of fresh Pacific salmon. Potential sales were intended to come from local sports fishermen who wanted their salmon processed, as well as from area consumers. It soon became apparent, however, that to be economically viable a larger volume of sales would be necessary. Accordingly, a successful effort to sell to potential customers in eastern Canada, the U.S., and Europe was launched, with sales increasing from $375,000 to $1.9 million per year in two years. The increase in sales was accompanied by an increase in average order size, which seriously strained the physical and financial resources of the company.

The plant was running at capacity, and over capacity during peak production periods in the pre-Christmas season. This was the result of several factors. The freezer (cold storage) and chill rooms were too small. An extra storage facility was being supplemented with a rented cold storage trailer, parked on the loading ramp, which was being used to store finished goods inventory. There was inadequate storage space within the plant for packaging material and other production supplies, such as boxes, plastic wrap and wood chips for the smoker. A portable "mini warehouse" was being rented for this purpose. The work space in the plant was inadequate during peak production periods when the work crew increased from six to twenty. In addition, crisscrossing product flows in the plant had reduced capacity and created an inefficient process. The plant's designers lacked previous experience with a smokehouse operation, and it had become evident that the original plant layout had not been done correctly.

The sales forecast projected a continued increase in total sales and in the size and number of large export orders. This presented a dilemma for Danny Watts.

SOURCE: "Nuu-chah-nulth Tribal Council Smokehouse Ltd.," The Centre for Aboriginal Management, Faculty of Management, The University of Lethbridge, 1992.

MANAGEMENT OF THE INTERNAL OPERATIONS

The area of operations management is one in which many small business owners have their greatest strength. They know how to produce a quality product or provide a quality service, and their prime interest often lies with this aspect of the business. As mentioned in earlier chapters, it is more typical for the entrepreneur to be weak in the areas of marketing and financial management than in managing the production process.

THE PRODUCTION PROCESS

The production process involves the conversion of inputs such as people, money, machines, resources, locations, and inventories into outputs — the products or services provided. An illustration of this application for manufacturing, wholesaling, retailing, and service businesses is shown in Figure 9.1. The owner-manager's task is to organize the production process of the business so that the outputs (product) can be produced efficiently. Incident 9.1 provides an illustration of how one First Nation is developing a service business out of the natural resources of the community. Incident 9.2 outlines how one entrepreneur processes deerskin to produce moccasins and dresses.

An important consideration for those wanting to establish a production process for traditional aboriginal products is the craftspeople and artisans that will be employed or contracted to produce the products. What makes many aboriginal products unique are the traditions and

FIGURE 9.1 Examples of Production Systems

Type of Business	Inputs	Process	Outputs
Apparel Manufacturer	Cloth, thread, buttons, beads, quills	Store→Cut→ Sew→Press→Ship	Dresses
Wholesaler	Large volume per order of each product	Store→Sort→ Package→Ship	Smaller volume of a product in each order
Retailer	A volume of each of many products to the ultimate customer	Store→Customer display→Package	Low volume of a few products to each customer
Laundry (service firm)	Dirty clothes	Sort→Wash→ Press→Store	Clean clothes

SOURCE: Adapted from Curtis E. Tate, Jr., Leon C. Megginson, Charles, R. Scott, Jr., and Lyle R. Trueblood, *Successful Small Business Management*, 3rd ed. (Georgetown, Ont.: Irwin-Dorsey of Canada, 1982), p. 244.

workmanship that go into them. Artisans and craftspeople may prefer to produce products using traditional methods, as is discussed in Incident 9.2, rather than adopt time-saving technology such as sewing machines. This may make it difficult to make commitments to buyers for delivery times and quantities to be supplied.[1]

INCIDENT 9.1
Majestic Location is Business Opportunity

Buffalo Point International Resort, established in 1976, has a mission statement to develop a world class tourism destination in harmony with the land, water and natural resources. It looks like they are on their way to accomplishing it.

Buffalo Point First Nation came into existence in 1873. Chief Ayashwash signed Treaty No. 3 on October 4 of that year at Northwest Angle. Located 240 km on Highway 12 from Winnipeg, on the southern shore of Lake of the Woods, this peninsula features Mother Nature at her best. It all starts with fishing for 20–30 pound pike in Buffalo Bay, the largest harbour in Manitoba. Buffalo Point also features boat trips, gorgeous sand beaches, hiking and biking through lush forested trails, rare flora and fauna, a wealth of berry picking, fishing derbies and historic landmarks.

Proposal 2000 is the finale to Buffalo Point's development plans. An 18-hole tournament play golf course is under construction, with a 40-unit hotel to complement it. The hotel will include a casino, theme suites, an indoor waterslide and swimming pool, a restaurant, lounge, convention facilities and the golf course clubhouse. There will also be outdoor recreation facilities and mooring for a cruise ship. Other attractions will include horse riding stables, a wildlife game farm and a native village. In the summer of 1994 they serviced more than 3,000 people, and in their 1995 fishing derby they had over 4,000 entries.

SOURCE: "Buffalo Point First Nation ambitions to become world-class tourist destination," *The First Perspective*, May 1995.

INCIDENT 9.2
Hand-tanned Moccasins Spell Business Success

Juliette Meness Ferguson grew up in the community of Kitigan Zibi Ansihinabeg (near Maniwaki, Quebec). Today, at age 65, Juliette has her own business making hand-tanned moccasins. She learned her skills from her mother, Theresa Meness. Juliette studied traditional designs in museums to create authentic Iroquois and Sioux-style moccasins, and Algonquin and Sioux-style dresses of deerskin.

Preparing deerskin for sewing is a lengthy process. Juliette collects the skins in the fall from hunters in the community, and then sprinkles them with bacon grease to start the softening process. Two days later, the skins are ready for the next step: soaking overnight in soapy water. She then wrings out the skins and starts the five to six-week stretching and rubbing stage. She then smokes the skins using old, rotten spruce wood as it produces a very pleasant odour and gives the skin a deep tan colour.

Following her mother's example, Juliette is passing her knowledge on to her children and grandchildren.

---

1   A. Saunders and J. Hannigan, "Canada's Northern Exporters," *Canadian Business Review*, Winter 1992, 32–35.

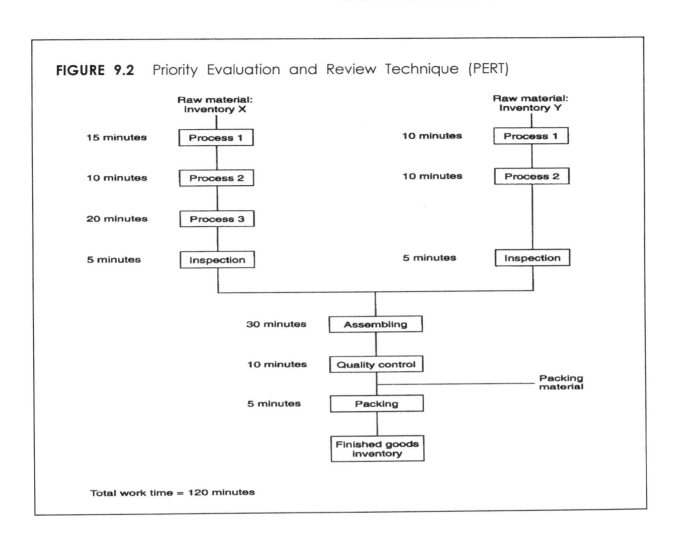

FIGURE 9.2   Priority Evaluation and Review Technique (PERT)

Juliette Meness Ferguson has succeeded in setting up a thriving small business based in her people's traditions, while at the same time keeping those traditions alive.

SOURCE: Adapted from Wendy MacIntyre, "Juliette Meness Ferguson: Hand-tanned Moccasins Spell Business Success," *Transition*, Vol. 7, No. 4, p. 4. Reproduced with the permission of the Minister of Supply and Services Canada, 1996.

The Program Evaluation and Review Technique and other flowchart systems have been developed to assist in organizing the production process. A simple example of such a system is shown below in Figure 9.2 for a manufacturing firm.

PHYSICAL FACILITIES

Planning the physical facilities was discussed briefly in Chapter 4 as part of the preparation of the feasibility analysis. Selection of the location for the business was also introduced in Chapter 4 as one of the steps in organizing a business.

While it is not necessary to review that information again, it is critical for the owner-manager to recognize that the physical facilities must be closely monitored and maintained to ensure that they are efficient, up-to-date and, in some instances, preserved. As was illustrated in Incident 9.1, facilities can include nature and natural resources. For businesses that rely on natural resources or the environment, for example fishing camps and tourist destinations, management of the environment is critical to long-term survival. Development of lands must be socially acceptable, environmentally sustainable, and economically feasible.[2]

Locations are never static, as populations, businesses, and traffic patterns shift, and government regulations change. This has caused many excellent locations to deteriorate over the years.

Some aspects of the physical facilities that should constantly be evaluated are illustrated in Figure 9.3. This table shows the differing levels of importance of physical facility characteristics depending upon the type of small business.

LAYOUT

Effective management of the interior layout of the business can greatly enhance productivity. And, as was shown in the Small Business Profile at the beginning of the chapter, can lead to problems if not planned properly. Small businesses use several types of layouts. The layout selected varies by industry and by the scope of operations. In determining layout it is advisable that a floor plan be drawn up to better utilize available space.

Layouts for Manufacturing Firms

Here are some of the key areas to consider in planning the interior and exterior of a manufacturing plant:

- Location of utility outlets for machines.
- Location of receiving and shipping areas for raw materials and finished goods.
- Safety aspects of the layout.
- Adequate lighting capability throughout.
- Provision for ease of maintenance and cleaning of the plant.
- Adequate storage space for raw and finished goods.
- Proper ventilation and air temperature controls.
- Adequate space for outdoor processing if necessary, e.g., tanning or drying.

Essentially three types of layouts are utilized by small manufacturing firms: product layout, process layout, and fixed-position layout.

Product Layout   This type of layout is suitable for the business that manufactures just one or only a few products and most closely resembles the production line of large factories. An example would be a company that specializes in the production of moccasins and mukluks. Although similar products, two separate production lines would be set up for each product. Each line would have its own leather and fur cutting, dying, beading, sewing, assembly and packaging functions. Figure 9.4 illustrates the floor plan of a typical product layout. The product layout generally allows for economy in both cost of and time required for production as each part of the manufacturing process is carried out in sequence.

---

2   Speech from Harry Bombay, "Developing Tourism at the Community Level," Proceedings from the Canadian National Aboriginal Tourism Association First National Symposium on Aboriginal Tourism, "The Quest Begins," Winnipeg, Feb. 23–25, 1995.

FIGURE 9.3   Business Building and Site-Rating Table

Factors	Retailing	Service	Manufacturing	Wholesaling
Building feature:				
Age	1	4	3	4
Space	1	3	1	4
Configuration	1	4	4	3
Appearance	1	3	3	4
Frontage	1	4	4	4
Access	1	2	1	1
Interior utilization:				
Floor space	2	3	1	1
Room dimensions	1	3	1	4
Ceiling heights	2	2	2	4
Stairways, elevators	3	3	1	1
Window space	1	3	4	4
Utility services	3	1	1	3
Improvement potential:				
Building exterior	1	3	4	4
Building interior	1	3	2	2
Site	1	2	3	4
Surrounding	2	2	3	4
Streets and walks	2	3	3	3
Access	1	3	2	1
Expansion	2	1	1	1
Site and environment:				
Street and service areas	1	2	2	3
Setback and frontage	1	3	4	4
Parking	1	2	2	3
Surrounding businesses	2	3	4	4
Area environment	2	3	4	4

KEY TO RATINGS:
1 = critical; 2 = very important; 3 = not ordinarily important; 4 = minimum importance

SOURCE: John B. Kline, Donald P. Stegall, Lawrence L. Steinmetz, *Managing the Small Business* (Homewood, Ill.: Richard D. Irwin, 1982).

Process Layout   The process layout is designed for factories that manufacture many different or custom-made products. In this layout similar processes are grouped together, and the product moves back and forth among these areas until completed. An example of such a factory is one that processes country meat for resale. Items such as seal, whale, caribou, goose, char, and cod are brought in, cleaned, cut, and packaged. While each item is different they all move through the same basic processes. The process layout is often more expensive and requires more management time to ensure efficiency. Figure 9.5 illustrates a process layout for a small factory.

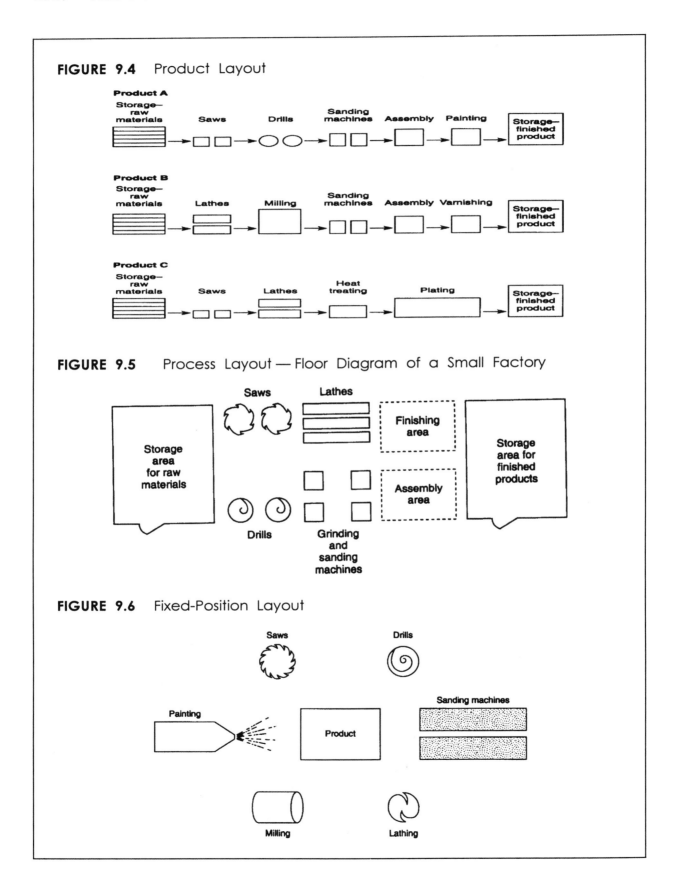

FIGURE 9.4 Product Layout

FIGURE 9.5 Process Layout — Floor Diagram of a Small Factory

FIGURE 9.6 Fixed-Position Layout

Fixed-Position Layout   In the fixed-position layout, the product remains in a fixed position throughout the manufacturing process; an example might be the carving of a large wooden canoe. The production processes move to the product. As one might expect, this type of layout is appropriate for very large and cumbersome products and is used infrequently by small businesses. Figure 9.6 illustrates the fixed-position layout.

Layouts for Retail Firms

As noted in Figure 9.3, interior layout is a very important factor in the success of a retail store. Sensitivity to cultural values, consumer needs, and shopping patterns is critical to the development of an effective layout. In planning the layout, the retailer will need to analyse several key areas.

The Allocation of Selling versus Nonselling Space   Experience in retailing shows that some areas of a retail store are more productive and draw more traffic than others. This phenomenon is illustrated in Figure 9.7. Generally, the space at the front and to the right is more productive space. Obviously, selling space should be planned for the most productive areas of the store. An additional consideration for businesses located in remote areas is the amount of space devoted to storage facilities. Because these businesses are not as likely to receive frequent shipments of products, (in some communities deliveries are made only one or two times per year), these business will be required to carry and store large amounts of inventory. Incident 9.3 is an example of a northern business that experiences this problem.

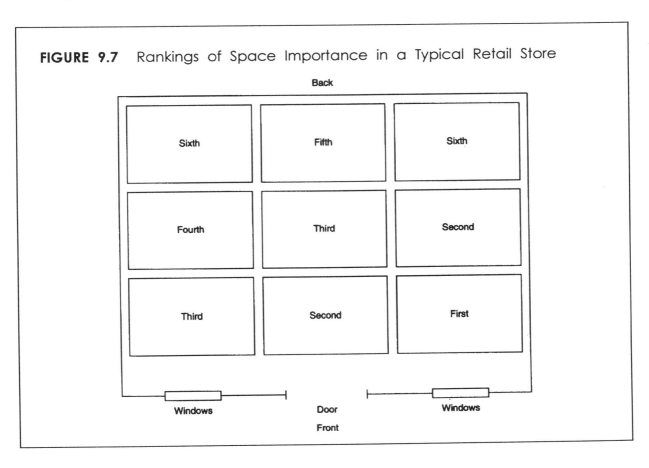

FIGURE 9.7   Rankings of Space Importance in a Typical Retail Store

INCIDENT 9.3 ——
41 Below but Getting Warmer

> North West Co. is the dominant retailer in Canada's north with 156 retail outlets in eight of the ten provinces and the territories. It is the largest private employer of native people in the country with a total of 3,700 employees across Canada and 470 in Alaska. It is also the largest Inuit art dealer in the world. Its 1992 revenues totalled $452-million with earnings of $15 million.
>
> What possible problems could a company this size and with such a captive market have? How to supply merchandise twice a week to isolated outposts. To supply its stores it relies on air, rail, ship, barge and a fleet of trucks that traverse thousands of kilometres over temporary winter roads. In 1992, for example, a winter road between Pickle Lake, Ont., and the Sandy Lake Nation was completed. This allowed supply trucks to make the six-hour trek. They deliver a one-year supply of fuel, sugar, flour and lard to warehouses in the isolated community. The rest of the year, it is only accessible by air.
>
> SOURCE: David Roberts, "41 below but getting warmer," *Globe and Mail*, February 1, 1994, p. B24.

Allocation of Space among Departments and/or Products   The same principle discussed above should be utilized in allocating space among departments and products, with the most profitable being placed in the high traffic areas if possible.

Classification of Merchandise   Chapter 7 discussed the classification of consumer goods — convenience, shopping, and specialty goods. Each merchandise classification may require a slightly different placement in the retail store, based on the purchase motives associated with that class of goods. For example, convenience items are often found close to heavier customer traffic flow. In an Arts and Crafts store, for example, small, impulse items such as beaded necklaces and earrings would be placed near the cash register. Shopping goods, such as moccasins, might be placed by competing brands, and specialty or demand items, such as art, in less accessible parts of the store.

Location of Displays and Products on the Shelf   The small retailer should acquire expertise in a number of display techniques. Placement of merchandise on the shelf or counter can lead to increased sales as certain areas are more productive than others. Merchandise placed at eye-level and at the end of aisles generally sells better.

Two types of layouts are used by retail stores: the grid layout and the free-flow layout.

■ Grid Layout

The grid layout is organized with customer convenience and retailer efficiency in mind. Grid layouts have traditionally been used in such stores as supermarkets and hardware stores. Figure 9.8 illustrates a grid layout.

■ Free-Flow Layout

Some types of merchandise are purchased in a more relaxed atmosphere where the customer spends more time browsing. For such merchandise, it is common to use the free-flow layout which is illustrated in Figure 9.9. This type of layout is suited for clothing, art, and many specialty types of merchandise.

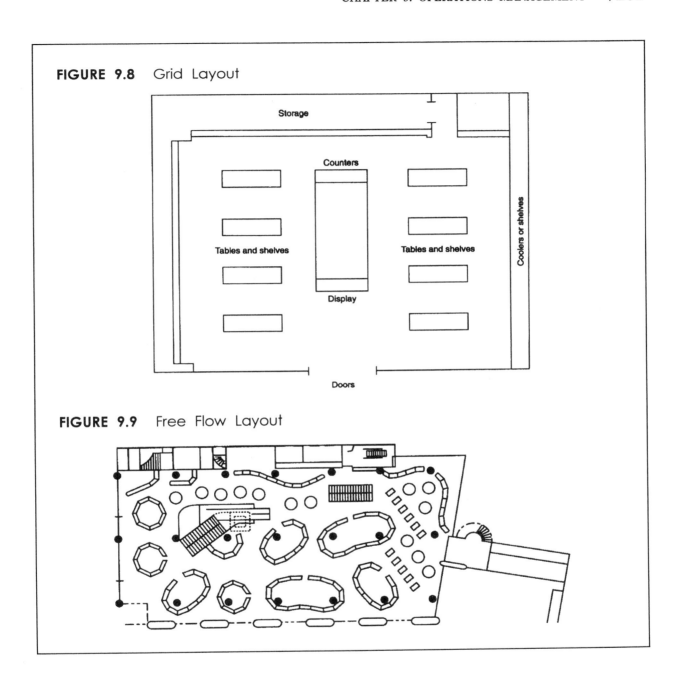

FIGURE 9.8 Grid Layout

FIGURE 9.9 Free Flow Layout

Many larger retail stores use combinations of the grid and free-flow layouts. Most small retailers, however, generally use one or the other.

Layouts for Service Firms

Because there is such a diversity in the operations of service firms, it is difficult to provide standard information on layouts. Some service firms, such as restaurants, more closely approximate the layouts of retail stores. Many of the principles discussed above for retailing would apply here. For those service firms that are more similar to manufacturing, such as repair firms, the principles of manufacturing layouts may be more appropriate.

Considerations in Establishing Tourism Facilities   There is continuing growth in the number of First Nations tourist operations, and this is the largest growth sector in the aboriginal economy. In 1993 there were approximately 1,300 native tourist operations, employing more than 50,000 native people in the industry.[3] This growth is due, in part, to increasing land claims settlements and access to an abundance of natural resources. Twenty percent of Canada's land mass is already controlled by aboriginal people and it is estimated that by the year 2000 they could control 30%, with land claim settlements totalling over $7 billion.[4]

Tourism operations can take many forms, for example, recreation facilities, nature trails, fishing and hunting expeditions, guiding, arts and crafts retailers, and cultural demonstrations. Each service operation has its own unique set of guidelines and operational considerations that must be addressed. There are, however, some common factors.

Most tourism operations will have an impact on the community in which they are centred, so it is important to carefully plan any developments. Plans must take into consideration the land, the community, and the culture.[5]

- What will the impact of the operation be on the land? Will water supplies be affected? Will there be an increase in pollution? Can the land support the expected number of tourists? Will there be conflicts with other land users in the area, such as traplines and logging groups?
- Does the community have the infrastructure to support the operation? Are there adequate roads? Water supply? Are there facilities to feed and shelter tourists if necessary? Does the community support the development? Have elders been consulted along with other community members who will be impacted by the project? Do they support and want the infrastructure that may be required to get the operations started? For example, if tourists will be brought into the community, will roads have to be constructed? Are the roads wanted by those living in the community?

  One of the difficulties for those considering developing tourism operations in northern communities is the lack of infrastructure. While there is vast potential for attractions such as adventure tours and "ecotourism," many of the people that can afford such trips, i.e., baby boomers, want first class facilities and services. These are amenities that are not developed in many northern communities.[6]
- Have cultural leaders been consulted on what can be shared and what needs to be protected? Are there certain ceremonies and lands that should not be open to tourists? Will the operations jeopardize traditions, beliefs, and the way of life? Are products and services being sold and not the culture and its people?

Home-based Businesses

Studies have shown that running a home-based business represents the fastest growing sector in the North American economy. It has been estimated that one million home-based businesses are operating in Canada[7] and by the year 2000, as many as 40% of Canadian

---

3   Ken Becker, "Native peoples are finding success in tourism," *Globe and Mail*, Wednesday, July 7, 1993, D3.
4   "New directions: federal support for Aboriginal business," *Aboriginal Business*, July/August 1994, 12–13.
5   "The stranger, the native and the land," Canadian National Aboriginal Tourism Association, Red Mango Pictures, 1994.
6   A. Saunders and J. Hannigan, "Canada's Northern Exporters," *Canadian Business Review*, Winter, 1992, 32–35.
7   Anne Crawford, "Quality of life comes first for entrepreneurs: study," *Calgary Herald*, April 25, 1994, D1.

workers will be working from home at least part-time[8]. The majority of all new businesses are started as home businesses, and they are more common in smaller and more remote communities. One of the biggest advantages of operating as a home-based business is lower operating costs. It can also be ideal for people who want to operate a business as well as care for family. Increased technological sophistication, such as computers and FAX machines, also makes it easier to run a business from one's home.

Chapter 4 briefly discussed some of the issues to consider when deciding to operate a home-based business. Additional operational considerations include:

- Are there any ordinances that restrict operating a business from a home?
- Is there proper insurance coverage? Homeowners' policies may not be valid if damage is caused by business operations. Some businesses may also require extra liability insurance.
- Can space be allocated between work and living areas? Working at home can be fatiguing in that there is no change in setting. Separating work and non-work space can provide some change.
- Will customers or suppliers be coming to the business? Is there space available to accommodate this? Is the business accessible?
- Is there adequate storage space for supplies and inventory? How will this space be allocated?
- Is there adequate lighting and is it effective? Will it cause shadows or glare that make it difficult to work?
- Is the power supply adequate to operate office or other types of equipment?
- Is there adequate ventilation for equipment (office or otherwise)?

PURCHASING AND CONTROLLING INVENTORIES

The cost of purchasing and holding inventories can be substantial. Because a small business generally has limited economic resources, it is critical that such a firm give inventory management a high priority. The following sections discuss areas about which the small business owner should be knowledgeable when purchasing and controlling inventories.

Sources of Supply

Chapter 7 discussed various aspects of the distribution channel from the seller's point of view. The same principles apply in this section but from the buyer's position. The owner-manager should know which suppliers are available. Purchases can usually be made directly from the manufacturer, from an agent of the manufacturer, from a wholesaler, or from a retailer. While there are considerable variations among industries, most small businesses purchase their inventories from wholesalers. Wholesalers generally carry a full line of products so the small retailer does not have to deal with many different suppliers. Additionally, many manufacturers do not have representatives in smaller and more remote communities, so retailers will not have much choice in suppliers and may have to utilize the services of wholesalers.

---

8   Anne Crawford, "At-home business booming," *Calgary Herald*, May 31, 1993, C1.

Many owner-managers import merchandise that uses sources of supply from other countries. In this case, many of the concepts discussed in Chapter 7 with respect to exporting may be applicable.

One question most small businesses face is whether to purchase from one supplier or many. In purchasing from only one supplier, the buyer is assured of consistent quality and will probably receive favourable treatment such as discounts and guaranteed supply in case of shortages. On the other hand, other suppliers may offer lower prices from time to time. The business may also spread risk by purchasing from many suppliers. The small business owner must weigh these pros and cons in making this decision. Incident 9.4 illustrates the possible tradeoffs when choosing suppliers.

INCIDENT 9.4
Standoff Supermarket

Daniel Weasel Moccasin, manager of the Standoff Supermarket in Standoff, Alberta had to decide if he should add another grocery wholesale firm to supply the supermarket.

Daniel expected three things from his suppliers: good service, competitive prices and reliable delivery. Service was partly a matter of the supplier carrying the goods he needed. Service also included attention from suppliers' sales personnel. They needed to inform him of special offers and provide information on product pricing. Reliable delivery was also essential, since a shortage of goods would result in lost sales.

Daniel also felt it was important to have control of the supplier relationship. He did not want to be dependent on the terms that an individual supplier might attempt to impose. To avoid this situation, he had found it useful to carry competing product lines and stocked both Pepsi and Coke, for example. His experience with bread suppliers confirmed his belief that two suppliers were better than one. Originally the Supermarket had dealt solely with McGavin's bakers. During one summer Daniel found he needed to fill a large order of bread on one day's notice. McGavin's was unable to provide the bread. Daniel called Weston's, and they delivered the required amount the next day. He was impressed with Weston's service and price, which was less than McGavin's charged. Shortly afterwards he informed McGavin's he would no longer need their bread. In their desire to retain some share of the business, McGavin's agreed to match Weston's price. As a result, Daniel carries both brands of bread at substantially lower prices than before.

Adding another supplier had several advantages. It would bring a wider product line to his customers, particularly in generic food items. The new supplier had more appealing packaging on their generic line. By buying from both suppliers Daniel would be informed of both firm's special offers and could choose the best deals. He also expected better service since both would be anxious to keep his business.

There were also several disadvantages. The new supplier demanded stricter payments, which Daniel felt was because they "seemed not to trust an Indian." Additionally, he would risk the Supermarket's relations with their current supplier. This was his biggest single supplier and he has maintained strong ties to them. Over the years salesmen from the original supplier had assisted him in learning about the retail grocery business and running a more efficient, computerized operation.

Daniel had to decide if the tradeoff was worth the risk.

SOURCE: "Standoff Supermarket," The Centre for Aboriginal Management, Faculty of Management, The University of Lethbridge, 1991.

Evaluating Suppliers

As was illustrated in Incident 9.3 certain criteria are generally used to evaluate suppliers in making the purchase decision. Following are some of the more common criteria.

Dependability   The owner-manager should evaluate how dependable the prospective supplier will likely be. Dependability will undoubtedly be more important for some companies and even for some types of products than others.

Cost   Obviously the cost of inventories will play a major role in supplier selection for the small firm.

Services Offered   Typical services that can be offered by the supplier are delivery, discounts, credit, promotion, and technical assistance. Delivery services can be a significant criteria for some businesses. Many suppliers will not deliver goods to businesses located in more remote communities and if they do they usually require large minimum orders that are not suitable or are too costly for many small businesses. In these instances it may be advantageous for several micro-entrepreneurs in a community to collectively negotiate with suppliers to increase their bargaining power.

It may also be advantageous to use the services of someone like Vincent McComber, whose company Northern Creek Enterprises operates a bulk distribution business that sells to centres located on native territories and owned by native people.[9] McComber, originally from Kahnawake, says that aboriginal communities pay too much for products, partly because of all the "middle men" involved in transactions. "By taking the buying power of the 1,600 aboriginal communities in this country, you can source goods very cheaply," according to McComber.[10]

Determining Order Quantities

Estimating the quantities of inventories to order will require several essential items of information.

Order Lead Time   The time taken to process the order at both shipping and destination points as well to transport the item(s) should be estimated. This is called **order lead time** and is illustrated by the distance between points B and C in Figure 9.10. Recently many businesses which require large stocks of inventory have instituted a Just-In-Time inventory policy. In this approach, the order is placed so that the inventory arrives "just-in-time" to be utilized in the production process. This system is appropriate for manufacturers that have computer capabilities, are confident in the dependability of suppliers and require large amounts of inventory. As was illustrated in Incident 9.3, for some businesses the order lead time may be from six months to one year because of inaccessibility and the mode(s) of transportation required to ship goods.

Sales or Production Estimate   The owner-manager will need to make a realistic projection of inventories to be sold or consumed in the manufacture of the finished product for the period. Methods of obtaining this type of information were discussed in Chapter 3. Such a rate of sale throughout the period is shown by the diagonal line A–C, in Figure 9.10.

---

9   Karen McCall, "Bulk buying keeps money home," *Windspeaker*, January 3–16, 1994, 8.
10   *Ibid.*

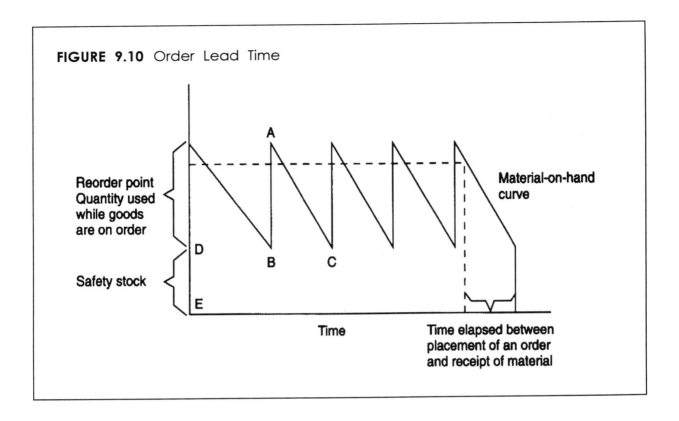

FIGURE 9.10 Order Lead Time

Minimum Inventory Levels Required   No business wants to run out of inventory, especially if the inventory consists of important items. It is therefore common to carry a minimum basic inventory for many items. This is often called **safety stock** and is shown as the distance between D and E in Figure 9.10. The size of safety stock usually depends on such factors as importance of the inventory, volatility of demand, and dependability of sources of supply.

Inventory Currently on Hand   The owner-manager should have an accurate estimate of inventories on hand. To monitor current inventory levels in a continuous manner, a perpetual inventory system can be used. Details of this type of system will be discussed later in this chapter. For many businesses, a perpetual system requires a computerized inventory system. As mentioned in Chapter 8, an increasing number of small businesses can now afford such systems. Once current inventory levels have been determined, the owner-manager can incorporate these amounts into various methods to determine order quantities.

Methods of Determining Order Quantities   Some of the more common methods used to determine order quantities follow.

■ Minimum Turnover Method

This method utilizes the inventory turnover formula (discussed in Chapter 8) for the business in determining amounts of inventory required. For example, if inventory turnover for the business is 4 (four times per year) and projected sales for the period are $200,000, then the required inventory is calculated as follows:

$$\frac{Sales}{Inventory} = Inventory\ turnover$$

$$\frac{\$200,000}{\text{Inventory}} = 4$$

$$\text{Inventory} = \frac{\$200,000}{4} = \$50,000$$

Hence, the required inventory for the period is $50,000.

■ Maximum and Minimum Method

Some small businesses set acceptable maximum and minimum limits on inventory levels. Whether inventory is measured in dollar amounts or number of units, reaching these limits indicates when it is time to order and specifies the amount to order. This method is utilized frequently by small businesses for merchandise of lower unit values.

■ Open to Buy Method

This method of calculating order quantities, used extensively in retailing, uses the following formula (the components were discussed earlier):

Open to buy =   Planned purchases – Merchandise on order – Merchandise on hand

where

Open to buy =   Inventories that can be purchased
Planned purchases =   Planned sales + Estimated reductions + Planned end of period stock – Beginning stock

■ Economic Order Quantity (EOQ)

This formula has been used infrequently in small business but may be helpful for important items or in manufacturing businesses. It allows for the calculation of the minimization of the ordering and storing costs of inventory. Generally speaking, if ordering costs are higher (more frequent orders), storage costs are lower (less inventory required). Through this formula, the owner-manager can arrive at the least cost combination of ordering and storage costs.

The EOQ formula for dollar amounts is as follows:

$$EOQ = \sqrt{\frac{2AB}{i}}$$

where

A = Annual or period demand in dollars
B = Costs of making an order, dollars
i = Inventory carrying costs (storage costs) expressed as a percentage of inventory value

If the economic order quantity is desired in units the formula is:

$$EOQ = \sqrt{\frac{2AB}{PI}}$$

where

PI = Unit price

Although this formula has proved unwieldy for many small businesses in the past, the increased accessibility of computers may allow more businesses to take advantage of the EOQ formula in the future.

■ A-B-C Analysis

This method of inventory management recognizes that some items of merchandise are more important to the business than others. The level of importance is influenced by such factors as higher sales, high unit value levels, higher profitability, or importance in the manufacture of the finished product.

With A-B-C analysis the most important inventory (A items) is watched more closely to ensure that they are managed efficiently. The B and C items, being less important, may require less detailed monitoring and control. Figure 9.11 gives an example of the A-B-C analysis.

Administration of the Buying Process   The owner-manager should be familiar with the mechanics of purchasing. Knowledge of the different kinds of discounts and purchase terms and conditions is essential, as are efficient receiving, checking, and marking of merchandise to minimize inventory costs and reduce shrinkage.

Inventory Control

As discussed earlier, efficient purchasing requires proper monitoring and control practices. Three essential aspects of inventory control are determining the unit of control, the method of valuing inventories, and the method of monitoring inventory levels.

Unit of Control   Most firms keep track of their inventories by dollar amounts. This is called **dollar inventory control**. Dollar inventory control is suitable for firms with large amounts of inventory at a relatively low per unit value.

FIGURE 9.11 A-B-C Analysis

	A Items	B Items	C Items
Percent of total inventory value	65%	25%	10%
Percent of total list of different stock items	20%	20%	60%
Inventory method used	Minimum turnover EOQ Maximum turnover	Minimum turnover	Eyeballing
Time Allocation	Time-consuming and precision needed	Less time-consuming estimates	Rough estimates only

Some businesses that have relatively small amounts of inventory keep track of inventories in numbers of units. This method is called **unit control.**

Valuation   Generally accepted accounting principles allow inventories to be valued at the lower of cost or market value. It is very important that an accurate valuation of inventory levels be calculated, because, as Figure 9.12 shows, inventory levels have a direct effect on the net income of the business at the end of the period.

Monitoring   There are essentially two methods of monitoring inventories. The first, periodic inventory, involves physically counting and recording the merchandise to determine inventory levels. Periodic inventory calculation is required at least once each year for income tax purposes. It is costly and time-consuming to carry out, however, so most businesses use this method no more frequently than required. For businesses located on reserves (where income taxes are not applicable) it is still recommended that a physical count of inventory be done once per year for control purposes. A physical count helps to determine if there are any discrepancies between what has been recorded and what actually exists. Differences can highlight problem areas such as loss, spoilage, and theft.

The second type of inventory monitoring, perpetual inventory, involves continuous recording of inventory increases and decreases as transactions occur. Historically this type of system was feasible only for a small business with low levels of high-unit-value inventory. Recently, however, microcomputer database management programs have made the perpetual inventory system a reality for many small businesses.

Security of Inventory   Preventing loss of inventory (shrinkage) is a major challenge for most small businesses. The business should develop a detailed procedure for ordering, receiving, marking, handling and monitoring all inventories. The system selected will vary depending on the type of business.

FIGURE 9.12 Valuation of Inventories

Sales – Cost of goods sold – Other expenses = Net Income

where

Cost of goods sold = Beginning inventory + Purchases – Ending inventory

Using the relationships in these formulas, one can see that if ending inventory is overstated, cost of goods sold will be understated by the same amount and net income overstated by that same amount. Therefore, a valuation error of $100 will translate into either an overstatement or an understatement of net income by $100.

SUMMARY

1. The production process involves the conversion of inputs such as people, money, resources, machines, and inventories into outputs — the products or services provided.

2. The physical facilities must be continually monitored, as the conditions that contribute to their effectiveness will not remain static.

3. The three types of layouts utilized by small manufacturing firms are the product layout, process layout, and fixed-position layout. The product layout is used when the business manufactures large numbers of just one or a few products. The process layout is designed for factories that manufacture smaller numbers of many different or custom-made products. The fixed-position layout is used for very large or cumbersome products.

4. In planning the interior layout of a retail store, the retailer needs to analyse the allocation of selling versus nonselling space, the allocation of space among departments and/or products, classification of the merchandise, and the location of displays and products on the shelf.

5. The two types of layouts used by retail stores are the grid layout and the free-flow layout. The grid layout, typically used in a supermarket, is organized with customer convenience and retail efficiency in mind. The free-flow layout has an atmosphere more relaxed and conducive to browsing. This type of layout is suited for art, clothing, and many specialty types of merchandise.

6. When establishing tourism operations the impact on the land, the community, and the culture must be considered.

7. When establishing a home-based business operational factors to consider include restrictive ordinances, insurance, space allocation, accessibility, power, lighting, and ventilation requirements.

8. It is important for the small business manager to be aware of the sources of supply, and the constraints which entrepreneurs in remote communities may face. One question most small businesses face is whether to purchase from one supplier or many. The owner-manager should understand the relative merits of using one versus many suppliers.

9. In estimating the quantities to order, the essential items of information required are the order lead time, the sales or production estimate, minimum inventory levels required, and the inventory currently on hand.

10. Some methods used to determine order quantities are the minimum turnover method, which uses inventory turnover calculations; the maximum and minimum methods, which indicate the time and amounts to order; the open-to-buy method used in retailing; the economic order quantity, which calculates the minimization of the ordering and storage costs of inventory; and A-B-C analysis, which prioritizes types of inventory.

11. Three essential aspects of inventory control are determining the unit of control, determining the method of valuing the inventories, and determining the method of monitoring inventory levels.

CHAPTER PROBLEMS AND DISCUSSION QUESTIONS

1. What kind of layout should be used for the following manufacturing firms?
   a. A fish processing company
   b. A manufacturer of traditional clothing
   c. Joe's garage

2. What kind of layout should be used for the following retail firms?

    a. A gift/art store

    b. An auto parts shop

    c. A small grocery store/gas bar

3. Answer the following questions regarding the location of the following food items in a grocery store.

    a. Where are the bread and milk located? Why?

    b. Where are the chocolate bars and candy located? Why?

    c. Where on the shelf are the top namebrand items located? Why?

    d. Where are the high-margin items positioned in the store and on the shelf? Why?

4. Visit a small retail store or manufacturing plant and evaluate the layout.

5. Frank Gull is opening a new video store, but he has not determined which VCR supplier to use. Frank has narrowed the choice to two sources. Supplier 1 is newly established and is selling the units for $260 apiece. Supplier 2 is a well-established firm and sells the units for $275 each, with a 7% discount on orders over 50. Evaluate each supplier from the information given. With this information, develop different scenarios in which Frank would choose supplier 1 or supplier 2.

6. Josephine Buffalo, owner of Buffalo Galleries, must determine how much inventory to purchase and in what amounts. For the upcoming year she has forecast $500,000 in sales. She has calculated that the average ordering cost is $50, and the average inventory holding cost is 5%. Her average inventory turnover is 3.4.

    a. Calculate the per-order quantities in dollars.

    b. Calculate the required inventory for the year.

    c. How many times during the year should Buffalo order?

7. Interview three businesses and determine which inventory ordering system they use and why.

8. Interview a small business owner to learn why he or she selected a particular supplier. Find out what criteria were important to the owner in making the choice.

9. In establishing a Guiding Operation what factors related to layout and location would you have to consider?

SUGGESTED READINGS

Berman, Barry, and Joel R. Evans. *Retail Management: A Strategic Approach*. New York: Macmillan, 1991.

Hodgetts, Richard M. *Effective Small Business Management*. New York: Harbrace, 1986.

Notzke, Claudia. "Aboriginal Tourism Development in the Western Arctic." Research Report. University of Lethbridge. November 1995.

Siropolis, Nicholas C. *Small Business Management* Boston: Houghton Mifflin, 1990.

Total Quality Control: A Winning Strategy for Small Business. Montreal: Federal Business Development Bank, 1990.

C H A P T E R   1 0

Personnel Management

Patricia Elemans

CHAPTER OBJECTIVES

☐   To explain the importance of personnel management to the small business.

☐   To illustrate the methods of planning for hiring and training of employees.

☐   To discuss skill areas the owner-manager can strengthen to improve personnel management practices within the small aboriginal organization.

☐   To consider the characteristics and problems of operating a family business.

☐   To describe the procedures of administering a small business payroll.

☐   To review the legal requirements relating to personnel for the small business.

☐   To discuss some of the unique personnel issues in managing aboriginal enterprises.

SMALL BUSINESS PROFILE
Doreen Janvier
DMJ Enterprises

For Doreen Janvier, a 29-year-old former resident of the Janvier reserve, south of Fort McMurray, Alberta, the desire to go into business stemmed directly from concerns about the health of her community.

The vision for DMJ Enterprises started to materialize in 1990 when Janvier's sister invited her to a weekend alcohol abuse workshop in her home community. It was there that she started thinking about ways to help members of her community find self-esteem and a brighter future. Her vision was to start a business that would employ the people she wanted to help and give them brighter futures. "I know I wouldn't feel good about myself if I wasn't working," says Janvier, who runs a company supplying workers for the oilsands giant Syncrude's heavy equipment wash bays and for AlPac's tree planting operations.

"Those people who are working will have self-esteem. They'll feel good about themselves. That's where all this started."

Despite Janvier's lack of business experience and unusual starting point for a business idea, DMJ Enterprises was launched in 1990 with 14 employees, all from Janvier. The company now boasts an all-native, 25 member staff and is in the process of hiring 40 new employees for AlPac. All employees are hired out of Janvier and Fort McMurray.

SOURCE: Doreen Janvier and "Altruism motivates Fort McMurray entrepreneur," *Windspeaker*, Canada's National Aboriginal News Publication, January 4, 1993, p. 9.

PERSONNEL MANAGEMENT AND SMALL BUSINESS

Management in an organization has often been defined as getting things done through other people. The small business owner is in fact a personnel manager, even though his or her main strength or interest may lie in the production, financial, or marketing aspects of the business.

Often the owner is reluctant to learn personnel administration fundamentals because he or she feels that these principles apply only to larger organizations. The result may be personnel problems such as frequent turnover of staff, absence of motivation and initiative, lack of harmony among employees, high absenteeism, frequent grievances, and high overall employee costs. The incidence of these problems appears to be high in small businesses. A study of 77 successful entrepreneurs indicated that owner-managers' number one headache was personnel.[1] The same study pointed out that the demands of running the business usually prevented owner-managers from paying as much attention to their employees as they should.

As the business grows, the owner-manager's workload generally expands. Because there is a limit to what one person can do, the business may suffer if the owner fails to hire new employees and delegate responsibilities to them.

The reputation of a business in the community can be affected by employees' satisfaction with their jobs, and in a small community a business's personnel policies may come under particular scrutiny. The level of employee satisfaction can be enhanced or lowered by the owner-manager's use of personnel management principles. This is especially true in the retail and service industries. Motivated and competent personnel is one characteristic of business that the competition may find difficult to duplicate.

Given all these factors, it is important that the entrepreneur have some knowledge of personnel administration principles to be able to sustain the success of the business. This chapter covers planning for personnel, hiring, and ongoing personnel management in the small business.

PLANNING FOR PERSONNEL

There are four personnel planning steps for an organization listed below. This section discusses each of these steps briefly.

1. Determine Personnel Requirements
2. Set Organizational Structure
3. Prepare Job Descriptions
4. Develop Personnel Policies

Determine Personnel Requirements   The first step in planning for personnel is to determine the number of jobs or tasks to be done, the level of expertise required, and the number of people needed to perform these tasks. This process may already have been carried out as part of the feasibility analysis discussed in Chapter 3. Incident 10.1 illustrates what can happen to a company if the personnel requirements are not planned effectively.

---

1   Psychological Motivations Inc., "Dobbs Ferry, New York," *Venture*, May 1986, 26.

INCIDENT 10.1
Poor Planning of Personnel Requirements Can Lead to Trouble

Eskasoni Chief Alison Bernard wants to give the bankrupt Gold Eagle fisheries a second chance. Since buying the former Nova Aqua fish farm in a receivership sale in 1991, Bernard's band in Cape Breton, Nova Scotia, has invested $3 million in the fishery. A series of bad management strategies forced the fishery to file for bankruptcy, leaving the band with a total $5 million debt.

"We are convinced that if it is run properly it could be viable," Bernard said. "There were too many people working there to start with. They had between 80 and 100 people working where only 40 to 50 people are needed," he said. With high salary costs and money owing to feed suppliers, the farm had to declare bankruptcy while in the midst of a restructuring plan.

SOURCE: "Bankrupt fishery has swimming chance," *Windspeaker*, Canada's National Aboriginal News Publication, April 26, 1993, p. 7.

Set Organizational Structure   The second step in personnel planning is to integrate the tasks and employees so that the owner can visualize how the different parts of the plan will work together. This formalized plan is commonly called an **organizational chart**. In the very small (two- or three-person) business the organizational chart may simply be a division of responsibilities, as in Figure 10.1. In a larger business, the organizational chart shows the lines of responsibility for each member of the organization. An organizational chart for a small retail grocery store appears in Figure 10.2.

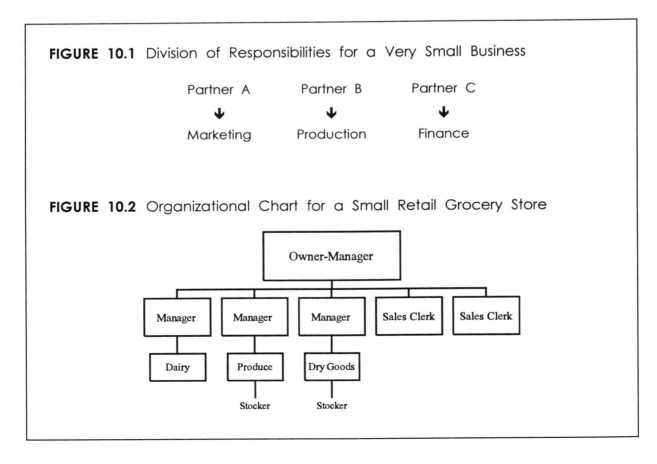

FIGURE 10.1 Division of Responsibilities for a Very Small Business

Partner A	Partner B	Partner C
↓	↓	↓
Marketing	Production	Finance

FIGURE 10.2 Organizational Chart for a Small Retail Grocery Store

Each business may possess unique characteristics that dictate how to set-up the organization chart. Some of the more common approaches are to organize by (1) function performed, such as sales, purchasing, or promotion; (2) type of merchandise or department, as in Figure 10.2; or (3) geographic territory.

In setting up the organizational structure, some rules of thumb have been found to contribute to a successful operation:

- Each employee should report to only one supervisor. This arrangement is called **unity of control** or **command**.
- Similar functions should be grouped together if possible.
- There is a limit to an individual's span of control. **Span of control** is the number of people who can be directly supervised by one person. The proper span of control varies according to the combined characteristics of the manager, the co-workers, and the job.

Prepare Job Descriptions   The third step in personnel planning is the preparation of job descriptions and specifications. Before hiring employees, a detailed listing of the job or task duties (job descriptions) must be made. The job description explains briefly what is to be done, how it is to be done, and why it is done. This information goes into the job specification — a statement of the skills, abilities, physical characteristics, and education required to perform the job. Part of the job description may be included in the policy manual. Figure 10.3 illustrates a job description and specifications for an employee of a small business.

FIGURE 10.3 Job Description and Specifications — Sales Manager, Art Gallery

Job duties (description):

Reports to the general manager.
Directly responsible for floor sales personnel.
Travels to trade shows, meets with distributors and artists to select
    merchandise.
Sets store displays and store promotions.
Prices merchandise.
Suggests markdowns on slow items.
Controls inventory.
Authorizes merchandise returns.
Maintains good customer relations at all times.
Takes care of written correspondence concerning sales.
Does any other task relevant to his job, as requested by the general
    manager.

Personal requirements (specifications):

High school diploma or equivalent.
At least two years' experience in a similar job. Preferably some background
    in art.
Initiative; "instinct" for sales; convincing manner; aptitude for managing
    people.
Self-disciplined; good appearance; willing to work overtime.

Develop Personnel Policies   The fourth step in personnel planning is to develop personnel policies formally. Including these policies in an employee policy manual can help prevent many personnel problems. For the very small business, this may simply be a list of do's and don'ts. An example of this is in Lyle Scout's small business plan beginning on page 277 of the Checklists and Examples section. A larger business may provide a booklet to each new employee.

Policy manuals are used infrequently in small business, and if in English may be of limited use in aboriginal communities where not everyone reads and writes that language; (Incident 10.4 profiles a company that writes their policy manual in both Cree and English). The resulting uncertainty that can occur may create serious employee difficulties. The common areas to be covered in a policy manual are described below. Minimum standards for many of these areas are set by government labour departments in each province and the territories.

- **Job descriptions** clearly outline the duties, responsibilities, and reporting lines for employees, as mentioned previously.
- **Working conditions** include such things as hours of work, coffee breaks, and other expectations of management.
- **Holiday and leaves** outline statutory holidays, paid vacations, and procedures for taking a leave of absence for personal reasons or to pursue seasonal activities such as hunting or fishing.
- **Remuneration and pay** consist of a listing of details of the payroll such as date of payment, time periods included, and reviews of pay levels.
- **Employee benefits** provided by the firm such as bonuses, profit sharing, and employee discounts should be clearly stated.
- **Grievance procedures** consist of a description of the procedure employees are to follow if they have a concern or grievance within the organization.

THE HIRING PROCESS

Once the personnel plan has been developed, the next step is to review various sources for potential employees and make the selection.

Sources of Employees

A discussion of the potential sources of employees for small business follows.

Recruitment from within the Community   As is illustrated in Incident 10.2 recruiting employees from within the community can have many benefits for both the business and the community as a whole.

INCIDENT 10.2
Store Benefits Entire Community

> More than 475 people gathered to celebrate the opening of Sonias Grocery Mayfair, in Hobbema, Alberta. The 1,080 square metre facility is a complete store, with a full complement of meat, dairy and produce items, as well as a bakery and deli.
>
> As project coordinator, Melvin Nepoose, with Samson Management, has seen the store grow from a concept on the drawing board to an enterprise employing 27 band members.

"This is owned by our own people and the location is ideal — right at the centre of Hobbema," said Nepoose. "We're retaining money in the community. The convenience is the major benefit because we don't have to go to town to buy our supplies and the store offers competitive prices."

"But another big thing is that we've created training and employment opportunities," he added.

Community spirit has been so supportive of the local endeavour, when uniformed staff filed out to watch the opening speeches, they received a spontaneous round of applause from the audience.

Sonias Grocery is part of the Samson Band's new 2,160 square metre mall and gas bar. The combined gas bar and convenience store employ about nine people.

SOURCE: "Convenience and competitive prices make new supermarket shoo-in success," *Windspeaker*, Canada's National Aboriginal News Publication, July 18–31, 1994, p. R2.

Recruitment from within the Business   For most organizations, recruiting from within is the most common course if current employees have the qualifications. Hiring an outsider to perform a supervisory job instead of someone within the organization usually has a negative and disruptive effect on the business.

Other Businesses   To reduce training costs, employees from competing firms or similar industries can be hired. Such employees generally will have some background in the industry and/or business that can be easily transferred. The recruiter, however, will have to be careful to avoid a negative reaction from the competition, particularly in smaller markets and communities.

Employee Referrals   Present employees may be asked to recommend acquaintances to fill available jobs. This method has the advantage of giving some prior knowledge of the individual's background, but it may have negative effects if the new employee proves unsatisfactory.

Advertising   Some small businesses advertise for employees in local newspapers, community centres or band offices. The cost of this type of advertising is minimal.

Employment Agencies   Private and government employment agencies are also sources of employees. Canada Manpower offices have lists of employees looking for work, and the Canadian Council of Aboriginal Business offers a referral service for corporations looking for aboriginal candidates. The Council's "Aboriginal Choice Placement Services" aims at "helping employers find top-notch aboriginal employees in an extensive range of professions" and has a database of more than 1,500 candidates.[2]

Educational Institutions   Some small businesses that require employees with technical expertise use universities or colleges as sources. These sources can be helpful in manufacturing and some service businesses and are increasingly being used in retailing.

Hiring Family and Friends   Often there is pressure on owner-managers to hire family and/or friends. This can be particularly strong in smaller communities. Although hiring these people can offer significant benefits, there is also the potential for problems if they do not

---

2   "Native placement agency set up," *Vancouver Sun*, September 15, 1993, D3.

perform satisfactorily. It can be very difficult to reprimand or, if necessary, fire a friend or family member. To minimize potential problems the manager can try to ensure that the best candidate for a job is hired based on the criteria in the job description, and from the information on the application form and in the interview. It is also important that job duties, policies, and procedures are set out clearly so that all employees are familiar with them and performance can be assessed relative to these guidelines.

Contracting   Many businesses today are using term contracts to obtain needed services instead of hiring individuals as part of the business's permanent team. An individual or individuals may be hired for a specified period of time to complete a particular project. The advantage to the employer is that he or she can hire individuals with expertise in a specific area for a short period of time. The advantage to the contracted individuals is that they know when a job will start and end and have clearly specified responsibilities.

The Screening Process

Once potential employees have been identified from one or more of the above sources, the owner-manager faces the task of selection. Several screening devices can be used to aid in the selection of employees; a competition between work teams such as that used by Mishtuk Corporation (Small Business Profile, Chapter 12) is also a possibility.

Application Form   Many small businesses do not use an application form. If new employees are hired infrequently, such a formal document may be unnecessary. However, the application form can be a valuable screening tool and a time-saver for the owner. An application form need not be lengthy to be helpful, as Figure 10.4 illustrates. The owner-manager must be careful not to violate provisions of the Human Rights Act in preparing the application form.

The Employment Interview   Although the application form may screen out several potential employees, an interview is usually required to make the final decision. The employment interview is particularly important for jobs requiring interpersonal contact, as it allows the interviewer to judge appearance, poise, and communication ability. A helpful tool in interviewing is an interview guide, which focuses the discussion and provides a constant base of information with which to compare applicants. Figure 10.5 illustrates an interview guide. Again, human rights legislation precludes the use of certain questions during an employment interview and the owner-manager should be aware of such legislation.

Checking References   The third screening device is the checking of references. Most application forms require the applicant to list both personal and business references; business references are valuable because they provide information regarding the individual's past work record, and personal references may provide additional information about his or her character and reliability.

Checks made by telephone or in person with business references are preferred to written responses, as the writer of a letter of reference may have little or no idea of the requirements of the job. Also, past employers are sometimes reluctant to write uncomplimentary letters of reference. Specific questions should be asked about the candidate's performance, as well as whether the employer would consider rehiring the person.

FIGURE 10.4 Application for Employment of a Small Business

Name_____	First Name_____
Address (Home)_____	Tel_____
Address (Work)_____	Tel_____
S.I.N. _____	
Languages Spoken _____	Written_____

Secondary Education

Years_____   School_____   City_____   Diploma_____

Postsecondary Education

Years_____   School_____   City_____   Diploma_____

Work Experience
(begin with most recent)

From:_____   To_____   Employer_____

Title_____   Duties_____

Salary_____   _____

Reason for leaving_____   _____

Work Experience

From:_____   To_____   Employer_____

Title_____   Duties_____

Salary_____   _____

Reason for leaving_____   _____

Other Information

References:

	Name	Address	Title
1.			
2.			
3.			

Signature_____   Date_____

Notification of the Hiring Decision

Once the hiring decision has been made, an offer of employment should be made to the successful applicant. Where possible, this notification should be in writing, with a clear indication of the terms and conditions associated with the job. All unsuccessful applicants should also be notified. Failure to provide this courtesy can have a detrimental effect on the reputation of the business.

FIGURE 10.5 Interview Guide for a Small Business

Job: _____

Applicant: _____

Interviewed by: _____

Date: _____

Check off or comment on the items you observed or found out. Do not guess at the other items; leave them blank. Not all items are relevant for every job. Your answer should be "yes" or "no," "we cannot hire," "maybe," or "not certain." You can qualify your yes or no under "Comments."

	Yes/No	Comments

Evaluate the applicant on the following:

1. Work experience necessary to perform the job satisfactorily.
2. Skills with machines, tools, equipment.
3. Skills with job procedures.
4. Experience with special projects.
5. Formal education.
6. Trade or vocational education.
7. On-the-job training.
8. Will need training for this job.
9. Ability to get along with supervisor.
10. Ability to get along with fellow employees.
11. Ability to work as a member of a team or work group.
12. Applicant's comments about former supervisor.
13. Applicant's plans.
14. Attendance record.
15. Punctuality.
16. Safety record.
17. Health.
18. Physical strength to perform job.
19. Good work habits.
20. Supervisory experience.
21. Prefers to work alone.
22. Primarily interested in money.
23. Prefers non-financial rewards.
24. Likes the work.
25. Blames others.
26. Flexible; can adjust to changes.
27. Has a part-time job.
28. Off-the-job activities.

PERSONNEL MANAGEMENT ——————————————————————

Once the employee has been hired, the owner-manager's responsibility is to see that the employee is properly trained, satisfied with the working conditions, and — probably most importantly — motivated to work hard and show initiative. Most small businesses are not in a position to hire a professional personnel manager to ensure that these desirable conditions exist. However, the owner-manager can foster these conditions by using the concepts of personnel management discussed next.

The Introduction Period

The first few months on the job are crucial to the employee's overall satisfaction and length of stay with the business.

The First Week   One of the most frequently mentioned characteristics of good working conditions is that the owner-managers make the employees feel that they are part of the organization.[3] Much can be done in the first week to communicate to the employee that he or she is a valued member of the business. The new employee should be introduced to co-workers, shown the locations of employee facilities, informed of any company regulations, and encouraged to ask for additional information if needed. If a new employee is coming in as an outsider to a community, the owner-manager may want to introduce the employee to community activities such as sporting events, barbecues, and other gatherings. In any event, the manager should talk with employees frequently during the introductory period and not simply leave them alone to read the company policy manual.

Many employers find it helpful to set some short-term goals which the employee can work toward within the first week or two. These goals can be discussed at the conclusion of the agreed-upon time. This approach communicates not only that the employer is interested in the employee but also that the business is results and goal-oriented.

The Probationary Period

Most employers find it advantageous to use a probationary period of three to six months for new employees. The probationary period allows the employer to further assess a new employee's suitability for the job. At the conclusion of a satisfactory probation period the employee becomes permanent and may be entitled to a pay increase and other benefits of a permanent employee.

Training

The purpose of a training program is to increase productivity. As illustrated in Incident 10.3, training programs can be used not only to teach employees about the requirements of the job, but also to introduce them to the culture of their customers and fellow employees. A successful training program can reduce employee turnover, decrease the need for supervision, and increase employee morale. Properly trained employees acquire a sense of worth, dignity,

3   Robert Levering, Milton Moscowitz, and Michael Katz, *The 100 Best Companies to Work for in America, 1984* (Scarborough, N.Y.: New American Library, 1985).

and competence, as well as increasing their skill level. Businesses use many forms of employee training. Some of the more common are discussed next.

INCIDENT 10.3
41 Below but Getting Warmer

It's 41 degrees below and the parking lot beside Sandy Lake's newest building is filling up with snowmobiles. Dozens of people, their kids in tow in wooden toboggans, have made the morning expedition from their homes in this sprawling Cree-Ojibway community. Their destination: the village's new "general store."

The store in Sandy Lake, a remote community 600 kilometres northeast of Winnipeg, represents a new direction for the North's dominant retailer, North West Co. It offers not just basic fare — groceries, hardware and apparel — but also fast food, a deli, a bakery, banking and a post office.

The new store signals an emerging partnership between the Winnipeg company and its customers — the native Indians and Inuit. North West knows it is here as a guest of the Sandy Lake First Nation. Instead of simply dropping into the community it must bargain the terms of its continued presence. The $1.5 million store is a joint venture, with profits shared between retailer and band. Mr. Sawanas, the chief at Sandy Lake, likes the idea of his community taking a stake in its major retailer. The band took out a $1.5 million mortgage to finance the building, which is being leased back to the company. The band also receives a percentage of gross sales, amounting to $80,000 the first year. The mortgage should be repaid in 12 years but the lease is for 50 years — a deal that spells more profit for the band.

Earl Boon, North West's vice-president of corporate development, indicated that at least 27 of the 37 outlets, to be built or renovated by North West in the next two years will be what the company calls its Tomorrow Stores — that is, joint ventures with individual Indian bands, such as in Sandy Lake. The company is the dominant retailer in Canada's north with 156 retail outlets. It also has 21 stores in Alaska.

Native people make up 90% of North West's customers — and a lot of its employees. Thirty-five of the staff of 38 in the Sandy Lake store are aboriginal. They have been trained on-site by the local manager with the help of a customized training manual (available in English or Cree). About 1,700 of 3,700 employees on North West Co.'s $40-million payroll are natives, making it the largest private employer of aboriginal people in Canada.

Len Flett, a Cree from Cumberland House, Sask., who is North West's store development director, says management realized the need to become more culturally sensitive. "We have to be careful as a company that our goals don't clash with those of our customers — the native people of the North. We have to make sure our goals are compatible with the bands." Inside North West Co., non-native staff receive cross-cultural training rather than being dropped into the North unprepared.

SOURCE: David Roberts, "41 below but getting warmer," *Globe and Mail*, February 1, 1994, p. B24.

On-the-Job Training   This is the least structured and most frequently used method by small business. It is perhaps the best method of training for routine and repetitive types of work. The business may assign another employee to work closely with the new one in a buddy system or apprenticeship.

Formal Classroom Training   Large organizations utilize many varieties of formal class-room training, but only a few have been used by small businesses. One such system is a cooperative type of program with an educational institution. This allows an employee to attend classroom instruction and training on a part-time basis. In Canada, the government provides financial assistance for employee training programs. These programs will be discussed later in this chapter. Some businesses hold seminars periodically in which they bring experts from various fields to the business.

The Owner-Manager as Personnel Manager

Time Management   One critical aspect of successful people management is efficiently managing one's own time. Time management is often difficult to apply in the small business, particularly for people who work at home and also have family obligations. So many operating crises and interruptions take place in the normal course of a day that the owner-manager may feel the advice of time management literature is impossible to employ. The segmented, deadline-based time orientation of the mainstream business world may also clash with an aboriginal community's traditional way of organizing and scheduling activities. However, some basic time management concepts can be used successfully in the small aboriginal business. Some of the more important concepts are discussed below.

■ Reexamine and Clarify Priorities

Priority planning may be long or short term. Long-term planning involves setting objectives for the owner and business to meet over a period of months or years. Long-term objectives, discussed in Chapters 3 and 4 as part of the establishment of the business, provide direction for the firm.

Short-term priority planning deals with the utilization of time on a daily or weekly basis. It involves prioritizing tasks and working on those that are the most important.

■ Analyse Present Time-Consuming Activities

This step requires keeping a diary of the daily activities of the owner-manager. Most people find the results of this step surprising. Often they find they spend time on less important items at the expense of those that are more important.

■ Implement Time Management Principles

The owner-manager may be able to eliminate common time-consuming activities by implementing the following practices:

- Avoid procrastinating on difficult but important decisions.
- Use the most productive time of the day for the more important decisions or analyses. For some people this may be early in the day, and for others it may be later. Many have found it beneficial to schedule routine or unenjoyable tasks in their least productive time.
- Read only relevant information. Stop reading and start searching. Use travel, waiting, or otherwise unoccupied times for reading.
- Use letters less and the telephone and electronic mail more. If possible, only handle letters once in a given period of time.
- Operate with a minimum of meetings. Make sure meetings are results-oriented.
- Delegate as much work as possible, recognizing that the owner-manager is still ultimately responsible for the decision or action.

Motivation and Loyalty

Successful managers are able to generate strong loyalty from their employees. They also succeed in motivating employees to work hard and be creative. They have open communication lines that provide a comfortable work environment. It is no accident, however, that these conditions exist in some companies and not in others. Some owner-managers understand and are able to apply critical principles of human relations management. Two important principles are working conditions and employee needs.

Working Conditions   Employee satisfaction with general working conditions has been shown to reduce employee turnover. Although these factors may have minimal motivational impact, they are important in developing loyalty to an organization.[4] Working conditions that may have this effect are the physical characteristics of the workplace, the level of supervision, relationships with co-workers, and company policies.

Employee Needs   Understanding employee needs and providing the means whereby an employee can fulfill them can be a powerful motivational tool for the owner-manager.[5] Needs may include adequate pay, feeling a valued part of the organization, the possibility for advancement, extra responsibility or authority, recognition by management, esteem by peers, a sense of achievement, job challenges and, for some, the ability to maintain aspects of their traditional lifestyle. Incident 10.4 highlights how some of these needs can be met when operating a seasonal business. One real challenge for the owner-manager is to encourage employees to have the same interest and enthusiasm for the business that he or she has.

INCIDENT 10.4
Northern Emak Outfitting

> On a remote coastal lake on the east side of Victoria Island, which lies 200 miles north of the Arctic Circle, brothers George and Gary Angohiotok operate a fishing camp. They are majority partners in a company called Northern Emak Outfitting Ltd; "emak" is the Inuit word for "waters." The camp offers fishermen from around the world the opportunity to catch arctic char in Char Lake. Bill Tait, who operates Adventure North Expeditions Ltd. in Yellowknife, and Jerome Knapp, a well-known journalist, are the other partners in Northern Emak.
>
> Each season Northern Emak employs about seven guides and a cook. It plays an active role in providing training and employment opportunities for people in the community. Both George and Gary are certified guides. Although they do not require certification from their guides, they do encourage them to become certified to improve their employability. Through their work with the business, the young guides are able to develop invaluable "people" skills.
>
> In the summer months George operates the fishing camp, and in the winter months he is a guide for big game hunters. He still does repair work on Yamaha equipment on a part-time basis, and he hunts on the land and provides meat for his family. George appreciates the blend of a traditional lifestyle with a modern way of earning a living. Bill also sees this mix of opportunities as crucial: "The answer to making tourism

4   Frederick Herzberg, *Motivation to Work* (New York: John Wiley & Sons, 1959).
5   Abraham H. Maslow, *Motivation and Personality* (New York: Harper & Row, 1970).

work here is not to offer jobs as chambermaids. Opportunities should combine more naturally with the cultural interests of the people."

SOURCE: Wanda Wuttunee, "Northern Emak Outfitting Inc.," The Centre for Aboriginal Management, Faculty of Management, The University of Lethbridge, 1991.

FAMILY BUSINESSES

Many small businesses are owned and operated as family enterprises. Estimates of the extent of ownership within a single family indicate that 70–90% of all businesses in Canada are family owned and operated.[6] Despite the predominance of family businesses in Canadian society, relatively few survive into the second and third generations. Personnel administration in family businesses can be even more complex than in non-family businesses. If the unique considerations in operating a family business are not recognized and planned for, they can cause considerable difficulties.

Potential Problems in a Family Business   Several problems may surface in the family-owned business. Recognition of these potential difficulties is essential for the owner-manger and even for the other family members so that they can take steps to prevent them.

■ Higher Emotional Level

Because of existing family relationships, some of the business decisions and evaluations may be more emotionally charged than they would be in a non-family setting. For example, the evaluation of performance or supervision affecting a family member employee, if it is done at all, may be biased positively or negatively because of the relationship. Family members often bring their personal feelings and stress to the business, which often precludes them from making objective decisions.

■ Blurring of Roles

In many family-owned businesses, the personal and business roles of individual family members may become blurred. For example, the chief executive officer or manager of the business may in practice not really be in control because of his or her junior role in the family. This often occurs when children have "taken over" the business but their parents still exert informal pressure on the children and the business.

■ Inadequacy

The problem of inadequacy may arise in the family business in two areas. The first situation involves the relative who assumes the position of chief executive or head of the company because of birthright, but may lack the experience, education, intelligence, or work ethic required to manage the business successfully. The second situation involves hiring a less qualified family member. Helping out a less capable family member may lead to disappointment and damage to the business and can have a disruptive effect on the non-family employees.

■ Non-family Employee Attitudes

One common characteristic of family-owned businesses is high turnover of non-family employees. Many young employees see no chance for promotion to management in the company

6   Jennifer Low, "Dad, When Are You Going to Let Go?", *Profit Magazine*, October 1991, 20.

because they are not part of the family. As a result, they may gain experience in the business but then leave for other organizations that offer a better opportunity for promotion.

■ Objectives of Family Owners

In most family businesses, more than one member of the family owns shares or has an ownership interest in the business. Because these owners may be from different generations, have different levels of involvement in the business, and have various backgrounds and needs, differences of opinion regarding the operations of the business are common. For example, owners who are actively involved in building up the business often want to reinvest more of the earnings in the business. The non-active owners or shareholders, on the other hand, may want their share of the profits to be distributed as dividends or payment to themselves.

Running a family business can offer many benefits to the family and to the community. They can offer an opportunity to provide on-the-job training and background for a young person that might not be possible otherwise. The parent-owner can assess the young person's progress and level of preparation over a longer period of time than would be possible if hiring an outsider to manage the business. In addition, the owner-manager's business philosophy and style may be taught to the next generation apprenticing for management and ownership of the business.

Principles of Success for Family Businesses   The preceding section has demonstrated the many difficulties that can arise in a family business. These difficulties may be detrimental to the success of the business and damaging to family relationships. The following practices may help prevent some of the aforementioned difficulties from arising.

Recognize the Importance of Objectivity   Evaluations and supervision involving family members should be done on an objective basis. Care should be taken to ensure that consistent policies are followed for both family and non-family employees.

■ Create Clear Role Structures

A clear definition of the roles, objectives, and responsibilities of all associated family members may help to overcome the difficulty of blurring of roles.

■ Ensure Competence

Providing the heirs with technical and practical training along with increased decision-making authority is vital. This may involve encouraging the family member to acquire necessary skills at a college, a university, or with another business before returning to become fully involved.

■ Provide Incentives for Non-family Employees

To maintain the loyalty of non-family employees and ensure that they stay with the company, the owner-manager can devise various rewards and incentives. These incentives can be financial or may involve including employees in decision-making and educational programs.

■ Clarify Objectives of Family Owners

To prevent disharmony resulting from differing objectives of family members, it is important to clarify formally the long and short-term objectives of the company. These might include objectives in such areas as expansion and distribution of profits.

■ Keep Communication Lines Open

Perhaps the most effective aspect of operating a family business successfully is open communication. Given many potential areas of conflict, differences of opinion must be communicated to the relevant parties before they develop into serious problems.

PAYING EMPLOYEES

Small business owners face stiff competition from large companies and even from the government in paying their employees. This is particularly true in northern communities where government jobs pay substantially more than smaller companies can. Incident 10.5 illustrates this and other problems faced by northern entrepreneurs. Many small business owners think they cannot afford to meet this competition; however, the value of a key employee cannot be overstated for many small businesses. As a result, many owner-managers have recognized that they must be competitive in paying key employees or offer other benefits such as flexible hours or work sharing.

INCIDENT 10.5
Personnel Challenges Magnified in Northern Business

Fred Carmichael, Miki O'Kane and Sheila O'Kane own, operate and manage Western Arctic Air and Antler Tours. Both are successful companies. Western Arctic Air conducts business year-round and operates a fleet of ten aircraft. It provides regular service to Aklavik, Fort McPherson, Old Crow and Tuktoyaktuk. There are ten pilots, six maintenance crew, and six office personnel in the summer, and about ten employees total in the winter.

One of the biggest challenges in operating a business is dealing with staffing issues, and this challenge is magnified when operating in a small northern community. Miki indicates that staffing has always been a problem: "We bring up our pilots from the south and most of the time they are here for a short time only. We are a stepping stone to the airline industry." Fred explains, "It has come to the point where now it's very expensive. Even though they are qualified pilots, we have to go through a training program in our own company to get them on-line. It's really costly. We've found that as soon as they get experience then they are gone."

Miki points out that another problem they face is that "this is very much a government town and a lot of the 'good jobs' are the government jobs because the pay is high. It makes it really hard for private enterprise to hire. Some of our workers want the experience and then when the first government job comes along, they go, and I don't blame them for doing it. The benefits are better — they get northern allowance. They get hourly wages that are higher than anywhere else in Canada, I'm sure, for the kind of work done. But it certainly makes it a lot more difficult for the small businessperson trying to employ and keep staff."

Antler Tours has also had problem connecting with outfitters and guides in surrounding communities. Through Fred's contacts they were able to identify their initial tour guides, but it has been difficult to expand. Sheila states, "A subsistence lifestyle is still important. So there are seasons when people aren't as available. There are local people here and we try whenever possible to give them time off when they want it. It's difficult because we start getting things ready for the summer about May and a lot of them like to be out on the land, hunting and trapping. We try to accommodate everyone as much as possible. That's what makes a company, it's the people around you. Happy workers."

SOURCE: Wanda Wuttunee, "Western Arctic Air Ltd.," The Centre for Aboriginal Management, Faculty of Management, The University of Lethbridge, 1991.

Employees are concerned not only about absolute but also about relative wage levels. This means employees are usually aware of and concerned about their level of pay relative to those of their co-workers. Employee pay levels are difficult to keep confidential in a small business. Often a wage increase to one employee will be seen by other employees not as a reward for that employee but as a decrease in pay for themselves. This, of course, can cause unrest within the organization.

Wage levels are set using both external and internal factors as a guide. Externally the owner-manager may want to assess wage levels in similar or competing industries in the same community. Many provincial governments publish wage survey data that can assist in this regard. Most owner-managers can find out what the wage levels are in their community by an informal survey. Other external considerations in arriving at wage levels might be the cost of living, the demand/supply situation for employees, and government regulations. Internal considerations used by employers in setting salary levels are ability to pay, employee performance levels and requirements, and, as just mentioned, relative pay relationships.

Remuneration can offer employees security and also have a motivational effect. There are many methods of paying employees, each with advantages and disadvantages. The owner-manager needs to tailor the pay plan to meet the needs of the employees and the goals of the organization. Figure 10.6 lists some of the more common methods of paying employees in small businesses and describes their advantages and limitations. Many organizations use combinations of these plans.

Fringe Benefits

Although a recent survey found that fewer than half of Canadian small businesses offer incentive plans,[7] increasingly a small business needs to provide fringe benefits to attract and retain employees. Some benefits becoming common in industry today are employee discounts, pension plans, disability and life insurance, and dental insurance. Other work-related fringe benefits the business might offer to increase employee satisfaction and motivation are job rotation and flexible hours.

Job Rotation   With job rotation employees are periodically allowed to exchange jobs with other employees. This program can not only increase employee interest and motivation but also assists in training workers.

Flexible Hours   Some firms have experienced increases in productivity by allowing employees to work at times other than the typical 9-to-5 schedule common in many industries. This can be an important benefit for individuals with family considerations. Some firms also schedule their operations so that individuals can participate in culturally important seasonal activities.

CONTROLLING AND EVALUATING EMPLOYEE PERFORMANCE ────────

Many of the practices previously mentioned contribute to a more motivated and loyal work force. So that this motivation be directed toward the achievement of the firm's objectives, the owner-manager needs to evaluate progress toward goals and objectives and work with employees to ensure their progress. This can be done through a regular performance appraisal or regular private meetings with each employee. Discussions can include giving praise and

---

7 "Small Business Magazine's First Annual Survey of Canada's Entrepreneurs," *Small Business*, June 1987, 49–53.

FIGURE 10.6 Salary Plans for Small Businesses

Type of Plan	How Calculated	Advantage	Limitation	Types of Businesses Using the Plan
Salary	Per hour or per month	Security; Simple	Lack of incentive	Many businesses; Routine tasks
Commission	Percent of sales	Incentive	Lack of control	Automobile sales; Housing industry; Some retail products requiring extra selling effort
Cash bonus on individual performance	Bonus upon reaching objectives or quota	Security; Incentive	Can be complicated	Retailing; Manufacturing
Profit sharing on company performance	Percent of profits distributed	Incentive; Cooperation in organization	Can be complicated; Amounts too small to motivate	Manufacturing; Retailing
Stock bonus	Predetermined percent to employees based on objectives	Long-term interest in organization; Incentive	Some employees want only cash	Manufacturing

encouragement; looking at individual needs, personal concerns and problems regarding the job; giving feedback on job performance; sharing of information; discussing possible training needs, managerial and organizational problems and opportunities, obstacles and aids to improvement and organizational values; and the setting of goals by the owner and employee.

HANDLING GRIEVANCES

Employee grievances, or concerns, arise in most organizations. They can have a negative effect on the morale of the organization, but they can also be positive and helpful if handled properly. Where cultural norms preclude direct interpersonal conflict, employee grievances may remain unresolved. To encourage employees to voice their concerns, the owner-manager may:

1. Implement a standard procedure through which employees can express grievances. If at all possible, a grievance should be expressed to the immediate supervisor. This procedure should be laid out in the policy manual (if there is one).
2. Assure employees that expressing their concerns will not jeopardize or prejudice their relationship with the employer. A wise employer will recognize that many grievances are legitimate and, if acted upon, can help the organization.
3. Establish a minimum of red tape in processing complaints. Employees need to feel that someone is really listening to their concerns.
4. Understand that some employees may be hesitant to raise a concern directly. In these situations, a suggestion box can be effective.

Unionization and Small Business

Most small businesses do not have unions operating within the organization. As a firm grows, however, and as employees become further removed from the owner, the possibility of union-related activity increases. The owner-manager should recognize that unions are formed when a majority of employees believe that a union would better serve their employment needs than the existing system. Effective human relations policies can go a long way toward discouraging union establishment in the firm. Some small businesses in certain industries may be required to hire unionized employees.

In both of these situations, there are requirements for both the employer and the union as set out in the Labour Relations Act of each province.

GOVERNMENT REQUIREMENTS AND ASSISTANCE

The owner-manager should be aware of relevant government labour laws and programs that affect the management of personnel. A brief discussion of such laws and programs for all levels of government follows.

Federal Government

The federal government provides training and employment programs to 400,000 Canadians each year. Through the Canadian Jobs Strategy approximately $1.7 billion is spent to increase training and expand opportunities.[8] Some specific programs of Jobs Strategy include the following:

- **Job entry programs** provide training for unemployed or undertrained people for up to one year.
- **Skill shortage and skill investment programs** provide financial assistance and training for up to three years for skill upgrading as a result of technological change.
- **Job development programs** provide training and financial assistance for the unemployed, disadvantaged persons, women, disabled persons, mature people, and visible minorities.
- **Innovation programs** provide funds to test new solutions to labour market related problems.
- **Community futures programs** help finance local committees for development training and employment initiatives in areas experiencing economic hardship.

---

8 *Small Business in Canada*, 1990, 61.

There are also programs set up specifically for aboriginal employers and employees, for example the Aboriginal Internship Program. This is a wage subsidy program that encourages employers to provide work experience and training to recent aboriginal graduates of post-secondary institutions. For more information on each of the above programs, contact your local Canada Employment Centre or the Canadian Council for Aboriginal Business.

The federal government also has some legislation in the areas of employment standards and hiring practices. Because of overlaps in jurisdiction with the provinces, details are discussed in the next section. These jurisdictions for the various programs and standards are illustrated on page 307 of the Checklists and Examples section.

Provincial Government

Each province and territory in Canada, through its manpower or labour department, has set labour standards with which every owner-manager should be familiar. The agencies that administer these standards are listed on page 340 of the Information Resources section. Some of the more important are discussed briefly below.

Job Discrimination   Each provincial government has passed legislation concerning human rights in the workplace. Entitled Bills or Codes of Human Rights and administered by provincial Human Rights Commissions, provincial legislation has jurisdiction over businesses not federally owned or regulated. Like their federal counterparts, these provincial regulations are designed to prevent discrimination in the workplace.

Pay & Employment Equity   Recently some provinces and the territories have enacted legislation to ensure equality of pay and employment opportunity regardless of gender, race, religious affiliation, or ethnic origin.

Working Conditions and Compensation   Numerous legal requirements govern the conditions under which retail employees work. Of importance to the small business owner are wage and hour requirements, restrictions on the use of child labour, provisions regarding equal pay, workers' compensation, unemployment benefits, and the Canada Pension Plan.

Employment Standards   Both the federal and provincial governments administer a considerable amount of legislation related to employment standards and labour relations. At both levels of government, Ministries of Labour have primary responsibility in this field of regulation. In addition, both levels have legislation that allows for the establishment of unions and collective bargaining agents in the form of provincial labour relations acts and the federal Canada Labour Code. The Canada Labour Code also deals with many aspects of fair labour standards, labour relations, dismissal procedures, severance allowances, and working conditions. Similarly, each province enforces statutes covering minimum wage rates, hours of work, overtime, holidays and leaves, termination notices, employment of young people, and information requirements on the statement of earnings and deductions. There is a considerable body of case law involving aboriginal organizations and the Canada Labour Code, especially in the area of unjust dismissal. In order to avoid litigation managers should ensure that they are familiar with and follow the guidelines set out in the Canada Labour Code.

Employment Safety and Health   Employment safety and health programs are designed to reduce absenteeism and labour turnover. Most provinces have passed industrial safety acts to protect the health and safety of workers. These laws govern such areas as sanitation, ventilation, and dangerous machinery. In addition to legislation, provincial governments, as well as employers, provide programs and training designed to accomplish similar purposes.

Workers' Compensation   Workers' Compensation is an employee accident and disability insurance program that is compulsory for certain industries under provincial law. Businesses that are operated on a reserve and are not incorporated are not required to pay workers' compensation, but may do so on a voluntary basis. Bands may also purchase voluntary coverage for employees of band businesses. If a business incorporates, it then becomes subject to provincial legislation and, depending on the nature of the business, will be required to pay workers' compensation (see Incident 10.6). Compensation covers employees who are accidentally injured while working or are unable to work as a result of a disease associated with a particular occupation. While these programs vary among provinces, they generally provide for medical expenses and basic subsistence during the period of disability. Employers help pay for the program through assessment from the Workers' Compensation Board. The assessment rates, which many provinces have recently increased, represent a substantial operating expense; thus they must be planned for and managed with considerable care.

INCIDENT 10.6
Sarcee Gravel Products Inc. versus Alberta

Sarcee Gravel Products Inc. was engaged in the extraction of gravel from land within the reserve of the Tsuu T'ina Nation. The shares of Sarcee were held by the chief and band council in trust for the benefit of band members. All assets of Sarcee were owned by another company whose shares were also held in trust for band members. All profits from the business of gravel extraction went to the band.

The Alberta Workers' Compensation Board ruled that Sarcee was required to contribute to the Accident Fund established under the provincial Workers' Compensation Act out of which workers' compensation payments were made. The legislation provided that the Act did not apply to an "industry carried on by an Indian or band on a reserve." Sarcee appealed to the WCB Appeals commission which affirmed the initial ruling, in part, on the basis that the exemption in the legislation did not apply because Sarcee was not in the same position as an Indian band. The Appeals Commission also stated that Sarcee would have an unfair advantage over non-Indian gravel companies if it were not required to contribute to the Accident Fund. Sarcee applied for judicial review of the Appeals Commission decision.

The court ordered that the matter be returned to the Appeals Commission for further consideration. It was not unreasonable for the Appeals Commission to decide that the exemption in the legislation applicable to an industry carried on by an Indian band did not apply to a corporation controlled by an Indian band. A corporation has an independent legal status from its shareholders. Furthermore, it was not unreasonable for the Appeals Commission to decline to pierce the corporate veil (in order to treat Sarcee and the band as in essence the same entity and thus allow Sarcee to benefit from the exemption which applied to the band). Piercing the corporate veil was a discretionary matter within the Appeals Commission's jurisdiction.

The Appeals Commission took an irrelevant factor into consideration reflected in its statement that not requiring Sarcee to contribute to the Accident Fund would result in an unfair advantage to Sarcee. There was no evidence on this matter before the Commission and the Commission would not have had any particular expertise on this topic. Accordingly the matter should be remitted to the Appeals Commission for re-consideration.

SOURCE: Sarcee Gravel Products Inc. v. Alberta (Workers' Compensation Board), *The First Perspective*, August 1995.

Wage Subsidy Programs   These programs provide financial assistance for up to six months for small businesses that hire unemployed persons.

Provincial Training Programs   These programs provide job training and skill development incentives to upgrade the labour force. Often such programs include a wage subsidy to small businesses that hire new employees. Contact your provincial labour department (see page 340 of the Information Resources section) for details of these programs.

Municipal Governments

Local or municipal government regulations related to industry generally are confined to such areas as licensing, zoning, hours of operation, property taxes, and building codes. For example, two issues of debate relate to Sunday openings of retail stores and smoking in public areas such as restaurants. Generally, jurisdiction has been left to the municipal government by the provinces.

Municipal authorities also exercise an especially strong influence over food establishments. For instance, a municipal licensing system for restaurants and other food services establishments may be in effect. Also, health inspectors may make periodic and sometimes unannounced inspections.

RECORD-KEEPING FOR EMPLOYEES

Every employer should maintain an employee file that includes such information as the employee's original application form, work record, salary level, evaluation reports, and any other pertinent information. One of the most important employee record-keeping tasks for the owner-manager is completing the payroll. There are several essential steps in managing a payroll system for employees.

Employee Remittance Number   For those employees that are subject to income tax (refer to Chapter 11) the owner-manager collects employee income tax on behalf of the government as a deduction from the employee's wage. Before remitting this amount to the Receiver General, the employer must obtain a remittance number, available by contacting the nearest office of Revenue Canada. Along with the remittance number, the appropriate tax deduction tables and forms will be provided.

Payroll Book   The employer should obtain a payroll book or record which contains space for recording time worked as well as the required deductions. These books can be obtained from most business supply or stationery stores.

Monthly Remittance   As mentioned above, each payday the employer is required to make the appropriate deductions and remit these, as well as the employer's share, to Revenue Canada. For those employees that are tax exempt, Unemployment Insurance and Canada Pension Plan deductions do not have to be made. However, according to Revenue Canada's *Employers' Guide* to *Payroll Deductions*, "under CPP employers can include in pensionable earnings any non-taxable salary or wages paid to Status Indians. Although you do not have to deduct CPP from non-taxable income paid to a Status Indian, you may choose to provide your Status Indian employee with optional CPP coverage. You can elect to do this by completing and filing the form *Application for Coverage of Employment of an Indian in Canada Under the Canada Pension Plan Whose Income is Exempt Under the Income Tax Act*, available at any income tax office. However, once you do this, you cannot revoke the election, and you have to cover all employees."[9]

For those employees whose income is taxable, or the portion thereof, deductions for Canada Pension Plan and Unemployment Insurance, along with the employer's contributions, must be remitted to Revenue Canada. This remittance is made on a prescribed form containing the remittance number, the current payment amount, and a cumulative record of payments to date.

Year-End Statements At the end of the calendar year, the employer is required to total and reconcile the year's remittances with Revenue Canada's totals. This is done on a T4–A summary form provided by Revenue Canada.

It is also the employer's responsibility to fill out for each employee a record of earnings and deductions for the year on the T4 slip. The T4 slip is completed by reviewing totals from the payroll book and is required to be sent to the employee by the end of February of the following year.

SUMMARY

1. Sound personnel management is a key to the success of a small business because motivated and competent personnel are one aspect of a business that may be unique and difficult to duplicate.
2. The organizational chart integrates tasks and employees so that the owner can visualize how the different aspects of the plan will work together.
3. Developing policies to cover such areas as job descriptions, working conditions, holidays and leaves, remuneration, and employee benefits may be an effective way to prevent many personnel problems.
4. Some of the potential sources of employees for small business are recruitment from within a community, promotions, other businesses, employee referrals, advertising, employment agencies, and educational institutions.
5. Screening devices used in hiring employees include an application form, the employment interview, and references.
6. An interview guide helps focus the interview and provides a constant base of information with which to compare applicants.
7. Much can be done to ensure that a new employee has a smooth transition into the job. The new employee should be introduced to co-workers, shown the locations of employee facilities, informed of any company regulations, and encouraged to ask for more information if needed.
8. Two important principles of human relations management are to provide satisfactory working conditions and to understand and provide for employee needs.
9. The unique problems of a family business are higher emotional levels, blurring of roles, inadequacy, non-family employee turnover, and differing objectives among family members.

---

9 "Employers' Guide to Payroll Deductions, 1993 to 1997," *Revenue Canada Customs, Excise and Taxation*, T4001.

10. Remaining objective, creating clear role structures, providing training, providing incentives for non-family employees, clarifying objectives of family members, and keeping communication lines open can help to overcome some of the potential difficulties of managing a family business.

11. Compensation plans that are used by small businesses are straight salary, straight commission, cash bonus plans, stock bonus plans, and combination plans.

12. Two common fringe benefits available to employees are job rotation and flexible hours.

13. Some important principles in grievance management are developing a clear procedure for expressing grievances, assuring employees that expressing their concerns will not jeopardize or prejudice their positions, ensuring a minimum of red tape in the grievance process, and providing a method for non-vocal or hesitant employees to use the process.

14. The steps in administering a payroll system are to obtain an employee remittance number, obtain a payroll book, make the appropriate deductions and remit them with the employer's share to Revenue Canada, total and reconcile the year's remittance at the end of every calendar year, and send out T4s.

CHAPTER PROBLEMS AND DISCUSSION QUESTIONS

1. Discuss the relative advantages and disadvantages of the various compensation plans used in small businesses.

2. What industries can you think of where profit-sharing would not be successful? Why?

3. Discuss the relative advantages and disadvantages of the different types of fringe benefits for a small manufacturing company. If possible, interview employees of such a business to find out which of these benefits are the most attractive.

4. Recently a small business increased the wages of its employees, but its productivity is still inadequate. What could be some possible reasons for this low level of productivity?

5. Interview two small business owners to find out their personnel policies and how they communicate these policies to their employees.

6. Ask three employees of small businesses what they like or dislike about their jobs. What personnel policies could be used to remedy the dislikes?

7. Determine how three employees of various small businesses were recruited for their present positions. What seems to be the most popular source to recruit employees for small businesses? Why?

8. A band-owned salmon-smoking operation hopes to hire its new manager from within the community. The band targeted a bright, recent high school graduate to attend college in Vancouver. But after the first year of classes the trainee returned home to say he had decided to go into social work. What are some of the band's alternatives?

9. Six months ago you hired a young women to work as a sales clerk in your art gallery. Her performance for the first five months was exceptional. She has the highest sales of all of your staff, and customers frequently comment on what an excellent sales associate she is. You were considering promoting her to assistant manager. Over the past month however, she has frequently been late for work, she has called in sick five times and has taken several days off to attend to family matters. Other staff are starting to get upset because they are having to cover her shifts. You spoke with her two days ago and she assured you matters were in control and that she would not miss any more work. She did not show up for work today. What is your next step?

SUGGESTED READINGS

Baumback, Clifford M. *How to Organize and Operate a Small Business*. Englewood Cliffs, N.J.: Prentice-Hall, 1988.

Dolan, Shimon L. and Randall S. Schuler. *Personnel and Human Resource Management in Canada*. New York: West Publishers, 1987.

Innes, Eva. *The 100 Best Companies to Work For in Canada*. Toronto: Harper and Collins, 1990–91.

Small Business in Canada, Industry, Science and Technology Canada, 1991.

C H A P T E R   1 1

Aboriginal Tax Issues

——————————————————————————— *Gordon D. Dixon*

CHAPTER OBJECTIVES

☐   To provide an overview of income tax exempt, and taxable, aboriginal business situations.

☐   To identify the different income tax rules for aboriginal proprietorships and corporations.

☐   To illustrate a number of the common rules when a business is taxable.

☐   To discuss some of the planning opportunities available because of the imposition of income taxes.

☐   To identify situations where provincial and federal sales taxes apply to business transactions.

SMALL BUSINESS PROFILE
Dan Gravelle
Quarter Circle "O" Longhorns

Dan Gravelle is an entrepreneur. He also happens to be an Indian. As the owner of Quarter Circle "O" Longhorns in Grasmere, B.C., he raises longhorn cattle, helped establish a duty-free shop on the U.S.-Canada border, and is the band manager of the Tobacco Plains First Nation.

Ranching longhorn cattle alternatively to domestic cattle means that Gravelle can access a different market. This change in product was based on knowledge of trends in the food industry and best use of land and maintenance requirements.

When it comes to financing aboriginal businesses, "You have to have a tremendous amount of patience with the bureaucracy," says Gravelle. "We have to present a sound business plan and exhibit sound business knowledge. We have to put up collateral. We have to go through the same hoops as anyone else, if not more."

Gravelle's ranch keeps him busy, but he's looking for other ways to make money from his herd of longhorns besides the conventional manner. He leases them out for rodeo events and has approached film and video makers with the idea of using the cattle for movie "extras."

"I like to take an idea and see it grow," explains Gravelle. "I'm not the only one. There are many of us. It's important to get rid of the stereotypes and be positive role models for our children. We have to let them know that they can get into business too. Education is a must if they're to see what's out there for them. Operating your own business successfully means hard work and perseverance. It's the same for all races."

SOURCE: Michael Lawrence, "Shattering the myths," *Kootenay Business Magazine*, June 1993, pp. 4–5.

"If you believe what you hear on the street, Indians in Canada don't pay tax. This is one of the myths and misunderstandings that surrounds the issue of taxation and Indians in Canada... We often hear of Indian groups that pursue their business plans without regard for the tax consequences, ready to fight Revenue Canada (or any other tax authority) if they are reassessed for taxes. While this is certainly an option, we believe this course of action to be imprudent. Most disputes can be avoided at a venture's outset if it is properly structured... Avoiding conflict invariably costs less than engaging in it."

SOURCE: "First Nations and Canadian Taxation," KPMG, 1994, p. 1.

Previous chapters presented brief outlines on taxation issues and aboriginal businesses. As has been noted, various taxes are levied by federal, provincial, and municipal governments. For the most part, these taxes are levied on particular activities or property and their calculation is relatively straightforward. Typically, income taxes prove to be the most complicated issue for Canadian businesses and for aboriginal businesses in particular; and, as the above quotation indicates, planning for the existence of taxes is less expensive than fighting the system. As of the date of this writing, tax on income for aboriginal businesses is a constantly evolving area and currently is subject to a number of different interpretations. The purpose of this chapter is to identify the two main areas of the taxation of aboriginal businesses. These two areas are (1) those situations where income is exempt from tax, and (2) those situations where income earned by an aboriginally owned business is subject to income tax.

EXEMPTIONS TO TAX

Historically, section 87 of the Indian Act has provided the basic exemption from income tax for aboriginal communities and individuals. This section states that personal property of an aboriginal person or band situated on a reserve is exempt from income tax imposed by any of the levels of government. Income is considered to be personal property and it follows that any business owned by an aboriginal person or band which is situated on a reserve is personal property of that person or band and is therefore exempt from income tax. Métis and Inuit communities and individuals and non-Status aboriginal persons do not fall within this exemption and are subject to tax. Corporations are not considered to be Indians, even if all of the shares of the corporation are owned by aboriginal people living on a reserve, and are therefore also subject to tax.

The question of when residency is established on a reserve is critical in determining whether the business qualifies for the exemption from tax. In the most simple of cases, the common facts of an aboriginal person locating and conducting business on the reserve should establish that the business is resident on the reserve and therefore exempt from tax. For example, renting a building on reserve property and conducting the business of a leather tanning manufacturer out of the building would establish that the business was resident on the reserve. Conversely, conducting the same business out of a rented building in a nearby town not on reserve property would establish that the business was not resident on the reserve and is therefore subject to tax.

In many circumstances, the simple facts may not determine residency. For example, an aboriginal person operates a construction business that erects prefabricated houses on the land owned by the purchaser. The actual business activity takes place on many different job sites over the course of the year with the majority of construction taking place off-reserve. In this case, residency of the business may be thought to be off-reserve since the actual work takes place on land not associated with reserve property. However, residency does not necessarily mean where the actual work takes place. Additional factors which would assist in establishing that the business was in fact located on the reserve include:

1. Location of the books and records of the business.
2. The location of the business office and the place of management.
3. The location of business contracts, documents, and safekeeping equipment.
4. The location where payments for supplies or services are made and where revenues are received.

If all of the above factors point to a reserve location, it may establish that the business was resident on the reserve and therefore free from tax. Since the establishment of reserve residency is critical when determining the tax status of the business, care and attention should be taken at the outset of business operations. In many situations, professional advice should be sought.

INCIDENT 11.1
Band Business Tax-Exempt

> A court decision preventing Revenue Canada from charging a Manitoba band-owned business corporate tax could have far reaching effects on other native businesses.
>
> In a precedent-setting decision, Tax Court of Canada Judge D.G.H. Bowan ruled the Opasquaiak Band, located in The Pas, 470 kilometres northwest of Winnipeg, has the same tax status as a municipality and the band-owned Otineka Development Corporation Ltd. is therefore exempt from paying any corporate tax.
>
> By arguing that the band government was in fact a municipal government, Otineka, as a band-owned business, would be exempt because municipal-owned corporations in Canada are exempt from paying corporate taxes to either federal or provincial governments.
>
> The band provides services to band members in a large number of areas that include education, health care and other social services. All monies made from band-owned businesses go toward maintaining or improving essential services like roads, sewer, or emergency services. The band also regulates water supplies and sewers, garbage disposal and weed and animal control. It controls public games, amusement and bee-keeping and restricts the use of slingshots and bows and arrows. The band is also planning an infrastructure upgrade that could reach $8 million, and the band is not looking to Ottawa for any of it.
>
> "As providers of essential social and community services, the Opasquaiak have earned, deservedly, the reputation in Canada for being a model of self-government," Bowman wrote in his January 28 decision. Bowman's decision could have ramifications for other bands in Canada. "It's a decision with national implications."
>
> SOURCE: "Band business tax-exempt," *Windspeaker*, Canada's National Aboriginal News Publication, February 14–27, 1994, p. 2.

Reserve bands or the governing bodies of the reserve are also exempt from tax under the Indian Act. Band-owned businesses located on a reserve are exempt from income tax. Recently, as indicated in Incident 11.1, it was established that a business owned by a band and operating on off-reserve property was also exempt from income tax. This particular band exhibited a level of operations in providing services to the residents of the reserve which were consistent with the level normally assumed by a non-reserve municipal government. Any profits earned by the band-owned business were used to maintain or increase services to the residents of the reserve. Since the band was operating as a "municipal government," the tax exemption for municipalities was used to provide tax-free income for the band operations. These circumstances may now provide that any business owned by a band, or any subsidiary of the band council such as economic development operations, may now be free to establish business operations anywhere and be tax exempt. Again, when contemplating the establishment of a business off-reserve, professional guidance may be necessary.

NON-EXEMPT BUSINESSES

All businesses located off-reserve owned by individuals and all non-band owned incorporated businesses, regardless of location, are subject to income tax. Since the majority of businesses are subject to income tax, aboriginal business owners-managers should, at a minimum, be aware of the impact of income taxes on fundamental business operations and the differences in tax treatment of certain business activities. These business activities can also be broken into which taxable entity, an individual or corporation, conducts the business, and how that entity is taxed. As will be seen, choosing the correct business entity may affect how and how much the business pays in tax.

Business Entities — Individuals

In order to understand the tax differences in how a business is taxed, the starting point is determining in what form the business should be carried out. Generally speaking, a business can be conducted as a proprietorship, partnership or corporation. These legal structures were examined in Chapter 4. For tax purposes, only people and corporations are taxed. Therefore, when business is conducted as a proprietorship, the person who owns the business is taxed on the income generated by the business. Similarly, the partners of a partnership are taxed on the income of the partnership or, in other words, neither the proprietorship nor the partnership is taxed.

The Canadian tax strategy, following the theory of progressive taxation, is that the more one earns, the more one pays in tax. The progressive federal income tax rate, and the provincial tax rates, are identified in the Checklists and Examples section on page 308. As indicated on page 308, as income rises for individuals, the various levels of government extract an increasing portion for tax. Since individuals are taxed on the income a business earns when the business is run as a proprietorship or partnership, and as income increases so does the amount of tax paid, the more successful an individual is, the more tax that person will pay.

As an example of the progressive rate structure, assume an individual runs a proprietorship whose business is repairing snowmobiles (See Figure 11.1). The business is not resident on a reserve and is therefore subject to tax. In the first year of operations, the business earns $29,600. If the province where the business was located had a 52.5% provincial tax rate, the individual would pay $7,671 in total taxes; $5,030 to the federal government and $2,641 to the provincial government. In the next year the business doubles its income to $59,200, which would result in a tax bill of $12,726 to the federal government and $6,681 to the province for a total of $19,407. Income increased by 100% but the total tax liability increased by 153%. The individual is still financially better off by earning the additional income in the second year of operations; however, the actual amount of additional income earned is less than it would have been if the tax rate had not increased.

If the business is unsuccessful in the first years of operations, individuals have an opportunity to use the tax system to reduce an otherwise payable tax liability. Following the concept that income earned by a business is taxable in the hands of the owner, losses incurred by a business are deductible by the owner. For example, an individual operates a business that manufactures traditional clothing which incurs losses totalling $10,000 in the first year of operations. This same individual also operates a sculpturing business which generates $59,200 in income. Assuming the same facts as the previous paragraph, if the sculpturing operation income was included in the individual's income, a total tax liability of $19,404 would be generated. Since the losses from the clothing business can be used to reduce the income generated from the profitable business, income subject to tax is now reduced to $49,200. This reduction in income also reduces the tax liability by $3,965 for a total net tax liability to the federal and provincial governments of $15,439.

The rationale for allowing the individual to deduct losses from an unsuccessful business operation against the income of a successful one is a simple one. Since governments are willing to share in the success of a business by levying a tax liability on any income generated by a business, they are also willing to assume a share of the risks associated with unsuccessful business ventures. By allowing the overall income of all business to be offset by the losses of unsuccessful business operations, the individual saves funds by having the total tax bill reduced. In the foregoing example, these savings amounted to $3,965.

FIGURE 11.1 Progressive Taxation Rates: An Example

	Year 1	Year 2
Business Income	$29,600	$59,200
Federal Tax		
17% × 29,600	$ 5,030	$ 5,030
26% × (59,200 – 29,600)	—	7,696
Total Federal Tax	5,030	12,726
Provincial Tax		
52.5% × 5,030	2,641	
52.5% × 12,726		6,681
TOTAL TAX	$ 7,671	$19,407

$$\text{Percentage increase in income} = \frac{\$59,200 - 29,600}{\$29,600} = 100\%$$

$$\text{Percentage increase in taxes} = \frac{\$19,407 - 7,671}{\$7,671} = 153\%$$

Prior to 1995, an individual who operated his or her business as a proprietorship or partnership had the option of selecting any day within a calendar year as the fiscal year-end for the business. In many circumstances, the careful attention to this year-end selection could have resulted in a significant tax deferral for the individual. Effective for 1995, all proprietorships and partnerships now must have a fiscal year end of December 31st. This change in the legislation by the federal government has resulted in proprietorship income being reported in the same calendar year as it is earned, thus eliminating any possibility of deferring tax on the income to a subsequent year. Most businesses which are currently operated as proprietorships or partnerships will have a maximum of 10 years before the full effect of the rules takes place. Individuals should consult with the business's professional advisors to ensure proper procedures are in place in order to plan for these rule changes.

Business Entities — Corporations and their Owners

Many business owners fail to separate the tax status of themselves as owners/employees and the tax situation of the company. Since owners can wear two hats, one as an employee of the company and the other as the owner, the overall tax situation can become complex. It is therefore important, for tax and business purposes, to keep the operations of the incorporated business very clearly separated from any financial transactions the aboriginal owner may have with the company. The following section will first identify the more common tax rules that affect corporations and then address the tax consequences of financial transactions between the owner and his or her company.

Corporations   Corporations owned by aboriginal people, whether situated on or off reserve, are not subject to the general exemption found in the Indian Act and are therefore taxable entities; Waswanipi Mishtuk Corporation (Small Business Profile, Chapter 12) is one such corporation. When corporations earn business income, the owners of the corporations, unlike proprietorships and partnerships, are not taxed on that income in the year the corporation earned the income but only when the corporation distributes the income to its shareholders through the payment of dividends. Since corporations are separate from their owners, the corporations pay tax on any income, after the deduction for expenses, before earnings can be distributed. Page 309 of the Checklists and Examples section identifies the tax rates for corporations.

Small corporations controlled by Canadians are generally taxed at a tax rate of approximately 20% lower than other corporations. A small corporation is a corporation which earns income from an active business but does not earn more than $200,000 of income in the year. Active business income is any business income that is not income from renting land and buildings or investing in income-producing property such as bonds, guaranteed investment certificates, or shares of corporations. Most small incorporated businesses engaged in the manufacture or selling of merchandise, or services, qualify for this reduced tax rate.

Expenses   The incorporated small business owner should be familiar with those expenses that are deductible in the calculation of taxable income. In order to be deductible, the expense must first meet the test that it was needed to produce or earn business income. Obviously, expenses that are not business related cannot be deducted by the business. The second test is that there must be proof that the expense was in fact incurred. The taxpaying corporation must ensure that adequate receipts are kept. In many cases, the owner may personally pay for business expenses and then be reimbursed by the company. If the company or the owner does not keep the receipt, the expense would not be deductible. While some expenses may appear to be too small to justify keeping track of them, if the tax rate is 20%, every nondeductible expense of $5 will result in an additional and unnecessary tax liability of $1.

Deductible Expenses

Accounting and Legal Fees   Most legal and accounting fees are deductible provided they are not personal expenses, such as fees paid for the preparation of a personal tax return. Legal fees paid for incorporating a business are not deductible in the year the company is created but deductible over a number of years.

Advertising   Advertising expenses are deductible in the year the advertising is contracted for.

Business Entertainment   Business entertainment and promotional expenses, such as meals with prospective or current customers, are 50% deductible. Certain entertainment expenses including golf course fees and club memberships are not deductible.

Interest Expenses   If a business borrows money to pay for ongoing expenses such as new items for resale in a mini-mart, interest on the borrowed funds is deductible. When the same business borrows funds to buy new shelving for the mini-mart and the shelves are expected to last for ten years, interest on the borrowed money is also deductible. There is very little distinction between what is purchased with the loan. The basic test is that the money must be used to earn income from the business.

Repairs and Improvements   Repairs are payments made to keep cars operating, premises looking appealing, etc. These types of expenditures are deductible. Improvements are payments made to extend the life of an asset, such as a new engine for a car. These types of expenditures increase the value of the asset, like the car, and are not deductible when the payment is made. Payments such as these are deductible over a number of years in the future following the Capital Cost Method.

Capital Cost Allowance   Items purchased by a business which are expected to last more than one year are not deductible in the year the item is purchased but are deductible over the life of the item. The tax system uses the Capital Cost Allowance method of determining the amount which may be deductible in any particular year and is the replacement for depreciation. The system adds the cost of the newly purchased item to the total cost of other items that have the same approximate life. It then multiplies this total by a fixed percentage, such as 10% for example, to determine the amount which may be deducted in any particular year. The amount which is deducted for tax purposes is then subtracted from the total cost. This new total is multiplied by the percentage to obtain the next year's deductible amount. See Figure 11.2 for a more precise numerical example. This system can become complex, and the business owner can seek the advice of an accountant for more exhaustive calculations.

Travelling Expenses   In many cases, such as a musical group performing traditional dances across a province, business is conducted at several locations. Transportation expenses including

FIGURE 11.2 Capital Cost Allowance: An Example

Pays Plat Outfitters Ltd. fiscal year end is December 31. The company had the following purchases of snowmobiles:

- 1996 purchased 4 Ski-doo snowmobiles for $6,000 each
- 1998 purchased 3 Arctic Cat snowmobiles for $7,000 each
- 1998 sold 2 Ski-doo snowmobiles for $2,000 each

The maximum amount of Capital Cost Allowance (CCA) which could be claimed for each of the three years is calculated as follows:

		Class 8 *CCA 20%*
Beginning balance — Jan. 1, 1996		$ 0
Purchases		
4 Ski-doos × $6,000		$24,000
Balance Dec. 31, 1996		24,000
Less 1/2 net purchases*		(12,000)
Balance Dec. 31, 1996		12,000
CCA 1996 (20% × $12,000)		(2,400)
		9,600
Add 1/2 net purchases		12,000
Beginning balance — Jan. 1, 1997		$21,600
CCA 1997 (20% × $21,600)		(4,320)
Beginning balance — Jan. 1, 1998		17,280
Purchases		
3 Arctic Cats × $7,000	21,000	
Dispositions		
2 Ski-doos × $2,000**	(4,000)	
Net Purchases	17,000	17,000
Balance Dec. 31, 1998		34,280
Less 1/2 net purchases		(8,500)
Balance Dec. 31, 1998		25,780
CCA 1998 (20% × $64,030)		(5,156)
		20,624
Add 1/2 net purchases		8,500
Beginning balance — Jan. 1, 1999		$29,124

NOTES:
*In the year assets are purchased, only one half of the purchase price may be claimed for CCA.
**When assets are sold, the lesser of the selling price or cost is subtracted from the ongoing balance.

gas, oil, and car and truck rental costs necessary to move the dancers and their equipment are deductible. Hotel and meal costs while travelling and at the various locations where the performances take place are also legitimate expenses and are deductible.

Office Expenses   Whether an office is located in a rented building or in a room in the business owner's home, expenses necessary to run the office are deductible. If the office is in the home of the owner, expenses such as gas or oil for heat, electricity, water, repairs to the office, and insurance on the home are deductible for tax purposes. The amount deductible from the total of these expenditures depends on the size of the office. For example, if the office occupies one room in a 5-room house, 1/5 (or 20%) of the total expense can be deducted against the income of the business. The remainder of the expenses are considered personal expenses of the owner and are not deductible.

FINANCIAL TRANSACTIONS BETWEEN THE OWNER AND THE COMPANY

If a business is successful, the aboriginal owners-managers of the business may pay themselves a salary for work performed and/or they may pay themselves dividends on the shares owned. In other cases, it is common to find that the owner-manager of a company has loaned money to the corporation with the expectation that the company will pay interest to the owner on the debt and, eventually, repay the debt in full. These three types of common financial transactions between owner-managers and their company have different tax effects for the two parties involved.

■ Corporate Perspective; Salary

Payment of salaries to the aboriginal manager would be for work performed as an employee of the company and be deductible to the corporation as an expense of doing business.

■ Corporate Perspective; Dividends

Payment of dividends to the owner of the shares is considered to be a return on the investment of the owner. These payments are not deductible for tax purposes to the corporation.

■ Corporate Perspective; Interest

When an owner of a corporation loans funds to the corporation, the interest paid by the corporation on the debt is a tax deductible expense to the corporation.

■ Personal Perspective; Salary

The tax status of the receipt of salary by the aboriginal owner-manager is dependent on three distinct factors: (1) residence of the manager, (2) residence of the corporation, and (3) where the manager performs the work for the corporation. Figure 11.3 outlines these three factors and the tax result of salary receipts by the aboriginal manager. These guidelines are very general in nature, and provide the tax result in most situations where the three factors exist. Caution should be exercised since the results expressed in the table are based on current law and administrative interpretation.

■ Personal Perspective; Dividends

The tax status of the receipt of dividends by the aboriginal owner of the corporation is not as clear cut as the receipt of salary. Generally, if the corporation and aboriginal owner

FIGURE 11.3 Tax Status of Salary

Manager resident on Reserve	Corporation resident on Reserve	Work performed on Reserve	Tax Status of Salary
YES	YES	YES	EXEMPT
YES	YES	NO	EXEMPT
YES	NO	YES	EXEMPT
NO	YES	YES	EXEMPT
YES	NO	NO	TAXABLE
NO	YES	NO	TAXABLE
NO	NO	YES	TAXABLE
NO	NO	NO	TAXABLE

are resident on the reserve, dividends received by the owner will be tax exempt. In most other cases, the owner of the shares will include the dividends in taxable income.

On a different note, the ownership of shares in a corporation allow a certain degree of income splitting. For example, if the aboriginal owner of a business owned all the shares of the company and the company is taxable, only the owner would be taxed on the dividend income when paid. If other individuals were involved in the share ownership, such as members of the original owner's family, dividend income would be taxed in the hands of the other owners. It is possible to have a spouse and children of the owner own shares in a corporation and therefore effectively share income of the company with family members. Figure 11.4 indicates that for a three-member family, each member owning an equal number of shares, the tax savings on dividend income may be the total tax liability when compared to the situation where there is only one owner.

■ Personal Perspective; Interest

It is common practice to have shareholders of corporations loan money to their companies. This strategy allows companies to obtain necessary operating funds without having to approach a bank or trust company, and it provides some flexibility of repayment of both the principal and interest to the shareholder. Owners may wish to accumulate money in the company and only pay interest when there is enough cash available for the payment. While the company may still record a tax deductible interest expense each year, the deferral of the actual payment of interest may not go beyond three years from that date of recording the interest expense by the company.

The tax status of the receipt of interest by the owner is unclear at this time. If both the shareholder and the corporation are resident on a reserve, and the documentation substantiating the loan is in the shareholder's possession, any interest payment made by the company to the shareholder would appear to be a tax exempt receipt by the owner. If only the documentation for the loan is in the owner's possession on the reserve, it is less likely, but still possible for the interest receipts to be tax exempt for the owner. Careful planning is necessary to ensure that the interest payments fall in the tax exempt category.

FIGURE 11.4 Dividend Example

The Canadian tax system operates on the notion that income first earned in a corporation and then paid out as dividends to the owner should only be taxed once. To accomplish this, the corporation pays tax on the income it has earned and the owner is allowed a tax credit when dividends are paid. The mechanism first adds 25% of the amount of dividend paid to the actual cash dividend, and then allows a tax credit of 13.33% of this total amount as a deduction against the tax liability. Utilizing this credit mechanism allows individuals to minimize the tax effects of dividend income by having these dividends paid to other family members who own shares in the company. The following numerical example illustrates the amount of tax which may be saved. The first column assumes that the company has one shareholder who has no other income. The second column assumes there are three owners, each owning 1/3 of the shares and therefore receiving 1/3 of the dividends.

	One Owner		Three Owners
Dividend Income	$71,250		$23,750
1/4 Gross-up	17,813		5,938
Taxable Income	$88,763		$29,688
Federal Tax	$21,304		$ 5,058
Less: personal tax credits	(1,098)		(1,098)
Dividend tax credit (13.33% × $88,763)	(11,832)	(13.33% × $29,688)	(3,960)
Basic Federal Tax	$ 8,374		NIL
Federal Surtax (3% × $8,374)	251		NIL
Provincial Tax (50% × $8,374)	4,187		NIL
Total Tax	$12,812		NIL

The overall result is that by having family members own shares in the corporation, it is possible for the family to have the same amount of dividends as one owner, but in doing so, the family may be able to save $12,812 in tax liabilities.

GOVERNMENT TAX-RELATED PROGRAMS

At the time of writing, there are no programs within the income tax structure which deal specifically with aboriginal businesses. There are, however, a small number of tax related programs which apply to all businesses. The small business tax rate and the somewhat generous Capital Cost Allowance method have been identified above and are automatically available for all businesses which qualify. Two additional programs are available and both require specific activity on the part of the business.

■ Investment Tax Credit

For the Atlantic provinces and the Gaspé only, an investment tax credit of 10% is available on the purchase of new buildings or equipment. The property must be used in a specific business which includes any manufacturing, farming, logging or natural resource businesses. The investment tax credit is calculated as 10% of the cost of the new building or equipment and reduces the federal tax liability.

■ Scientific Research and Development Tax Credit

All businesses, regardless of location, may apply for a tax credit on expenditures which have been made for scientific research. Scientific research is narrowly defined and adequate professional advice should be sought beforehand. The tax credit is calculated at 20% of the qualified expenditures.

PROVINCIAL SALES AND GOODS AND SERVICES TAX

Provincial Sales Tax

All provinces, with the exception of Alberta and the Territories, levy a sales tax identified by a variety of names. In all cases, businesses are the collecting agents for the provinces, charging the tax at the point of sale and submitting the amounts customers have paid to the various provincial governments. Of importance to small business, the exemptions for aboriginal people purchasing goods or services are dependent on the particular provinces' legislation. Some provinces exempt aboriginal purchases of goods and services regardless of where the purchase takes place (Saskatchewan), some only exempt on reserve purchases (Ontario), while others exempt only the purchase of on-reserve goods and expect sales tax to be paid for services (New Brunswick). In at least one case, an aboriginal government has agreed to collect the provincial tax for the province (Incident 11.2). In all circumstances of provincial sales tax, only persons and band councils or band-owned corporations are exempt from payment. All other corporations are therefore not exempt.

INCIDENT 11.2
Fort Folly First Nation's Casino Closer to Reality

Fort Folly First Nation in New Brunswick and Dion Entertainment of British Columbia held a sod-turning ceremony on April 3rd at the site of the 2,787 square-metre (30,000 square-foot) gaming facility expected to open in approximately four months. The $1.9 million project is a partnership between Blue Raven (the corporation the band set up to run the bingo centre) and Dion Entertainment, with Blue Raven owning 51 % of the casino and Dion the rest.

The gaming agreement enables Fort Folly to operate High Stake bingos with jackpots up to $75,000 and video lottery terminals. In addition, Fort Folly may have mega bingos with jackpots of $150,000 twice a year. Under this agreement, the band will collect provincial sales tax for the province while the province will return a percentage of this revenue to the First Nation for economic and community development projects.

SOURCE: Adapted from "Fort Folly First Nation's casino closer to reality," *Transition*, Vol. 8, No. 2, May 1995, p. 9. Reproduced with the permission of the Minister of Supply and Services.

Goods and Services Tax

The Goods and Services Tax (GST) is a 7% tax levied by the federal government at the point of sale. As with the provincial sales taxes, businesses are the collectors of the tax. Unlike the provincial sales taxes, businesses also must pay the GST. The tax is levied on most goods and services purchased by businesses and also levied on most sales by businesses to consumers. When the tax is paid on purchases, businesses are allowed to offset this amount with the tax collected from consumers, only sending in or receiving the difference. Figure 11.5 offers the numerical calculation of the tax.

Purchases   For on-reserve purchases, an aboriginal, band or unincorporated band organization will not be subject for the payment of goods and services. Off-reserve purchases of goods will be exempt from GST only if the property is delivered to the reserve by the seller. Off-reserve purchases of services will be exempt only if the service is provided on the reserve and it is provided to an aboriginal person or an aboriginally operated proprietorship or partnership. For example, if a non-reserve plumber is required to fix the faucets in a restaurant operated by an aboriginal person and the business is on the reserve, the business operator is exempt from paying GST on the plumber's services.

Sales   As Incident 11.3 indicates, the collection of GST on sales of its goods or services by aboriginally run businesses is not without its controversies. Currently, a business is required to collect GST on sales of its goods or services if those sales are made to off-reserve customers. Aboriginal persons and aboriginally run businesses located on a reserve are not required to pay GST, and the selling business is not required to collect GST from these customers.

INCIDENT 11.3 ——
Roseau River Reserve Rebel Prepared to Battle Taxman

Marvin Atkinson's convenience store is rapidly becoming a symbol of native sovereignty and an instrument of economic development for this reserve north of Emerson, Manitoba. Atkinson is refusing to charge provincial and federal sales taxes on purchases by non-band members. Lawrence Henry, chief of the Roseau River Anishinabe First Nation, says the band is solidly behind Atkinson. Atkinson said he's only getting a small percentage of his business from non-reserve residents. His goal — and that of the band council — is to have more band members shop at home. At the moment, the 1,450 member band (900 of whom live on the reserve) obtain most of their groceries, dry goods and other consumer needs off the reserve — much of it in nearby Letellier and Dominion City.

FIGURE 11.5 GST Calculation Example

Purchases of Inventory	$5,000	
GST Paid (7% × $5,000)		$350
Sales of Inventory	$7,000	
GST Collected (7% × $7,000)		$490
GST Owed to Federal Government		$140

"We're trying to win back some of those customers," Atkinson said. "The whole idea is to keep that money in the community here and have it circulate a few times before it leaves."

SOURCE: *Winnipeg Free Press*, August 1, 1992, p. A14.

CONCLUSION

The imposition of taxes on the non-aboriginal community has been a controversial and complex problem for over 75 years. The developing aboriginal business community, because of the various factors, are now educating themselves about the existence of taxes and their impact on business decisions. It is not only taxes imposed by the current levels of government that aboriginal businesses must concern themselves with but also the possibility, in the future, of on-reserve governments looking to a form of taxation in order to broaden the flow of funds for band purposes.

For example, many reserve governments have opted for a system of property tax on non-aboriginal businesses operating or leasing property on a reserve. Despite the obvious cultural, legal, and historical arguments and opinions, it may be that aboriginal governments will enter into income taxation systems of at least non-aboriginally operated businesses. It should be noted that the original agreement in 1975 between the governments of Canada and Québec and the Grand Council of Crees and the Northern Quebec Inuit Association, known as the James Bay and Northern Québec Agreement, provided for the powers of taxation for community purposes to be given to the local governments. Aboriginal business leaders are adapting to these shifting forces of taxation and give every appearance that they will continue to do so. Entrepreneurs, such as Dan Gravelle (Small Business Profile), should do the same.

SUMMARY

1. The establishment of the residency of a business is important in establishing its tax status.
2. Aboriginal persons may conduct business as a proprietorship, partnership, or as owner of a corporation. The tax rules are very different for each type of business organization.
3. Operating a business as a proprietorship may protect all of the income of the business from tax in certain situations.
4. Corporations are taxable and are separate from their owners. Some expenses by corporation require analysis in order to determine if they are deductible by the corporation.
5. The Capital Cost Allowance method is a way of deducting the costs of assets over a number of years and must be used by all businesses for tax purposes.
6. Financial transactions between a corporation and its owner(s) can be confusing if they are not separated from the owners. Owners of corporations who also act as employees of the same corporations can withdraw funds from the corporation as salary or dividends. The tax treatment of each form of withdrawal is different.
7. In certain circumstances, the salary to the owner-manager may be tax exempt. With some careful planning, the tax on dividends received by the owner may be reduced.
8. Provincial sales taxes are not universal. The provinces differ in their treatment of the sales tax when purchases are made by aboriginal persons.
9. The federal Goods and Services Tax must be paid and collected by corporations. Aboriginal persons may not have to pay the GST if goods are delivered to them on a reserve.

CHAPTER PROBLEMS AND DISCUSSION QUESTIONS ——————————

1. What does Section 87 of the Indian Act provide? To whom does it apply?
2. Suppose you are resident on a small reserve near a large city. How would you go about setting up a construction business to minimize the income tax you might have to pay?
3. What kind of deductible expenses might you incur in the following businesses:
   a. traditional dance troupe
   b. home-based catering business
   c. snowmobile repair shop
   d. hairdressing salon
   e. incorporated construction company
4. Investigate the policies of three different provinces on GST exemptions for aboriginal transactions.
5. Review several back issues of *The First Perspective* for their summaries of recent legal decisions. Describe the cases that involve aboriginal taxation law.
6. With reference to Figure 11.3, what would be the tax status of the following businesses:
   a. Mishtuk Corporation (Profile, Chapter 12)
   b. Northern Emak Outfitting (Incident 2.3)
   c. Juliette Meness Ferguson (Incident 9.2)
   d. Standoff Supermarket (Incident 9.4)
   e. LRS Landscaping (Chapter 13, p. 277)

SUGGESTED READINGS ——————————

Indian Act Taxation and Exemption. Vancouver: Continuing Legal Education Society of British Columbia, 1995.
New Developments in Aboriginal Tax and Finance. Toronto: Insight Press, 1996.
Reiter, Robert A. *Tax Manual for Canadian Indians*. Edmonton: First Nations Resource Council, 1990.

Part 4

Looking to the Future

Part Four focuses on long-term management of the aboriginal small business. If a business is being managed effectively and the result is increasing sales and profitability, the owner-manager will be faced with the question of expansion. If growth of the business is desired, some changes will be required within the organization. Chapter 12 discusses the preparations that will be needed in such a situation. This chapter also looks briefly at the methods of transferring ownership of the business to someone else, including the involvement of other family members in the business. Finally, this chapter considers what kind of tribal businesses might genuinely be considered "small aboriginal businesses."

C H A P T E R   1 2

Aboriginal Business Growth

Katherine Beaty Chiste

CHAPTER OBJECTIVES

☐   To describe the potential problems that success and growth can bring to the small business.

☐   To discuss the desirability of growth for the aboriginal small business.

☐   To review the characteristics of the stages in the business life cycle.

☐   To discuss how to sustain the business despite the difficulties created by growth.

☐   To illustrate the importance of planning for growth.

☐   To review three possible outcomes for the business: transfer to a family member, sale to an outsider, and closing down.

☐   To consider what kind of band, settlement or tribal business might genuinely be considered "aboriginal small business."

SMALL BUSINESS PROFILE
WASWANIPI, QUEBEC
Waswanipi Mishtuk Corporation

Waswanipi Mishtuk Corporation is a forestry operation owned and operated by a Cree community in northern Quebec. The Waswanipi Band, numbering nearly a 1,000 people, has a demographic structure in which half the population is under the age of 20; providing employment for young band members in Cree territory rather than seeing them leave home and migrate south was a prime motive instigating the development of Mishtuk Corporation.

Band leadership mobilized community support behind the forestry project, striving to meet the concerns of traditional hunters and trappers of the community as well as determining the level of technological sophistication which would be appropriate for the logging activities.

After a Special General Assembly of the Band, it was decided to incorporate Mishtuk. While the eight members of the elected Band Council were selected as Mishtuk's founding Board of Directors, it was anticipated that this formulation would change over time to include other band members and even non-natives with expertise in the forestry business. A community member with commercial experience was selected to act as Mishtuk's first manager.

To help them decide on the best logging technology, the company opened up a competition between "hi-tech" feller-buncher operators and conventional chainsaw operators; the "hi-tech" crew proved to be the more productive and reliable option. From a pilot project in 1982, Mishtuk has developed into a successful logging operation a decade later. Although the exploitation of Cree forests by Cree loggers is not uncontroversial, Mishtuk's proponents continue to make the case that the company provides jobs as well as needed band revenues to the Waswanipi community.

SOURCE: Ignatius E. La Rusic, "Managing Mishtuk: The Experience of Waswanipi Band in Developing and Managing a Forestry Company." The Centre for Aboriginal Management, Faculty of Management, The University of Lethbridge, 1992).

SMALL BUSINESS AND GROWTH

Short-term success and subsequent growth do not always lead to a trouble-free business operation. Often success and growth may compound the complexities and difficulties of managing the business.

In order for the owner-manager to avoid the pitfalls of growth, it is essential that steps be taken early in the life of the business to ensure long-term viability. There are three concepts that can give the owner-manager the knowledge to deal with growth problems. The first is to have an understanding of the life cycle of the business in order to plan effectively for the future. Second, the owner-manager should understand some of the more common growth problems a business is likely to face. Third, there are things that the owner-manager can do to plan effectively for growth in his or her business.

THE BUSINESS CYCLE

The business cycle of the small enterprise is similar to the product life cycle that was discussed in Chapter 8. For small businesses that have only one or two products, their business cycle and the life cycle of their product may be one and the same. Figure 12.1 illustrates the shape and characteristics of a life cycle for a small business. The length of time a business stays in one stage is dependent upon several variables. Many small businesses take several years to move through the life cycle while others pass through all four stages within a couple of years.

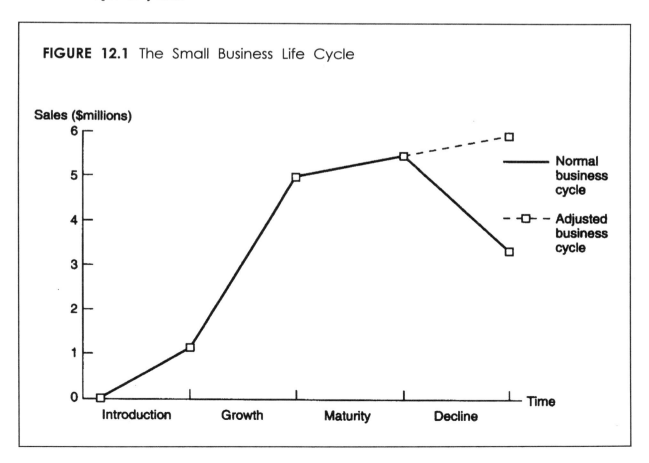

FIGURE 12.1 The Small Business Life Cycle

Introduction

Stage one is the start-up stage of the small business. It is characterized by expenditures made for product development and introductory promotion and also by low profits, particularly at the beginning of the stage. Stage one also usually includes a narrow market, a limited product line, and the owner-manager's involvement in most aspects of the business. North Waters Fishing Seminars, Incident 12.1, is at this stage of its business cycle.

Growth

The growth stage of the business cycle is usually characterized by establishment of a market share, or acceptance, and expansion of the product line or markets. It may also take the form of internal or external expansion such as a merger or franchising. During this period sales grow at an increasing rate. At the end of the growth stage, however, competitive pressures begin to be felt. These require changes in business strategy.

INCIDENT 12.1
North Waters Fishing Seminars

> Ken Dokis had just finished reading his nephew's first draft of a business plan. He had been asked to be an investor in his nephew's venture, and Ken felt honoured that Billy was asking for his advice. Ken had been involved with gaming, hunting, trapping, guiding, and fishing at Nipissing First Nation for most of his 51 years. Billy's idea was to start a fishing seminar business that would take advantage of the boom in sports fishing throughout northern Ontario.
>
> Billy hoped to establish North Waters Fishing Seminars as a mobile business catering to what he believed was an untapped market. He would travel to numerous resorts in the North Bay area marketing his seminars, selling fishing equipment, and teaching fishermen the latest fishing techniques. He believed there was little competition in the region and that the potential for growth was only restricted by his own skills and the amount of money he could get to start.
>
> North Waters would be organized as a sole proprietorship. The short-term plan was to open for business at the beginning of the fishing season on May 21, 1996. If the concept proved to be successful in the North Bay area, the plan was to expand into different markets throughout Ontario. It was also Billy's long-term goal to get enough business to hire his two life-long friends, Brian and Sam Mawabe, who had fished with him for many years.
>
> SOURCE: Adapted from John Pliniussen, "North Waters Fishing Seminars," B.E.S.S. Program, Faculty of Management, University of Lethbridge, 1995.

Maturity

Stage three is characterized by a levelling of sales due to increased competition and/or a decrease in demand. During this stage the owner-manager must make some important strategy decisions to avoid moving into stage four. Of necessity the strategy of the business will become more competitive, a stance which not all individuals may find comfortable. Such strategies may involve the addition of new products, the expansion to new markets, or the adjustment or improvement in some way of existing products.

Decline

As shown in Figure 12.1, stage four involves a decrease both in sales and profits. Unless action is taken to reverse this trend, the business will end up a failure.

PROBLEMS CREATED BY GROWTH

In order to anticipate growth difficulties and to make plans to minimize them, the owner-manager should be aware of some of the problems that can be expected to accompany growth. These are discussed below.

■ Owner-Manager Fatigue and Stress

Increased stress levels are caused when the scope of the business and the magnitude of its demands increase. Two entrepreneurs who found that a brother-sister partnership eased some of the load are described in Incident 12.2.

■ Lack of Communication

As the scope of operations grows, the closeness that may once have existed is no longer present. Many owner-managers have resented this loss of closeness and have even curbed their growth objectives as a result.

■ Lack of Coordination

Different aspects of the business may become specialized and less concerned with the whole operation as a business grows. This often results in increased conflicts between departments and/or individuals within the organization. Employees, who in the early stages of the company life cycle may have performed many duties, are often reluctant to give up some of those duties to specialists.

■ Community Expectations

In a small inter-related community, where community values may not favour individual acquisition of wealth, success and growth of a business may present a dilemma for the owner-manager. On the one hand, he or she may become the subject of jealousy or disapproval from other community members. On the other hand, she or he may come under pressure to share the material gains of the business rather than reinvest for future growth.

■ Shortage of Cash

Growth and expansion require financing that often has not yet been generated by the business operations. Merchandise may have been sold but cash not yet received, even though there is still a requirement for new inventories.

■ Low Profitability

Low profitability is not uncommon in fast-growing businesses. Several of the fastest growing companies in Canada lost money in 1991 and others profits were small.[1] In these cases, considerable expenses have been incurred in research and development of markets during the growth period.

---

1 "Canada's Fastest Growing Companies, 1992," *Profit Magazine*, June 1992, 22–23.

■ Breakdowns in Production Efficiency

Lack of production efficiency as evidenced by schedules not being met, increases in quality assurance problems, and consumer complaints are common in rapidly growing companies.

■ Lack of Information

Lack of information with which to evaluate how the business is performing often accompanies rapid growth, especially for owner-managers who began with more enthusiasm than technical skills. As the scope of the business outgrows manual information retrieval, a more automated system is often required to generate the required data.

■ Decreasing Employee Morale

This is evidenced by higher employee turnover and absenteeism. As new people are added to the firm to accommodate growth, time is often not taken with them in training. Existing employees work harder in growth companies and may not receive adequate recognition for their efforts. This can lead to employee discontent.[2]

Any one of the above problems can spell disaster for an otherwise potentially successful small business. In order to prevent such problems from developing, the owner-manager can prepare himself or herself and the business to handle growth in several ways.

INCIDENT 12.2
Family Partnership Offers Freedom, Co-operation

Can a family business partnership survive and thrive? In this column we meet a couple who have known each other since childhood and are in business for themselves. Clifford Atkinson and Juanita Hoflin joined together in a brother-sister partnership to own and operate Triangle Greenhouses Ltd. in St. Paul, Alberta.

Atkinson and Hoflin often talked of owning their own business. When Hoflin called him looking for a partner to acquire a greenhouse in Bonnyville, he decided to give it a try. That first greenhouse did not pan out, but they followed a lead to their present location in St. Paul. In February 1994, after nearly a year of hard work and frustration, the sale was final.

With the help of several of the staff they managed to get things organized and ready for the busy spring season. Many long hours and days followed. With no experience in plants, Atkinson soon got a crash course in seeding, transplanting, spraying, watering, and fertilizing. They shared the work and day-to-day operations of the greenhouse and discovered they had interests in different areas of the business.

Like any business start-up, Hoflin and Atkinson had a number of problems to overcome. The season started off with a break-in and many unforseen expenses. Some immediate renovations were needed to improve the customer service area. Equipment broke down and had to be replaced. The previous owner went to work for the competition and took some of her customers with her.

The good news is the first season is behind them now. They get a lot of support from their families, and the partnership arrangement means that Atkinson can spend time with his wife and Hoflin can be with her husband. The partnership gives them someone to work business problems out with. Instead of working 24 hours a day, they can occasionally scoot away from the business for a break. For them, a partnership allows more freedom and more opportunity for service for their customers. Hoflin says,

2 Paul Winberg, "Growing Pains," *The Magazine That's All about Small Business*, May 1984, 26.

"When a satisfied customer drops in to tell you his garden is wonderful, or someone you spent a little extra time with brings you a home-made pumpkin pie, it is all worth it!"

SOURCE: Heather Halpenny, *Windspeaker*, Canada's National Aboriginal News Publication, February 1995, p. 25.

EVALUATING THE GROWTH QUESTION

The owner-manager should answer four important questions before proceeding to expand the business.

Is the Business One that Can Grow?   A preliminary step in dealing with the question of growth is to evaluate whether the product or business is one that can grow. Restricted or remote markets or products that have volume production restrictions, such as traditional aboriginal crafts, are ones that are difficult to expand. Many service businesses that rely on the special expertise of the owner also fit in this category.

Is the Business Owner Prepared to Make the Effort?   Expanding a business will require additional time and effort on the part of the owner-manager and perhaps his or her family. The decision the owner-manager must make is whether he or she is ready to increase effort and prepare for the stress or be content with a less demanding but smaller business. Many successful small businesses have chosen not to grow for precisely this reason.

Does the Owner-Manager Have the Capabilities to Grow?   The owner-manager should assess whether the needed capital, labour, and expertise can be obtained to deal with growth effectively. Some of these specific areas will be discussed in the following section.

How Should the Owner-Manager Pursue Growth?   If growth is desired, several different approaches may be taken in pursuing it. Incident 12.3 describes a company which has been expanding on several fronts. The most common growth strategies are as follows:

1. Pursue new markets for the product or service. This may involve different geographic or demographic markets.
2. Increase sales of existing products by increasing the frequency of use. This can be done through increased promotion.
3. Add new products or alter old products.
4. Find new uses for the product or service.
5. Acquire other small companies.

INCIDENT 12.3
Goodfish Lake Band Launches Major Business Expansion

A Cree band will soon be doing business with an American oil company dry-cleaning, mending, and manufacturing coveralls for oil workers. On February 15th in Edmonton, the Exxon Corporation from Houston, Texas will sign a new contract with the Whitefish Lake Band from northeastern Alberta. As well, two Alberta oil companies — Suncor Inc. and Syncrude Canada Ltd. — will sign five-year extensions of current dry-cleaning and mending contracts.

The contracts are the result of a recently completed expansion worth nearly $2 million of the Goodfish Garment and Sewing Company. The company, which is run by the band, currently employs 20% of the 600 of 1200 reserve residents eligible to work, according to Band Chief Ernest Houle. With a larger building and dry-cleaning operation, it will employ 200 people around the clock.

The band borrowed $170,000 from the Alberta Indian Investment Corporation and pumped $700,000 of its own into the expansion, adding a sewing factory and expanding the building where the dry-cleaning operations were housed.

Indian Association of Alberta president Roy Louis congratulated Houle and the council on its initiatives: "You have shown a lot of native politicians, who think they are leaders, that the world is not flat. Our people won't fall off if they take on the awesome challenges of the world off the reserve," said Louis.

"We can excel and flourish. That's the name of the game for the next decade," he declared. "We are the aboriginal people in this country. We are survivors. We aren't going anywhere except forward."

SOURCE: John Holman, *Windspeaker*, Canada's National Aboriginal News Publication, February 2, 1989, p. 4.

GROWTH PLANNING

Once the decision has been made to expand and the method of expansion has been determined, a plan should be developed. A growth plan is a blueprint of future actions.

The Growth Plan

In Chapter 4 the essential elements of the start-up business plan were discussed. Many similarities exist between the start-up plan and the expansion plan.

■ Set Objectives

The first step in the planning process is to set the objectives the business hopes to accomplish. As mentioned previously it is important to set objectives specifically so that the outcomes can be measured. This may include dollar sales, market share percentage, or dollar profits.

■ Determine Alternatives

This step includes identifying possible strategies to achieve the set objectives. It also involves forecasting the possible outcomes of different alternatives.

■ Select Best Alternatives

Alternatives are selected with a view toward long-term success. The components of this success are the company's capability and the potential growth of the area.[3]

Understanding the Requirements of Growth

Rapid growth will require some fundamental changes within the organization. Some of the requirements of growth are the following:

---

3   Richard M. Hodgetts, *Effective Small Business Management*. Reproduced by permission of Academic Press Inc., 1982, 197.

■ The Requirement for Greater Management Depth

The owner-manager must realize that expanding the business will require an accompanying expansion of management depth, that is, more skills or harder work on his or her behalf. Because he or she may already be stretched to the limit, the owner-manager may have to hand over some of the management responsibilities to subordinates. This involves training and delegation, two personnel practices owner-managers are often hesitant to incorporate into their management style. As is illustrated in Figure 12.2, the owner must spend more time thinking and less time doing. This also means that the owner-manager must move from task delegation to functional delegation, allowing key people to manage various areas of the business. In addition, greater management depth can be achieved through the use of functional specialists outside of the company. Such people as accountants, lawyers, directors, or mentors could be helpful at this stage, although in a small or remote community such help may be difficult or expensive to access.

■ The Requirement of Capital

Any expansion of the business will require additional money. This is needed to finance additional productive capacity, inventory, or personnel. Unless the business has a solid debt-equity ratio and a steady cash flow, it may have difficulty obtaining this needed financing. Chapter 6 included a discussion of financing sources. One way to achieve a high growth level even with limited capital may be to franchise the business or the idea. Although becoming a franchiser requires a certain amount of capital, franchising may allow a firm to expand rapidly without large amounts of funds.

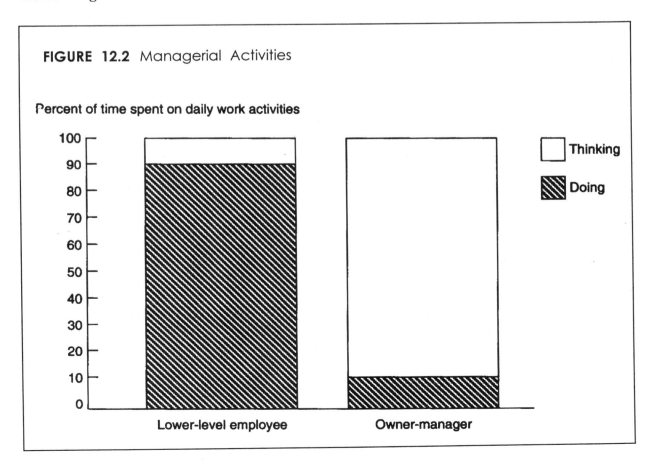

FIGURE 12.2 Managerial Activities

■ The Requirement of Financial Information

Often increased sales may obscure the fact that the profitability of the business is declining or even negative. As the business grows it is increasingly difficult, though more important, for the owner-manager to obtain accurate information about his or her profitability and productivity. The use of computers by many small businesses has greatly helped in this area. Owner-managers should regularly project future financial requirements so that cash shortages do not occur.

■ The Requirement of Organizational Change

As the owner-manager realizes that he or she can no longer be involved in every aspect of the business, the organizational structure will require alteration. This is necessary to allow a clear understanding of reporting and responsibility centres in the business. The result is to reduce the owner's span of control and to direct more of the owner's time to the planning and long-term strategy development of the business. It can also allow the owner greater time to foster coordination within the firm.

At the same time the owner-manager must resist the temptation to "overdo" the bureaucracy of the organization. An entrepreneurial culture (which likely contributed to the business success in the first place) must be retained if growth is to continue.

■ The Requirement of Management Controls

As a business grows it is more difficult to control. Through the use of informational and organizational methods a system of goals, performance levels, and evaluations can then be put into place. As was discussed in Chapter 9, the use of computers in small business has greatly enhanced the owner-manager's ability to control all aspects of a business. Such measures as ratio analysis, inventory turnover, margins, and cost controls are examples.

■ The Requirement of Monitoring the External Environment

The final growth requirement is that the owner-manager must focus more of his or her attention on the external environment of the business. These external forces serve as a guide to the long-term strategic planning that he or she should now become engaged in. Important external forces discussed in Chapter 7 are technological change, competition, consumer demand, social and cultural norms, changing legislation, and the state of the economy.

LONG-RANGE PLANNING

Because of the time, effort, money and commitment owner-managers have put into their ventures, they generally want their businesses to continue to grow and prosper in the future. To ensure that this continuity will exist for a business, the owner-manager needs to plan early for the time when he or she will no longer be in charge.

There are three possible outcomes for the business that the owner-manager can anticipate. One outcome is transferring the business to heirs and keeping it in the family. The unique situation of family owned businesses is discussed in Chapter 10. Or, a business may close down, be put into receivership, or go into bankruptcy. Finally, if the owner-manager is not able or does not wish to keep the business in the family, the decision may be to sell all or part of the business to someone outside the family. Each of these outcomes is discussed briefly below.

Transferring the Business to Family Members

Some of the most common methods of transferring ownership to one's family include the following:

Through a Will   In this case ownership of a business does not pass to the heir until the owner dies. Although this approach may enable the owner-manager to keep a reasonable amount of control over the business until the heirs are of an age and competence to assume their responsibilities, it may not lead to an orderly transfer of the business.

For registered Indians who are ordinarily resident on a reserve, the making of wills and the distribution of estates is governed by the *Indian Act* and the *Indian Estate Regulations*.[4] The wills of registered Indians who do not live on reserve and aboriginal people who are not registered Indians are treated the same as the wills of non-aboriginal Canadians.[5] Where land itself is involved in a will, it is worth noting that a band's reserve land cannot be left to a person who is not a band member.

Purchase and Sale of the Business   A purchase and sale agreement can remain flexible within the family to accomplish the objectives of both the owner and the heirs. Gradually purchasing a business may provide incentive to the heirs to maintain a continuing interest in the business while allowing the parents to maintain control for a reasonable amount of time. Many small business owners find an advantage to including a "buy-sell" agreement in their will so that family members who wish to carry on the business may purchase shares from family members who do not.

Gifting Program   In the absence of gift taxes, part or all of the business may be gifted to the heir(s).

Life Estate   This is used primarily where the significant assets are real property. This method transfers the ownership or title of land or buildings to the heir with the condition that the previous owner has a position of control until he or she dies. Immediately upon death the title automatically passes to the heir.

Closing Down or Going Bankrupt

A second possible outcome for the business, generally a result of unsatisfactory performance, involves closing down, being placed into receivership, or going bankrupt. Closing down is much easier for an unincorporated business than for a limited company. In theory, the incorporated company is required to file dissolution forms and notify government agencies.

If a business is performing unsatisfactorily, a major creditor may appoint a receiver and have the business placed in receivership. The receiver enlists the services of another agency in an attempt to manage the business out of financial difficulty. As this may be difficult to do, receivership is often a forerunner to bankruptcy.

A second option is for the business owner to consult an accountant. If the accountant recommends seeking a licensed trustee for bankruptcy, an assignment usually takes place. When this happens, the small business assigns its assets to the trustee, who in turn meets

---

4   Shin Imai, Katharine Logan and Gary Stein, *Aboriginal Law Handbook* (Scarborough, ON: Carswell, 1993), 181.
5   *Ibid.*

with the creditors. The assets are converted to cash and distributed to the creditors to repay as much of the debt as possible.

Selling the Business to Outsiders

A third possible outcome is sale of the business. If the owner-manager is not able or does not wish to keep the business in the family, he or she may decide to sell to someone outside the family. In this case, the last few years' performance of the business will affect the purchase price. Many aspects of selling a business were discussed in Chapter 5, from the potential purchaser's point of view. The seller must now consider the informational requirements of purchasers and make this information available to prospective buyers. Particularly important is information on the financial condition of the business as represented by the financial statements.

Another critical area in selling the business includes the terms of sale; timing of payments may have certain tax consequences. Often the purchaser wants the previous owner to remain in the business in an advisory capacity, and this arrangement can be included in the purchase agreement.

Sometimes a small business that has been successful but has a need or desire for a significant amount of capital sells shares to the public. In this case, the corporate status changes from a private to a public company. The advantages and disadvantages of this form of equity investment were discussed in Chapter 6.

A small business within an aboriginal community may be perceived as "belonging" to more than just the individuals who are operating it. If an outsider were to come into a community, purchase the business and commence operations, relations with local customers and the community's socio-political infrastructure may change. In some cases tribal governing structures have stepped in to operate local aboriginal businesses, with varying degrees of success.

TRIBAL SMALL BUSINESSES

A number of aboriginal business ventures which have received attention in both Canada and the United States are tribal ventures rather than individual proprietorships and partnerships. Yet many of these fall within the definition of small business established in Chapter 1.

Both in Canada and the United States, standard definitions of a small business include both quantifiable and non-quantifiable variables. One common measure is number of employees. In Canada, for example, the Department of Industry, Science and Technology considers a "small business" to employ fewer than 100 in a manufacturing industry and fewer than 50 in a non-manufacturing industry. By these standards, tribal ventures such as Mishtuk Corporation (see Small Business Profile in this chapter) still fall in the category of small business.

Another quantifiable measure is the level of sales and profits achieved by a business. Canada's Ministry of State for Small Business defines a small business as one which has less than $2 million in sales annually. By these standards, again, many tribal ventures qualify. For example, a proposed "electricity farm" for the Peigan Nation in Alberta would cost $15 to $18 million to build but would generate $1.5 million in revenues annually and employ four to six band members full-time.[6]

---

6   "Band Plans Wind-Generated Electricity 'Farm,'" *Native Issues Monthly*, August 1993, 16.

Finally, one of the most important non-quantifiable indicators of a small business is the role the owner or owners play in managing the day-to-day operations of the business. Where the owner is also the "owner-manager," the business usually falls into this category. With band or settlement owned businesses, the degree to which the band, more particularly its governing structures, can be productively involved in day-to-day management is the subject of much vibrant discussion.

As the profile of Mishtuk Corporation, above, suggests, some band-owned businesses start out with a nearly complete overlap between band council and band business management and therefore can expect some of the stresses and strains of the "owner-manager" model. Still, band businesses which experience a more "arms-length" relationship with political structures in their community may benefit from band council's support. The closing Incident for this chapter describes such a business in an Algonquin community in Ontario.

INCIDENT 12.4
Building a Community Greenhouse

> Pride has grown in the community of 350 Algonquin [Long Point First Nation] about 100 miles southeast of Rouyn-Noranda as their ever-expanding gardening project provides a focus for useful activity and brings new skills to people in the area. The project has offered some temporary work; it is beginning to develop new markets in the region and holds much promise of permanent jobs in the long term.
>
> It began when plastic was used to convert the roof of an old barn into a rudimentary greenhouse. Today, it is a $400,000 project that includes a new, year-round greenhouse that is moving Winneway towards agricultural self-sufficiency.
>
> "We did a bit of agriculture a long time ago here, with personal gardens and stuff like that, but we are mostly a nation of hunters and fishermen," says Jules Paiement, who is coordinating the project. "For us to go out and kill a moose is nothing, but to grow tomatoes or potatoes, that is something. We say, 'Can it be done?' Yes, it can be done if we put our hearts and minds to it."
>
> It was 1993 when Paiement first approached Chief Jimmy Hunter and his council with the idea of a greenhouse. The council agreed, and a committee, the Winneway Kitigan, was formed to organize the project. The council's support ever since the beginning has been an extremely important part of the project's success to date.
>
> In the first year, Winneway Kitigan built the greenhouse, using the old barn roof, and began an outdoor gardening project, growing vegetables like carrots and potatoes. Then this summer, a greenhouse "kit" was purchased and floated into the community on a barge. A crew of 14 prepared the area and constructed the greenhouse with the help of an engineer. Now it has 800 tomato plants and 400 cucumber plants.
>
> "I am doing some sales to the outside market, little towns around here that are not native," says Paiement, and the Winneway produce has an additional selling point: "This year all the gardens were organic!"
>
> SOURCE: *mawo'mi*, 1994, pp. 20–21.

SUMMARY

1. There are three concepts that can give the owner-manager the knowledge to deal with growth problems. First the owner-manager can review the business life cycle. Second the owner-manager can be aware of the common growth problems that arise. Finally,

the owner-manager can be aware of the things he or she can do to plan effectively for growth.

2. The four stages of the business cycle include introduction, growth, maturity, and decline.

3. The problems that can be anticipated as a result of growth are increased fatigue and stress for the owner-manager, lack of communication, lack of coordination, shortage of cash, low profitability, breakdown in production efficiency, lack of information, and possible decreasing employee morale.

4. In deciding upon growth the owner-manager should ask four important questions: (1) Is the business one that can grow? (2) Am I, as the business owner, prepared to make the effort? (3) Do I have the capabilities to handle growth? (4) How should I pursue growth?

5. The three steps in developing a growth plan for a small business are: (1) set objectives; (2) identify all the possible strategies or alternatives that would achieve the objectives; and (3) choose the best and most viable alternative.

6. The requirements of growth are greater management depth, increased capital, financial information, organizational change, less management control, and increased owner-manager attention to the external environment of the business.

7. To ensure long-term continuity of the business, the owner-manager needs to plan early for the time when he or she will no longer be in charge.

8. There are three possible outcomes for the business: (1) transferring the business to heirs and keeping it in the family; (2) closing down, being placed into receivership or going bankrupt; and (3) selling the business to outsiders.

9. The most common methods of transferring ownership to one's family include the following: a will, a purchase and sale, a gifting program, and a life estate.

10. If a decision is made to sell to outsiders, the business owner will have to be prepared to provide information on the financial condition of the business.

11. It may be difficult to sell a small business in an aboriginal community to anyone from outside the community.

CHAPTER PROBLEMS AND DISCUSSION QUESTIONS

1. Refer to Figure 12.1 and describe how the business cycle might unwind for North Waters Fishing Seminars.

2. Which of the problems created by growth, as developed in the chapter, could be experienced by North Waters? Explain.

3. The owner-managers of a small successful hairdressing company want to expand their business. The growth objective for the company is to have 35% of the local hairdressing market in two years' time.
   a. What steps could be taken to determine feasibility of their expansion?
   b. Outline an brief expansion plan.

4. What recommendations for expansion would you have for the following companies?
   a. Steinhauer Guiding (Incident 3.1)
   b. Wickaninnish Gallery (Incident 6.6)
   c. Abenaki Associates (Incident 8.3)
   d. Juliette Menness Ferguson (Incident 9.2)

5. Interview the owner-manager of a successful small business and evaluate the potential for further growth. Would you recommend expansion for this firm? Why or why not?

6. Visit three small businesses that you suspect might have varying sales levels and determine the market, product, and degree of owner-manager involvement each of the businesses have. Do your results show significant similarity to those in Figure 12.2? Explain.

7. Your aunt and uncle have just made you the manager of your family's grocery store. Since the transition, problems have seldom been brought to your attention, and you have received little feedback on your instructions. What problems might be evident? How would you solve these problems?

8. Interview the manager of a family-owned and operated business. What unique problems are evident?

9. Interview the owner of a small business operating in an aboriginal community. What are his or her options for transfer of the business?

10. Your father has made you president of the family sand and gravel company. You want to computerize the payroll and the accounts payable and receivable, but your father doesn't see the need for extra expense when expenses are already high? How would you resolve this conflict?

SUGGESTED READINGS

Anderson, Robert L. *Managing Growth Firms*. Englewood Cliffs, N.J.: Prentice-Hall, 1987.

Barach, Jeffrey A., Joseph Gantisky, James A. Carson, and Benjamin A. Doochin. "Family Business: The Next Generation." *Journal of Small Business Management*, April 1988, pp. 49–56.

Entrepreneurial Communities: A Handbook for Local Action. Westcoast Development Group, 1993.

Joiner, B. and S. Reymard. *Fourth Generation Management: The Business Consciousness*. New York: McGraw Hill, 1994.

Naisbitt, J. *Global Paradox: The Bigger the World Economy, the More Powerful its Smallest Player*. New York: W. Morrow, 1994.

Siropolis, Nicholas C. *Small Business Management*. Boston: Houghton Mifflin, 1990.

Torrence, Ronald W. *In the Owner's Chair: Proven Techniques for Taking Your Business from 0 to $10 Million*. Englewood Cliffs, N.J.: Prentice-Hall, 1991.

Part 5

Reference

C H A P T E R   1 3

Checklists, Tables and Examples

CHAPTER OBJECTIVES

☐ To provide checklists which potential aboriginal entrepreneurs can use to:
- develop a small business plan;
- develop a marketing plan for their business;
- make a decision about purchasing a computer;
- make a decision about purchasing a business; and
- make a decision about becoming a franchise.

☐ To outline, in tabular form, useful information about:
- small business advertising;
- use of financial ratios for the small business;
- relevant labour legislation;
- federal and provincial tax ratios; and
- licences and taxes applicable to the small business.

☐ To give an example of a well-developed small business plan for a landscaping operation on Alberta's Blood Reserve.

CHECKLIST FOR A SMALL BUSINESS PLAN
(from Chapter 4)

1. Have specific business objectives been set? At the end of one or five years, what will the size of the business be in gross sales? In production level? In number of employees? In market share? In profit?

2. Has a market approach been developed?
   a. Who is the target market in terms of age? Residence? Occupation? Income level? Education? Lifestyle?
   b. What is the target market purchasing behaviour for this or similar products? Where are purchases made? When are purchases made? What quantities are purchased?
   c. Why does the target market purchase this or similar products? Which characteristics are preferred? What other factors influence the purchase?
   d. What external constraints will affect the business? Existing or pending legislation? State of the economy? Competition? Social or cultural trends? New technology?
   e. Which product characteristics will be developed? Quality level? Amount of depth? Type of packaging? Patent protection? Extent of warranty protection? Level of service?
   f. How will the product get to the consumer? What channel of distribution will be used? Length of the channel? Intensity of channel distributors? Legal arrangement within the channel? Type of physical transportation?
   g. How will the product be promoted? What are the promotional objectives? Which media are to be used? How much will be spent on production? Who is the target of the promotion? What is the promotional theme? What is the timetable for promotion?
   h. What price levels will be set for the product? Which price policies will be instituted? What factors will influence pricing? How important is price to the target market?

3. Has the location been selected?
   a. In what trading area or community will the business be established? What is its economic base? Its attitude toward new businesses? Its saturation level in terms of competing businesses? Its costs?
   b. What specific site will be selected? Is it accessible to supplies, employees, and the target market? What is the site cost? What restrictions on site use exist? What is the history of the site? Who are the neighbouring businesses? What are the physical characteristics of the site?

4. Have the physical facilities been determined?
   a. What building, equipment, and start-up supplies will be needed? What are the costs? What are the depreciation rates of the fixed assets? Which building codes or standards are relevant? Which permits are required? What insurance is required?
   b. How will the physical facilities be organized? Is the production process efficient and safe? Has the interior layout been carefully planned? Is the exterior facade attractive?
   c. How will the inventories be managed? What initial inventory is required? How will inventory levels be monitored? How will inventory be valued? What method will be used to carry out inventory ordering?

5. Has a financial plan for the business been made?
   a. What are the financial requirements of the business? What are start-up costs? Ongoing operating costs? What are projected sales, expenses, income, and cash flow?
   b. Which sources of funding will be used? How much equity? Debt? Which sources will be utilized? Private? Commercial? Government?

    c. What bookkeeping system will be instituted?

    d. How will the financial information be used? Which accounts evaluated? How often? By whom?

6. Has a personnel plan been developed?

    a. What is the administrative structure? Is there an organizational chart? A responsibility and reporting procedure? Have job descriptions and specifications been developed? Will community members be hired preferentially?

    b. Have personnel policies been developed? What are the hours of work? Pay levels? Employee benefits? Conditions and standards of employment? Grievance procedures? Will employees be allowed time off for traditional and seasonal activities?

    c. How will the business recruit employees? Where will employees be found? How will they be screened? What guidelines will be used in selection? How will they be trained?

7. Have legal requirements been investigated?

    a. Has the legal structure for the business been determined?

    b. Have the relevant licences and taxes been researched?

    c. Has patent protection been obtained if necessary?

BUSINESS PLAN — SCOUT LANDSCAPING (from Chapter 4)

Business Plan
Table of Contents

I. **Business Objectives**

    I.1. Short Range Objectives

    I.2. Long Range Objectives

II. **Marketing Approach**

    II.1. Description of Target Market

    II.2. The Competition

    II.3. Uncontrollables

        II.3.1. The Weather

    II.4. Economy

        II.4.1. The Local Economy

        II.4.2. The National Economy

    II.5. Political

III. **Market Strategy**

    III.1. Product

    III.2. Pricing

    III.3. Promotion

IV. **Location**

    IV.1. Trading Area

Business Plan:
LRS Landscaping

Owner-Manager: Lyle R. Scout
Blood Indian Reserve
Standoff, Alberta

Background

LRS Landscaping, as the name suggests, will be a landscaping business owned and managed by Lyle Scout. It will be located on the Blood Indian Reserve in southern Alberta and will offer its services to residents of that area.

The business will offer basic, inexpensive landscaping services to new homeowners on the Blood Indian Reserve. The owner-manager has chosen this line of service because it can be entered into fairly cheaply, takes advantage of assets already controlled by the owner-operator, and is an area in which he has some experience.

The need for this service on the Blood Reserve is apparent. Although there are dozens of new homes built each year on the reserve, few are left with anything resembling a front yard. Most often the aftermath of the construction is a rough, denuded patch of land that, more often than not, has several piles of refuse and dirt left behind by the construction crews. Homeowners presently have the choice of doing their own landscaping, hiring someone else to do it, or leaving it as it is. Unfortunately, the last solution seems to be the prevalent one.

Lyle Scout, the proposed owner and manager of this business, as previously noted, has had some experience in this area. He has worked several summers as a maintenance assistant and grounds keeper for the Blood Tribe Department of Education. As well, he has done work of this nature privately.

The service will range from a basic service to include fencing and planting trees if requested, but it is expected that most jobs will consist of levelling and sodding.

The business will run for approximately four months a year, partially because of seasonal and weather constraints, and partially because the largest part of the business is intended to be conducted during the summer, when the owner-operator is not attending school. However, some operations such as hiring and taking orders will be done in the months before and after the summer season. The bulk of the work will occur in the summer months, between April and September.

Business Plan

A well thought out business plan is crucial to the success of a fledgling business. The following pages will outline the business plan for LRS Landscaping, and will aid the owner-manager in establishing the business, obtaining required funding, and efficiently running and controlling the business after its establishment.

I. Business Objectives

Organizing a business is a great deal of work, and this work is done with specific ends in mind. The objectives of this business can be divided into short range and long range objectives.

l.1. Short-Range Objectives   The first short-range goal is to provide the owner-manager with summer employment while he attends school. Because the business will be run seasonally for the first year, it is important the business make more money than it costs the owner-operator in its limited window of operations. More specifically, the return from the business should be greater or at least equal to the best alternative employment of the owner-manager's labour and capital.

This can be calculated by taking what the owner-manager's best alternative employment would be and adding whatever return the owner-manager could gain from the money invested in the venture, and adjusting this for the relatively higher risk of operating a small business. However, it may prove profitable to operate the business at less than the above-specified amount, because other, intangible benefits will accrue to the owner from this venture. These include real-world entrepreneurial experience and the enhanced skills and knowledge that should follow.

In calculating the opportunity cost for the owner-operator's labour a wage of $7.50 per hour was used. Because of the owner-operator's relative inexperience and incomplete education, and because of the difficult job market, this figure most realistically reflects the probable return he could realize for his labour. In an informal survey of the rate of pay for jobs for which the owner-operator is qualified, a range of $6.00 per hour to $10.00 hour was noted.

Using the figure of $7.50 per hour, and assuming that there are four weeks per month, the owner operator's potential income can be calculated:

$$\$7.50/hr \times 40 \text{ hrs./wk} \times 16 \text{ weeks} = \$4,800$$

This figure does not include deductions for benefits or tax, transportation costs, and other costs coincident with working. These have not been included because they will apply whichever option is chosen.

Next, the return that the owner-operator could realize for his investment if he used it in another alternative employment should be calculated. Because the amount invested is and the time over which it will be invested is relatively small, this is not a large factor, but the calculations for it follows:

$$\$3,000 \times (1.0025)^{120} = \$4,048.06[1]$$

Therefore, the business should earn the owner-manager at least $1,048.06 on the capital invested over the period in which the business operates.

As well, specific performance objectives are required to guide the operation of the business and indicate the level at which the business should be run. The business must have a positive cash flow at the end of the first six months of operations equal to the amount the owner-manager had invested plus interest plus the money required to pay back the loan.

l.2. Long Range Objectives   Although the business is intended to run only seasonally, and only during the time that the owner-operator is engaged in attending university, there is the possibility that the business may be lucrative enough to warrant continuing its operation after graduation. Therefore, one long range goal for the business is keeping it going as a continuing operation if it can profitably continue outside the intended time span of operations.

---

1   This is using a daily interest rate of .25% compounded daily over four months (120 days). The interest rate was obtained from the Canadian Imperial Bank of Commerce, Lethbridge Branch, on April 18, 1994.

As well, the business may serve as a base for future entrepreneurial ventures. Growth, however, is not one of the long-term goals. If the business is to continue in future years, it will likely continue at the same size and number of employees.

II. Marketing Approach

II.1. Description of Target Market   The target market will be primarily new home-owners on the Blood Indian Reserve, these being defined as anyone who has acquired a new house within the last five to seven years. The rationale for the five-to-seven year cutoff is based on the assumption that, if the homeowner has left his or her yard in an unfinished state for a period of time longer than this, it is likely that he or she does not place a high a value on having an attractive yard and living space. While these people and others outside the target market may be interested in the service this business will offer, they will not be actively pursued as members of the target market. Sales to these people will be incidental, but will not be the main source of business for LRS Landscaping.

II.2. The Competition   There are no landscaping businesses located within the target market. Persons who desired this service in the past were left to their own devices or forced to look off the reserve to providers of this service in the neighbouring towns. With the advantages of providing the service GST free and the advantage to the business being able to operate tax-free, as well as with the use of programs that are designed to encourage and assist aboriginal entrepreneurs, this business can offer this service at a substantially lower price than off-reserve competitors and still meet the owner-manager's operating objectives and goals. However, it is also possible that businesses that provide this service in neighbouring areas may see the potential for sales and also try to enter this market, meaning that there may be more competition for the market than anticipated. Monitoring, advertising, and price checks will be used to address these concerns. Comparisons with businesses offering a similar service ranged from $4,000 to $5,000, depending on whether seed or sod was used.[2]

Dealing with the alternative of "doing it yourself" for the homeowner, the service must be priced so that it is an attractive alternative to the homeowner doing the work himself.

The only competitors that have not yet been accounted for are possible on-reserve competitors that could organize and begin operations in time to compete with us. While this is a definite possibility, especially if it becomes known that this business is operating profitably, and if it is known how little investment by the owner is required, it is hoped that the owner-operator's knowledge and planning should provide an edge against potential competitors. This source of competition should be watched carefully.

II.3. Uncontrollables   As with any business, there are factors which, although they are beyond the control of the owner-operator, can have a direct impact upon the business and its prospects of operating profitably. Therefore, the owner must gather information about uncontrollables as he becomes more familiar with the particulars of the business and monitor trends that may affect the business, as well as other unlooked-for threats that may affect the probability of the business. Additionally, there is the matter of the weather, which will be addressed separately.

---

2   Todd Lepard, Owner-Manager Accent Landscaping, Lethbridge Alberta.

■ II.3.1. The Weather

Because this business is involved in outside work, it is inevitable that some days will be lost to inclement weather. This factor obviously is beyond the owner-operator's control, but can be prepared for and worked around. The work week will be structured so that work time will be 40 hours per week, from Monday to Friday, 8 am. to 5 pm, with a break from noon until 1 pm. Although rain will make work impossible on some days, the amount of days that are likely to be lost can be calculated. An owner-manager of a landscaping business in the same geographic region was consulted on this matter and he estimated that he lost approximately 10 percent of his work days on average to rain.[3] He also noted that the number of days he lost to rain each season had increased in recent years and observed that southern Alberta seemed to be in the midst of a "wet" climatic cycle. Unfortunately, there is really no sure way to predict the weather, but the business must be aware that these problems exist and operate with this awareness to ensure that these problems do not threaten the venture's health and stability.

II.4. Economy

As may be expected, the conditions of both the local and national economies have strong effects on the success of small business start-ups. Accordingly, they should be analysed to see which relevant threats and opportunities they may hold for this business.

■ II.4.1. The Local Economy

The economy of the Blood reserve is depressed, permanently, it would seem. Employment rates are a fraction of what they are off the reserve. This narrows the target market somewhat. However, the low employment rates should benefit the business as it should be relatively easy to find inexpensive labour. As well, although incomes are generally below average on the reserve, income is quite stratified so that there is a sizeable group of people with significant amounts of disposable income.

■ II.4.2. The National Economy

As the economy of the country is somewhat distressed, and because the business will rely on some government incentives and assistance, the possibility exists that some government sources of support may be cut either during the business season or prior to it which may adversely affect the business.

II.5. Political

Politically, the Blood Reserve has recently been an unstable place, and this may affect the business. However, there are so many variables involved in this sphere that positive or adverse effects are difficult to ascertain, and even harder to gauge. Because there is practically no business community on the Reserve and because the band administration is the main employer, political changes could possibly affect the business. Every two years a new chief and council is elected. Although there is usually a strong carryover between incoming and outgoing councils, it is possible that a majority of new councillors may be elected that do not understand the importance of business to the Reserve, both presently and in the future. With this in mind, it would be wise to cultivate contacts with administrators in relevant departments so that the effects of this source of instability can be minimized.

---

3   Todd Lepard, Owner-manager Accent Landscaping, Lethbridge, Alberta.

III. Marketing Strategy

III.1. Product   The marketing strategy of LRS Landscaping involves offering an existing product to a new market. Landscaping is not a novel service. However, for one reason or another, it has not been targeted at or widely purchased by homeowners on the Blood Reserve. While some homeowners have chosen to do their own landscaping, most have done nothing at all to their front and back yard areas. The possible reasons for this are either that they have not found a suitable provider of this service or that landscaping is relatively unimportant to homeowners on the reserve.

I have spoken to several new home owners and I am counting on the former explanation although doubtless, there are some homeowners who care little for the condition of their yard and the grounds surrounding their house. The service offered is not different from others offered by owners of similar businesses. The service will be quite basic, both to keep time spent on each job to a minimum and to keep the cost of the service below comparable services offered by off-reserve suppliers.

III.2. Pricing   Pricing will be the main way of differentiating this service offered from other potential providers. By using cheap labour and government incentive and assistance programs, in addition to the fact that the owner-manager does not have to pay tax on his income or profits from this business, he can offer a comparable service at a far lower price than existing competitors and still maintain his required profit levels. As well, the fact that customers do not have to pay GST on the service if it is provided by the owner rather than by off-reserve competitors should provide a competitive edge to the owner-operator in the area of pricing. However, the effects of this factor are mitigated by the fact that businesses that have less the $30,000 in sales per year do not have to register for the GST.

As well, because of the aforementioned factors, the service must be priced so that it will provide an attractive alternative to those homeowners who are considering landscaping their own yards, but whose time may be profitably or enjoyably spent doing other things.

Ideally, the service will be priced so that the business can operate at full capacity and at the same time maximize its profits. Finding the proper price range will require some time after the establishment of the business, at least until a range of suitable prices can be established for this particular market, but a good starting point is covering all costs including opportunity costs. The initial price for the service will be $1,650. This price may be raised or lowered, depending on demand. This compares favourably with off-reserve businesses, which would charge between $4,000 and $5,000 for a comparable service.[4]

III.3. Promotion   This business will be opening a new market to an existing service, so advertising and promotion will be important in ensuring the viability of this venture. In the months prior to the start of operations, the goal of promotion will be to create an awareness of the business and the product. Higher than average advertising costs are expected because the market may be unfamiliar with this service and because it has not previously been specifically targeted for this service.

In keeping with the rest of the business, advertising will be done using as economical of means as possible. Advertising costs for the proposed business have been calculated at $661.40

---

4   Todd Lepard. Owner-manager Accent Landscaping, Lethbridge, Alberta.

for five months of advertising. This includes advertisements in newspapers that are circulated on the Blood Reserve, including the Cardston Chronicle and the Blood Tribe Community News. As well, leaflets and advertisements on community billboards and store/agency windows will be used to heighten awareness of this service and may help draw in consumers from outside of the target market, ie. those who are not new homeowners by the definition used in this business plan but who still may desire the service. Too, word of mouth advertising is a viable way of publicizing the service and this can be done through my many relatives and friends on the Blood Reserve. Finally, going door-to-door is an option, because it will be obvious just who the potential customers are (the ones with unfinished yards). However, this is a less attractive option, because it is a rural setting which will mean that the distances covered in going door-to-door are substantially greater than in other markets and will result in higher advertising costs.

The advertisements will emphasize that the service will be inexpensive, that it is owned and operated by a member of the Blood Tribe, that it will be providing summer employment for Blood students, and that it will be GST free.

Advertising will begin a month (newspapers) to two months (leaflets, notices, etc.) prior to the beginning of operations.

IV. Location

IV.1. Trading Area

■ IV.1.1. Economic Base

The geographic area is very well defined. The Blood Indian Reserve is located in south-western Alberta, close to Lethbridge on the east, Fort Macleod on the north, and Cardston on the west. The reserve is the largest in Canada geographically, with a population of 4,015 as recorded in the 1991 Canada Census.[5] The primary area of economic activity on the Reserve is agriculture and the population is predominantly rural, and it does not have much private enterprise beyond farming and ranching, although in recent years several small businesses have been established. It is defined as a Reserve under the Indian Act of Canada and thus has well defined boundaries.

Beyond the areas of ranching and farming the only other significant source of income is administrative positions in the Blood administration and local government. In recent years several new business have opened up on the reserve, including three new gas stations, a convenience store, a local newspaper, and a couple of auto repair businesses. As well, there are a number of economic development and small business incentive programs available to residents and members of reserves who wish to start up businesses that will contribute to economic self-sufficiency and employment. The Canadian Aboriginal Economic Development Strategy, administered by Industry, Science, and Technology Canada, provides several programs designed to assist aboriginal commercial ventures. Many of the goals enumerated in the CAED Strategy are applicable to this venture, including increasing earned income among Aboriginal people, increasing Aboriginal employment, and broadening the base of Aboriginal businesses.[6]

---

5 Statistics Canada. *Profile of census divisions and subdivisions in Alberta. Part A.* Ottawa: Supply and Services Canada, 1992. 1991 Census of Canada. Catalogue number 95–372, [p.] 34.
6 Industry, Science, and Technology Canada. *Canadian Aboriginal Economic Development Strategy*, 8.

■ IV.1.2 Competition

There is no company or entity offering a comparable service on the reserve. However, because of the presence of three commercial centres in close proximity to the reserve it is expected that some competition may come from businesses in these areas. The major commercial centre in the region is Lethbridge, a city of approximately 65,000 located east of the Blood Reserve and connected to the reserve by a paved secondary road. As well, both Fort Macleod and Cardston are located close to the borders of the reserve. There are 30 landscaping services located in areas near the target market area, with the largest share being located in Lethbridge (24). These competitors offer a variety of services, including many services that LRS Landscaping will not offer. It is possible that some customers may be interested in landscaping but want a more elaborate or professional service than LRS Landscaping is able to provide. However, many of these competitors specialize in distinct segments of the landscaping services market, such as industrial and commercial design and landscaping, Japanese design, professional horticultural and design services, and environmentally friendly services. In perusing the Yellow Pages advertisements for these businesses, it was noticed that none of them target the Blood Indian Reserve or its residents.

VI.2. Specific Site   Because the proposed business is a service and the work that it does will be done on site, the specific site is less important than it would be if the business were involved in retailing or some other service industries. I have chosen to run the business from my home on the Blood Reserve. To ensure that potential customers will be able to reach me whether I am at home, at work, or somewhere else, I have decided that a cellular phone will be necessary. Basing the business in my place of residence will lessen some of the risk of starting up this business.

As well, because my home is located on the Blood Reserve and because I will be earning my income on the Blood Reserve any income from the business will not be subject to federal or provincial income taxes.[7] This enables the business to realize more net profit than if it were located off-reserve on the same amount of sales and also will cut down on the amount of paperwork that will have to be done by the owner-manager. One downside of being located on-reserve (as well as having all of my assets located on-reserve) is that obtaining financing from private funding institutions is nearly impossible, because section 89 of the Indian Act restricts the pledging of on-reserve property belonging to an Indian or an Indian Band as security for a loan.[8]

Because I have based the business in my home, I have used my average rent and utility expenses as the site costs for the proposed business, at $300/month. The site costs total $2,234. As well, my home on the Blood Reserve is located in the far southwestern corner of the reserve, meaning that transportation between home and work each day will cost me a significant amount over the course of the summer. However, I have not included this in any of my calculations because I would incur the same costs regardless of whether I worked for myself or worked for someone else.

Because the goal of the business is to make a profit in the first year of operations, insurance will be minimal. Liability insurance will cost $500 per year. Equipment insurance will cost an additional $25 per year.[9]

---

7   Reiter, Robert A. *A Legal Guide To Conducting Business On Indian Reserves.* 3rd printing. First Nations Resource Council, 1990.
8   Indian and Northern Affairs Canada. *Commercial Development Lending Programs: Support for Business Development.*

LRS Landscaping Plan
Site Costs, May 1994–August 1994

Rent and Utilities	$1,200	($300/month)
Telephone:		
Cellular Phone	250	Denis Cellular
Hookup	98	Denis Cellular
Estimated Monthly Charges	300	($50/month) Denis Cellular
Provincial License	60	Alberta Consumer & Corporate Affairs
Insurance:		
Liability Insurance	500	Astro Insurance
Equipment Insurance	25	Astro Insurance
Bond	250	Astro Insurance
TOTAL	$2,683	

V. Physical Facilities

V.1. Start-Up Supplies   The main piece of equipment is a Roto-Tiller. A BCS 8hp Roto-Tiller that has been used as a demo can be obtained for $1,800.[10] As noted above, it will cost an additional $25 to insure it. In addition, a truck will be necessary to haul the equipment and transport the owner-manager to and from the work site. The owner-manager already owns a 1981 Ford pickup which will serve this purpose, so no purchase is necessary. It is valued at $1.000.

In addition, tools and equipment necessary to the business must also be purchased. This includes such things as shovels, rakes, wheelbarrows and the like. It was estimated that the necessary tools and equipment can be purchased for approximately $500.[11]

Besides other common start-up costs, a cellular phone will be necessary to operate the proposed business efficiently. In addition, the hookup fee must also be paid in advance. The other start-up costs are quite standard.

LRS Landscaping
Start-Up Supplies

Equipment:		
1 BCS 8hp. Roto-tiller	$1,800	Master Farm Supply
Miscellaneous tools and Implements	500	Accent Landscaping
Office Supplies	100	Accent Landscaping
Telephone	250	Denis Cellular Phone
Hookup charge	98	Denis Cellular Phone
Two months charges	100	Denis Cellular Phone
Insurance (prepaid):		
Liability	500	Astro Insurance

---

9   Astro Insurance, Lethbridge, Alberta.
10   Master Farm Supply, Lethbridge, Alberta.
11   Todd Lepard, owner-manager, Accent Landscaping, Lethbridge, Alberta.

Equipment	25	Astro Insurance
Vehicle	450	Astro Insurance
Bond	250	Astro Insurance
License	60	Alberta Consumer and Corporate Affairs
Advertising:		
Newspaper Advertisement	227	Cardston Chronicle-Globe; Blood Tribe Community News
Other	100	
TOTAL	$4,460	

VI. Financial

VI.1. Feasibility Analysis

■ VI.1.1. Target Market and Trade Area

Each year on the Blood Reserve several new houses are built. It was estimated that 100 new houses have been built on the Blood Reserve in the last five years and that in the coming year, a minimum of 26 houses and a maximum of 52 houses will be built.[12] However, it is more than likely that some of these homeowners have already done their own landscaping and that others may not feel that this service is worth the price. However, this will still leave a number of potential clients who can be targeted as the main market for this service, as well as providing a fresh source of potential clients each year. As well, competition must be considered, although there are no competitors situated within the trade area. For the purpose of this business plan, the target market will be 126 households.

■ VI.1.2. Market Potential

Because this service is being targeted at this market for the first time, there is no market information on sales of this service to this area. However, an informal series of interviews and queries of some new homeowners, quoting a proposed price of $1,650, indicated that approximately one third of those spoken to were both interested in the service and had the ability to pay for the service.

$$42 \text{ homes} \times \$1,650 = \$69,300$$

■ VI.1.3. Market Share

Calculating the market share and potential net revenues for the proposed business requires first assessing the total capacity of the service available to the market area, or the market potential. After the capacity of the proposed business is calculated, the market share can be derived.

Although no other businesses in this field specifically target this market, there are several landscaping businesses in Lethbridge and the surrounding area, and their services are available to those who are interested. Many of these competitors offer more involved and sophisticated services than those that this firm is able to provide. It is difficult to calculate how much of the target market may be lost to these competitors. I have arbitrarily assigned half the market

---

12 Blood Tribe Department of Housing, Lenora Many Fingers, Standoff, Alberta.

to off-reserve competitors, on-reserve competitors, and do-it-yourselfers to reflect the uncertain status of this market.

Capacity of proposed business: There are 87 days available for working. A landscaper I interviewed said that he lost approximately 10% of his working days to rain. Taking into account delays for rain and inclement weather over the summer and statutory holidays, the proposed business has a capacity of 20 jobs.

Calculation of Market Share

$$\frac{20 \text{ homes}}{42 \text{ homes}} = 47.6\%$$

Adjustments to Market Share

Because of both the newness of this business and the fact that this service has not previously been offered to this market previously, I have taken approximately 10% off the market share, resulting in a 38% market share.

■ VI.1.4. Projected Net Income

A market share of 38% translates to a total of $26,334 in sales, rounded off to $26,400. This translates into 16 jobs over the summer, well within the capacity of the proposed business, even taking bad weather into account.

VI.2. Financing

■ VI.2.1. Start-Up Costs and Cash Flow

According to the cash flow statement, an initial opening balance of $6,000 will ensure that the opening balance at the start of each month is never negative, although in May the balance will drop to below $1,000. For the months of March and April, before operations begin, the disbursements total $2,160.56. Once operations begin, I will require a deposit of half the price of the job ($825) both to lessen my risk and to help pay for the materials and labour while working. This is why the receipts are divided into deposits (those made by customers) and collections, which will be due 30 days after the completion of the job.

With an opening balance of $3,000 (the investment required by the owner-manager), a loan of $3,000 will also be required to get the business past the first months until revenues catch up with expenditures. The crucial month is May, when the balance dips to $293.16. This is the month in which the equipment will be acquired. In all the other months of operation the balance never dips below $2,000, and in most cases, is substantially higher. It may be necessary to arrange for a line of credit or some contingency funding to sustain the business through this stage.

VI.3. Sources of Financing   I have chosen to divide the financing between owner's equity and a loan. A $3,000 investment by the owner-manager is not an unreasonable expectation, and can be raised by working during the school year or if necessary, can be obtained by leasing my land on the Blood Reserve. The other $3,000 will be obtained from the Federal Business Development Bank, through its Challenge program for summer students.[13] This program provides a loan of $3,000 to a student at the start of the summer which, if repaid

---

13   Telephone interview with Federal Business Development Bank, Lethbridge Branch.

before mid-October, is interest free. The final September balance of $9,865.60 will cover this loan (as well as my investment and the required rate of return on the investment) and thus allow the proposed business to acquire the necessary funds interest free. If I am unable to obtain funds through the FBDB, I will attempt to obtain financing from the Aboriginal Business Development, administered by ISTC. This program provides low-interest loans to aboriginal entrepreneurs who wish to establish commercially viable businesses.

VI.4. Accounting System   The number of transactions that flow through the business will be relatively small, therefore a simple accounting system can be utilized. A one-book manual system of recording and classifying transactions will be used, keeping track of the date and description of receipts and disbursements and classifying them as either expense, revenue, or balance sheet items on the same page.

VI.5. Credit Policy   LRS Landscaping will require a deposit equal to half the total price of the contracted job. This will serve two purposes. First, it will lessen the risk imposed upon the owner-manager in the event that the person backs out of the contract and secondly it will break the price of the service into two more manageable portions. The remaining portion will be due 30 days after the completion of the job, after which a penalty of 5% will be imposed for each month overdue.

When accounts are overdue the first step will be to send a letter to the client politely reminding him or her that the remainder of his or her bill is still unpaid and that he or she will be liable for the 5% penalty. The provision for the penalty will be included in the initial agreement. If the account remains overdue 45 days after completion, another less polite letter will be mailed to the client demanding both the remaining portion of the fee and the penalty and offering to take partial payments if full payment is not possible. If this elicits no response, a letter will be sent after 60 days threatening legal action. Finally, if the bill is remains unpaid, there are two options: legal action or writing the debt off as a bad debt. While neither of these options are attractive, they may be necessary. Fortunately, the business will have legal recourse against the person because it is a proprietorship owned by a treaty Indian on an Indian reserve and therefore can sue other treaty Indians for nonpayment. This would not be the case if the business were incorporated.

VI.6. Financial Evaluation   Monthly statements of income and cash flow will be prepared by the owner and compared both to projected statements and standard industry ratios of profitability, performance, and liquidity. If any serious deficiencies or worrisome trends are noted, measures can then be taken to address the problem before it develops into something that could threaten the existence of the business. As well, quarterly and yearly statements of income and cash flow, as well as balance sheets will be prepared, and ratios will be calculated from these statements.

VII. Personnel

VII.1 Administrative Structure   The hours at LRS Landscaping will be from 8 am to 5 pm. with a one hour break for lunch from 12 to 1. As well, there will be two short breaks during the day, at 10 am. and 3 pm. The business will employ two people, the owner-manager at $7.50 per hour and one employee at $6.00 per hour. It is expected that the business will pay 16 weeks of wages, so the salary and wage expenses will be:

Owner-manager
(40 hours/week × 16 weeks @ $7.50/hr) $4,800
Employee
(40 hours/week × 16 weeks @ $6.00/hr) $3,840
                                    TOTAL $8,640

Because the proposed business will be relatively small, the structure will be simple, with the employee under the owner-manager. The owner manager will be responsible for all administrative, financial, and supervisory duties, while the employee will be responsible for his or her share of the physical work and any other miscellaneous duties that the owner-manager may be unable to do at the time, restricted, of course, to work and the job site. The owner-manager will also keep a journal of his activities classified into his functions such as labouring, record keeping, accounting, planning, etc.

VII.2. Employee Recruitment

First, it is necessary to compose a job description for the employee so that he or she will be aware of what the job entails before accepting or rejecting an offer of employment.

- **Duties**: levelling and sodding work and heavy lifting. Occasionally take orders on telephone.
- **Responsible to**: owner-manager of LRS Landscaping.
- **Requirements**: must be physically fit and strong enough to do the physical work this job requires, must be able to learn to use roto-tiller.
- **Personal**: must enjoy outdoors work, must be punctual, and will not object to working occasional weekends if necessary.

Recruitment should not be a problem. The owner-manager of a landscaping business in southern Alberta said that he did not even have to advertise for employees, that instead, people came to him looking for work.[14] The job requires only one employee and pays at a rate comparable to other similar jobs in the area. The Hire-a-student service will be used to refer possible employees to the business. The owner-manager will then personally interview the person, informing him or her of the job description and what would be expected of him or her if employed at LRS Landscaping. It is expected that finding a satisfactory candidate will not take long.

VII.3. Evaluation and Training

Employees will be hired on a seasonal, full-time basis, so a lengthy period of evaluation and/or probation will not be possible. Because the owner-manager will be working alongside the employee on the job site, evaluation and feedback on the quality of the employee's work will be relatively straightforward. The atmosphere on the job site will be very casual, and a good relationship between the employee and the owner-manager will go a long way toward ensuring the business is productive and profitable. If any serious problems in the employee's quality of work or attendance or punctuality are noted, the employee will be informed and will be warned.

Training will be minimal. Basically, the job requires unskilled labour, and the time required to learn how to operate the roto-tiller will be negligible.

---

14 Todd Lepard, owner-manager, Accent Landscaping, Lethbridge, Alberta.

VII.4. Policies   Although the work atmosphere will be quite informal, some policies will be necessary to ensure that no problems or misunderstandings develop between the employer and employee. These policies will clarify what is expected of the employee and what the employee can expect of the employer.

* the employee will be paid the Wednesday after each two week period of work
* the employer will notify the employee at least one week in advance if he or she is required to work at times not within the regular work week.
* employees are expected to arrive at work on time and leave only at the end of the working day. The employee will be docked for any lateness over an hour during a week.
* the employee will notify the employer as soon as possible if he or she cannot be at work at any time.
* wages will be $6.00 per hour.
* the employee will be allowed one paid sick day per month.
* use of alcohol and/or drugs on the job or on the work site will not be tolerated, and will result in dismissal.

VIII. Legal Requirements

LRS Landscaping will be a sole proprietorship. There are several reasons why this form of organization has been chosen. First, it is simple and inexpensive to start. There will be no need to worry about share structure, a corporate charter, or any of the other paperwork that accompanies incorporation. However, this is a minor reason for not choosing incorporation. The main reason that the business will be a sole proprietorship is that a corporation cannot be an "Indian" under the Indian act. It instead is a separate legal entity and therefore would be liable for income tax, even if it owned by in Indian person.[15] There are some disadvantages to being a sole proprietorship. The main disadvantage of sole proprietorships is that they have difficulty obtaining financing. It is hoped that by obtaining financing through the FBDB Challenge program or the ISTC Aboriginal Business Development Program these difficulties can be mitigated.

Alberta Consumer and Corporate Affairs requires that landscaping business that take any money in advance of completing a job must have both provincial license and a $5,000 bond.[16] Both of these requirements have been taken care of in the financing section of the business plan. The cost of the license is minimal, and the bond will cost $250 according to a local insurance company.[17] As for any local regulations pertaining to the Blood Reserve, there are no requirements for sole proprietorships on the Blood Reserve to have any sort of local or municipal license. As well, there is no local tax on businesses located on the Blood Reserve owned by Blood Indians.

---

15 Reiter, Robert A. *A Legal Guide to Conducting Business on Indian Reserves.* 3rd printing. First Nations Resource Council, 1990.
16 Telephone interview with person from Alberta Consumer and Corporate affairs.
17 Astro Insurance, Lethbridge, Alberta.

LRS Landscaping
Projected Income Statement
for the year ended December 31, 1994

		% of Revenue	
Revenue:			
Sales	$26,400.00	100.00%	Feasibility Study
Cost of Goods Sold	7,200.00	27.27%	Bos Sod Farms
Gross Margin	19,200.00	72.73%	
Expenses:			
Manager's Salary	4,800.00	18.18%	@ 7.50/hr.
Employee wages	3,840.00	14.55%	@ 6.00/hr.
Maintenance and Repair	500.00	1.89%	Accent Landscaping
Rent and Utilities	1,200.00	4.55%	p. 19
Telephone hookup	98.00	0.37%	Denis Cellular
Telephone expenses	300.00	1.14%	Denis Cellular
Office Supplies	100.00	0.80%	Accent Landscaping
Insurance:			
Liability	500.00	1.89%	Astro Insurance
Equipment	25.00	0.09%	Astro Insurance
Vehicle	450.00	1.70%	Astro Insurance
Bond	250.00	0.95%	Astro Insurance
License	60.00	0.23%	Alberta Consumer and Corporate Affairs
Depreciation:			
Roto-Tiller	360.00	1.36%	See Schedule of Depreciation
Vehicle	200.00	0.76%	
Advertising	651.40	2.51%	Blood Tribe Community News; Cardston Chronicle-Globe
Total Expenses	$13,544.40	50.55%	
Net Profit	$ 5,855.60	22.18%	

LRS Landscaping
Projected Cash Flow Statement
for year ended December 31, 1994

Receipts:		
Sales	$26,400.00	Feasibility Study
Loan	3,000.00	FBDB Challenge Program
Total Receipts	$32,400.00	
Disbursements:		
Rent and Utilities	1,200.00	$300/mo. (p. 19)
Wages	8,640.00	p. 30
Cost of Goods Sold	7,200.00	$1.50/sq.yd. delivered (GST free) Bos Sod Farms
Bond	250.00	Astro Insurance
Licence	60.00	Alberta Consumer and Corporate Affairs
Insurance	975.00	Astro Insurance
Advertising	641.40	Cardston Chronicle-Globe; Blood Tribe Community News
Telephone	648.00	Denis Cellular Phone
Equipment	2,300.00	Master Farm Supply, Accent Landscaping
Loan Repayment	3,000.00	p. 27
Office Supplies	100.00	Accent Landscaping
Maintenance/repairs	500.00	Accent Landscaping.
Total Disbursements	$25,534.40	
Net Inflow (Outflow)	$ 6,865.60	

Notes on Financial Statements

Income Statements   Although the vehicle was already owned by the owner-manager, I have included its depreciation as an expense on the income statement. Although the business is situated on an Indian reserve and therefore not subject to income tax I have used the rate of depreciation described the Capital Cost Allowance in calculating depreciation. This facilitates comparison with other businesses and industry averages. Similarly, I have depreciated the roto-tiller at 20% per year as well. One final note on depreciation should be included. Although the CCA is supposed to be assessed on a yearly basis, I have included the year's depreciation over the period during which the assets were used in the business. I did not include depreciation for either the telephone or the miscellaneous tools and implements because these items generally do not lose value or wear out. While allocating their cost via depreciation expenses may have been possible, I have included not done this, because the amount would have been negligible, and the term over which they were to be depreciated is more uncertain than with machinery.

The telephone expenses break down to a monthly charge of $24.50 with airtime charges above that. When interviewing the person from Denis Cellular I asked him to estimate the total monthly charges for a business like mine and $50 per month was the figure he quoted me. As well, the range of cellular telephone prices ranged from $100 to $500, and he said that $250 was a reasonable estimate.

Although the insurance for the liability and equipment is assessed on a yearly basis, I have allocated these costs over a six month time span because they will not be used either before or after that time period. The insurance agent I spoke to said that they only offered these types of insurance on a yearly basis. The same is true with the license and the bond.

Cash Flow Statement   In the cash flow statement, the specific rates for advertising are $5.32 per week for advertising in the Chronicle-Globe and an initial charge of $50 plus $45 for each subsequent advertisement in the Blood Tribe Community News. These newspapers were chosen because together, they cover most of the Blood Reserve.

Sources

Balderson, D.W. *Canadian Entrepreneurship and Small Business Management. Second Edition.* Richard D. Irwin, Inc. Burr Ridge, Illinois: 1994.

Gardner-O'Toole. *Aboriginal People and Taxation.* Ottawa: Library of Parliament, September 1992.

Reiter, R.A. *A Legal Guide to Conducting Business on Indian Reserves.* Third Printing. First Nations Resource Council. 1990.

Statistics Canada. *Profile of Census Divisions and Subdivisions in Alberta — Part A.* Ottawa: Supply and Services Canada, 1992. 1991 Census of Canada.

Industry and Science Canada. *Aboriginal Business Development Program.*

Indian and Northern Affairs Canada. *Building A Future: DIAND and the Canadian Aboriginal Economic Development Strategy.* Ottawa: 1993.

Industry, Science, and Technology Canada. *Aboriginal Economic Programs. Policy Guidelines.* Volume 1. Ottawa: August 17, 1990.

Interviews

- Federal Business Development Bank. Lethbridge Branch.
- Todd Lepard. Accent Landscaping, Lethbridge, Alberta.
- The Canadian Imperial Bank of Commerce, Lethbridge Branch.
- The Cardston Chronicle-Globe, Cardston, Alberta.
- Blood Tribe Community News, Standoff, Alberta.
- Lenora Many Fingers, Blood Tribe Department of Housing, Standoff, Alberta.
- Bos Sod Farms.
- Master Farm Supply, Lethbridge, Alberta.

COMMON LICENCES AND TAXES THAT APPLY TO ——————— THE SMALL BUSINESS (BY JURISDICTION) (from Chapter 4)

Topic	Comment	Municipal	Provincial	Federal
Licence and Permits				
City business permits		X		
Zoning by-laws	Applicable to certain provinces	X		
Land use regulations		X		
Business, school, water, taxes		X		
Provincial corporation income tax, estate taxes			X	
Capital tax (Ontario, Quebec, Manitoba, Saskatchewan, B.C.)	Applicable only to these provinces		X	
Quebec place of business tax	Applicable only to Quebec		X	
Sales and Excise Taxes				
Provincial excise tax	For consumer goods, must obtain a certificate from Department of Revenue, and vendor collects sales tax from consumer			X
Federal corporation income tax				X
Goods and Services Tax (GST)	Generally 7%, but certain goods exempted, e.g., foodstuffs			X
Revenue Canada Excise Branch Federal Sales and Excise Tax Office	Manufacturers or producers can obtain a manufacturing licence for sales tax exemption on raw material purchased			X
Export/import permit	All Canadian importers and exporters must obtain permit			X
Federal sales and excise taxes on imported goods	Levied on duty-paid value of some items			X
Custom duties on imported goods	Amount levied varies according to type of goods imported as classified by Canadian customs			X

CHECKLIST OF CONSIDERATIONS IN PURCHASING A BUSINESS ———
(from Chapter 5)

The Industry
1. What are the sales and profit trends of the industry?
2. What is the degree of competition, and what competitive changes have taken place?
3. What is the nature of competitor strategies?
4. What is the state of the economy in the market, and how is performance of the business affected by changes in the economy?
5. What existing or pending legal restrictions affect the operations of the business?
6. What social or cultural concerns affect the industry?
7. Are there any potential competitive or trading area changes that might affect the business?

The Previous Owner
1. Why is the previous owner selling the business?
2. Has the reputation of the previous owner contributed to the success of the business?
3. Will the previous owner help you by providing assistance and advice after the sale?
4. Is the previous owner willing to finance all or part of the purchase?
5. Will the previous owner be starting a competitive business after the sale?

Financial Condition of the Business
1. Is the financial information that has been provided accurate and indicative of the business performance?
2. What is the past history of profits going back at least five years?
3. Has the business gained or lost market share in the past five years?
4. How do the various financial ratios for the business compare with industry averages?
5. Does the business have a strong identity with customers or clients, and can this be maintained?
6. What prospects does the business have for increasing market share and profitability in the future?
7. If the business is currently unsuccessful, what are the chances that this can be improved with an infusion of capital and/or management expertise?
8. What value is being placed on goodwill?

Condition of Assets
1. Are there any special terms or conditions associated with the liquid assets?
2. Are the accounts receivable collectible?
3. Is the inventory old or obsolete?
4. Are the building and equipment up-to-date and paid for?
5. Are taxes and service costs paid on land?
6. Is the location good? Is it increasing or decreasing in value?
7. Is the lease good? What are the terms and conditions of the lease?

Quality of Personnel

1. Do the employees of the business compare favourably with the industry in productivity and expertise?
2. Will the employees stay on with the business after the sale?
3. Has the business been progressive in meeting competitive demands regarding wage rates and employee benefits?

Condition of External Relationships

1. Can favourable relations be maintained with suppliers?
2. Are financial sources appropriate and adequate, and can they be maintained?
3. Does the business have a strong support staff such as a lawyer, an accountant, and a consultant; and can they be retained if needed?

Condition of the Records

1. Can the purchaser obtain key records such as credit files, personnel files, customer lists, sales reports, and contracts?

A SAMPLING OF CANADIAN FRANCHISERS (from Chapter 5)

Franchisor	Number of Units Owned	Total Units Operated	Initial Fee ($)	Royalty (%)	Investment Required ($)
Bonanza	–	51	40,000	4.8	350–400,000
Budget Rent A Car	–	375	15,000	10	varies
Century 21 Real Estate	–	425	20,000	6	60–70,000
College Pro Painters	–	2%	–	10	2,500
Dairy Queen of Canada	–	406	30,000	4	600–1,100,000
Magicuts	18	149	18,000	7 (1.5 adv)	60,000
McDonalds Restaurants	236	230	250,000	9 (16 adv)	650,000+
Midas Muffler	35	184	25,000	5	225,000
Ramada Inns	40	590	35,000	3	varies
Second Cup	3	147	20,000	9	175–225,000
Tim Hortons	–	420	15,000	3 (adv)	230,000
Zippy Print	10	80	40,000	5	135,000

Source: Franchise Annual 1990, Info Franchise News, St. Catherines, Ontario LZR 6W8.

A CHECKLIST FOR THE POTENTIAL FRANCHISEE ——————— (Questions to answer affirmatively before going into franchising) (from Chapter 5)

About the Franchiser

1. Has the franchiser been in business long enough (five years or more) to have established a good reputation?
2. Have you checked Better Business bureaus, Chambers of Commerce, government agencies, Association of Canadian Franchisers, industry associations, or bankers to find out about the franchiser's business reputation and credit rating?
3. Did the above investigations reveal that the franchiser has a good reputation and credit rating?
4. Does the franchising firm appear to be financed adequately so that it can carry out its stated plan of financial assistance and expansion?
5. Have you found out how many franchisees are now operating?
6. Have you found out the "mortality" or failure rate among franchisees?
7. Is the failure rate small?
8. Have you checked with some franchisees and found that the franchiser has a reputation for honesty and fair dealing among those who currently hold franchises?
9. Has the franchiser shown you certified figures indicating exact net profits of one or more going operations which you have personally checked yourself?
10. Has the franchiser given you a specimen contract to study with the advice of your legal counsel?
11. Will the franchiser assist you with:
    a. A management training program?
    b. An employee training program?
    c. A public relations program?
    d. Obtaining capital?
    e. Good credit terms?
    f. Merchandising ideas?
    g. Designing store layout and displays?
    h. Inventory control methods?
    i. Analyzing financial statements?
12. Does the franchiser provide continuing assistance for franchisees through supervisors who visit regularly?
13. Does the franchising firm have an experienced management trained in depth?
14. Will the franchiser assist you in finding a good location for your business?
15. Has the franchising company investigated you carefully enough to assure itself that you can successfully operate one of its franchises at a profit both to it and to you?
16. Have you determined exactly what the franchiser can do for you that you cannot do for yourself?

The Product or Service

17. Has the product or service been on the market long enough to gain good consumer acceptance?
18. Is it priced competitively?

19. Is it the type of item or service the same consumer customarily buys more than once?
20. Is it an all-year seller in contrast to a seasonal one?
21. Is it a staple item in contrast to a fad?
22. Does it sell well elsewhere?
23. Would you buy it on its merits?
24. Will it be in greater demand five years from now?
25. If it is a product rather than a service:
    a. Is it packaged attractively?
    b. Does it stand up well in use?
    c. Is it easy and safe to use?
    d. Is it patented?
    e. Does it comply with all applicable laws?
    f. Is it manufactured under certain quality standards?
    g. Do these standards compare favourably with similar products on the market?
    h. If the product must be purchased exclusively from the franchiser or a designated supplier, are the prices for you, as the franchisee, competitive?

The Franchise Contract

26. Does the franchise fee seem reasonable?
27. Do continuing royalties or percent of gross sales payment appear reasonable?
28. Are the total cash investment required and the terms for financing the balance satisfactory?

The Franchise Contract

29. Does the cash investment include payment for fixtures and equipment?
30. If you will be required to participate in company-sponsored promotion and publicity by contributing to an advertising fund, will you have the right to veto any increase in contributions to the fund?
31. If the parent company's product or service is protected by patent or liability insurance, is the same protection extended to you?
32. Are you free to buy the amount of merchandise you believe you need rather than being required to purchase a certain amount?
33. Can you, as the franchisee, return merchandise for credit?
34. Can you engage in other business activities?
35. If there is an annual sales quota, can you retain your franchise if it is not met?
36. Does the contract give you an exclusive territory for the length of the franchise?
37. Is your territory protected?
38. Is the franchise agreement renewable?
39. Can you terminate your agreement if you are not happy for some reason?
40. Is the franchiser prohibited from selling the franchise out from under you?
41. May you sell the business to whomever you please?
42. If you sell your franchise, will you be compensated for the goodwill you have built into the business?
43. Does the contract obligate the franchiser to give you continuing assistance after you are operating the business?
44. Are you permitted a choice in determining whether you will sell any new product or service introduced by the franchiser after you have opened your business?

45. Is there anything with respect to the franchise or its operation that would make you ineligible for special financial assistance or other benefits accorded to small business concerns by federal, provincial, or local governments?
46. Did your lawyer approve the franchise contract after he studied it paragraph by paragraph?
47. Is the contract free and clear of requirements that would call upon you to take any steps which are, according to your lawyer, unwise or illegal in your province, country, or city?
48. Does the contract cover all aspects of your agreement with the franchiser?
49. Does it really benefit both you and the franchiser?

Your Market

50. Are the territorial boundaries of your market completely, accurately, and understandably defined?
51. Have you made any study to determine whether the product or service you propose to sell has a market in your territory at the prices you will have to charge?
52. Does the territory provide an adequate sales potential?
53. Will the population in the territory given you increase over the next five years?
54. Will the average per capita income in the territory remain the same or increase over the next five years?
55. Is the existing competition in your territory for the product or service not too well entrenched?
56. Are you prepared to give up some independence of action to secure the advantages offered by the franchise?
57. Are you capable of accepting supervision, even though you will presumably be your own boss?
58. Are you prepared to accept rules and regulations with which you may not agree?
59. Can you afford the period of training involved?
60. Are you ready to spend much or all of the remainder of your business life with this franchiser, offering this product or service to the public?

SOURCE: Adapted from Wendell O. Metcalf, "Starting and Managing a Small Business of Your Own," *The Starting and Managing Series*, Vol. 1, 3rd ed. (Washington, D.C.: Small Business Administration, 1973), pp. 50–55.

ADVERTISING AS PRACTISED BY SELECTED SMALL BUSINESSES ——— (from Chapter 7)

Type of Business	Average Ad Budget (% of sales)	Favourite Media	Other Media Used
Gift stores	2.2	Weekly newspapers	Yellow Pages, radio, direct mail, magazines
Hair-dressing shops	2.0–5.0	Yellow Pages	Newspapers (for special events), word of mouth
Home furnishing stores	1.0–3.2	Newspapers	Direct mail, radio
Pet shops	2.0–5.0	Yellow Pages	Window displays, shopper newspapers, direct mail
Restaurants and food services	0.3–3.2	Newspapers, radio, Yellow Pages, transit, outdoor	Television for chain or franchise restaurants
Shoe stores	0.5–0.8	Newspapers, direct mail, radio	Yellow Pages (especially for specialty shoe vendors)
Bars and cocktail lounges	1.0–1.2	Newspapers (entertainment section), local magazines, tourist bulletins	Specialties
Bookstores	1.5–1.6	Newspapers, shoppers, Yellow Pages	Direct Mail
Building maintenance services		Direct mail, door-to-door, Yellow Pages	Signs on company vehicles and equipment
Camera shops (independent)	2.0–3.5	Direct mail, handouts, Yellow Pages	Newspapers (except large urban)
Drugstores (independent)	1.0–3.0	Local newspapers, shoppers	Direct Mail (list from prescription files)
Dry cleaning plants	0.9–2.0	Local newspapers, shoppers, Yellow Pages	Store front, ads, pamphlets on clothes care
Equipment rental services	1.7–4.7	Yellow Pages	

Adapted from Dennis H. Tootelian and Ralph M. Gaedeke, *Small Business Review* (Sacramento, CA: Goodyear Publishing Company, 1978), pp. 154–55; and Dun and Bradstreet Operating Statistics, 1990. Dun and Bradstreet, Toronto.

CHECKLIST FOR A MARKETING PLAN ————————————————
(from Chapter 7)

The Target Market

1. Has the target market been clearly defined geographically?
2. Has the target consumer been clearly identified?
3. What are target consumer characteristics: age, income, education, occupation?
4. What are target consumer lifestyle characteristics such as activities, interests, opinions, media habits, and personalities?
5. What are target consumer purchase characteristics such as what, when, where, and how much of the product or service they purchase?
6. What are the reasons the target consumer purchases the product?
7. Are there any government programs that can assist in marketing to the target consumer?

The Environment

1. What economic forces will affect the business?
2. What is the competitive situation? How many competitors? What are relative market shares? What is the nature of competitor strategies? What are competitor strengths and weaknesses?
3. What legal restrictions will impact on the marketing of the business?
4. Are there any social or cultural trends which will affect the business?
5. What adjustments have been made to accommodate any of the above environmental constraints?

The Product

1. What are the objectives and policies for the product?
2. How will the product be manufactured?
3. What is the estimated length of the life cycle for the product?
4. What can be done to increase rate of adoption of the product?
5. How does the target consumer classify the product?
6. What will be product quality, depth, and variety?
7. What warranty and service standards will be set?
8. Does the product or service possess the features or characteristics the target consumer wants?

Distribution

1. What channel options are available to reach the target consumer?
2. Can the product be marketed best through a shorter direct channel or a longer indirect channel?
3. Who are potential buyers for the product?
4. What trade shows exist for the industry?
5. What level of intensity should exist in the distribution channel?
6. Will the selected distribution channel provide the product to the target consumer at the right place, at the right time, and in the right quantities?

Price

1. What price policies have been set?
2. What price is the target consumer willing to pay?
3. How important is price to the target consumer?
4. What levels of mark-up are required to cover selling and overhead costs?
5. What are competitor prices and how do they compare with our product price?

Promotion

1. What are the objectives of the promotional program?
2. Does the theme reflect target consumer needs and attitudes?
3. What specific media will be selected to carry the message to the target consumer?
4. Is personal selling required for the product?
5. How much will be spent on promotion?
6. What is the timing of the promotional program? Has a calendar timetable been prepared for this?
7. How will the results of the promotion be evaluated?
8. Will the business offer credit to the target consumer? If so, what procedures will be followed to screen, monitor, and collect accounts?

CHECKLIST FOR BUYING A SMALL BUSINESS COMPUTER ——————
(from Chapter 8)

1. Take an introductory computer course or read a book on small business.
2. Invest in independent consulting advice.
3. Determine the potential benefits your organization can obtain from EDP (electronic data processing).
4. Examine your existing systems and their deficiencies.
5. Define your information needs.
6. Estimate your current costs.
7. Prepare and send out a request for proposals.
8. Consider feasibility questions:
   a. Will it work?
   b. Will it pay?
   c. Will we use it?
   d. Will it cause adverse effects?
9. Avoid potential risks:
   a. Availability of proper personnel.
   b. Availability of suitable computer programs.
   c. Continued support of software.
   d. Expendability of the equipment.
   e. Security of the computer installation.
   f. Security of files and programs.
   g. Availability of a disaster recovery plan.
   h. Adequate formal management and personnel discipline.
   i. Careful selection of the computer system.
10. Deal carefully with suppliers:
    a. Get everything in writing.
    b. See a realistic demonstration.
    c. Check the suppliers' references.
    d. Negotiate a contract.
11. Develop and follow an implementation plan:
    a. Form a conversion and installation team.
    b. Involve top management.
    c. Plan your conversion carefully.
    d. Emphasize careful system testing.

SOURCE: Harvey S. Gellman, *A Buyer's Guide to Small Business Computers* (Toronto: The Canadian Information Processing Society, 1979), p. 12.

USE OF FINANCIAL RATIOS FOR A SMALL BUSINESS (FOOD STORE WITH ASSETS LESS THAN $100,000) (from Chapter 8)

Ratio	Method of Computation	Last Year	Previous Year	Industry Average*	Explanation
LIQUIDITY					
Current Ratio	Current assets ÷ current liabilities	1.5 times	1.4 times	1.3 times	Satisfactory: This retailer has the same ability (a bit better) as is common in the industry.
Quick Ratio	(Current assets – Inventories) ÷ Current liabilities	.7 times	.5 times	.5 times	Same as above.
PRODUCTIVITY					
Inventory Turnover	Cost of goods sold ÷ Average inventory (at cost) or Sales ÷ Average Inventory (at retail)	17 times	16 times	14.9 times	Good: This retailer has a higher turnover rate than the average retailer. This may indicate a higher sales level or lower inventory levels.
Collection	Average inventory at retail ÷ Daily credit sales	7 days	9 days	2.8 days	Poor: The collection period is longer than average which may indicate the need to tighten the credit policy; however, it seems that some action has already been taken.

...continued

...continued from previous page

Ratio	Method of Computation	Last Year	Previous Year	Industry Average*	Explanation
PROFITABILITY					
Gross Margins	Gross Sales – Cost of goods sold or a percent of sales	5%	6%	N/A	
Profit on Sales	Net profit (before tax) ÷ Gross sales	.4%	.5%	1.3%	Poor: The inventory may be old or prices may be too low.
Expense Ratio	Expense Item ÷ Gross Sales	14%	15%	N/A	Good: The company is making an effort to cut expenses.
Return on Investment	Net profit (before tax) ÷ Owner's equity	3.1%	1.5%	1.3%	Good: This company is more profitable than most in the industry. It is clear that action is being taken to improve profitability of this firm.
DEBT					
Total Debt to Equity	Total debt ÷ Owner's equity	120%	100%	58.9%	Poor: This retailer depends more on debt financing than is common in this industry. And more debt has been taken on in the past year.

*Based on Dun and Bradstreet, *Canadian Industry Norms and Key Business Ratios, 1993*, Food Stores with assets under $100,000.

LABOUR LEGISLATION JURISDICTION (from Chapter 10)

Topic	Comments	Municipal	Provincial	Federal
Minimum age: contact provincial department of labour	Varies among provinces		X	
Minimum wage: contact minimum wage commission	Each province has its own industrial relations legislation		X	
Hours of work, annual vacations, holidays; contact provincial department of labour	Varies among provinces; general standard is two weeks; other holidays depend on the province		X	
Workers' compensation; contact provincial workers' compensation commission	Contributed by employer		X	
Industrial safety and health contact provincial department of labour	Major jurisdiction from provinces; some federal jurisdiction		X	
Unemployment insurance; contact Canada Employment and Immigration Commission	Contributed by employer			X
Canadian pension plan; contact Revenue Canada, District Taxation Office	Except in province of Quebec, where contributions are made to Quebec Pension Plan and both employer and employee contribute			X
Employment equity	Contact provincial department of labour; Ontario has legislation; Some federal guidelines		X	
Hours of operation	Contact city hall	X		

FEDERAL INCOME TAX RATES FOR INDIVIDUALS ——————
(from Chapter 11)

Taxable Income	Tax Rate*
Up to $29,590	17%
$29,591 – $59,180	$5,030** + 26% of next $29,590
$59,181 and over	$12,724*** + 29% on remainder

*the taxable income brackets are indexed for annual inflation in excess of 3%. A surtax of 3 percent must be added after taking any personal credits in account.
** calculated as 17% of $29,590 = $5,030 (rounded)
*** calculated as $5,030 + 26% of $29,590 (rounded)

1994 PROVINCIAL TAX RATES (PERCENT OF FEDERAL TAX) ——————
(from Chapter 11)

	Provincial Rates		Provincial Rates
British Columbia (a)	52.5%	Nova Scotia (h)	59.5%
Alberta (b)	45.5%	Prince Edward Island (i)	59.5%
Saskatchewan (c)	50.0%	Newfoundland	69.0%
Manitoba (d)	52.0%	Northwest Territories (j)	45.0%
Ontario (e)	58.8%	Yukon	52.0%
Quebec (f)			
New Brunswick (g)	69.0%		

NOTES: Not all provinces have publisher their respective budgets; therefore these rates are subject to change.

(a) A surtax of 30% applies to B.C. tax exceeding $5,300. An additional surtax of 20% applies to B.C. tax exceeding $9,000

(b) A surtax of 8% of basic Alberta tax in excess of $3,500 and a flat tax of 0.5% of Alberta taxable income are levied

(c) There is a flat tax of 2% of net income and a surtax of 15% on Saskatchewan tax (including flat tax) in excess of $4,000. An additional "Deficit Surtax" of 10% is applicable to basic Saskatchewan tax plus the flat tax.

(d) A flat tax of 2% of net income and a surtax equal to 2% of net income in excess of $30,000 are levied in Manitoba.

(e) For 1994, a surtax of 20% applies to Ontario tax exceeding $5,500 plus an additional surtax of 10 % on Ontario tax exceeding $8,000.

(f) Quebec collects its own taxes at the rates noted below.

(g) A surtax of 8% applies to basic New Brunswick tax in excess of $13,500.

(h) For 1994, a surtax of 20% applies to Nova Scotia tax in excess of $7,000 plus an additional surtax of 10% on tax payable in excess of $10,499.

(i) A surtax of 10% applies to basic P.E.I. tax in excess of $12,500.

(j) A surtax of 5% applies to Yukon Territory tax in excess of $6,000.

1994 Quebec Tax Rates

Taxable Income	Tax on Lower Limit	Tax Rate on Excess
$ 0–7,000	$ –	16.0%
7,000–14,000	1,120	19.0%
14,000–23,000	2,450	21.0%
23,000–50,000	4,340	23.0%
50,000 and over	10,550	24.0%

NOTES: Residents of Quebec receive a reduction of their federal taxes equal to 16.5% of Basic Federal tax. Quebec imposes a surtax of 5% of Quebec tax exceeding $5,000 plus 5% of Quebec tax exceeding $10,000.

A tax reduction is granted to 2% of the excess of $10,000 over tax payable after deducting non-refundable tax credits. This tax reduction declines as taxes payable approach $10,000.

FEDERAL AND PROVINCIAL CORPORATE TAX RATES (EFFECTIVE JANUARY 1, 1994) (from Chapter 11)

	Small Business Corporations	Other Corporations
Federal Rates	12.84%	28.84%
Provincial Rates		
British Columbia	10.0%	16.0%
Alberta	6.0%	15.5%
Saskatchewan	8.5%	17.0%
Manitoba	9.5%	17.0%
Ontario	9.5%	15.5%
Quebec	5.75%	8.9%
New Brunswick	9.0%	17.0%
Nova Scotia	5.0%	16.0%
Prince Edward Island	7.5%	15.0%
Newfoundland	5.0%	16.0%
Northwest Territories	5.0%	14.0%
Yukon Territory	6.0%	15.0%

C H A P T E R   1 4

Information Resources

CHAPTER OBJECTIVES

☐   To provide a list of print references for the aboriginal small business owner.

☐   To provide a list of government departments and other organizations where the small business owner can go for advice and information.

☐   To describe Aboriginal Business Canada and other sources of capital for the aboriginal small business.

☐   To list current Internet web sites relating to aboriginal business.

SOURCES OF INFORMATION FOR ABORIGINAL BUSINESSES ─────────
(from Chapter 3)

General Small Business Reference Books

ABC Assistance to Business in Canada, Federal Business Development Bank, 204 Richmond St. West, Toronto, Ontario, M5V 1V6, (416) 973–0062.

Canadian Small Business Guide, CCH Canadian Ltd., 6 Garamond Court, Don Mills, Ontario, M3C 1Z5.

The Financial Post Canadian Markets, Maclean Hunter Ltd., 777 Bay Street, Toronto, Ontario, M5W 1A7, (416) 596–5585. This book provides complete demographics for Canadian urban markets. It looks at 500 municipalities across Canada with populations greater than 5,000. [It includes data on demographics; income; manufacturing activity; television, radio, and newspaper statistics; other economic statistics; average and annual growth rate of the population; and future population projections.]

Handbook of Canadian Consumer Markets, The Conference Board of Canada, Suite 100, 25 McArthur Road, Ottawa, Ontario, K1L 6R3, (613) 746–1281. [This book includes data on provincial, rural, marital populations, etc.; employment; income; expenditures; production and distribution; and pricing.]

Handbook of Grants & Subsidies of Federal & Provincial Governments, CCH Canadian Ltd., 6 Garamond Court, Don Mills, Ontario, M3C 1Z5.

Index to Federal Programs & Services, Supply and Services Canada, Ottawa, Canada.

Key Business Ratios, Dun & Bradstreet Canada Ltd., P.O. Box 423 Station A, Toronto, Ontario. [Contains key business ratios for over 800 different types of businesses. Also, the U.S. affiliate of Dun & Bradstreet publishes "typical" balance sheets, income statements, and "common size" financial figure.]

Statistics Canada publications: Statistics Canada, Head Office, R.H. Coats Building, Tunney's Pasture, Ottawa, Ontario, K1A 0T6.

1. *Operating Results*. This report presents typical expenses, cost of goods sold, inventory, and net profit as a percent of sales for many different types of businesses. It presents results for both incorporated and unincorporated business and presents both mean and median results. Data is provided both by level of sales, and by province.

2. *Market Research Handbook*. This book presents data on selected economic indicators; government revenue; expenditures and employment; merchandising and services; population characteristics; personal income and expenditures.

3. *Family Expenditure in Canada*. This report provides information on family expenditures in Canada for a very detailed list of items.

4. *Census Data*. This can be obtained from local city halls. Census data will provide information on population growth rates, income level of schooling, and other facts. Census tracts for large centres can also be obtained from Statistics Canada.

5. *Small Business Profiles*. These reports provide complete financial operating report for many small businesses.

Periodicals/Trade Magazines particular to the type of business

For example:

Restaurateur if opening a new restaurant. These magazines often provide typical start-up and operating costs for a business. In addition there are several general small business periodicals, such as *Entrepreneur*, *Venture*, and *INC.* which can provide valuable ideas on starting a business.

Royal Bank of Canada, "Management Tips: Guide for Independent Business." [A series of books that assist in starting and running a business. Topics covered include: "How to Finance Your Business"; "Pointers to Profits"; "Good Management: Your Key to Survival."]

Managing for Success Series, The Institute for Small Business Inc., 1051 Clinton Street, Buffalo, New York, U.S.A. [Sixteen self-tutorials in business procedure written expressly for the independent business owner. It discusses important business topics, for example: Financing; Do-It-Yourself Marketing Plan; Planning and Budgeting; and Advertising and Sales Promotion. It provides illustrative case studies, detailed examples and workbooks and checklist pages that let you work out your business details along the lines detailed in the text.]

Industry, Science and Technology Canada. Provides several services for small businesses across the country. ISTC business service centres contain publications, videos and computer databases as well as counselling personnel.

Provincial Small Business Departments

These offices can be very useful to someone who operates or plans to open a small business. They can provide information on sources of financing for small business and so on. In Alberta, for example, the government publishes pamphlets on many aspects of running a small business as well as "Kind of Business Files" (KOB) which contain data on 100 types of small businesses such as financial ratios and market trends.

Minding Your Own Business, Federal Business Development Bank, Management Services, P.O. Box 6021, Montreal, Quebec, H3C 3C3. [This is a series of guides to starting and running a small business. They provide information on areas such as forecasting for an existing business; managing your current assets; retail pricing; attracting and keeping your retail customer; and buying a franchise. Federal Business Development Bank also publishes workbook case study pamphlets which are used in training seminars for entrepreneurs. Some of these topics are Total Quality Control, Developing a Financial Forecast, and How to Prepare a Market Study.]

Suggested Periodicals for Small Aboriginal Business

- *Aboriginal Business*
  Blue Mitt Media Corporation
  P.O. Box 23060
  2325 Preston Avenue
  Saskatoon, Saskatchewan S7J 2G2

- *Native Issues Monthly*
  Box 691 Station C
  St. John's, Newfoundland A1C 5M3

- *The First Perspective*
  General Delivery
  Scanterbury, Manitoba R0E 1W0

- *Entrepreneur Magazine*
  2311 Pontius Avenue
  Los Angeles, CA 90064
  (213) 477–1011

- *In Business*
  Jerome Godstein, Publisher
  Box 351
  Emmaus, PA 18049
  (215) 967–4135

- *INC.*
  Bernard Goldhirsh, Publisher
  38 Commercial Wharf
  Boston, MA 02110
  (617) 227–4700

- *Journal of Small Business &
  Entrepreneurship*
  Faculty of Management
  University of Toronto
  246 Bloor St. West
  Toronto, Ontario M5B 2K3

- *Journal of Small Business Management*
  Bureau of Business Research
  West Virginia University
  Morgantown, WV 26506
  (304) 293–0111

- *Venture*
  Arthur Lipper III, Chairman
  521 Fifth Avenue
  New York, NY 10175
  (212) 682–7373

- *Success*
  Lang Communications
  230 Park Ave
  New York, NY

- *Profit*
  CB Media Ltd.
  70 The Esplauade, 2nd Floor
  Toronto, Ontario

- *N.E.D.I. Notes*
  National Entrepreneurship
    Development Institute
  3601 St. Jacques West
  Montreal, Quebec

- *Windspeaker*
  15001–112 Avenue
  Edmonton, Alberta T5M 2V6

Organizations and Trade Associations that Assist Entrepreneurs

- *Aboriginal Business Canada*
  1st Floor West, 235 Queen St.
  Ottawa, Ontario K1A 0H5
  Provides assistance in preparing feasibility studies, business planning, establishing or expanding businesses, and help in operations and marketing. ABC is also empowered to invest in activities that improve the aboriginal entrepreneurial climate in Canada.

- *Aboriginal Economic Development
    National Board*
  Oversees the development of programs designed to assist aboriginal business in Canada. The chairman is Kenneth Thomas and this board operates as part of the Department of Industry, Science, and Technology in Ottawa.

- *Council for Advancement of Native
    Development Officers*
  This organization has received funding from the Royal Commission on Aboriginal Peoples to study the current and future training requirements for economic development relating to aboriginal peoples in Canada. Robin Wortman, Executive Director, (403) 453–6001.

- *First Nations Resource Council*
  14601–134 Avenue
  Edmonton, Alberta T5L 4S9
  Manages the Indian Management Assistance Program (IMAP), which matches university students with aboriginal communities and organizations for summer term work as

consultants. Clayton Blood, IMAP Director, (403) 453–6114.

- *Association of Collegiate
    Entrepreneurs (ACE)*
  University of Western Ontario
  UCC Building Room 268
  London, Ontario N6A 3K7

- *Business Counselling Group*
  Communications Branch
  Dept. of Industry, Science and
    Technology

- *Entrepreneurship and Small Business
    Office*
  235 Queen Street
  Ottawa, Ontario K1A 0A5

- *Business Information Centre*
  Federal Business Development Bank
  204 Richmond St. West
  Toronto, Ontario M5V 1V6
  (416) 973–0062

- *The Canadian Chamber of Commerce*
  120 Adelaide Street West
  Suite 2109
  Toronto, Ontario M5H 1T1
  (416) 868–6415

- *Canadian Council of Better Business
    Bureaus*
  2180 Steeles Ave. West, Suite 219
  Concord, Ontario M6P 4C7
  (416) 922–2584

- *Canadian Federation of Independent Business*
  4141 Yonge Street, Suite 401
  Willowdale, Ontario M2P 2A6
  (416) 222–8022

- *Canadian Organization of Small Business*
  Toronto Office
  150 Consumers Road, Suite 501
  Willowdale, Ontario M2J 4V8
  (416) 492–3223

- *Centre for Entrepreneurial Management*
  29 Greene Street
  New York, NY 10013
  (212) 925–7304

- *Federal Business Development Bank*
  Counselling Assistance for Small Business

  901 Victoria Square
  Montreal, Quebec H2Z 1R1

- *International Council for Small Business Canada*
  204 Richmond St. West, 5th Floor
  Toronto, Ontario M5V 1V6

- *Small Business Network*
  52 Sheppard Avenue West
  Willowdale, Ontario M2N 1M2
  (416) 221–8040

- *National Entrepreneurship Development Institute*
  3601 St. Jacques West
  Montreal, Quebec

- *Small Business Institute*
  1070 West Broadway, Suite 310
  Vancouver, B.C. V6H 1E7

LISTING OF PROVINCIAL DEPARTMENTS FOR SMALL BUSINESS ——— (from Chapter 3)

Alberta
Economic Development:
  Small Business Assistance
17th Floor, 10025 Jasper Ave.
Edmonton, T5J 3Z3
(403) 427–3685

British Columbia
Ministry of Economic Development
B.C. Enterprise Centre
750 Pacific Boulevard South
Vancouver, B.C.
(604) 660–3900

Manitoba
Department of Business Development and
  Tourism and Small Business and
  Regional Development
155 Carlton St.
Winnipeg, R3C 3H8
(204) 945–2422

New Brunswick
Department of Commerce and Technology
Small Industry and Regional Development
Centennial Bldg., P.O. Box 6000
Fredericton, E3B 5H1
(506) 453–3606

Newfoundland
Department of Development and Tourism
Local Industry Support Services
Atlantic Place, Water Street
St. John's, A1C 5T7
(709) 576–2702

Northwest Territories
Department of Economic Development and
  Tourism
Business Development
P.O. Box 1320
Yellowknife, X1A 2L9
(819) 873–7229

Nova Scotia
Department of Development
World Trade and Convention Ctr.
1800 Argvie St.
P.O. Box 519 Halifax
B3–2R
(902) 426–7850

Ontario
Ministry of Industry, Trade, and Technology
Hearst Blk., 900 Bay St.
Toronto, M7A 2E1
(416) 965–1586

Prince Edward Island
Department of Industry
Business Development
Shaw Bldg., Box 2000
Charlottetown, C1A 7N8
(902) 892–5445

Quebec
Ministere du Commerce
Exterieur et du Development, Technologique
Place Mercantile, 6e–7e et 10e étages
770, Rue Sherbrooke Ouest
Montreal, H3A 1G1
(514) 643–5275

Saskatchewan
Department of Tourism and Small Business
Bank of Montreal Bldg.
2103 11th Ave.
Regina, S4P 3V7
(306) 787–2207

Yukon
Department of Economic Development:
  Mines and Small Business
Business Development Office
2131 Second Ave.
Whitehorse, Y1A 2C6
(403) 667–3011

LISTING OF UNIVERSITIES AND GROUPS THAT HAVE ———— STUDENT CONSULTING PROGRAMS (from Chapter 3)

These programs offer consulting projects done on all aspects of business by senior commerce/business students under the supervision of the university faculty. There are two purposes to these programs:

1. To provide a low-cost consulting service to small business.
2. To provide a useful and practical learning experience for senior commerce/business students.

Nova Scotia
- *Atlantic Business Consultants Ltd.*
  6094 University Avenue
  Halifax, Nova Scotia B3H 1W7

- *Coburg Consultants*
  6152 Coburg Road
  Halifax, Nova Scotia B3H 1Z5

British Columbia
- *Geoffrey Dalton, Coordinator*
  Faculty of Business Administration
  University of British Columbia
  Burnaby, B.C. V5A 1S6

- *David Boag*
  University of Victoria
  P.O. Box 1700
  Victoria, B.C. V8W 2Y2
  (604) 721–6060

The Province of British Columbia has several Business Development Centres. For more information, contact:

- *Gary L. Bunney*
  Director of Academic/
    Technical Programs
  Ministry of Post-Secondary Education
  (604) 387–6181

Ontario

- *Prof. Clem Hobbs, Faculty Coordinator*
  School of Business
  Carleton University
  Ottawa, Ontario K1S 5B7

- *Prof. P. Shonoski, Faculty Coordinator*
  School of Business Administration
  Lakehead University
  Thunder Bay, Ontario P7B 5E1

- *Prof. Dave Gillingham, Faculty Coordinator*
  School of Commerce & Administration
  Laurentian University
  Sudbury, Ontario P3E 2C6

- *Dr. R.S. Adamson, Faculty Coordinator*
  School of Business & Economics
  Wilfrid Laurier University
  Waterloo, Ontario N2L 3C5

- *Dr. A.W. Richardson, Faculty Coordinator*
  Faculty of Business
  McMaster University
  Hamilton, Ontario L8S 4M4

- *Reid McWilliam, Program Manager*
  Small Business Management Program
  Mohawk College
  P.O. Box 2034
  Hamilton, Ontario L8N 3T2

- *Prof. John McKirdy, Faculty Coordinator*
  School of Business
  Queen's University
  Kingston, Ontario K7L 3N6

- *Prof. Jim Forrester, Faculty Coordinator*
  School of Business
  Ryerson Polytechnical Institute
  50 Gould Street
  Toronto, Ontario M5B 1E8

- *David Litvak, Faculty Coordinator*
  Faculty of Administration
  University of Ottawa
  Ottawa, Ontario K1B 6N5

- *Prof. Wally Smieliauskas, SBC Faculty Coordinator*
  Faculty of Management Studies
  University of Toronto
  246 Bloor Street West
  Toronto, Ontario M5S 1V4

- *Prof. Murray Bryant, SBC Faculty Coordinator*
  Faculty of Management Studies
  University of Toronto
  246 Bloor Street West
  Toronto, Ontario M55 1V4

- *J.F. Graham, Faculty Coordinator*
  School of Business Administration
  The University of Western Ontario
  London, Ontario N6A 3K7

- *Dr. M. Ragab, SBC Faculty Coordinator*
  Faculty of Business Administration
  University of Windsor
  401 Sunset Avenue
  Windsor, Ontario N9B 3P4

- *Dr. W.B. Crowston, SBC Faculty Coordinator*
  Faculty of Administrative Studies
  York University
  4700 Keele Street
  Downsview, Ontario M3J 1P3

Ontario has several colleges and universities that run innovation centres. The innovation centre developed specifically for small business is listed below; for further information on other innovation centres, contact the Ontario Ministry of Industry, Trade, and Technology.

- *Ryerson Innovation Centre*
  Ryerson Polytechnical Institute
  350 Victoria Street
  Toronto, Ontario M5B 2K3

Saskatchewan

University of Regina operates a student consulting service on an informal basis. Students involved in this service have completed a number of different projects for a small number of organizations. They are now considering formally establishing the student consulting service.

- *Faculty of Administration*
  University of Regina
  Regina, Saskatchewan S4S 0A2

- *Business Consulting Services*
  College of Commerce
  University of Saskatchewan
  Saskatoon, Saskatchewan S7N 0W0

Manitoba

- *M.B.A. Student Consulting Program*
  (May–August)
  Department of Business Development and
  Tourism
  Winnipeg Enterprise Development Centre
  2nd Floor, 1329 Niakwa Rd.
  Winnipeg, Manitoba

Alberta

- *Student Consulting Group*
  Faculty of Management
  University of Lethbridge
  4401 University Drive
  Lethbridge, Alberta T1K 3M4

- *Faculty of Management*
  University of Calgary
  2500 University Drive N.W.
  Calgary, Alberta T2N 1N4

- *Faculty of Business*
  University of Alberta
  202 Faculty of Business Building
  Edmonton, Alberta T6G 2R6

INCORPORATION OF COMPANIES AND ASSOCIATIONS
(from Chapter 4)

Federal
Registrar of Companies
Place du Portage, Phase 2
Ottawa-Hull K1A 0L5

Alberta
Registrar of Companies
Alberta Consumer & Corporate Affairs
Century Place
9803 102A Ave.
Edmonton, Alta. T5J 3A3

British Columbia
Registrar of Companies
Minister of Consumer and Corporate Affairs
940 Blanshard St.
Victoria, B.C. V8W 3E6

Manitoba
Corp. & Business Names
Registration Branch
Dept. of Consumer & Corporate Affairs
Woodsworth Bldg., 405 Broadway
Winnipeg, Man. R3C 3L6

New Brunswick
Registrar of Companies
Consumer & Corporate Services Branch
Dept. of Justice
Box 6000
Fredericton, N.B. E3B 5H1

Newfoundland
Registry of Deeds
Companies & Securities
Dept. of Justice
Confederation Building
St. John's, Nfld. A1C 5T7

Nova Scotia
Consumer Services Bureau
5639 Spring Garden Rd.
2nd Floor, Box 998
Halifax, N.S. B3J 2X3

Northwest Territories
P.O. Box 1320
Yellowknife, N.W.T. X1A 2L9

Ontario
Companies Branch
Minister of Consumer & Commercial
  Relations
555 Yonge St., 2nd Floor
Toronto, Ont. M7A 2H6

Prince Edward Island
Dept. of Provincial Secretary
Box 2000
Charlottetown, P.E.I. C1A 7N8

Quebec
Dept. of Consumer Affairs
Cooperative & Financial Institutions
6th Floor, 800 Pl. d'Youville
Quebec, P.Q. G1R 4Y5

Saskatchewan
Corporations Branch
Saskatchewan Justice
1871 Smith Street
Regina, Sask. S4P 3V7

Yukon
Department of Consumer and Corporate Affairs
Box 2703
Whitehorse, Yukon Y1A 2C6

TRADE ASSOCIATIONS TO ASSIST FRANCHISERS AND FRANCHISEES (from Chapter 5)

- *Canadian Franchise Association*
  595 Bay St., Suite 1050
  Toronto, Ont., M5G 2C2
  (416) 625–2896

- *International Franchise Association (IFA)*
  1350 New York Avenue
  #900 Washington, DC
  20005

- *International Franchise Opportunities*
  11 Bond St.
  St. Catherines, Ont., L2R 4Z4
  (416) 648–2923

- *Retail Council of Canada*
  Franchise Division
  Suite 212, 214 King St. West
  Toronto, Ont., M5H 1K4
  (416) 598–4684

SOURCES OF CAPITAL
(from Chapter 6)

Aboriginal Business Canada

This program supports the continued growth in the numbers and the capability of aboriginally owned and operated businesses. The program improves access to business financing, increases management capacity, and enhances the business climate for aboriginal entrepreneurs.

In addition to a range of direct-funded and non-funded business assistance, Aboriginal Business Canada supports the network of Aboriginal Capital Corporations in providing important community-based commercial lending services, and helps to improve the entrepreneurship climate through support to business conferences, studies and information products. The program acts as an advocate in government for the interests of aboriginal business.

Who is Eligible?

Canadian Status Indians and Non-status Indians, Métis, Inuit people, partnerships, profit and non-profit groups, and other entities that are majority owned or controlled by aboriginal people are eligible.

What are the Eligibility Criteria?

Proposals are assessed individually, on their merit, taking into account:

- amount of client equity
- management experience
- markets
- viability/profitability
- other sources of financing

How Much Financial Assistance is Available?

Each proposal is assessed according to its needs and overall financing package.
- Financing may be repayable or non-repayable, depending on the size of the contribution and the conditions surrounding the proposed project. Loan insurance is also an available option.
- For information about possible levels of support for various types of projects, please request a copy of *Aboriginal Business Canada and You* from the office listed below.

How Do You Apply?

The fist step is to contact the nearest Aboriginal Business Canada office to discuss the project with an officer.

Clients will complete a "Statement of Intent", providing the information required to determine if proceeding to a full business plan in appropriate.

Where Can You Apply?

Atlantic Regional Office

* Aboriginal Business Canada
Industry Canada
1801 Hollis Street, 4th Floor
PO Box 940, Station M
Halifax, Nova Scotia B3J 2V9
Tel (902) 426–2018
Fax (902) 426–2624

Quebec/Eastern Arctic Regional Office

* Aboriginal Business Canada
Industry Canada
800 Tour de la Place Victoria, Suite 2604
P.O. Box 280
Montreal, Quebec
Tel (514) 283–1828
Fax (514) 283–1843

Ontario Regional Office

* Aboriginal Business Canada
Industry Canada
Dominion Public Building, 4th Floor
1 Front Street West
Toronto, Ontario M5J 1A4
Tel (416) 973–8800
Fax (416) 973–2255

* Aboriginal Business Canada (sub-office)
Industry Canada
Time Square
1760 Regina Street South
Sudbury, Ontario P3E 3Z8
Tel (705) 522–5100
Fax (705) 522–5225

Central Regional Offices

* Aboriginal Business Canada
Industry Canada
3300 Portage Avenue, Room 608
P.O. Box 3130
Winnipeg, Manitoba R3C 4E6
Tel (204) 983–7316
Fax (204) 983–4107

* Aboriginal Business Canada (sub-office)
Industry Canada
119–4th Avenue South, Suite 401
Saskatoon, Saskatchewan S7K 5X2
Tel (306) 975–4329
Fax (306) 975–5334

Western Regional Offices

* Aboriginal Business Canada
Industry Canada
650 West Georgia Street, Suite 810
P.O. Box 11551
Vancouver, British Columbia V6B 4N8
Tel (604) 666–3871
Fax (604) 666–0238

* Aboriginal Business Canada (sub-office)
Industry Canada
Canada Place, Suite 545
9700 Jasper Avenue
Edmonton, Alberta T5J 4C3
Tel (403) 495–2954
Fax (403) 495–4172

Other Aboriginal Business Canada offices

* Aboriginal Business Canada
Industry Canada
235 Queen Street, 1st Floor West
Ottawa, Ontario K1A 0H5
Tel (613) 954–4064
Fax (613) 957–7010

* Aboriginal Capital Corporations
Aboriginal Business Canada
Industry Canada
3300 Portage Avenue, 7th Floor
P.O. Box 3130
Winnipeg, Manitoba R3C 4C6
Tel (204) 983–5136
Fax (204) 983–8954

For further information, please contact Aboriginal Business Canada, Industry Canada at (416) 973–8800.

SOURCE: Aboriginal Business Canada, Industry Canada.

Provincial Equity Capital Programs

British Columbia
- Small Business Venture Capital

Alberta
- Small Business Equity Corporation

Saskatchewan
- Equity financing available through SEDCO (Saskatchewan Economic Development Corporation)

Manitoba
- Venture Capital Program

Ontario
- Small Business Development Corporations Program
- Venture Investments Corporations

Quebec
- Societés de placement dans l'entreprise Quebecoise

- Societés de developpement de l'entreprise Quebecoise

New Brunswick
- Venture Capital Support Program

Nova Scotia
- Nova Scotia Venture Corporations

Prince Edward Island
- Small Business Development Corporations
- Venture Capital Program

Newfoundland
- Venture Capital Program

SOURCE: "Provincial Venture Capital Corporations: A Comparative Analysis," *Journal of Small Business & Entrepreneurship — Canada* 4, no. 5 (Fall 1986), p. 22.

FEDERAL GOVERNMENT ASSISTANCE PROGRAMS ———— TO SMALL BUSINESS (from Chapter 6)

Program	Type of Assistance	Limits	Purposes	Contact Offices
Aboriginal Economic Programs	Up to 40% equity to aboriginal projects. Financial assistance throughout the business cycle, feasibility studies, business planning, establishing or expanding business operations, and follow-up business services. Support for marketing, innovation or R & D projects, covering up to 75% of project costs. Support clients who require funds to offset inventory costs Up and running businesses get special services such as accounting and consulting or training in management.	Varies by type of program and assistance provided.	Support and encourage the formation and growth of aboriginal businesses in Canada. Trade and market expansion. Increased adaption of technology to aboriginal businesses. Development of aboriginal youth entrepreneurs.	Aboriginal Economic Programs Industry Canada 1st Floor West 235 Queen Street Ottawa, Ontario K1A 0H5 (613) 954–4064
Small Business Loans Act	Provides guarantees on loans for a variety of capital purposes.	No refinancing of existing debt. Annual revenues can't exceed $2 million. Interest prime plus 1%. Maximum 10-year repayment period.	Improve and modernize equipment and buildings; purchase land.	All approved lenders.

Program	Type of Assistance	Limits	Purposes	Contact Offices
Program for Export Market Development	Shares costs of specific export marketing efforts. Encourages and assists export.	Provides up to 50% of the costs incurred by a company in penetration of new markets. Repayable if sales are made.	Specific project bidding; market identification; participation in trade fairs abroad; bringing in foreign buyers; export consortia development; sustained export market development.	I.S.T.C. regional offices.
Self-Employment Incentive Program	Provides temporary grants while entrepreneurs establish business.	$200 per week.	To assist with living expenses while an entrepreneur establishes a business.	Employment and Immigration Canada.
Atlantic Canada Opportunity Agency	Financial assistance for economic development and capital costs.	Varies by type of project and industry.	Improve the economic viability of businesses in Atlantic Canada and encourage entrepreneurship.	ACOA offices in Atlantic Canada.
Western Economic Diversification Fund	Financial assistance through grants.	Maximum amount of assistance depends on which tier the applicant is in. Level of support depends on nature of the project, need for support, value and government economic objectives.	Promote industrial and regional development in Western Canada.	I.S.T.C. regional offices.

...continued

...continued from previous page

Program	Type of Assistance	Limits	Purposes	Contact Offices
Small Business Development Bank	Assistance through reduced interest rates on loans.	Eligible small business corporations that use all their assets in an active business. One-to-five year loan. Specific time restriction on past loans to qualify.	Relieve the financial burden of interest rates on the small businessperson.	All approved lenders.
Technology Outreach Programs	Financial assistance.	Small businesses can access information, receive grants and loans for implementing new technology.	Promote innovation and use of new technology.	Industry Science and Technology Canada.
Federal Business Development Bank	Loans and equity investment.	Extend debt financing to small businesses. Can also extend venture capital to small firms wanting to expand.	Increase viability of small business.	FBDB.
Industrial Research Assistance Program	Financial assistance through grant and technical assistance.	Varies according to which aspect of the program is applied for.	Increase the calibre and scope of industrial research and development through the use of available technology.	Industrial Research Assistance.

TALE'AWTXW ABORIGINAL CAPITAL CORPORATION ————— (from Chapter 6)

Our Organization   Tale'awtxw Aboriginal Capital Corporation is a Native-owned and controlled lending institution fully funded by federal government through the Aboriginal Economic Programs.

The company is registered under the British Columbia Companies Act and will initially operate two offices situated at Chemainus and North Vancouver.

Corporate and Management Structure   The policy and direction of the company are managed by a board of directors consisting of representatives from the Coast Salish Economic Development Commission, banking expertise, Native business persons and an accountant.

The day to day operations are managed by a general manager who will have a complement of business development and business loan specialists.

Services Provided   Tale'awtxw will provide Native entrepreneurs of Coast Salish ancestry and members of the United Native Nations:

1. Business loans for the acquisition, implementation, or expansion of any Native owned or controlled viable enterprise located within the geographic area encompassed by the Coast Salish Nation.
2. External delivery services to the client wishing to access the Aboriginal Business Development Program.
3. Advice to entrepreneurs on business planning and programs available to them. These programs can provide assistance for capitalization, working capital, and training. In many cases this will complement loan funding provided by TACC.

Types of Loans Provided

■ Capital Loans
Usually used for the acquisition of fixed assets.

■ Working Capital
Required to conduct the day to day affairs of an enterprise.

■ Equity Loans
Usually used to leverage private loan funds from private lending sources.

■ Bridge Financing
Is sometimes required to facilitate assistance offered through the Aboriginal Business Development Program.

■ Loan Guarantees

Interest Rates   Interest rates are set by the board of directors and are reviewed quarterly.

Combination of Funding Sources   When one or more funding agencies have committed to the project, the loans from TACC can only be disbursed once the client has formal approval from these funding sources.

Equity   To qualify for a loan, the applicant must demonstrate that they have a minimum of 10% equity. This equity may take the form of cash, contributed assets and in some cases, personal labour (sweat equity).

Business Plan Guidelines   Contact the TACC office closest to where the business is to be located. Our loans officer will provide you with further information and a general guide on developing a business plan.

How to Apply for a Loan

1. All applicants will be required to submit a complete and comprehensive business plan.
2. Individuals will be required to complete a personal statement of affairs which should accompany the business plan.
3. Businesses located on reserve land must obtain a band council resolution support and a resolution of access to enable TACC to conduct business on that particular reserve.

Reactive — Not Proactive   Tale'awtxw does not assist clients with the actual development of the business plan. However, our loans officer can provide information regarding the content of such plan.

Loan Amounts and Turnover Time on Applications   Limitations on loan amounts may apply and turnover time on applications may vary. For complete information contact the TACC office nearest you.

The major sections to be addressed in a business plan are:

- Description of the Industry
- Description of Your Business
- The Market
- The Target Customer
- Marketing Strategy
- The Competition
- Location
- Source and Application of Funds
- Description of the Facilities
- Management and Personnel
- Sales and Credit Terms
- Pricing
- Description of the Production Process
- Advertising
- Licenses and Permits
- Major Suppliers
- Other Professional Services Required
- Strengths and Weaknesses
- Long Range Plans
- Critical Risks and Assumptions
- Sales Forecasting
- Cash flow Analysis — Years 1, 2 and 3
- Pro-forma Financial Statements — Years 1, 2 and 3

You can also include the following as appendices:

- Resumes of Key Personnel
- Letters of Support
- Certificates/Diplomas
- Photographs

Tale'awtxw Aboriginal Capital Corporation
Personal Data Sheet — North Vancouver Office

Tale'awtxw Aboriginal Capital Corporation
Personal Data Sheet - North Vancouver Office

(Please complete all sections on both pages)

Surname	First Name	Initial
Applicant		
Spouse		

Name of Employer	Number of Years	Monthly Salary
Applicant		
Spouse		

Contact Person	Telephone Number
	Home:
	Work:

Present Address (Please include postal code)	Previous Address (If less than two years at current address)

PERSONAL INFORMATION

DATE OF BIRTH:	SIN:
MARITAL STATUS:	NO. OF DEPENDENTS: (Including spouse)
ABORIGINAL ANCESTRY: (Please check one) ☐ Coast Salish ☐ Métis ☐ U.N.N. ☐ Other	BAND/UNN/MÉTIS LOCAL: NUMBER:
BANK AND ACCOUNT NUMBER:	BRANCH ADDRESS:

BUSINESS INFORMATION

Business Location	Number of Jobs Created/Maintained	Amount of Loan Request
☐ On Reserve ☐ Off Reserve	_____ Male _____ Female	$

Personal Data Sheet - North Vancouver Office

FINANCIAL INFORMATION

ASSETS	AMOUNT		LIABILITIES (Acct' No.)	BALANCE OWING	MONTHLY PAYMENTS
Cash	$		1.		
Household	$		2.		
1.	$		3.		
2.	$		Mortgage Holder		
3.	$		Rent		
Automobile (Year/Make Model)	$		(A) Total Liabilities:		
Real Estate	$		(B) Total Assets:		
TOTAL ASSETS	$		(A-B) NET WORTH		

PERSONAL DEBTS

CREDITOR	REASON FOR DEBT	ORIGINAL AMOUNT OF DEBT	BALANCE OUTSTANDING	REPAYMENT TERMS

PERSONAL REFERENCES

NAME	ADDRESS	PHONE NUMBER

CONSENT

I hereby authorize the person or corporation to whom this application is submitted to obtain such credit reports or other information as may be deemed necessary in connection with the establishment and maintenance of a credit account or for any other direct business requirement.

This consent is given pursuant to Chapter 78, Section 12, of the Credit Reporting Act, R.S.B.C. 1979.

SIGNATURE: _____ DATE: _____

SIGNATURE OF SPOUSE:_____ DATE: _____

FOR OFFICE USE ONLY

BUSINESS SECTOR	

FINANCIAL ASSISTANCE PROGRAMS AND AGENCIES ———— TO SMALL BUSINESS (from Chapter 6)

Native Development Corporations

The purpose of these corporations is to make investments in businesses in their region, or outside, to create long-term cash flows and/or employment and enhance skills for people. Usual targets are commercial infrastructure such as real estate, airlines, hotel, and some resource development businesses.

CAEDS (Canadian Aboriginal Economic Development Strategy)

CAEDS was created in 1989 to help native people with long-term employment through business development. (This program is currently under review.)

- **CEDOs**: Community Economic Development Organizations are the main vehicles of investment. Created to help design and make investments in local ventures, CEDOs are accountable to their communities.
- **ROPs**: Regional Opportunities Programs identify region-wide opportunities (mines, tourism etc.) through planning and levering other help programs. ROPs may not make direct investments.

First Peoples' Fund

The First Peoples' Fund is a program of the Calmeadow Foundation. It is a private sector initiative designed to assist First Nations communities to establish and operate their won micro-enterprise loan funds. Loans are offered at commercial interest rates and range form $300 to $3000. Loans are offered to self-employed people within borrower circles of 4–7 people who approve and guarantee each others loans. No collateral or equity contributions are required. Loan funds are administered by the communities themselves with the support of First Peoples' Fund.

Guaranteed Loan Program

This program is administered through Indian and Northern Affairs Canada (INAC). Its objective is to provide guarantee backing for unincorporated Indian and Band businesses on reserves needing financial aid from approved lending institutions. It provides commercial lenders with security not available to them under Section 89 of the Indian Act. The program is available to any unincorporated Canadian Status Indian or Inuit individual and group and, other entities which are majority owned by Aboriginal people.

Settlement Investment Corporation

Administered through Industry Science Canada/Aboriginal Capital Corporations this program is designed to encourage and assist Métis entrepreneurs to start businesses and expand their existing business by giving loans. It gives business loans up to $100,000 and agriculture loans up to $50,000. Applicants must be a resident member of a Métis Settlement.

Alberta

Alberta Indian Investment Corporation   The A.I.I.C. provides interest-bearing loans to Indian entrepreneurs for the purpose of establishing, acquiring, modernizing or expanding a business. Equity financing may also be available. Loans are generally for periods of up to 5 years. Applicants must have: a business plan which shows that their business will be profitable; contribute their own equity as a portion of the total financing of the business; have adequate collateral security; and have a good credit rating. Applicants must meet the following criteria: must be a Status Indian who has resided in Alberta for at least one year; if a corporation or partnership, the Status Indian must own at least 51% of any shares, participate in more than 51% of profits, and must be active in managing the business; 50% of revenue must be guaranteed in Alberta; and the applicant's head office must be in Alberta.

Apeetogosan (Métis) Development Inc.   To provide the Métis and Non-Status Indian people of Alberta with business financing and related services; to administer and allocate funds that will be instrumental in the economic development and self-sufficiency of the Métis and Non-Status Indians of Alberta. The program provides commercial loans for start-up or expansion for a for-profit business. Assistance in are areas of feasibility analysis, business planning, accounting, marketing and general management support is available. Applicants must be either a Métis or Non-Status Indian over 18 years of age, or groups, organizations and business owned by Métis or Non-Status Indian, must be resident of Alberta and the head office of the business must be located in Alberta; and it must be a for-profit commercial entity.

Indian Agri-Business Corporation (IABC)   To provide direct and indirect financing for Alberta Indian farmers. Available to Alberta Treaty individuals or groups.

Native Venture Capital Company Limited   The objective of this program is to bring together sound business ideas from the Alberta Native community and necessary financing to translate ideas into reality. It normally invests in situation where significant equity financing is not otherwise available. Native Venture will invest as a shareholder with the Native entrepreneur and remain as an equity partner within the business until pre-determined economic goals are achieved (usually a 10-year plan is established) at which time the Native entrepreneur is encouraged to buy out the investment. Investments are made in new and/or existing Native enterprise. Native Venture expects to make a reasonable, risk adjusted rate of return. Normally Native Venture will invest up to 50% of equity or debt capital up to a maximum of $300,000 in each company. The enterprise must operate in Alberta and must be controlled by Albertans of Indian ancestry (Status Indians, Métis, Non-Status Indians); where majority control is not held, the business must be of significant benefit to Native Albertans.

British Columbia

First Citizens' Fund Loan Program   The primary objective of the program is to enhance Native Indian economic development through start-up, expansion and/or upgrading of Native businesses. The objective of the loan program is to support Native Economic Development through: the enhancement of Native business management skills; the creation of successful new Native-owned/operated businesses; and expansion of existing Native business employment opportunities.

The B.C. Development Corporation   The BCDC is a provincial crown corporation set up to further economic development in British Columbia through financial, advisory, and information services. Under its low-interest loan plan, the BCDC provides funds for establishing, modernizing, or expanding manufacturing and processing industries.

The Small Manufacturers Assistance Program and the Assistance to Small Enterprise Program   These programs create jobs by assisting with the establishment, expansion, or modernization of small manufacturers as well as other assistance to small enterprises in the province. These programs provide interest-free, forgivable loans to British Columbia companies, which may be used for start-up, expansion, or modernization.

Manitoba

Design Assistance for Small Projects   This cost-shared program will pay up to 50 percent of design costs to improve product, graphics, and packaging to a maximum contribution of $1,000.

Venture Capital Company Program   This program aims to stimulate the flow of equity capital into Manitoba businesses by providing an investment vehicle for the private sector. The province participates jointly on a 35/65 percent basis with private investors who must contribute $25,000 at the time the venture capital company is registered and a minimum of $65,000 within one year.

New Brunswick

Department of Commerce and Development   The minister of Commerce and Development may provide financial assistance to aid and encourage the establishment or development of manufacturing or processing industries in the province. Assistance may take the form of a direct loan, bond guarantee, or acquisition of shares in a company.

Financial Assistance to Small Industry   This program makes interest-free forgivable loans to new or existing industries, for purposes of start-up, modernization, or expansion. Loans are calculated on the basis of approved capital costs.

Newfoundland and Labrador

The Newfoundland and Labrador Development Corporation   This crown corporation is funded jointly by the federal and Newfoundland governments. It is mandated specifically toward small business. The NLDC offers both term loans and equity finance, although it does not guarantee loans.

Northwest Territories

Department of Indian and Northern Affairs Canada (DIAND)   The Commercial Services Division of DIAND promotes economic development in the NWT, and coordinates all major federal economic development initiatives in the North. The Canada/NWT Economic

Development Agreement is one of several programs the Federal Government funds to expand the local economy through small business, tourism and resource projects.

GNWT — Economic Development and Tourism   Programs to help start or expand business in any sector. Priority on employment creation in less developed communities.

■ Business Credit Corporation

Provides term loans, guarantees and contract security bonding to NWT businesses unable to secure financing or where commercial serves are not available. The maximum available to any business or group of related business is $1 million.

■ N.W.T. Development Corporation

Develops and operates businesses that will create employment and income; promotes diversification and stability. May operate as a working partner in joint ventures, or as sole owners and mangers. Initial business losses, or preset subsidies, may be absorbed as alternatives to social assistance.

■ Business Development Fund

A multi-part incentive program to help all business of any size regardless of stage of development. Each program has different limits and criteria. Types of assistance available: Grants to small business, planning and development; pilot and demonstration projects; business creation or expansion; market development and project promotion; business skills; and business relief.

Nova Scotia

Small Business Development Corporation   This program provides loans to businesses having annual sales of less than $2 million or employing less than 50 people. Interest rates are fixed for the life of the loan, and repayment terms are flexible.

Industrial Estates Limited Financing Program   This program is designed to provide appropriate loan financing to new or expanding manufacturing operations. The minimum loan financing available under this program is $250,000. Repayment is normally by way of a 20-year amortization.

Product Development Management Program   This program aims to assist manufacturers in developing new products and upgrading the design quality of existing products. Grants under the program provide up to 75 percent of the product development costs submitted by a consultant designer. The maximum grant is $15,000 per project.

Ontario

Aboriginal Business Ventures Program   This program offers loans to new companies to a maximum of $15,000 if approved by a participating financial institution. The applicant must make a cash equity contribution equal to at least 50% of the loan amount, of which at least 10% of the loan amount but be the applicants own cash equity. The remaining balance, up to 40% of the amount, can come from other sources such as Band loans, federal loans and/or agency grants. The loan must be used to cover costs directly related to the start-up of a new business or to cover costs directly related to the expansion of an existing business.

MNDM — Aboriginal Internship Program (AIP)   AIP is a wage subsidy program that encourages employers in Northern Ontario to provide valuable work experience and training to recent Aboriginal graduates of post-secondary programs. Northern employers, including private sector employers, non-profit organizations, First Nations, tribal councils, social/economic organizations, municipalities and school boards are all eligible. They will provide a subsidy of 75% of wages to a maximum of $10.50/hour.

Ontario Development Corporation   This agency and its complementary development corporations within Ontario stress the importance of small business and the desirability of a private sector share in small business financing. Although commencement of repayment may be deferred, loans may be interest-free or at a rate lower than the ODC's prevailing rate.

Small Business Development Corporation Program   This program acts as a private sector investment firm in which individuals and corporations are encouraged to buy equity. These firms then invest in small businesses eligible under the act. Money invested may be issued only for expansion or improvement of fixed assets, development, or start-up debt. Corporations investing in SBDCs are granted a credit of 25 percent against Ontario corporations income tax.

Prince Edward Island

Department of Industry and Commerce   The P.E.I. Department of Industry and Commerce administers five general assistance programs. Those occupied with direct assistance are run jointly with DREE. Eligible recipients of these programs are manufacturers and services in the small business sector.

Quebec

Quebec Industrial Development Corporation   This crown corporation aims at spreading economic power within the population, improving and rationalizing the business structure. Assistance may come in the form of a rebate on the company's borrowing cost, a loan at the usual market rate, a loan guarantee, or an acquisition of a minority interest in a company.

Small Business Assistance Program   This program was established to assist firms that, although usually profitable and well managed, face temporary working capital shortages. Financial assistance takes the form of an interest subsidy and loan guarantee.

Saskatchewan

Business Loans: Treaty and Status Indians   The Saskatchewan Indian Equity Foundation (SIEF) Businesses Loans program is responsible for the provision of business loans to Treaty and Status Indian People in the province of Saskatchewan. The program is designed to assist both new and existing business.

Sasknative Economic Development Corporation (SNEDCO) Small Business Loans Program   SNEDCO is a Saskatchewan Métis-owned and operated business development organization, whose sole purpose is to assist in the creation of viable Métis, or non-status aboriginal People Business ventures. It provides the following programs: capital loans, working capital loans, supplementary equity loans, bridge loans, loan guarantees and business advisory services. Only Métis and non-status Aboriginals residing in Saskatchewan are eligible to apply for loans.

Northern Business Development and Northern Saskatchewan Economic Development Revolving Fund The Small Business Branch provides business support services including the identification and evaluation of business opportunities, management counselling, and skills training to northern businesses and residents. The branch also provides pathfinding, assistance and information to northern businesses and residents on government programs and initiatives. The program provides business loans to eligible northern residents, including fishing, trapping and wild rice loans.

Saskatchewan Indian Agriculture Program The program serves as a training opportunity for individuals of aboriginal ancestry for the agriculture and food industry. The objective is directed at the development of economically viable farm units and to improve the productive capacity of Indian lands.

The Saskatchewan Economic Development Corporation (SEDCO) This crown corporation is a major internal provincial government vehicle of economic development, and as such deals with enterprises of all sizes and sectors. There is no upper limit on loans, and interest rates are set according to type of loan and current market conditions.

Sask Power Northern Enterprise Fund (SPNEF) The program is designed to provide assistance to both new and existing northern businesses. Eligible projects include: the creation of a new business, the purchase of an existing business, expansion of an existing business, business improvement, business refinancing and working capital.

Yukon

Yukon Small Business Assistance Program This program offers both financial and nonfinancial assistance to entrepreneurs wishing to start a new business as well as those wishing to expand an existing business. Financial assistance takes the form of loans and loan guarantees.

AGENCIES PROVIDING EXPORT ASSISTANCE
(from Chapter 7)

* *Department of Industry, Science and Technology*
1st Floor, East Tower
235 Queen Street
Ottawa, Ontario
K1A 0H5

This Federal Government department, which has a branch devoted to aboriginal business issues (Aboriginal Business Canada), provides assistance in designing marketing plans, provides information and liaison with other government departments, and administers specific programs such as the following:

* *Promotional Projects Program*: This program promotes Canadian goods and services abroad through trade fairs, missions, and other foreign contacts.

* *Program for Export Market Development (PEMD)*: This program shares part of the financial risk associated with foreign trade by providing grants to the entrepreneur for foreign travel to identify markets, participate in trade fairs, and bring foreign buyers to Canada.

* *World Information Network for Exports (WIN Exports)*: This is a computer-based information system designed to assist in matching foreign needs to Canadian capabilities.

* *Technology Inflow Program*: This program is designed to help locate, acquire and adopt foreign technologies by promoting international collaboration.

* *New Exporters to Border States (NEBS); New Exporters to U.S. (NEXUS); New Exporters to Overseas (NEXOS)*: This program provides counselling assistance as well as organizing trade missions to businesses who are planning to export to these areas.

* *Aboriginal Business Canada*
(A division of the Department of Industry, Science and Technology)
Industry Canada
235 Queen Street, 1st Floor West
Ottawa, Ontario K1A 0H5

* *Export Development Corporation (EDC)*
Box 655
Ottawa, Ontario
K1P 5T9

The EDC is a crown corporation of the federal government that provides three services to exporters.
1. *Export insurance*: This is a protection service for the exporter to insure payment for export sales in the event of buyer default or detrimental foreign government action.
2. *Export guarantees*: Guarantees can be provided to financial institutions to assist exporters in obtaining financing for the export operations.
3. *Export financing services*: The EDC also has authorization to provide medium and long-term financing for exporters to help them compete in the international marketplace.

* *Canadian Commercial Corporation (CCC)*
Bental Tower IV
P.O. Box 49158
Vancouver, B.C.
V7X 1K8

CCC is a crown corporation that responds to requests from foreign governments and international agencies seeking Canadian goods and services by attempting to match these requests with suitable sources of supply.

- *Canadian International Development Agency (CIDA)*
200 Promenade du Portage
Hull, Quebec
K1A 0G4

CIDA is a federal agency that administers Canada's development cooperation programs around the world, many of which employ private consultants, contractors, suppliers, and manufacturers to underdeveloped countries.

- *Canadian Export Association (CEA)*
Suite 250, 99 Bank Street
Ottawa, Ontario
K1P 6B9

The CEA is a national non-profit association concerned with improving the environment for Canadian exporters. It provides information, contacts, education, and lobbying support for exporters.

- *External Affairs and International Trade Canada*
125 Sussex Drive
Ottawa, Ontario
K1A 0G2

The Trade Commissioner Service is a referral service which maintains an extended network of trade offices in other countries; its primary focus is to assist Canadian companies seeking export markets. A directory of the trade offices throughout the world may be obtained through the Department of External Affairs or the Department of Industry, Trade, and Commerce.

LISTING OF PROVINCIAL AND TERRITORIAL LABOUR DEPARTMENTS ——
(from Chapter 10)

Alberta
Department of Labour
10808 99 Ave.
Edmonton, Alberta T5K 063
(403) 427–2723

British Columbia
Ministry of Labour
Parliament Building
Victoria, B.C. V8V 114
(604) 327–1986

Manitoba
Manitoba Labour
Norquay Building, 401 York Ave.
Winnipeg, Manitoba R3C 0P8
(204) 945–4079

New Brunswick
Department of Labour and
    Human Resources
Chestnut Complex, 470 York St.
P.O. Box 6000
Fredericton, N.B. E3B 5H1
(506) 453–2342

Newfoundland
Department of Labour
Beothuk Building, Crosbie Place,
St. John's, Newfoundland
Mailing Address: Confederation Building
St. John's, Newfoundland A1C 517
(709) 576–2722

Northwest Territories
Labour Standards Board of the
    Northwest Territories
P.O. Box 2804
Yellowknife, N.W.T. X1A 2L9
(819) 873–7924

Nova Scotia
Department of Labour
5151 Terminal Rd., 6th Floor
P.O. Box 697
Halifax, N.S. B3J 2T8
(902) 424–6647

Ontario
Ministry of Labour
400 University Ave.
Toronto, Ontario M7A 1T7
(416) 965–4101

Prince Edward Island
Department of Fisheries and Labour
Sullivan Building, 16 Fitzroy St.
P.O. Box 2000
Charlottetown, P.E.I. C1A 7NB
(902) 892–3493

Quebec
Ministere du Travail
425, Rue St. Amable
Quebec, G1R 4Z1

Ministere du Travail
255, Boul. Cremazie
Montreal, H2M 1L5
(514) 543–2422

Saskatchewan
1870 Albert St.
Regina, Saskatchewan S4P 3V7
(306) 787–2396

Yukon
Workers' Compensation Board
3rd Floor, 4110–4 Ave.
Whitehorse, Yukon Y1A 2C6
(403) 667–5877

INTERNET WEB SITES RELATING TO ABORIGINAL BUSINESS ————————

■ Aboriginal Business Canada [http://www.vli.ca/clients/abc/abenaki/]
A home page with links directing the user to the following:

a. Aboriginal Business Canada
b. National Aboriginal Economic Development Board
c. Profiles in Aboriginal Business Leadership

This is the most interesting and relative site to BESS.

■ "Aboriginal Business and the Internet"
[http://www.vli.ca/clients/abc/intro.htm]
Discusses the proactive process towards entrepreneurship using the information highway as a medium.

■ "The development of tourism in aboriginal communities across Canada"
[http://www.vli.ca/clients/abc/chata/cover.htm]
A table of contents (links) page. Topics include tourism in aboriginal communities across Canada and aboriginal workshops.

■ First Nations Resource Library [http://www.com/westward/nitacat.html]
A list of publications relating to aboriginal business.

■ The Inuvialuit Corporation Group [http://www.discoveryplace.com/Inuvialuit/]
A multipage summary of the corporations that the Inuvialuit are currently involved in.

■ Saw-Whet Communications [http://www.saw-whet.ca/]
A native-owned company providing computer-related services and training for First Nation clients.

■ Aboriginal Youth Business Council [http://www.aybc.org]
A website supporting young entrepreneurs.

■ Thunder Bay Native Business Association
[http://www.tradenet.ca/Mizhinawae/]
This is a site being developed to provide a forum for native businesses to come together and share ideas. Included are links to other aboriginal business sites.

■ Northern Ontario Native Tourism Association
[http://www.tradenet.ca/Nonta/]
Promotes native entrepreneurs in regards to outpost camps and lodges.

■ "Spirit of Aboriginal Enterprise" [http://gamma.omnimage.ca/spirit/]
Another good site linking browsers to aboriginal websites.

■ Environmental Systems Technology
[http://mfginfo.com/cadcam/environmental/est.htm]
A business advertisement specializing in computer software related to cleaning contracts.

■ Other sites of Interest [http://www.infobahnos.com/waseskun/sites.html]
This is a broad index of internet sites relative to aboriginal issues and organizations.

CHAPTER 15

Index

A

Abenaki Associates 140
aboriginal business in Canada
    export potential 16
    funding 321–336
    increases 7
    information and assistance 313–315
    performance 5
    taxation 241
aboriginal Business Canada (ABC) 116, 321–323
    export program 16, 337
    start-up assistance 45
Aboriginal Business Magazine 64
Aboriginal Capital Corporations 117, 327
Aboriginal Choice Placement Services 219
aboriginal community attributes
    culture 42
    financial capital access 41
    human capital 42
    location and size 41
    natural resources 41
    political sovereignty 40
Aboriginal Global Investment Corporation 123
aboriginal management courses 9
aboriginal mortgage restrictions, circumventing 109, 123
Accountant
    counselling source 46
    financial statements 75, 165
    franchising role 101, 102
    loan proposal use 128
    purchasing business, role 91, 96
    for tax advice 242
    trustee in bankruptcy 267
accounting, essential part of business 75
accounting cycle 163–168
    classifying transactions 165
    journal entries 164
    summarizing data 165
accounting system
    accrual based 180
    for small business 168–171
accounts receivable
    evaluating a business 92
    factor companies 121
    for a credit program 186
ACCs 117
Adventure North Expeditions 111, 226
advertising (*see also* promotion)
    for employees 219

    for franchising 98
    as practised by small business 154, 301
    start-up cost 112
    tax deductible 246
Alberta Native Guide Services 40
Amarok Country Foods 162
Angohiotok, George and Gary 29, 111, 226
Antler Tours 229
Arctic T-shirt company 11
asset value, method of determining a price for small business 93
assets, evaluating a business 92
Association of Canadian Franchisers 104, 298
Atkinson, Clifford 66, 262
Atkinson, Marvin 252
autonomy 13

B

balance sheet 165
    for a loan proposal 128
Ballard, Brent 64
band as counselling source 46
band as financing source 118, 127
bank credit cards 187
banker, counselling source 46
bankruptcy 267
bartering 165
Bellerose, Roland 30
Bernard, Alison 216
Bernard, Mark 143
bingo licences 80
Blue Raven bingo centre 251
bookkeeping 163
book value 93
break-even point 177
budget
    setting the promotional 158
    short-term planning 175
Buffalo Point International Resort 194
business cycle 259–261
business failure
    incompetence 32
    inexperience 32
    pitfalls 25
    risk 24
business losses, tax deduction 244
business opportunity evaluation 39–59
    aboriginal community attributes 40–42
    breaking into market 43–44
    information collection 44–50
    non-quantitative factors 39–40

ACKNOWLEDGEMENTS ———————————————————

The editor and contributors would like to gratefully acknowledge the following:

* Dean George Lermer and the Faculty of Management at the University of Lethbridge for providing a home for this project in the B.E.S.S. (Business Enterprises and Self-Governing Systems of Indian, Inuit and Métis Peoples) Program.

* Nova Corporation of Calgary for their financial support of and interest in B.E.S.S.

* Randy Hoffman, Drew Ellis, and Captus Press Inc. for their enthusiasm and technical support.

* Jim Clark of the Faculty of Management for teaching our flagship course in Aboriginal Entrepreneurship and developing the accompanying overheads.

* *Windspeaker*, Canada's National Aboriginal News Publication, *The First Perspective* and *Native Issues Monthly*, for their generosity in allowing reprints.

* Cover artist Frederick A. Lepine, Hay River, Northwest Territories, for offering the theme "define yourself *yourself*".

* All students, past and present, for their participation and contribution to the ongoing development of the B.E.S.S. Program.

K.B.C.
August, 1996